SOMETHING ABOUT THE AUTHOR®

Something about
the Author *was named
an "Outstanding
Reference Source,"
the highest honor given
by the American
Library Association
Reference and Adult
Services Division.*

ISSN 0276-816X

SOMETHING ABOUT THE AUTHOR®

Facts and Pictures about Authors
and Illustrators of Books for Young People

volume 198

GALE
CENGAGE Learning™

Detroit • New York • San Francisco • New Haven, Conn • Waterville, Maine • London

GALE
CENGAGE Learning

Something about the Author, Volume 198

Project Editor: Lisa Kumar

Editorial: Dana Ferguson, Amy Elisabeth Fuller, Michelle Kazensky, Jennifer Mossman, Joseph Palmisano, Mary Ruby, Marie Toft

Permissions: Dean Dauphinais, Aja Perales, Jhanay Williams

Imaging and Multimedia: Leitha Etheridge-Sims, John Watkins

Composition and Electronic Capture: Amy Darga

Manufacturing: Drew Kalasky

Product Manager: Janet Witalec

Gale
27500 Drake Rd.
Farmington Hills, MI, 48331-3535

LIBRARY OF CONGRESS CATALOG CARD NUMBER 62-52046

ISBN-13: 978-1-4144-2170-4
ISBN-10: 1-4144-2170-2

ISSN 0276-816X

This title is also available as an e-book.
ISBN-13: 978-1-4144-5744-4
ISBN-10: 1-4144-5744-8
Contact your Gale sales representative for ordering information.

Printed in the United States of America
1 2 3 4 5 6 7 13 12 11 10 09

Contents

Authors in Forthcoming Volumes

Below are some of the authors and illustrators that will be featured in upcoming volumes of *SATA*. These include new entries on the swiftly rising stars of the field, as well as completely revised and updated entries (indicated with *) on some of the most notable and best-loved creators of books for children.

Daniel Bar-el ▮ Bar-el, a writer and storyteller based in Canada, is the author of the unusual ABC picture book *Alphabetter,* in which readers can help characters search the pages for hidden objects. An early childhood educator, Bar-el is also the author of the award-winning picture books *Things Are Looking Grimm, Jill* and *Such a Prince,* both of which feature the author's upbeat humor.

Kyrsten Brooker ▮ Brooker studied interior design before deciding to become a children's book illustrator. Her multimedia collage art, which has earned both critical praise and awards, is a feature of picture books ranging from Kathleen Krull's nonfiction *They Saw the Future: Oracles, Psychics, Scientists, Great Thinkers, and Pretty Good Guessers* and Caroline Lazo's *Someday When My Cat Can Talk,* a fanciful story in which Brooker's richly textured images are studded with brocaded fabrics, pearls, wallpaper, and other found objects.

*Michael Coleman ▮ Coleman's books for young people range from detective fiction to sports stories to nonfiction and picture books. A former computer programmer and academic in his native England, the prolific Coleman made his debut with the middle-grade novel *Triv in Pursuit.* His more-recent books include the novels *Weirdo's War, Tag, The Snog Log,* and *On the Run,* as well as the sports-themed "Foul Football" and "Angels F.C." series.

Rita de Clercq Zubli ▮ A preteen living in Sumatra when World War II broke out, de Clercq Zubli disguised herself as a boy and taught herself Japanese in order to survive the Japanese occupation of her homeland. In her memoir *Disguised: A War Memoir* readers learn about de Clercq Zubli's efforts to avoid detection, her adventures working as a translator for the Japanese, and her work aiding camp inmates by using advantages gained through her privileged position.

Peter Fergusen ▮ Ferguson is a comic-book and editorial artist who is based in Montreal, Quebec, Canada. In addition to illustrating young-adult novels and children's books, including the works in Michael Buckley's popular "Sisters Grimm" series, his humorous and at times eerie art has won praise from numerous critics.

Robert Kinerk ▮ A former journalist and playwright, Kinerk teams up with artist Steven Kellogg to produce the large-format picture books *Clorinda* and *Clorinda Takes Flight.* In addition to these humorous stories, which lyrically depict a bright-eyed cow with unusual aspirations, the Massachusetts-based author has also written the critically praised picture books *Timothy Cox Will Not Change His Socks* and *Bear's First Christmas.*

*Wendell Minor ▮ Even those who do not read picture books or visit art galleries have likely encountered the work of Minor, an award-winning artist whose illustrations appear in books by such noted children's book authors as Jean Craighead George, Margaret Wise Brown, Carl Sandburg, and Alice Schertle. His style, which has been lauded for its classic elements, graces books including *Red Fox Running, Julie and the Wolves,* and *Ghost Ship,* as well as original self-illustrated books.

Kathy Osborn ▮ Well known for her fine-art paintings, as well as for her collaboration with writer Jacqueline Carey in the illustrated adult novel *Wedding Pictures,* Osborn is also an illustrator of children's books. Her highly colored gouache images have a static, staged quality that shows the modernist influence of artist Edward Hopper. Working in a three-dimensional art form, Osborn is also known for creating modernist doll houses featuring a colorful collage of retro design elements.

*Anne Spudvilas ▮ Spudvilas is an acclaimed Australian illustrator and portrait painter who works predominantly in oils on canvas. Her art has been featured alongside texts by a number of well-known children's writers, among them Isobelle Carmody, Margaret Wild, Ian Bone, Sophie Masson, and Gary Crew. The haunting, large-format picture book *Woolvs in the Sitee* is one of several collaborations between Spudvilas and Wild that have earned the women both critical praise and recognition.

*Jacqueline Wilson ▮ Wilson is one of Great Britain's most beloved writers for young readers. Her middle-grade novels, which include the critically acclaimed *The Story of Tracy Beaker, The Illustrated Mum,* and *Candyfloss,* have been translated into dozens of languages and several have been adapted for television. Wilson's many honors include the Smarties Prize and the British Book Awards Children's Book of the Year; in 2005 the prolific writer was also named Britain's fourth children's laureate.

Introduction

Something about the Author (*SATA*) is an ongoing reference series that examines the lives and works of authors and illustrators of books for children. *SATA* includes not only well-known writers and artists but also less prominent individuals whose works are just coming to be recognized. This series is often the only readily available information source on emerging authors and illustrators. You'll find *SATA* informative and entertaining, whether you are a student, a librarian, an English teacher, a parent, or simply an adult who enjoys children's literature.

What's Inside *SATA*

SATA provides detailed information about authors and illustrators who span the full time range of children's literature, from early figures like John Newbery and L. Frank Baum to contemporary figures like Judy Blume and Richard Peck. Authors in the series represent primarily English-speaking countries, particularly the United States, Canada, and the United Kingdom. Also included, however, are authors from around the world whose works are available in English translation. The writings represented in *SATA* include those created intentionally for children and young adults as well as those written for a general audience and known to interest younger readers. These writings cover the entire spectrum of children's literature, including picture books, humor, folk and fairy tales, animal stories, mystery and adventure, science fiction and fantasy, historical fiction, poetry and nonsense verse, drama, biography, and nonfiction. Obituaries are also included in *SATA* and are intended not only as death notices but also as concise overviews of people's lives and work. Additionally, each edition features newly revised and updated entries for a selection of *SATA* listees who remain of interest to today's readers and who have been active enough to require extensive revisions of their earlier biographies.

Autobiography Feature

Beginning with Volume 103, many volumes of *SATA* feature one or more specially commissioned autobiographical essays. These unique essays, averaging about ten thousand words in length and illustrated with an abundance of personal photos, present an entertaining and informative first-person perspective on the lives and careers of prominent authors and illustrators profiled in *SATA*.

Two Convenient Indexes

In response to suggestions from librarians, *SATA* indexes no longer appear in every volume but are included in alternate (odd-numbered) volumes of the series, beginning with Volume 57.

SATA continues to include two indexes that cumulate with each alternate volume: the Illustrations Index, arranged by the name of the illustrator, gives the number of the volume and page where the illustrator's work appears in the current volume as well as all preceding volumes in the series; the Author Index gives the number of the volume in which a person's biographical sketch, autobiographical essay, or obituary appears in the current volume as well as all preceding volumes in the series.

These indexes also include references to authors and illustrators who appear in *Gale's Yesterday's Authors of Books for Children, Children's Literature Review,* and *Something about the Author Autobiography Series.*

Easy-to-Use Entry Format

Whether you're already familiar with the *SATA* series or just getting acquainted, you will want to be aware of the kind of information that an entry provides. In every *SATA* entry the editors attempt to give as complete a picture of the person's life and work as possible. A typical entry in *SATA* includes the following clearly labeled information sections:

PERSONAL: date and place of birth and death, parents' names and occupations, name of spouse, date of marriage, names of children, educational institutions attended, degrees received, religious and political affiliations, hobbies and other interests.

ADDRESSES: complete home, office, electronic mail, and agent addresses, whenever available.

CAREER: name of employer, position, and dates for each career post; art exhibitions; military service; memberships and offices held in professional and civic organizations.

MEMBER: professional, civic, and other association memberships and any official posts held.

AWARDS, HONORS: literary and professional awards received.

WRITINGS: title-by-title chronological bibliography of books written and/or illustrated, listed by genre when known; lists of other notable publications, such as plays, screenplays, and periodical contributions.

ADAPTATIONS: a list of films, television programs, plays, CD-ROMs, recordings, and other media presentations that have been adapted from the author's work.

WORK IN PROGRESS: description of projects in progress.

SIDELIGHTS: a biographical portrait of the author or illustrator's development, either directly from the biographee—and often written specifically for the *SATA* entry—or gathered from diaries, letters, interviews, or other published sources.

BIOGRAPHICAL AND CRITICAL SOURCES: cites sources quoted in "Sidelights" along with references for further reading.

EXTENSIVE ILLUSTRATIONS: photographs, movie stills, book illustrations, and other interesting visual materials supplement the text.

How a *SATA* Entry Is Compiled

SATA editors examine a wide variety of published sources to gather information for an entry. Biographical and bibliographic sources are consulted, as are book reviews, feature articles, published interviews, and material sometimes obtained from the biographee's family, publishers, agent, or other associates. Whenever possible, the author or illustrator is sent a copy of the entry to check for accuracy and completeness.

Entries that have not been verified by the biographees or their representatives are marked with an asterisk (*).

Contact the Editor

We encourage our readers to examine the entire *SATA* series. Please write and tell us if we can make *SATA* even more helpful to you. Give your comments and suggestions to the editor:

Editor
Something about the Author
Gale, Cengage Learning
27500 Drake Rd.
Farmington Hills MI 48331-3535

Toll-free: 800-877-GALE
Fax: 248-699-8070

Something about the Author Product Advisory Board

The editors of *Something about the Author* are dedicated to maintaining a high standard of excellence by publishing comprehensive, accurate, and highly readable entries on a wide array of writers for children and young adults. In addition to the quality of the content, the editors take pride in the graphic design of the series, which is intended to be orderly yet inviting, allowing readers to utilize the pages of *SATA* easily and with efficiency. Despite the longevity of the *SATA* print series, and the success of its format, we are mindful that the vitality of a literary reference product is dependent on its ability to serve its users over time. As literature, and attitudes about literature, constantly evolve, so do the reference needs of students, teachers, scholars, journalists, researchers, and book club members. To be certain that we continue to keep pace with the expectations of our customers, the editors of *SATA* listen carefully to their comments regarding the value, utility, and quality of the series. Librarians, who have firsthand knowledge of the needs of library users, are a valuable resource for us. The *Something about the Author* Product Advisory Board, made up of school, public, and academic librarians, is a forum to promote focused feedback about *SATA* on a regular basis. The nine-member advisory board includes the following individuals, whom the editors wish to thank for sharing their expertise:

SOMETHING ABOUT THE AUTHOR

ABLOW, Gail 1962-

Personal

Born 1962.

Addresses

Home—Brooklyn, NY.

Career

Children's author and broadcast journalist. Has produced documentaries for national television networks, including Cable News Network, American Broadcasting Companies, and Public Broadcasting Service.

Awards, Honors

Knight fellowship, Stanford University, 2004.

Writings

A Horse in the House, and Other Strange but True Animal Stories, illustrated by Kathy Osborn, Candlewick Press (Cambridge, MA), 2007.

Sidelights

A veteran of the broadcast journalism industry, Gail Ablow turned to children's literature with *A Horse in the House, and Other Strange but True Animal Stories.*

Illustrated by Kathy Osborn, Ablow's book features sixteen short and unusual animal tales, including one about a family that adopted a horse as a house pet, another about a man who gave a fish mouth-to-mouth resuscitation, and another about a psychologist who treats poultry. While many of these stories seem far-fetched, Ablow documents the sources of her information, demonstrating to young readers the legitimacy of her tales.

Writing in *Booklist,* John Peters suggested the inclusion of external sources is important, as young readers might otherwise doubt the plausibility of several of the animal accounts without them. Peters commented favorably on *A Horse in the House, and Other Strange but True Animal Stories* as a whole, predicting that "even skeptical young readers will come back for more." Ablow's stories "are consistently interesting and worthy of inclusion," concluded a *Kirkus Reviews* contributor, while in *Horn Book* Susan Dove Lempke applauded the book's text and artwork, claiming that *A Horse in the House, and Other Strange but True Animal Stories* "will provide lots of laughs and some good anecdotes to retell at the dinner table."

Biographical and Critical Sources

PERIODICALS

Booklist, September 15, 2007, John Peters, review of *A Horse in the House, and Other Strange but True Animal Stories,* p. 64.

Horn Book, January-February, 2008, Susan Dove Lempke, review of *A Horse in the House, and Other Strange but True Animal Stories,* p. 103.
Kirkus Reviews, September 15, 2007, review of *A Horse in the House, and Other Strange but True Animal Stories.**

* * *

BABONI, Elena

Personal

Born in Mantua, Italy. *Education:* Studied art in Florence, Italy.

Addresses

Home—Italy.

Career

Art restorer, illustrator, and ceramicist. Has restored works of the Old Masters in Italy.

Illustrator

Claire and Nick Page, *The Summer Queen* (beginning reader), Make Believe Ideas, 2006.
Leena Lane, *Angels among Us,* Eerdman's Books for Young Readers (Grand Rapids, MI), 2007.
Roberta Fasanotti, *Faccia di cavolfiore,* Falzea (Italy), 2007.
Leena Lane, *Star of Wonder,* Abington Press, 2007.

Illustrator of several books published in Italy.

Books featuring Baboni's illustrations have been translated into several languages, including French and German.

Sidelights

Italian artist Elena Baboni creates textured illustrations that reflect her expertise as an art restorer who specializes in restoring the work of the Old Masters. In addition to appearing in several books published in her native Italy, Baboni's stylized, full-color acrylic paintings have also accompanied English-language texts, among them *Star of Wonder,* Leena Lane's account of the events of the very first Christmas.

In *Angels among Us* Baboni once again teams up with Lane to create a picture book with biblical themes. A large-format work that features what *Booklist* contributor Ilene Cooper described as "elongated and dramatic" angelic figures wearing "gowns of purple, red, and gold," *Angels among Us* shares stories from both the Old and New Testament that find heavenly helpers aiding Moses, Daniel, Mary, and others on earth by communicating messages from God. In *Publishers Weekly* a reviewer praised Lane's "simple language," adding that

the illustrator's "fuzzy, jewel-toned acrylic paintings create a dreamlike mood." Baboni also uses the texture gained by acrylics to evoke the ancient quality of biblical stories, according to *School Library Journal* critic Linda Israelson. As the critic added, the artist's "decorative" renderings "reinforce the unpredictable nature of the heavenly hosts" by depicting them in an exotic, multicultural manner.

Biographical and Critical Sources

PERIODICALS

Booklist, October 1, 2007, Ilene Cooper, review of *Angels among Us,* p. 71.
Kirkus Reviews, September 1, 2007, review of *Angels among Us.*
Publishers Weekly, August 27, 2007, review of *Angels among Us,* p. 95.
School Library Journal, November, 2007, Linda Israelson, review of *Angels among Us,* p. 109.**

* * *

BECKERMAN, Chad W.

Personal

Born in CT. *Education:* Rhode Island School of Design, B.F.A. (illustration), 2000.

Addresses

Home—New York, NY. *E-mail*—chadwbeckerman@gmail.com.

Career

Book designer and illustrator. Scholastic, Inc. (publisher), New York, NY, former design assistant; HarperCollins, New York, NY, designer, then senior designer at Greenwillow Books for four years; Harry N. Abrams, New York, NY, associate art director, 2006-08, art director for Amulet and Abrams Books for Young Readers, beginning 2008. Illustrator of book covers.

Illustrator

Sid Fleishman, *Disappearing Act,* Greenwillow (New York, NY), 2003.
Delia Ephron, *Frannie in Pieces,* Laura Geringer Books (New York, NY), 2007.

Biographical and Critical Sources

PERIODICALS

Booklist, November 1, 2007, Ilene Cooper, review of *Frannie in Pieces,* p. 40.

Chad W. Beckerman (Photograph courtesy of Chad W. Beckerman.)

Horn Book, May-June, 2003, Betty Carter, review of *Disappearing Act,* p. 345.

Kirkus Reviews, September 1, 2007, review of *Frannie in Pieces.*

Kliatt, September, 2007, Myrna Marler, review of *Frannie in Pieces,* p. 11.

Publishers Weekly, September 24, 2007, review of *Frannie in Pieces,* p. 73.

School Library Journal, May, 2003, Steven Engelfried, review of *Disappearing Act,* p. 150.

ONLINE

Chad W. Beckerman Home Page, http://chadbeckerman. com (February 2, 2009).

Career Cookbook Web site, http://www.thecareercookbook. com/ (August 27, 2006), Paul Maniaci, interview with Beckerman.

*   *   *

BLAKE, Francis

Personal

Born in England. *Hobbies and other interests:* Gardening.

Addresses

Home—London, England. *Agent*—Three in a Box Inc., http://threeinabox.com. *E-mail*—francis@francisblake. com.

Career

Illustrator.

Awards, Honors

International Reading Association Children's Book Award Notable Book citation, 2003, for *From Head to Toe* by Janice Weaver.

Illustrator

Anna Jean, *Clubhouse Stories: Parallel Parables for Young Teens,* Bible Reading Fellowship (Oxford, England), 1999.

Sue Doggett, *Advent Angels: A Host of Stories, Crafts, Puzzles, and Things to Do for the Days of Advent,* Bible Reading Fellowship (Oxford, England), 1999.

Jenny Hyson, *Love Is Full of Surprises,* Barnabas (Oxford, England), 2000.

Lucy Moore, *The Gospels Unplugged: 52 Poems and Stories for Creative Writing, Drama, and Collective Worship,* Bible Reading Fellowship (Oxford, England), 2002.

Veronica Heley, *Stories of Everyday Saints: 40 Stories with Bible Links and Related Activities,* Bible Reading Fellowship (Oxford, England), 2002.

Janice Weaver, *From Head to Toe: Bound Feet, Bathing Suits, and Other Bizarre and Beautiful Things,* Tundra Books (Plattsburgh, NY), 2003.

Janice Weaver, *The A to Z of Everyday Things,* Tundra Books (Toronto, Ontario, Canada), 2004.

Lucy Moore, *The Lord's Prayer Unplugged: A Wealth of Ideas Opening up the Prayer in Ten Sessions,* Bible Reading Fellowship (Oxford, England), 2004.

Jan Andrews, *Stories at the Door,* Tundra Books (Toronto, Ontario, Canada), 2007.

Also author and illustrator of several short cartoon chapbooks.

Sidelights

London-based artist Francis Blake has been an illustrator for as long as he can remember. Blake's cartoon-style drawings, rendered in ink and tinted with water colors, appear in several books by author Janice Weaver that entertain and inform at the same time. Their 2003 collaboration, *From Head to Toe: Bound Feet, Bathing Suits, and Other Bizarre and Beautiful Things,* covers unusual fashion trends throughout history and across the world. The numerous fun facts are "lavishly illustrated with witty color drawings," according to *Kliatt* contributor Janet Julian. In *School Library Journal* Lynda Ritterman called Blake's images "humorous," while in *Canadian Review of Materials* Lorraine Douglas predicted that "the book's text and whimsical drawings . . . will appeal to a wide range of readers."

In *The A to Z of Everyday Things* Weaver and Blake inspire readers to reconsider an assortment of common items through interesting histories, and their focus ranges from alphabets to colors to numerals. "Blake's illustrations are the perfect accessories to pull together Weaver's textual wardrobe," Julie Chychota remarked in a *Canadian Review of Materials* appraisal. "The drawings that mark the start of each chapter are often amusing in their own right; they are funnier still as readers come to understand them within the context of the text," Chychota added.

Blake also collaborated with Weaver on *Stories at the Door,* a collection of folktale retellings. According to *Booklist* reviewer Carolyn Phelan, "the lively stories are well matched by Blake's jaunty, colorful, and often comical line-and-wash artwork." "Bright coloured, whimsical illustrations abound, adding fun and interpretation to each story," Carolyn Cutt similarly remarked in *Resource Links,* while in *Canadian Review of Materials* Ruth Scales McMahon asserted that "Blake's colourful collaboration adds life, humour, depth and entertaining sidelights to [Weaver's] . . . tales."

Biographical and Critical Sources

PERIODICALS

Booklist, January 1, 2008, Carolyn Phelan, review of *Stories at the Door,* p. 70.
Kirkus Reviews, September 15, 2007, review of *Stories at the Door.*
Kliatt, January, 2004, Janet Julian, review of *From Head to Toe: Bound Feet, Bathing Suits, and Other Bizarre and Beautiful Things,* p. 32.
Resource Links, October, 2007, Carolyn Cutt, review of *Stories at the Door,* p. 12.
School Library Journal, February, 2004, Lynda Ritterman, review of *From Head to Toe,* p. 170.
Voice of Youth Advocates, August, 2004, review of *From Head to Toe,* p. 243; April, 2005, Mary Ann Harlan, review of *The A to Z of Everyday Things,* pp. 73-74.

ONLINE

Francis Blake Home Page, http://www.francisblake.com (January 19, 2009).

Francis Blake's entertaining art is a highlight of Jan Andrews' picture book Stories at the Door. (Illustration copyright © 2007 by Francis Blake. All rights reserved. Reproduced by permission of Tundra Books of Northern New York in the United States.)

Canadian Review of Materials, http://www.umanitoba.ca/cm/ (September 5, 2003) Lorraine Douglas, review of *From Head to Toe;* (December 10, 2004) Julie Chychota, review of *The A to Z of Everyday Things;* (October 12, 2007) Ruth Scales McMahon, review of *Stories at the Door.**

*   *   *

BROWN, Elbrite

Personal

Born in Philadelphia, PA. *Education:* University of the Arts (Philadelphia, PA), earned bachelor's and master's degrees.

Addresses

Home—PA.

Career

Illustrator, artist, and art instructor. Has worked as a public school art teacher in Philadelphia, PA, and in New Jersey.

Awards, Honors

Coretta Scott King/John Steptoe New Talent Award, American Library Association, 2004, for *My Family Plays Music.*

Illustrator

Judy Cox, *My Family Plays Music,* Holiday House (New York, NY), 2003.
Ellen B. Jackson, *Cinnamon Brown and the Seven Dwarfs,* Viking (New York, NY), 2006.
Karen Deans, *Playing to Win: The Story of Althea Gibson,* Holiday House (New York, NY), 2007.

Sidelights

Artist Elbrite Brown provided the cut-paper illustrations for *My Family Plays Music,* a children's picture book with a text by Judy Cox. Narrated by a young African-American girl, *My Family Plays Music* depicts a multiracial family's love for a variety of musical styles, from Mom's preference for country music to Dad's enjoyment of classical works. With a sister in the marching band and a brother in a rock-and-roll group, the book's young narrator not only experiences a variety of musical genres, but also joyfully participates in each one of them in her own way.

In recognition of his work for *My Family Plays Music,* Brown earned a Coretta Scott King/John Steptoe New Talent Award from the American Library Association, as well as favorable comments from several reviewers. His "paper-cut illustrations vibrate with color and—almost—with sound," wrote GraceAnne A. DeCandido

Elbrite Brown brings the world of athlete Althea Gibson to life in his artwork for Karen Deans' picture book **Playing to Win.** (Illustration copyright © 2007 by Elbrite Brown. All rights reserved. Reproduced by permission of Holiday House, Inc.)

in a *Booklist* review of the book, while *School Library Journal* contributor Jane Marino claimed that Brown's "cut-paper illustrations are vibrant and filled with energy."

Brown teams up with author Karen Deans, adding mixed-media illustrations to Deans' book about tennis great Althea Gibson. *Playing to Win: The Story of Althea Gibson* shares with young readers the story of the first African-American woman to win Grand Slam tennis championships at Wimbledon, the French Open, and the U.S. Open. Gibson's early life is revealed through a picture-book format that relates some of the difficult experiences in the young tennis star's life, such as riding on segregated buses in the South and eventually breaking the color barrier of the previously all-white U.S. Lawn Tennis Association. In general, wrote *School Library Journal* reviewer Judy Chichinski, "the multimedia illustrations are well matched to the power

and fluidity of the text." A *Kirkus Reviews* critic praised Brown's use of "perspective and color to amplify emotion," while *Booklist* contributor Carolyn Phelan concluded that the artist's "mixed-media collage illustrations bring the story to life," creating a "visually dynamic picture-book biography."

Biographical and Critical Sources

PERIODICALS

Booklist, October 15, 2003, GraceAnne A. DeCandido, review of *My Family Plays Music,* p. 417; September 1, 2007, Carolyn Phelan, review of *Playing to Win: The Story of Althea Gibson,* p. 137.
Kirkus Reviews, September 1, 2003, review of *My Family Plays Music,* p. 1121; July 15, 2007, review of *Playing to Win.*

Publishers Weekly, October 6, 2003, review of *My Family Plays Music,* p. 83; August 27, 2007, review of *Playing to Win,* p. 89.

School Library Journal, October, 2003, Jane Marino, review of *My Family Plays Music,* p. 116; September, 2007, Judy Chichinski, review of *Playing to Win,* p. 182.*

* * *

BURGESS, Melvin 1954-

Personal

Born April 25, 1954, in Twickenham, Surrey, England; son of Christopher (an educational writer) and Helen Burgess; married Avis von Herder (marriage ended); married Judith Liggett; children: Oliver von Herder, Pearl, Sam. *Politics:* "Left."

Addresses

Home—Manchester, England. *E-mail*—melvin@melvinburgess.net.

Career

Writer.

Member

Society of Authors.

Awards, Honors

Carnegie Medal shortlist, British Library Association, 1991, for *The Cry of the Wolf,* 1993, for *An Angel for May,* 1994, for *The Baby and Fly Pie,* and 2000, for *The Ghost behind the Wall;* Whitbread Award shortlist, Carnegie Medal, and London *Guardian* Award for Children's Fiction, all 1997, and "Carnegie of Carnegies" shortlist, 2007, all for *Junk;* Lancashire Children's Book Award, for *Bloodtide; Los Angeles Times* Book Award for young-adult fiction, 2004, for *Doing It.*

Writings

The Cry of the Wolf, Tambourine Books (New York, NY), 1990.

Burning Issy, Andersen (London, England), 1992, Simon & Schuster (New York, NY), 1994.

An Angel for May, Andersen (London, England), 1992, Simon & Schuster (New York, NY), 1995.

The Baby and Fly Pie, Andersen (London, England), 1993, Simon & Schuster (New York, NY), 1996.

Loving April, Andersen (London, England), 1995.

Junk, Andersen (London, England), 1996, published as *Smack,* Holt (New York, NY), 1998.

Tiger, Tiger, Andersen (London, England), 1996.

Earth Giant, Putnam (New York, NY), 1997.

Kite, Andersen (London, England), 1997, Farrar, Straus & Giroux (New York, NY), 2000.

The Copper Treasure, illustrated by Richard Williams, A & C Black (London, England), 1998, Holt (New York, NY), 2000.

Bloodtide, Andersen (London, England), 1999, Tor (New York, NY), 2001.

Old Bag, illustrated by Trevor Parkin, Barrington Stoke (Edinburgh, Scotland), 1999.

The Birdman, illustrated by Ruth Brown, Andersen (London, England), 2000.

Billy Elliot (novelization of a screenplay by Lee Hall), Scholastic (New York, NY), 2001.

The Ghost behind the Wall, Andersen (London, England), 2001, Holt (New York, NY), 2003.

Lady: My Life as a Bitch, Andersen (London, England), 2001, Holt (New York, NY), 2002.

Robbers on the Road ("Tudor Flashbacks" series), A & C Black (London, England), 2002.

Highwayman ("Tudor Flashbacks" series), A & C Black (London, England), 2002.

Doing It, Andersen (London, England), 2003, Holt (New York, NY), 2004.

Bloodsong (sequel to *Bloodtide*), Andersen (London, England), 2005, Simon & Schuster (New York, NY), 2007.

Sara's Face, Andersen (London, England), 2006, Simon & Schuster (New York, NY), 2007.

Adaptations

Junk was adapted as a play by John Retallack, Methuen Drama (London, England), 1999; *An Angel for May* was adapted as a motion picture directed by Harley Cokeliss, screenplay by Peter Milligan, Children's Film and Television Foundation, 2002; *Bloodtide* was adapted as a play produced in York, England, 2005; *The Baby and Fly Pie* was adapted as a play produced in Manchester, England, 2005.

Sidelights

Described as the "godfather" of young-adult fiction in Britain, Melvin Burgess has combined fantasy with gritty realism in a succession of critically acclaimed novels which are unsettling and controversial. In such works as *The Cry of the Wolf, Junk,* and *Sara's Face,* Burgess has showcased his creative and unique views regarding the experience of adolescence. As the author once told *SATA,* "My books are about *anything* that interests me, but they nearly all have this in common: they are life seen from the under-side, not (usually) from on top."

Taking place in Surrey, England, *The Cry of the Wolf* features a young boy who inadvertently threatens the wild wolf population near his home. Ten-year-old Ben tells a stranger identified only as "the Hunter" about a wolf pack that lives in the forest nearby; the Hunter, on a mission to gain notoriety for killing the last of the wolves surviving in the wild in England, arms himself with a crossbow and hunts them down. "This is indeed

Cover of Melvin Burgess's dystopian fantasy novel Bloodtide, *featuring artwork by Jon Foster.* (Tom Doherty 2001. Reproduced by permission.)

a powerful first novel, and sinister too," noted a reviewer in *Junior Bookshelf.* Calling the novel "a dramatic and horrifying tale of the tragedy of extinction," Susan Oliver added in *School Library Journal* that *The Cry of the Wolf* is "an ecological thriller that will draw nature lovers and horror fans alike."

Tiger, Tiger recalls Burgess's first novel in its focus on the plight of animals. The story revolves around a Chinese businessman's attempts to use several hundred square miles in Yorkshire as a safari park featuring Siberian tigers, rare animals that are said to have magical properties. When one of the great cats—a female called Lila—escapes and encounters several children living in a nearby village, a merger between cat and human on both physical and intellectual levels is the result. "The adroit combination of fact and fantasy is expertly managed with no concession to the tenderhearted," explained a *Junior Bookshelf* critic, who also noted the story's use of the folklore of werewolves and human-to-animal shape shifting. Linda Newbery praised the work in *School Librarian,* declaring that *Tiger, Tiger* "ends with a poignant reflection on the status of wild animals in the modern world."

An Angel for May finds Tam, a twelve year old, upset over his parents' recent divorce. He spends a great deal of time roaming through the moors and the charred ruins of a farmhouse near his country home. On one of his rambles, Tam encounters an unusual homeless woman named Rosey who draws him fifty years into the past—the World War II era—where he meets a young retarded child named May. May helps Tam to put his own family situation into perspective and he, in turn, becomes an important, caring presence in her life. Calling the novel "a sad, strange little story," a *Junior Bookshelf* reviewer stated that Burgess's book "hits the right note throughout" and is written "with a restraint which is all the more moving for its quietness." Merri Monks, in a *Booklist* assessment, lauded *An Angel for May* as "a story of courage, moral development, friendship, and love."

In *Burning Issy* Burgess draws readers into the seventeenth century, depicting the life of a young, orphaned woman who befriends both white and black witches. In this era of superstition, when witch hunters and the church persecuted herbal healers and others with supposed "magical" powers, she is eventually accused of witchcraft. As the story unfolds, Issy, who was badly burned as a small child, realizes that her recurrent nightmares of fire are actually recollections of being almost burned alongside her mother, a convicted witch who was burned at the stake. When she herself is imprisoned, Issy is determined to escape, whatever the cost. Helen Turner, in a review in *Voice of Youth Advocates,* called the book "a riveting exploration into some dark corners of history." *Burning Issy* was also hailed by *Horn Book* contributor Nancy Vasilakis as "a compelling story with a thoughtful message on the destructive force of superstition."

From the distant past, Burgess moves ahead to the not-so-distant future in his novel *The Baby and Fly Pie.* The book's unusual title comes from the two main characters: Fly Pie, an orphaned teen surviving on the London streets as one of the scavenging "Rubbish Kids," and the infant daughter of a wealthy family whom Fly Pie and his friend Sham intercept during a kidnapping attempt gone awry. When the kidnapper dies of his wounds, the teens find themselves surrogate parents and must decide whether to return infant Sylvie to her distraught parents or hold out for ransom. While some reviewers deemed the novel too bleak to interest teens, the book received high marks from several critics. A *Junior Bookshelf* commentator noted that the novel's "topical theme and its sympathetic treatment, its social message and its refusal to compromise with the harsh reality of shanty town economy make it strong meat for early teenagers." *Booklist* contributor Anne O'Malley maintained: "The stunning characterizations, fascinating scenario, well-plotted, virtually nonstop action, and mounting suspense pull the reader right in from start to tragic end."

Winner of the 1997 Carnegie Medal and the London *Guardian* Children's Fiction Award, *Junk*—published in the United States as *Smack*—follows the story of two fourteen-year-old runaways, Tar and Gemma. Fleeing disturbing home environments, the two find their place among the squatters of Bristol and adopt a delinquent lifestyle that eventually includes shoplifting, prostitution, and heroin addiction. Critics praised Burgess for offering, without condescension, an accurate depiction of teen drug abuse. Writing in the London *Observer*, Neil Spencer noted the "absence of adult finger-wagging" in *Junk*. He went on to praise Burgess for leaving the book's ending open, but with "a sense of hope rather than despair" for the characters. Calling the novel "complex, multifoliate, and tremendously powerful," a contributor to *Books for Keeps* applauded the author's ability to capture the "addicts' self-deluding psychobabble," writing that "the chill authenticity of their ramblings is frightening."

Burgess also received critical praise for *Bloodtide*, which won the Lancashire Children's Book Award. Based on the thirteenth-century Icelandic Volsunga saga, *Bloodtide* is set many years later in a post-apocalyptic London where two warring human clans live among a breed of half-men. With character names and a story line taken from the famous saga, the story revolves around the power struggle between the Conors and the Volsons to see who will rule London. In the midst of the story, which is narrated by multiple characters, the leaders of the two clans hope to unite through a marriage between the head of the Conor clan and a fourteen-year-old girl named Signy. However, the Conors use the marriage as a trap and end up slaughtering the entire Volson clan. Only Signy and her twin brother survive the massacre, and the story follows them in their search for vengeance against the Conors. Amid the ensuing battle between the two clans, the Norse gods Odin and Loki play significant roles, just as they do in the Volsunga saga.

While praising *Bloodtide*, several literary critics warned readers of the tale's darker elements. According to a contributor for *Publishers Weekly*, *Bloodtide* "does not stint on graphic portrayals of violence." Sally Estes, writing in *Booklist*, called the work "a grim, disturbing dystopia." Despite such forewarning, Julia Eccleshare, who reviewed the book for the London *Guardian*, maintained that its "moments of tenderness offset the brutality." Estes described the story as one that "readers . . . won't forget."

In *Bloodsong*, a companion to *Bloodtide*, Burgess continues his reworking of Icelandic mythology. The novel centers on fifteen-year-old Sigurd, the only surviving member of the Volson clan, and his efforts to reunite his war-torn nation. Returning to London, Sigurd must slay a deadly, genetically modified dragon named Fafnir by using a magical sword forged from his father's dagger. "Burgess pulls no punches in his dark dystopian vision; classic themes of heroism, love, and betrayal are illustrated with violent imagery," Jennifer Hubert re-

marked in *Booklist*, and Paula Rohrlick wrote in *Kliatt* that *Bloodsong* is "an intense and involving read."

With *Lady: My Life as a Bitch*, Burgess again attracted controversy. Including scenes of teenage sex, *Lady* is about seventeen-year-old, angst-ridden Sandra Fancy, who is transformed into a dog after an encounter with a tramp. Far from perplexed by her metamorphosis, Sandra actually enjoys her new life because it allows her to pursue hedonistic pleasures without worrying about how human society will perceive her actions. In a *Bookseller*, interview, Burgess answered critics who accused him of endorsing amoral behavior. "People tend to write books for young adults and children that say, you can go anywhere and explore anything, so long as you come home at the end," he stated. "So it was a real pleasure to write a book where the female character left home at the end—and for all the wrong reasons." Despite its controversial subject matter, several literary critics lauded *Lady*, a *Bookseller* contributor calling it "a vivid account, both realistic, and fantastical, of a teenager's experiences, and one in which the morality is not reducible to a cautionary lesson." London *Daily Telegraph* critic Rachel Cusk dubbed the work a "funny, punchy, well-written, original book."

Burgess's *Doing It* also became the subject of much debate in England, even before it appeared in print. Geared for a mature teen readership, *Doing It* revolves around three seventeen-year-old boys and their relationships with women. As much of the work features frank discussions of sex, some reviewers found the dialogue inappropriate for teenagers, among them British children's laureate Anne Fine who called *Doing It* "filth, whichever way you look at it" in the London *Guardian*. Fine also disparaged the work as a "grubby book, which demeans both young women and young men." However, as Burgess himself has remarked, other reviewers noted that the title addressed a genre largely ignored in literature for teens: adolescent male romance. As the author explained on his home page, "I wrote *Doing It* because I do believe that we have let young men down very badly in terms of the kind of books written for them. . . . This is changing these days, and *Doing It* is my go at trying to bring young, male sexual culture into writing."

Considering the characters in *Doing It* "nice boys" who are simply interested in sex and what it involves physically as well as emotionally, Burgess defended his work to London *Evening Standard* critic Catherine Shoard by claiming that the criticism surrounding this work "confirmed my feeling that *Doing It* was a good thing to do. Lads of that age get terribly neglected because of these so-called moral guardians." Despite the controversy, several reviewers offered praise for the work. "From snogging to shagging to buggering, *Doing It* discusses it in a dizzying array of contexts, and it is relentlessly and refreshingly honest," noted *Booklist* critic John Green, and a contributor in *Publishers Weekly* noted that teenage readers "will welcome (and even be reassured by) a book that so accurately mirrors their new world view."

Burgess examines issues of celebrity and identity in *Sara's Face,* "a nightmarish, unforgettable story," observed a reviewer in *Publishers Weekly.* Narrated by a reporter with questionable ethics, the work concerns seventeen-year-old Sara Carter, a young woman obsessed with fame and physical beauty. Hospitalized after scarring her own face with an iron, Sara meets Jonathon Heat, a pop idol whose numerous cosmetic surgeries have left his own face in shreds, which he hides with a mask. When Jonathon invites Sara to recover at his compound, under the care of Dr. Wayland Kaye, a crazed plastic surgeon, the girl's friends and family begin to fear for her safety. "Although this rollercoaster of a ride is hurtling towards the one inevitable conclusion, it's thrilling nevertheless, gaining momentum and causing frantic page-turning as it nears its gruesome final stop," commented Philip Ardagh in the London *Guardian.* A critic in *Kirkus Reviews* also praised the work, calling *Sara's Face* "a gory nail-biter with ghastly sadness and maddening emotional incomprehensibility, exquisitely done."

Cover of Burgess's novel Sara's Face, *a realistic thriller that mixes medicine with mystery.* (Cover illustration copyright © 2008 by Getty Images. Reproduced by permission.)

One of the strengths of Burgess's writing, according to Elizabeth O'Reilly on the *Contemporary Writers in the UK* Web site, is "the way in which he shows acute sensitivity towards teenage feelings and experiences without fully endorsing or indulging the adolescent point of view." "Teenage qualities are really rather splendid," the author stated in a London *Guardian* essay. "The enthusiasm, the shyness and the energy are all good things. There's also the laziness, of course—but maybe a bit more time to stop and stare would be good for us all. We call them gauche and over the top, but maybe making mistakes is something people do when they're learning. Perhaps we could do with being a little more gauche ourselves."

Biographical and Critical Sources

BOOKS

Beacham's Guide to Literature for Young Adults, Volume 12, Gale (Detroit, MI), 2001.

PERIODICALS

Booklist, May 1, 1995, Merri Monks, review of *An Angel for May,* pp. 1571-1572; May 15, 1996, Anne O'Malley, review of *The Baby and Fly Pie,* p. 1586; October 15, 2001, Sally Estes, review of *Bloodtide,* p. 387; June 1, 2002, Anne O'Malley, review of *Lady: My Life as a Bitch,* p. 1716; April 15, 2003, Anne O'Malley, review of *The Ghost behind the Wall,* p. 1470; June 1, 2004, John Green, review of *Doing It,* p. 1716; May 15, 2007, Michael Cart, review of *Sara's Face,* p. 42; September 1, 2007, Jennifer Hubert, review of *Bloodsong,* p. 115.

Bookseller, August 3, 2001, interview with Burgess, p. 32; August 24, 2001, review of *Lady,* p. 24; September 2, 2005, John McLay, review of *Bloodsong,* p. 24.

Books for Keeps, May, 1997, review of *Junk,* p. 27.

Daily Telegraph (London, England), December 1, 2001, Rachel Cusk, review of *Lady,* p. 4; July 8, 2006, Nigel Richardson, review of *Sara's Face,* p. 9.

Evening Standard (London, England), April 25, 2003, Catherine Shoard, "The Truth about Teenagers."

Guardian (London, England), October 12, 1999, Lindsey Fraser, review of *The Copper Treasure,* p. 2; November 30, 1999, Julia Eccleshare, review of *Bloodtide,* p. 4; June 2, 2001, Fiachra Gibbons, "Children's Writer Courts Controversy with Lusty Teenager Goes to the Dogs in Kids' Pot-Boiler," p. 10; March 29, 2003, Anne Fine, review of *Doing It;* May 27, 2006, Melvin Burgess, "Then, Thank God, We Grew Up," p. 1; July 15, 2006, Philip Ardagh, review of *Sara's Face,* p. 20.

Horn Book, March-April, 1995, Nancy Vasilakis, review of *Burning Issy,* p. 193.

Junior Bookshelf, February, 1991, review of *The Cry of the Wolf,* pp. 29-30; June, 1992, review of *Burning Issy,* pp. 117-118; February, 1993, review of *An Angel for May,* pp. 26-27; April, 1994, review of *The Baby and Fly Pie,* p. 64; August, 1995, review of *Loving April,* pp. 142-143; August, 1996, review of *Tiger, Tiger,* pp. 146, 153-154.

Kirkus Reviews, April 1, 2007, review of *Sara's Face.*

Kliatt, May, 2007, Myrna Marler, review of *Sara's Face,* p. 8, and Paula Rohrlick, review of *Bloodtide,* p. 30; July, 2007, Paula Rohrlick, review of *Bloodsong,* p. 30.

Observer (London, England), March 30, 1997, Neil Spencer, review of *Junk,* p. 17; May 28, 2006, Stephanie Merritt, review of *Sara's Face,* p. 25.

Publishers Weekly, November 26, 2001, review of *Bloodtide,* pp. 62-63; March 4, 2002, review of *Lady,* p. 81; July 1, 2002, Emily Jenkins, "The British Invasion: PW Speaks to Five Authors Who Have Crossed the Atlantic and Found American Readers," p. 26; April 14, 2003, review of *The Ghost behind the Wall,* p. 70; April 26, 2004, review of *Doing It,* p. 67; February 19, 2007, review of *Sara's Face,* p. 170.

School Librarian, August, 1996, Linda Newbery, review of *Tiger, Tiger,* p. 117.

School Library Journal, September, 1992, Susan Oliver, review of *The Cry of the Wolf,* p. 250; July, 2002, Miranda Doyle, review of *Lady,* p. 114; July, 2003, Beth L. Meister, review of *The Ghost behind the Wall,* p. 124; June, 2007, Jill Heritage Maza, review of *Sara's Face,* p. 140.

Voice of Youth Advocates, April, 1995, Helen Turner, review of *Burning Issy,* pp. 19-20.

ONLINE

Contemporary Writers in the UK Web site, http://www.contemporarywriters.com/ (March 1, 2009), Elizabeth O'Reilly, profile of Burgess.

enCompass Culture UK Web site, http://www.encompassculture.com/ (April 1, 2007), Susan Tranter, interview with Burgess.

Melvin Burgess Home Page, http://www.melvinburgess.net (March 1, 2009).

Penguin Books Web site, http://www.penguin.co.uk/ (March 1, 2009), "Melvin Burgess."*

C

CARLS, Claudia 1978-

Personal
Born 1978, in Alsternähe, Germany. *Education:* Vorhaben an der Hochschule für Angewandte Wissenschaften (Hamburg, Germany), graduate.

Addresses
Home and office—Hamburg, Germany. *E-mail*—Schnabelfisch@die-besten-bilder.de.

Career
Illustrator and freelance artist.

Illustrator
Carl and Theodor Colshorn, retellers, *The Porridge Pot,* translated by Anthea Bell, Minedition (New York, NY), 2007.

Barbara Kindermann, reteller, *Servant of Two Masters* (adapted from a story by Carlo Goldoni), Kindermann (Berlin, Germany), 2007.

Sidelights
As a child growing up in Germany, Claudia Carls hoped to become an author as well as an artist. These dual interests led her to pursue a career in children's books, and she studied illustration and communication design at the Vorhaben an der Hochschule für Angewandte Wissenschaften in Hamburg, Germany. Although she is primarily an illustrator, Carls wrote on her home page that, because versatility is very important to her, she continues to create art in a variety of areas, experimenting in drawing, painting, and sculpture.

Among the books featuring Carls' illustrations is *The Porridge Pot,* a German folktale adapted by Carl and Theodor Colshorn that relates how a poor miller's wife runs off with the family's pot of porridge. The miller gives chase, and their daughter follows, but when the girl is unable to keep up, she is approached by a mysterious old woman who offers her advice that leads her to become a princess. "Extraordinary illustrations that blend clay sculpture and painting bring to life a lesser-known German folktale," noted Lee Bock in a *School Library Journal* review of *The Porridge Pot. Booklist* critic Janice Del Negro wrote that the "hyperrealistic, imagination-stretching details" in Carls' art "combine with a melange of architectural fragments and skewed perspectives," while a *Kirkus Reviews* contributor cited the artist's "surreal hyper-reality and dreamy textures for both color and form."

Biographical and Critical Sources

PERIODICALS

Booklist, September 1, 2007, Janice Del Negro, review of *The Porridge Pot,* p. 122.

Kirkus Reviews, September 1, 2007, review of *The Porridge Pot.*

School Library Journal, November, 2007, Lee Bock, review of *The Porridge Pot,* p. 104.

ONLINE

Claudia Carls Home Page, http://claudiacarls.de (March 9, 2009).*

*   *   *

CHAPPELL, Crissa-Jean

Personal
Born in Miami, FL. *Education:* University of Miami, M.F.A. (screenwriting), 1999, Ph.D. (film/literature), 2003.

Addresses

Home—Miami, FL. *Office*—P.O. Box 543, Miami, FL 33176. *Agent*—Kate Lee, International Creative Management, 825 8th Ave., New York, NY 10019. *E-mail*—me@crissajeanchappell.com.

Career

Writer and educator. Miami International University of Art and Design, professor of creative writing and film studies, 2001—. Former film critic, *Miami Sun Post.*

Awards, Honors

Florida Book Award Bronze Medal, Florida State University, 2007, and New York Public Library Books for the Teen Age citation, 2008, both for *Total Constant Order.*

Writings

Total Constant Order, Katherine Tegen Books (New York, NY), 2007.

Sidelights

Crissa-Jean Chappell has been writing as long as she can remember. "I used to steal pens out of my dad's pocket and 'draw' stories before I knew the words," she

Cover of Crissa-Jean Chappell's Total Constant Order, *featuring artwork by James Connelly.* (HarperTeen, 2007. Jacket art © James Connelly/ CORBIS.)

recalled on her home page. "I always dreamed of writing books. But I didn't know that I'd become a young-adult author." While she was studying writing in college, she began to focus her writing on adolescents. Writing for teens has proved to be a natural fit for the author; "I never got over that super high, super low feeling that everything is a big deal," Chappell admitted to Laura Isensee in the *Miami Herald.* "I'm always feeling like I'm on the outside, looking in, scratching my head and saying, 'what is that?'"

In her debut novel *Total Constant Order,* Chappell focuses on an outsider, fourteen-year-old Fin. Fin's family's recent move to Miami has been complicated by her parents' divorce. Now the girl can only deal with her anxiety by counting everything around her and washing her hands raw. Although the teen's therapist diagnoses obsessive-compulsive disorder (OCD) and prescribes medication, it does not help. What does is befriending Thayer, a classmate with attention deficit disorder whose unconventional outlook helps bring Fin understanding. "The ending goes on and on, which suggests that maybe there are no perfect answers for Fin," Myrna Marler noted in her *Kliatt* review of *Total Constant Order.*

"From the start, Chappell's portrayal of Fin's mental state is on target," a *Publishers Weekly* reviewer noted, adding that the author's debut novel would have benefited from more of "Fin's heart." *School Library Journal* contributor Caryl Soriano called *Total Constant Order,* "a brave attempt to explore the world of a teenager ravaged by both obsessive-compulsive disorder and depression." While *Booklist* writer Hazel Rochman found the descriptions of Fin's OCD "tiresome," she added that "what will hold readers are the witty observations of the high-school caste system." Chappell's "must-have story is fresh," Robbie L. Flowers concluded in *Voice of Youth Advocates,* the critic dubbing *Total Constant Order* "a breakthrough."

Chappell drew on her own experiences in writing *Total Constant Order.* She developed her own counting rituals as a child, and a tense night riding out Hurricane Andrew at home made her realize that OCD would always be part of her life. Although she learned to channel her nervous energy into writing, exploring Fin's story "actually made me more self-conscious because I had to focus on some dark places in my head," the author told Isensee. Nevertheless, Chappell advises young people with a similar problem: "You're not broken, you don't need to be fixed." Instead, she encourages them to find their own creative outlets.

Biographical and Critical Sources

PERIODICALS

Booklist, November 15, 2007, Hazel Rochman, review of *Total Constant Order,* p. 58.

Bulletin of the Center for Children's Books, February, 2008, Deborah Stevenson, review of *Total Constant Order,* p. 243.

Kliatt, November, 2007, Myrna Marler, review of *Total Constant Order,* p. 8.

Miami Herald, September 3, 2008, Laura Isensee, "Young Novelist, Drawn to Obsessive Rituals, Uses Writing to Order Her Life."

Publishers Weekly, December 3, 2007, review of *Total Constant Order,* p. 71.

School Library Journal, January, 2008, Caryl Soriano, review of *Total Constant Order,* p. 115.

Voice of Youth Advocates, April, 2008, Robbie L. Flowers, review of *Total Constant Order,* p. 42.

ONLINE

Crissa-Jean Chappell Home Page, http://www.crissajean chappell.com (January 20, 2009).*

*   *   *

CHAREST, Emily MacLachlan (Emily MacLachlan)

Personal

Daughter of Patricia (a children's book author) and Robert MacLachlan; married Dean Charest; children: Sofia.

Addresses

Home—Stow, MA.

Career

Children's book author.

Awards, Honors

Irma S. and James H. Black Book Award, Bank Street College of Education, 2006, for *Once I Ate a Pie.*

Writings

(Under name Emily MacLachlan, with mother, Patricia MacLachlan) *Painting the Wind,* illustrated by Katy Schneider, Joanna Cotler Books (New York, NY), 2003.

(With Patricia MacLachlan) *Bittle,* illustrated by Dan Yaccarino, Joanna Cotler Books (New York, NY), 2004.

(With Patricia MacLachlan) *Who Loves Me?,* illustrated by Amanda Shepherd, Joanna Cotler Books (New York, NY), 2005.

(With Patricia MacLachlan) *Once I Ate a Pie,* illustrated by Katy Schneider, Joanna Cotler Books (New York, NY), 2006.

(With Patricia MacLachlan) *Fiona Loves the Night,* illustrated by Amanda Shepherd, Joanna Cotler Books (New York, NY), 2007.

Sidelights

Emily MacLachlan Charest is the daughter of Newbery Medal-winning author Patricia MacLachlan, and she has joined her mother in creating several engaging picture books for young readers. The first collaboration between mother and daughter, *Painting the Wind,* has been followed by several other books, all noted for their engaging artwork. A story about a young boy's artistic development that features illustrations by Katy Schneider, *Painting the Wind* was praised by *Booklist* reviewer Julie Cummins as a "quietly told" tale that "goes to the heart of creativity in a way children will understand." The authors' go totally to the dogs in *Once I Ate a Pie,* a man's-best-friend confessional that is also enlivened by Schneider's detailed oil paintings.

In *Bittle* a dog and cat learn to accept a new baby in their human-run household, and here Charest and MacLachlan "humorously imagine the pets' grudging tolerance turning to bemused affection," according to a *Publishers Weekly* contributor. In the story, the new arrival—a baby girl—at first seems to preempt Nigel the cat and Julia the dog for attention, but when the infant likes to chase butterflies like Julia and tosses tasty tidbits from the highchair to the floor and a hungry Nigel, the pets become accepting. Illustrator Dan "Yaccarino's rubbery, boldly distinct figures reflect the vim and humor in this pets'-eye view of a new baby's homecoming," wrote a *Kirkus Reviews* critic, and in *School Library Journal* Kelley Rae Unger dubbed *Bittle* a "humorous and heartwarming" tale that captures the subtle way "a pet can seemingly become the ruler of a house."

Featuring artwork by Amanda Shepherd, MacLachlan and Charest tell a nighttime story in *Who Loves Me?* Here a young girl is reassured by the family's wise cat, and falls asleep knowing that many people love and care for her. Shepherd also contributes the art to Charest and MacLachlan's *Fiona Loves the Night.* In this picture book a young girl goes on a moonlit tour of her suburban world, observing the many sights and sounds that are unique to nature in the nighttime. "The story's serene, lulling rhythm creates a sense of safety, a balm for young readers," wrote Jessica Bruder in her *New York Times Book Review* appraisal of *Fiona Loves the Night.* The "jewel-toned highlights and lustrous shades of blue" in Shepherd's paintings for the book "keep the dark scenes lively," the critic added.

Biographical and Critical Sources

PERIODICALS

Booklist, August, 2003, Julie Cummins, review of *Painting the Wind,* p. 1980; June 1, 2004, Jennifer Mattson, review of *Bittle,* p. 1743.

Emily MacLachlan Charest teams up with her mother, Patricia MacLachlan, to create picture books such as **Fiona Loves the Night.** (Illustration copyright © 2007 by Amanda Shepherd. All rights reserved. Used by permission of HarperCollins Children's Books, a division of HarperCollins Publishers.)

Bulletin of the Center for Children's Books, October, 2003, review of *Painting the Wind,* p. 91; September, 2004, Deborah Stevenson, review of *Bittle,* p. 27.

Kirkus Reviews, April 15, 2003, review of *Painting the Wind,* p. 609; May 15, 2004, review of *Bittle,* p. 494.

New York Times Book Review, February 17, 2008, Jessica Bruder, review of *Fiona Loves the Night,* p. 16.

Publishers Weekly, July 5, 2004, review of *Bittle,* p. 55.

School Library Journal, May, 2003, Lee Bock, review of *Painting the Wind,* p. 125; June, 2004, Kelley Rae Unger, review of *Bittle,* p. 114; September, 2007, Mary Jean Smith, review of *Fiona Loves the Night,* p. 171.*

*   *   *

COCHRAN, Thomas 1955-

Personal

Born 1955, in LA.

Addresses

Home—West Fork, AR.

Career

Children's author and educator. English teacher, Fayetteville High School, Fayetteville, AR; former sports writer.

Writings

Roughnecks, Harcourt Brace (San Diego, CA), 1997.
Running the Dogs, Farrar, Straus & Giroux (New York, NY), 2007.

Sidelights

High school English teacher Thomas Cochran has earned favorable notice from critics for his novels *Roughnecks* and *Running the Dogs,* both of which feature themes likely to appeal to male readers. Called "a very promising first novel" by *Booklist* reviewer Jean Franklin, *Roughnecks* follows the story of Travis Cody, a high-school star football player for the Oil Camp Roughnecks. After making a game-losing bad play against a rival team, Travis earns another chance during the Louisiana state championships, an opportunity that might earn him a college scholarship. Standing in his way, however, is Jericho Grooms, an outstanding opponent from the Roughneck's cross-town rival, the Pineview Pelicans. Franklin lauded Cochran for creating "an appealing, positive character," in Travis, while a *Publishers Weekly* contributor contended that the strength of *Roughnecks* lies in Cochran's detailed narrative of the events leading to the championship game. "Unlike many sports novels," the critic observed, "the highlight here is the build-up to the game, rather than the game itself."

Cochran's elementary-grade novel, *Running the Dogs*, revolves around ten-year-old Talmidge Cotton. The son of an oil-rig worker, Talmidge looks forward to his father's return for the Christmas holiday, although he fears inclement weather might set the family's holiday plans awry. Compounding matters, the young boy's favorite beagles have become lost in the woods, forcing Talmidge to search for the wandering dogs at night. Although Talmidge had hoped that his father would recognize his sense of responsibility and allow him to hunt

Cover of Thomas Cochran's sports-themed novel Roughnecks, *featuring artwork by David Kahl.* (Cover illustration copyright © 1997 by David Kahl. Reproduced by permission of Houghton Mifflin Harcourt Publishing Company.)

at night with his dogs, being alone in the dark searching for the beagles now shakes the boy's self-confidence. "Cochran's greatest strength lies in evoking hushed yet intense moods," claimed Megan Lynn Isaac in a *Horn Book* review of *Running the Dogs*. While questioning the book's predictability, a *Kirkus Reviews* contributor nonetheless called *Running the Dogs* a "earnest and gentle story" that offers children a "pleasant reading" experience.

Biographical and Critical Sources

PERIODICALS

Booklist, September 17, 1997, Jean Franklin, review of *Roughnecks*, p. 220.
Bulletin of the Center for Children's Books, October, 1997, review of *Roughnecks*, p. 45.
Horn Book, January-February, 2008, Megan Lynn Isaac, review of *Running the Dogs*, p. 83.
Kirkus Reviews, November 1, 2007, review of *Running the Dogs*.
Publishers Weekly, August 4, 1997, review of *Roughnecks*, p. 76.
School Library Journal, October, 1997, Jack Forman, review of *Roughnecks*, p. 131.
Voice of Youth Advocates, December, 1997, review of *Roughnecks*, p. 315.*

*   *   *

COX, Judy 1954-

Personal

Born November 25, 1954, in San Francisco, CA; daughter of Walter Alan (a photographer) and Carol (a nurse) Houde; married Tim Cox (a school counselor), June 7, 1974; children: Christopher. *Education:* Lewis-Clark State College, B.A., 1979; Northern Arizona University, M.A., 1984. *Religion:* Presbyterian. *Hobbies and other interests:* Music, bird watching, reading, playing bass guitar.

Addresses

Home—Ontario, OR. *E-mail*—Gtrmouse@aol.com.

Career

Writer and educator. Welches School District, Welches, OR, teacher, 1985-92; West Linn-Wilsonville School District, West Linn, OR, teacher, 1996-2002; Ontario Public Schools, Ontario, OR, reading specialist, 2004—.

Member

International Reading Association, Authors Guild, Society of Children's Book Writers and Illustrators.

Awards, Honors

First place award, Oregon Association of American Mothers Short-Story Contest, 1993, for "When the Meadowlark Sings"; Children's Choice Award, 2001, Nevada Young Readers Award, 2002, and Beverly Cleary Award runner up, 2003, all for *Weird Stories from the Lonesome Café;* Children's Literature Choice listee, 2004 for *Go to Sleep, Groundhog!;* Coretta Scott King/John Steptoe New Talent Award, and Chickadee Award nomination, Maine Children's Choice Picture Book Project, both 2004, both for *My Family Plays Music* illustrated by Elbrite Brown; Top Ten Children's Books selection, *Time* magazine, 2005, and Bill Martin, Jr. Picture Book Award nominee, Kansas State Reading Association), Washington State Children's Choice Picture Book Award nominee, and Keystone State Reading Association Award nominee, all 2006, all for *Don't Be Silly, Mrs. Millie!;* Maryland Blue Crab Young Readers Honor Book designation, 2006, for *That Crazy Eddie and the Science Project of Doom;* Rhode Island Young Readers Award nomination, 2009, for *Puppy Power.*

Writings

Now We Can Have a Wedding!, illustrated by DyAnne DiSalvo-Ryan, Holiday House (New York, NY), 1998.
The West Texas Chili Monster, illustrated by John O'Brien, Bridgewater Books (New York, NY), 1998.
Third Grade Pet, illustrated by Cynthia Fisher, Holiday House (New York, NY), 1998.
Rabbit Pirates: A Tale of the Spinach Main, illustrated by Emily Arnold McCully, Harcourt/Browndeer Press (San Diego, CA), 1999.
Mean, Mean Maureen Green, illustrated by Cynthia Fisher, Holiday House (New York, NY), 2000.
Weird Stories from the Lonesome Café, illustrated by Diane Kidd, Harcourt (San Diego, CA), 2000.
Butterfly Buddies, illustrated by Blanche Sims, Holiday House (New York, NY), 2001.
Cool Cat, School Cat, illustrated by Blanche Sims, Holiday House (New York, NY), 2002.
My Family Plays Music, illustrated by Elbrite Brown, Holiday House (New York, NY), 2003.
Go to Sleep, Groundhog!, illustrated by Paul Meisel, Holiday House (New York, NY), 2004.
That Crazy Eddie and the Science Project of Doom, illustrated by Blanche Simms, Holiday House (New York, NY), 2005.
Don't Be Silly, Mrs. Millie!, illustrated by Joe Mathieu, Marshall Cavendish (New York, NY), 2005.
The Mystery of the Burmese Bandicoot, illustrated by Omar Rayyan, Marshall Cavendish (New York, NY), 2007.
Mrs. Millie Goes to Philly!, illustrated by Joe Mathieu, Marshall Cavendish (New York, NY), 2008.
Puppy Power, illustrated by Steve Björkman, Holiday House (New York, NY), 2008.
One Is a Feast for Mouse: A Thanksgiving Tale, illustrated by Jeffrey Ebbeler, Holiday House (New York, NY), 2008.
The Case of the Purloined Professor, illustrated by Omar Rayyan, Marshall Cavendish (New York, NY), 2009.
Pick a Pumpkin, Mrs. Millie!, illustrated by Joe Mathieu, Marshall Cavendish (New York, NY), 2009.

Also contributor of short stories, articles, poems, and essays to periodicals, including *Cricket, Spider, Highlights for Children, Children's Playmate, Instructor, Learning, Family Times, Single Parent, Family Fun, Hopscotch,* and *Poem Train.* Short stories included in anthology *Stories from Highlights,* Boyds Mill Press.

Sidelights

Judy Cox is the author of picture books and beginning chapter books, including *Weird Stories from the Lonesome Café, My Family Plays Music,* and *Don't Be Silly, Mrs. Millie!,* all of which have been praised for their jovial characters and humorous scenarios. Cox also works as an educator in a small school in rural Oregon. "I enjoy teaching," she remarked in an *Institute of Children's Literature* online interview with Mel Boring. "It informs my writing work, and my experience as a writer provides me with a richer background to help children read and write."

In her very first book, *Now We Can Have a Wedding!,* Cox's young narrator goes from kitchen to kitchen in the apartment house where she lives. In each, she helps out or merely observes as residents prepare a special dish to bring to the wedding feast for the girl's older sister and her betrothed, a young man who lives in apartment 4-B. "Without being didactic, the book is a showcase for ethnic diversity through gastronomy," contended Ilene Cooper in *Booklist.* Other critics voiced similar observations. "Cox cleverly combines the meanings of the terms 'melting pot' and 'pot luck,'" wrote a reviewer for *Publishers Weekly,* noting that the story is strengthened by the author's use of repetition and by emphasizing what the neighbors have in common: "their pleasure in preparing for a wedding and in sharing their traditions." Aided by DyAnne DiSalvo-Ryan's welcoming watercolor renditions of the various kitchens, the result is "a sweet and joyful twist on weddings," Patricia Pearl Dole concluded in *School Library Journal.*

The West Texas Chili Monster is a "goofy story about a chili cook-off that produces smells powerful enough to attract the attention of a roving space creature," wrote John Sigwald in *School Library Journal.* Cox employs the same brand of whimsical humor in her picture book *Rabbit Pirates: A Tale of the Spinach Main,* in which two old friends retire from pirating and open a restaurant in the Provence region of France. Though Monsieur Lapin and Monsieur Blanc wax nostalgic about their days on the open sea, they seem content enough to argue over old times, and prepare and serve food at the Spinach Main, their restaurant. Then a fox comes in one day and expresses the desire to see the cooks featured on the menu. Although Cox's scenario may have more appeal for adult readers than for these youngsters

Blanche Sims creates the artwork for Judy Cox's entertaining picture book Butterfly Buddies. (Illustration copyright © 2001 by Blanche Sims. All rights reserved. Reproduced by permission of Holiday House, Inc.)

who are reading *Rabbit Pirates,* Hazel Rochman nevertheless remarked in *Booklist* that many children will "recognize the tough-guy talk and enjoy the clever tricks the rabbits use to get rid of" the fox. A reviewer for *Publishers Weekly* described Cox's book as "a wonderful mix of humor, food and friendship, with just the right touch of je ne sais quoi."

Characteristic of the author's works, *Go to Sleep, Groundhog!* features an insomniac groundhog who wanders out of his burrow into several other holiday celebrations before finally making his annual appearance on his own special day. The book prompted *School Library Journal* reviewer Kathleen Kelly MacMillan to note that, "at last, Groundhog Day finally has an irresistible story to call its own," while a *Kirkus Reviews* writer described *Go to Sleep, Groundhog!* as a "toasty story of autumn and winter festivities" that is "ideal for bedtime" due to its "pleasing mood and gentle pacing."

While Cox has earned several awards for her writing, two books that have sparked a great deal of enthusiasm are *My Family Plays Music* and *Weird Stories from the Lonesome Café.* Within a family where everyone plays a different instrument—from pots and pans to a pipe organ—a young girl learns about rhythm by serving as

percussionist to each musician in *My Family Plays Music.* In addition to introducing a number of musical terms and profiling ten different musical genres through the performances of each of the girl's family members—from marching bands to orchestras to rock and roll—Cox's "upbeat" tale is "more a celebration of sound than a story," according to Jane Marino in *School Library Journal. Booklist* contributor GraceAnne A. DeCandido dubbed *My Family Plays Music* a "charmer" and a *Kirkus Reviews* writer noted that, in addition to learning about music, "it's the pride" Cox's young narrator "takes in her family, and her place in that family," that resonates with readers.

Winner of the Nevada Young Readers Award as well as several other honors, the chapter book *Weird Stories from the Lonesome Café* finds Sam and his uncle moving to the Nevada desert to escape the city's noise and bustle. Highly distracted by a novel he is hoping to write as soon as something interesting happens, Uncle Clem opens a restaurant, oblivious to the fact that he begins to assemble a very unusual staff indeed: the bread delivery man looks a whole lot like Elvis Presley, a Santa Claus character named Mr. C. and a skinny guy in a spaceship who could pass for E.T. soon ask to hire on, and behind the grill is none other than Big Foot! While Uncle Clem remains oblivious, Sam is quick to recognize that this is no ordinary restaurant. In *Booklist* Gillian Engberg noted that Cox's "first-person narrative is clever and playful," while Pat Leach commented in *School Library Journal* that *Weird Stories from the Lonesome Café* will also "appeal to more sophisticated older reluctant readers" due to the repetitive text and the humorous plot.

Other chapter books by Cox include *Mean, Mean Maureen Green* and *Butterfly Buddies,* both of which feature young girls learning to deal with social situations. In *Mean, Mean Maureen Green* third-grader Lilley learns to conquer her fear of a neighborhood bully, a ferocious dog, and riding her two-wheeler bike with the help of a friend and her father. The result is a "solid, well-paced chapter book," according to Engberg. *Butterfly Buddies* finds Robin eager to find approval with Miss Wing, a new teacher she adores—so eager, in fact, that she attempts to dress and act just like Miss Wing, with humorous results. Commenting on Cox's chapter books, *School Library Journal* contributor Debbie Whitbeck noted that in each work "readers will find much to relate to" in the actions of the young protagonists.

A pair of third-graders join forces in an effort to win their school's science fair in Cox's *That Crazy Eddie and the Science Project of Doom.* With his eye set on the top prize, Matt enlists the help of his outrageous best friend, Eddie, to construct a papier-mâché volcano. When Matt takes ill, however, Eddie announces the embarrassing details of his intestinal distress at school. Angry and ashamed, Matt damages the project, an act that also places his friendship in jeopardy. "Believable characters and situations . . . make this story easily ac-

Cox's picture book **Puppy Power** *comes to life in energetic graphite illustrations by Steve Bjorkman.*

cessible to newly independent readers," Kay Weisman stated in *Booklist,* and a *Kirkus Reviews* contributor wrote: "Fast-paced and realistic, this tale rings true for its young readers."

In *Puppy Power,* energetic, impetuous third-grader Fran finds it difficult to control her behavior at recess. Although the youngster lands a lead role in her school play, it comes with a condition: she must improve her conduct. When Fran begins taking her Newfoundland puppy, Hercules, to obedience school, the lessons seem to help the young dog owner as much as they do her pet. Laura Scott, writing in *School Library Journal,* complimented the book's "light tone, clear writing, ac-

tion, vivid descriptions, and realistic school and family scenarios," and a critic in *Kirkus Reviews* remarked that "the familiar situation will resonate with the early elementary set."

Cox's first book for more advanced readers was *Third Grade Pet.* In this 1998 work, a group of students vote to adopt a pet rat, and Rosemary, despite her disgust, is selected to be one of the animal's first caretakers. Critics applauded Cox's descriptions of her protagonist's initial fear of the rat and "how creepiness gives way to cuddly affection," as Rochman put it. Rosemary becomes so attached to Cheese the rat, in fact, that when a boy she does not trust is assigned to take Cheese home for the weekend, Rosemary kidnaps the pet and tries to hide it in her home. Cox's "writing has a clarity and an energetic freshness that keeps the rodential hijinks . . . realistic rather than corny and contrived," *Bulletin of the Center for Children's Books* reviewer Deborah Stevenson stated. Similarly, a critic for *Publishers Weekly* wrote that Cox properly keeps her focus on her human rather than rodent characters, and their "fresh and credible voices . . . give this brief, quick-moving novel plenty of life." Lisa Gangemi Kropp, writing in *School Library Journal*, compared *Third Grade Pet* to chapter books by Suzy Kline and Betsy Duffey, concluding that readers who enjoy those books "will feel right at home with this light and breezy story."

The Mystery of the Burmese Bandicoot, a second novel by Cox, concerns Frederick and Ishbu, a pair of rat brothers that escapes from a classroom cage and encounters the nefarious Big Cheese. Big Cheese is a possum who rules the rodent underworld, and this criminal kingpin asks the sharp-toothed siblings to steal the Burmese Bandicoot, a legendary statue. Frederick and Ishbu then flee aboard a ship that sinks during a storm, leaving them stranded on a tropical island. There they discover the figurine, which contains a poison that is deadly to humans. "Fast-paced and suspenseful, this is solid entertainment," observed a contributor reviewing *The Mystery of the Burmese Bandicoot* for *Kirkus Reviews.*

Cox puts her years of classroom experience to good use in *Don't Be Silly, Mrs. Millie!,* a picture book about a witty kindergarten teacher who loves puns. Mrs. Millie greets her students by reminding them to hang up their "goats," and she later invites them to snack on "parrot sticks and quackers." The author "keeps kids on their toes in this book of wordplay," Stephanie Zvirin commented in *Booklist,* and Erin Senig noted in *School Library Journal* that "Mrs. Millie's obvious substitutions make this story an appealing read-aloud." The pun-loving teacher makes return appearances in *Mrs. Millie Goes to Philly!* and *Pick a Pumpkin, Mrs. Millie!*

Cox once told *SATA:* "I am the oldest of five children. We grew up near San Francisco. Even when I was young, I loved to tell stories to my brother and sisters. As soon as I learned to read, reading became my favorite thing to do. I love books, the way they look, the way they feel, the way they smell. I wanted to be a part of that. I wrote my first story in third grade. In those days, students didn't have much chance to write stories in school. We only had 'creative writing' every other Friday. By the time I was eleven, I knew I wanted to be a writer when I grew up. I started a novel about six girls who had a club in a tree house. I wrote long descriptions and drew pictures of each of them. I got so involved planning my characters that I never finished the first chapter!

"In the sixth grade, a poem I wrote was published in the local newspaper. My grandmother was so proud of it, she framed it. It hung in her house for the rest of her life. I wrote without getting published again for many, many years! I wrote journals, essays, poems, short stories, picture books. I started several novels. I read somewhere that you have to write a million words before you write anything worth reading and I thought, 'I'd better get busy.' I wrote on an old refurbished manual typewriter my parents gave me when I graduated from high school. I wrote in longhand on yellow, lined tablets.

"After I married, my husband bought me an electric typewriter for Christmas because he liked one of my science-fiction stories, and I wrote on that. I sat on the screened sun porch of the old farmhouse we rented in Idaho, and I wrote my first children's novel, a mystery, on the backs of old dittos he brought home from his teaching job. I wrote in pencil and ink and marker. But I couldn't sell anything. I got discouraged, not realizing that all this practice was leading somewhere. I dreamed of being published. But it seemed as if my dreams would never come true.

"Finally, years and years later, I wrote an article about dinosaurs. I mailed it to *Instructor* magazine. They bought it! I was so excited! My husband and I went out for pizza to celebrate. But I didn't really start to write seriously again until I left teaching to stay home with my baby. I began to write every day. I'd turn on *Sesame Street* and write straight through until *Mr. Roger's Neighborhood* was over. When I heard Mr. Rogers sing his closing song, I knew it was time to stop.

"I started keeping a journal. I used to think nothing interesting ever happened to me. But I discovered the interesting stuff in the stuff in your head. Your dreams. Your fantasies. Your pretends, and wishes, and ideas. Once I knew that, I had lots to say after all. I use big spiral-bound notebooks and write my journal on one side of each page. The other side I use for story ideas. I started to send things out to magazines and book publishers. My husband calls me 'The Queen of Persistence' because I have more than 350 rejection slips. . . . Not everything I write gets published. But writing is like piano practice. You do it every day to keep in shape."

Biographical and Critical Sources

PERIODICALS

Booklist, February 15, 1998, Ilene Cooper, review of *Now We Can Have a Wedding!,* p. 1019; December 15, 1998, Hazel Rochman, review of *Third Grade Pet,* p. 749; October 15, 1999, Hazel Rochman, review of *Rabbit Pirates: A Tale of the Spinach Main,* p. 451; December 1, 1999, Gillian Engberg, review of *Mean, Mean Maureen Green,* p. 703; April 15, 2000, Gillian Engberg, review of *Weird Stories from the Lonesome Café,* p. 1542; October 15, 2003, GraceAnne A. De-

Candido, review of *My Family Plays Music*, p. 417; November 15, 2003, Jennifer Mattson, review of *Go to Sleep, Groundhog!*, p. 599; June 1, 2005, Kay Weisman, review of *That Crazy Eddie and the Science Project of Doom*, p. 1806; August, 2005, Stephanie Zvirin, review of *Don't Be Silly, Mrs. Millie!*, p. 2038; October 1, 2007, Kristen McKulski, review of *The Mystery of the Burmese Bandicoot*, p. 59; May 1, 2008, Kay Weisman, review of *Puppy Power*, p. 90.

Bulletin of the Center for Children's Books, February, 1999, Deborah Stevenson, review of *Third Grade Pet*, p. 198; April, 2000, review of *Weird Stories from the Lonesome Café*, p. 275.

Kirkus Reviews, October 1, 2002, review of *Cool Cat, School Cat*, p. 1465; September 1, 2003, review of *My Family Plays Music*, p. 121; December 15, 2003, review of *Go to Sleep, Groundhog!*, p. 1449; June 1, 2005, review of *That Crazy Eddie and the Science Project of Doom*, p. 634; June 15, 2005, review of *Don't Be Silly, Mrs. Millie!*, p. 680; August 15, 2007, review of *The Mystery of the Burmese Bandicoot*; April 1, 2008, review of *Puppy Power*; August 15, 2008, review of *One Is a Feast for Mouse: A Thanksgiving Tale*.

Publishers Weekly, February 9, 1998, review of *Now We Can Have a Wedding!*, p. 94; December 14, 1998, review of *Third Grade Pet*, p. 76; August 2, 1999, review of *Rabbit Pirates*, p. 83; April 24, 2000, review of *Weird Stories from the Lonesome Café*, p. 91; October 6, 2003, review of *My Family Plays Music*, p. 83; January 12, 2004, review of *Go to Sleep, Groundhog!*, p. 53.

School Library Journal, March, 1998, Patricia Pearl Dole, review of *Now We Can Have a Wedding!*, p. 168; June, 1998, John Sigwald, review of *The West Texas Chili Monster*, p. 103; February, 1999, Lisa Gangemi Kropp, review of *Third Grade Pet*, p. 83; June, 2000, Pat Leach, review of *Weird Stories from the Lonesome Café*, p. 104; October, 2001, Debbie Whitbeck, review of *Butterfly Buddies*, p. 113; September, 2002, Wendy S. Carroll, review of *Cool Cat, School Cat*, p. 183; October, 2003, Jane Marino, review of *My Family Plays Music*, p. 116; February, 2004, Kathleen Kelly MacMillan, review of *Go to Sleep, Groundhog*, p. 104; July, 2005, Debbie Stewart Hoskins, review of *That Crazy Eddie and the Science Project of Doom*, p. 72; October, 2005, Erin Senig, review of *Don't Be Silly, Mrs. Millie!*, p. 110; December, 2007, Sheila Fiscus, review of *The Mystery of the Burmese Bandicoot*, p. 120; June, 2008, Laura Scott, review of *Puppy Power*, p. 100; July, 2008, Martha Topol, review of *Mrs. Millie Goes to Philly!*, p. 68.

Time, November 30, 2005, Christopher Porterfield, review of *Don't Be Silly, Mrs. Millie!*

ONLINE

Institute of Children's Literature Web site, http://www.institutechildrenslit.com/ (June 9, 2005), Mel Boring, interview with Cox.

Judy Cox Home Page, http://www.judycox.net (March 1, 2009).

CRAIG, Joe 1979-
(Joe Alexander Craig)

Personal

Born December 31, 1979. *Education:* Emmanuel College Cambridge, M.A. (philosophy), 2002. *Hobbies and other interests:* Music, watching films, reading, collecting frogs, eating lunch, cooking, Aesop's fables, dancing Tango, playing poker, painting, eating Haribo sweets, playing five-a-side football and cricket.

Addresses

Home—London, England. *E-mail*—joe@joecraig.co.uk.

Career

Songwriter, musician, and author. Composer of music for play *Told You So*, produced 2002.

Awards, Honors

Most Promising Young Writer designation, Vivian Ellis Prize, 1999, for best first musical; Bolton Children's Book Award, 2006, for *Jimmy Coates: Killer*.

Writings

"JIMMY COATES" SERIES; MIDDLE-GRADE NOVELS

Jimmy Coates: Killer, HarperCollins (London, England), 2005, published as *Jimmy Coates: Assassin?*, HarperCollins (New York, NY), 2005.

Jimmy Coates: Target, HarperCollins (London, England), 2006, HarperCollins (New York, NY), 2007.

Jimmy Coates: Revenge, HarperCollins (London, England), 2007.

Jimmy Coates: Sabotage, HarperCollins (London, England), 2007.

Jimmy Coates: Survival, HarperCollins (London, England), 2008.

Sidelights

Joe Craig was born and raised in England, and attended Emmanuel College Cambridge, where he earned a degree in philosophy. Craig was interested in music from a young age and spent time writing songs during his formative years and following graduation. He earned a Vivian Ellis Prize for Most Promising Young Writer for his first musical in 1999. At Cambridge University he wrote for the Cambridge Footlights, as well as for the university's radio station, where he contributed to the *Ali and Joe Show*. Then, in 2002, he composed the score of *Told You So*, a musical production by playwright John Finnemore that was staged in London, England, over the Christmas holiday. It was not his intention to become a professional writer of children's novels, but the success of his "Jimmy Coates" series swiftly changed Craig's plans.

Jimmy Coates: Killer, which was published in the United States as *Jimmy Coates: Assassin?,* is the first book in Craig's novel series. Likened to other popular adventure stories for middle-grade readers, such as Anthony Horowitz's "Alex Rider" books, the novel features eleven-year-old Jimmy Coates. Jimmy soon discovers he has amazing powers, most notably the ability to perform fantastic, seemingly impossible physical stunts. That is not the only thing that Jimmy has discovered, however. There are men chasing him everywhere he goes, and only his special abilities keep him one step ahead. While avoiding his pursuers, Jimmy sets out to find the truth about himself, why his parents have been lying to him, and just who is out to get him. In a review for *School Library Journal,* Hillias J. Martin predicted that the "humorous mishaps and athletic thrills will leave middle-grade boys drooling for the next installment." *Jimmy Coates: Killer* went on to win the Bolton Children's Book Award from the University of Bolton.

Jimmy's adventures continue in *Jimmy Coates: Target.* In this installment, Jimmy has learned the truth: he's being hunted by a government organization called NJ7—the organization that created him. NJ7 built Jimmy to be a weapon—a highly trained and specialized assassin—and now that he has escaped from them they want him back. Jimmy knows he is still thirty-eight percent human, and his human part wants to be free. This freedom seems feasible until someone from the past comes after him, and this new threat has all the same abilities as Jimmy. A contributor to *Kirkus Reviews* remarked of *Jimmy Coates: Target* that the "roaring, constant action zooms along."

Jimmy Coates: Revenge, the third title in Craig's series, finds Jimmy and his friends escaping to the United States in a continued effort to hide from NJ7. Losing himself in the streets of New York City's Chinatown, Jimmy hopes that no one has tracked him. When he begins to have mysterious headaches and inexplicable flashes, Jimmy is suddenly faced with a whole new set of questions about who he is and what he can do.

In *Jimmy Coates: Sabotage* Jimmy continues his attempt to outwit the powers in charge of NJ7, even while fulfilling a dangerous mission that requires the stealth and invisibility of someone who, at least officially, does not exist. Jimmy returns yet again in *Jimmy Coates: Survival,* when the stakes go up even higher. Not only must Jimmy prevent a war, but now his family is in danger as well.

As Craig once commented: "Anybody can write a great story. There's no magic about it. You don't have to wait for inspiration. Nobody even really knows what 'inspiration' is. If you start with the hard work, the inspiration will follow. Or it won't—it doesn't matter. Working hard, using every scrap of your brain, and giving yourself the time and space to create something you care passionately about—that's enough.

Cover of Joe Craig's novel **Jimmy Coates: Target.** (HarperCollinsPublishers, 2006. Jacket art © 2006 by Stockdisc/Getty Images.)

"After several weeks of planning, I write 2,000 words a day until the first draft is finished, then I go back to the beginning for the rewriting, polishing, and editing. I've always liked what [nineteenth-century English novelist] Anthony Trollope said: 'Three hours a day will produce as much as a man ought to write.' (But it usually takes me a lot more than three hours a day!)

"Writing is a constant battle between my instinct and my intellect. I have to keep the two apart. First I have to write from my gut, not analysing anything and not worrying about how good it is. Then only when the first draft is finished do I go back and switch on the rational, critical part of my brain to rewrite.

"My aim is to make my books as gripping as they can possibly be! I love the feeling of not being able to put a book down."

Despite the success of the "Jimmy Coates" novel series, Craig remains interested in music and songwriting; he intends to continue to write songs and produce albums, even as he sends Jimmy off on more adventures. He performs his music periodically at various venues in the London area.

Biographical and Critical Sources

PERIODICALS

Booklist, May 1, 2005, Jennifer Mattson, review of *Jimmy Coates: Assassin?,* p. 1542; June 1, 2007, Todd Morning, review of *Jimmy Coates: Target,* p. 72.

Kirkus Reviews, January 15, 2007, review of *Jimmy Coates: Target,* p. 71.

Kliatt, March, 2007, Paula Rohrlick, review of *Jimmy Coates: Target,* p. 10.

School Library Journal, June, 2005, Hillias J. Martin, review of *Jimmy Coates: Assassin?,* p. 153.

Times Educational Supplement, April 21, 2006, "Destroy after Reading," p. 32.

Voice of Youth Advocates, August, 2005, James Blasingame, review of *Jimmy Coates: Assassin?,* p. 232; February, 2007, Jeff Mann, review of *Jimmy Coates: Target,* p. 538.

ONLINE

Bookbag, http://www.thebookbag.co.uk/ (January 7, 2008), Jill Murphy, review of *Jimmy Coates: Revenge.*

Edge of the Forest, http://www.theedgeoftheforest.com/ (January 7, 2008), Camille Powell, interview with Craig.

Families Online, http://www.familiesonline.co.uk/ (February 26, 2007), Jo Rogers, review of "Jimmy Coates" series.

HarperCollins Children's Books Web site, http://www.harpercollinschildrensbooks.co.uk/ (January 7, 2008), interview with Craig.

Joe Craig Home Page, http://www.joecraig.co.uk (January 7, 2008).

MyShelf.com, http://www.myshelf.com/ (January 7, 2008), review of *Jimmy Coates: Target.*

Teens Read Too, http://www.teensreadtoo.com/ (January 7, 2008), interview with Craig.

* * *

**CRAIG, Joe Alexander
See CRAIG, Joe**

D

DADDO, Andrew 1967-

Personal
Born February 18, 1967, in Australia; married; wife's name Jacqui; children: Felix, Bibi, Jasper.

Addresses
Home—Sydney, New South Wales, Australia.

Career
Author and entertainment personality. Host of television and radio programs for Australian Broadcasting Corporation, including *MTV, Olympic Sunrise,* and annual Logie Awards. Actor in television series, including *Round the Twist, Cluedo,* and *The Factory,* and in motion pictures, including *A Kink in the Picasso,* 1990, *Body Melt,* 1993, and *Ned,* 2003. Has also worked on *Australia's Funniest People* and *The Great Outdoors.*

Writings

Sprung!, illustrated by Terry Denton, Hodder Headline (Sydney, New South Wales, Australia), 2001.

Writing in Wet Cement, illustrated by Craig Smith, Hodder Headline (Sydney, New South Wales, Australia), 2002.

Sprung Again!, illustrated by Terry Denton, Mark Macleod (Sydney, New South Wales, Australia), 2002.

Creepy Cool, illustrated by Craig Smith, Hodder Headline (Sydney, New South Wales, Australia), 2002.

You're Dropped!, illustrated by Terry Denton, Mark Macleod (Sydney, New South Wales, Australia), 2003.

Dog of a Day, illustrated by Craig Smith, Hodder Headline (Sydney, New South Wales, Australia), 2003.

Dacked!, illustrated by Terry Denton, Hodder Headline (Sydney, New South Wales, Australia), 2003.

Flushed!, illustrated by Terry Denton, Hodder Headline (Sydney, New South Wales, Australia), 2004.

The Girl Trap, illustrated by Craig Smith, Mark Macleod (Sydney, New South Wales, Australia), 2004.

Chewing the Seatbelt, Walker (London, England), 2004.

Good Night, Me, illustrated by Emma Quay, Hodder (Sydney, New South Wales, Australia), 2005, published as *Goodnight, Me,* Bloomsbury (New York, NY), 2007.

Youse Two (young-adult novel), Hachette (Sydney, New South Wales, Australia), 2005.

It's All Good, Hachette (Sydney, New South Wales, Australia), 2006.

Muffin Top, ABC Books (Sydney, New South Wales, Australia), 2006.

Run, Kid, Run!, illustrated by Craig Smith, ABC Books (Sydney, New South Wales, Australia), 2007.

That Aussie Christmas Book, illustrated by Terry Denton, Scholastic Australia (Sydney, New South Wales, Australia), 2007.

I Do It, illustrated by Jonathan Bentley, ABC Books (Sydney, New South Wales, Australia), 2007.

Cheeky Monkey, illustrated by Emma Quay, ABC Books (Sydney, New South Wales, Australia), 2008.

Letters to Santa, illustrated by Michelle Pike, Scholastic Australia (Sydney, New South Wales, Australia), 2008.

Contributor to anthologies, including *My Dad's a Punk: Twelve Stories about Boys and Their Fathers,* edited by Tony Bradman, Kingfisher (Boston, MA), 2006.

Adaptations
Sprung! was adapted for the stage.

Sidelights
A popular member of the Australian entertainment industry, Andrew Daddo turned his hand to writing for children with *Sprung!,* the first of several books illustrated by Terry Denton. Since then, Daddo has penned a variety of stories, from picture books for the youngest set such as *I Do It,* to short chapter books such as *Writing in Wet Cement,* for students just learning to read independently. Daddo also entertains teenaged readers with his novel *Youse Two.*

Daddo's first published book for children, a picture book about a child's evening preparations for sleep, was published in the author's native Australia as well as in North America. Featuring artwork by Emma Quay, *Goodnight, Me* allows readers to observe the routine a young orangutan follows while settling himself in for the night. From limb to trunk, the creature addresses each of his body parts, thanking his feet for their work running all day and asking his tummy to rest for the night. After a goodnight kiss from Mom, the drowsy orangutan drifts to sleep, content that every part of him will wake refreshed the next morning. Comparing the book favorably to Margaret Wise Brown's bedtime classic, *Goodnight, Moon, School Library Journal* contributor Catherine Callegari deemed *Goodnight, Me* "perfect for bedtime or pajama storytimes." Writing in *Kirkus Reviews,* a critic suggested that Daddo's picture book offers a soothing "pattern for little ones to quiet their tired bodies and souls."

Biographical and Critical Sources

PERIODICALS

Kirkus Reviews, October 15, 2007, review of *Goodnight, Me.*

School Library Journal, December, 2007, Catherine Callegari, review of *Goodnight, Me,* p. 87.

ONLINE

Andrew Daddo Home Page, http://andrewdaddo.com.au (March 7, 2009).*

* * *

DALY, Nicholas
See DALY, Niki

* * *

DALY, Niki 1946-
(Nicholas Daly)

Personal

Born June 13, 1946, in Cape Town, South Africa; son of George (a carpenter) and Sarah Daly; married Judith Mary Kenny (an artist), July 7, 1973; children: Joseph, Leo. *Education:* Cape Town Technikon, diploma, 1970.

Addresses

Home and office—36 Strubens Rd., Cape Town, South Africa. *Agent*—Laura Cecil, 17 Alwyne Villas, London N1 2HG, England.

Career

Illustrator and graphic designer. CBS Record Company, London, England, singer and songwriter, 1971-73; junior art director for advertising agencies in Cape Town,

Niki Daly (Reproduced by permission.)

South Africa and London, 1973-75; freelance illustrator, 1975-79; East Ham Technical College, London, graphics teacher, 1976-79; Stellenbosch University, head of graphic design, 1983-89; David Philip Publishers, head of Songololo Books, 1989-92; The Inkman Company, facilitator of children's picture books, 1993—; author and illustrator. *Exhibitions:* Work has been exhibited at the Original Art Show of the Society of Illustrators, New York, NY, 1995.

Member

Writers and Illustrators Group (founding member).

Awards, Honors

Award for Illustration, British Arts Council/Provincial Booksellers, 1978 for *The Little Girl Who Lived down the Road; Horn Book* Honor List inclusion, 1987, and Parents' Choice Foundation Book Award for Literature, and Katrine Harries Award for illustration (South Africa), both 1988, all for *Not So Fast, Songololo; New York Times* Ten Best Illustrated Books listee, 1995, and Anne Izard Story Teller's Choice Award, 1996, both for *Why the Sun and Moon Live in the Sky;* International Board on Books for Young People Honor designation for illustration, 1995, for *All the Magic in the World* by Wendy Hartmann and 1996, for *One Round Moon and a Star for Me* by Ingrid Mennen; Parents' Choice Award, 1999, for *Bravo, Zan Angelo!;* Children's Africana Book Award Honor Book for Young Children designation, 2004, for *Once upon a Time.*

Writings

SELF-ILLUSTRATED FICTION; FOR CHILDREN

The Little Girl Who Lived down the Road, Collins (London, England), 1978.

Vim the Rag Mouse, Atheneum (New York, NY), 1979.

Joseph's Other Red Sock, Atheneum (New York, NY), 1982.

Leo's Christmas Surprise, Gollancz (London, England), 1983.

Not So Fast, Songololo, Gollancz (London, England), 1985, Atheneum (New York, NY), 1986.

Mama, Papa, and Baby Joe, Viking (New York, NY), 1991.

Papa Lucky's Shadow, Margaret K. McElderry (New York, NY), 1992.

(With Ingrid Mennen) *Somewhere in Africa,* illustrated by Nicolaas Maritz, Dutton (New York, NY), 1992.

Mary Malloy and the Baby Who Wouldn't Sleep, Golden (New York, NY), 1993.

Why the Sun and Moon Live in the Sky, Lothrop, Lee & Shepard (New York, NY), 1994.

My Dad, Margaret K. McElderry (New York, NY), 1995.

Bravo, Zan Angelo!, Farrar, Straus & Giroux (New York, NY), 1996.

(With Nola Turkington) *The Dancer,* Human & Rousseau, 1996.

(With Wendy Hartmann) *The Dinosaurs Are Back and It's Your Fault Edward!,* Margaret K. McElderry (New York, NY), 1997.

The Boy on the Beach, Margaret K. McElderry (New York, NY), 1999.

Pa's Perfect Pizza, Corgi (London, England), 2000.

Old Bob's Brown Bear, Farrar, Straus & Giroux (New York, NY), 2002.

Once upon a Time, Farrar, Straus & Giroux (New York, NY), 2003.

Ruby Sings the Blues, Bloomsbury (New York, NY), 2005.

A Wanderer in Og: An Amphigory Devised for Your Amusement, Double Storey Books (Cape Town, South Africa), 2005.

Pretty Salma, Frances Lincoln (London, England), 2006, published as *Pretty Salma: A Little Red Riding Story from Africa,* 2007.

Welcome to Zanzibar Road, Clarion Books (New York, NY), 2006.

Bettina Valentino and the Picasso Club, Farrar, Straus & Giroux (New York, NY), 2009.

"WALKER STORYTIME" SERIES; SELF-ILLUSTRATED

Ben's Gingerbread Man, Viking (New York, NY), 1985.

Teddy's Ear, Viking (New York, NY), 1985.

Monsters Are like That, Viking (New York, NY), 1985.

Just like Archie, Viking (New York, NY), 1986.

Look at Me!, Viking (New York, NY), 1986.

Thank You, Henrietta, Viking (New York, NY), 1986.

"JAMELA" SERIES; SELF-ILLUSTRATED

Jamela's Dress, Farrar, Straus & Giroux (New York, NY), 1999.

What's Cooking, Jamela?, Farrar, Straus & Giroux (New York, NY), 2001.

Where's Jamela?, Farrar, Straus & Giroux (New York, NY), 2004.

Happy Birthday, Jamela!, Farrar, Straus & Giroux (New York, NY), 2006.

ILLUSTRATOR

Kathleen Hersom, *Maybe It's a Tiger,* Macmillan (London, England), 1981.

Christopher Gregorowski, reteller, *Fly, Eagle Fly!,* Tafelberg (London, England), 1982, revised edition, Margaret K. McElderry (New York, NY), 2000.

Louis Baum, *I Want to See the Moon,* Bodley Head (London, England), 1984, Overlook Press (New York, NY), 1989.

Ruth Craft, *The Day of the Rainbow,* Heinemann (London, England), 1988, Viking (New York, NY), 1989.

Reviva Schermbrucker, *Charlie's House,* Viking (New York, NY), 1991.

Wendy Hartmann, *All the Magic in the World,* Dutton (New York, NY), 1993.

Ingrid Mennen, *One Round Moon and a Star for Me,* Orchard (New York, NY), 1994.

Cari Best, *Red Light, Green Light, Mama, and Me,* Orchard (New York, NY), 1995.

Dinah M. Mbanze, reteller, *The Magic Pot: Three African Tales,* Kwela Books (Cape Town, South Africa), 1999.

Dinah M. Mbanze, reteller, *The Berry Basket: Three African Tales,* Kwela Books (Cape Town, South Africa), 1999.

Christopher Gregorowski, reteller, *Fly, Eagle, Fly: An African Fable,* Margaret K. McElderry (New York, NY), 2000.

Philip Wells, *Daddy Island,* Barefoot Books (New York, NY), 2001.

Pat Thomson, *The Squeaky, Creaky Bed,* Random House (New York, NY), 2003.

Louise Borden, *The Greatest Skating Race: A World War II Story from the Netherlands,* Margaret K. McElderry (New York, NY), 2004.

Shutta Crum, *A Family for Old Mill Farm,* Clarion (New York, NY), 2007.

Sheila P. Moses, *Sallie Gal and the Wall-a-kee Man,* Scholastic Press (New York, NY), 2007.

Adaptations

Not So Fast, Songololo, was adapted as a videotape by Weston Woods, 1990.

Sidelights

Niki Daly is a highly acclaimed South African author/ illustrator whose picture books celebrate the imaginative powers of children and their magnificent everyday lives. Notable due to his ability to view the world from

Daly's popular self-illustrated picture books include **Pretty Salma,** *a retelling of the Red Riding Hood story.* (Illustration copyright © 2006 by Niki Daly. All rights reserved. Reproduced by permission of Clarion Books, an imprint of Houghton Mifflin Harcourt Publishing Company.)

a child's perspective, Daly depicts the world in a rainbow of shades that is reflective of multicultural modern South Africa. Indeed, many of Daly's solo efforts, as well as his illustrations for books by other authors, represent strongly African themes. In *Not So Fast, Songololo, Why the Sun and Moon Live in the Sky, The Boy on the Beach, Pretty Salma: A Little Red Riding Hood Story from Africa,* and the books in his self-illustrated "Jamela" series, Daly captures the intersection between modern life and myth that shapes black South African reality. As a writer, editor, and provider of art workshops, he has furthered the creation of a body of South African children's literature inclusive of all races and ethnic groups.

Daly first became involved in drawing by using pencil stubs handed down from an uncle who painted watercolor pictures. Born in South Africa, he traveled to London at age twenty-four in order to pursue a career in singing and songwriting, but ultimately worked as a commercial artist. As Daly once commented to *SATA:* "My interest in illustrating for children started after I settled in London. My first book, *The Little Girl Who Lived down the Road,* was written . . . simply as an excuse to draw the pictures, after realizing that a completed product was more useful to a publisher than trying an unknown illustrator on the work of an established writer. I was very encouraged by the favorable

reviews I received concerning the writing of *The Little Girl Who Lived down the Road*—which spurred me on to further books."

Partly inspired by the work of Maurice Sendak, *The Little Girl Who Lived down the Road* is the story of a day at the sea that "has the inevitability of the folk tale," according to a reviewer for *Junior Bookshelf.* This story "is ideal material for the oral story-teller," concluded the reviewer. Carolyn O'Grady wrote in the *Times Educational Supplement* that Daly creates "endearing creatures which make the most of a child's love of animals." Winner of the British Arts Council illustration award, this debut effort encouraged Daly to believe he could actually make a living writing and illustrating children's books.

Inspired by a collection of ornaments and toys arranged on the windowsill of his London studio, Daly next wrote and illustrated *Vim the Rag Mouse* about a toy mouse who lives on a similar windowsill and longs for adventures. A *Publishers Weekly* critic called this book "a welcome fantasy," while a writer for *School Library Journal* commented that the "story has lots of action and a satisfyingly resolved plot." *Joseph's Other Red Sock,* another one of Daly's early works, is a read-aloud story for young children. In the story, the hunt for a missing sock turns into imaginative play as it runs from one room to another. The clutter in Joseph's closet finally becomes a monster who has the sock perched on his ear. "Cheerful pastel watercolors highlight the nonchalant pictures, which have a messy, real-kid feel to them," remarked a reviewer in *Booklist.*

Returning to South Africa with his family in 1980, after ten years living abroad, Daly produced several traditional books for the very young. *Leo's Christmas Surprise* follows Leo and his family through their Christmas festivities. They blow up balloons, decorate the tree, and ice the cake while Grandpa Bob finishes the surprise gift he is making for Leo in the shed. *Growing Point* reviewer Margery Fisher lauded the book as a "good idea expressed in a spirited, individual manner." G. Bott noted in *Junior Bookshelf* that *Leo's Christmas Surprise* "has all the signs of qualifying as a Christmas favorite." Other books produced during this time include the toddler-sized "Walker Storytime" series: *Ben's Gingerbread Man, Teddy's Ear, Monsters Are like That, Just like Archie, Look at Me!,* and *Thank You Henrietta.* Lucy Ellmann, writing in the *Times Literary Supplement,* commented that these books "offer . . . down-to-earth instruction on child psychology."

When Daly and his family returned to South Africa, the country was experiencing great unrest as a result of apartheid. As the author/illustrator recalled to *SATA,* "I wrote and illustrated a number of books which reflected the lives of the children on the other side of the racial divide. In retrospect, I see these books (*Not So Fast, Songololo, Charlie's House, Papa Lucky's Shadow,* and *All the Magic in the World*) as half-way bridges between white and black children who live[d] separate and unequal lives determined by the appalling apartheid system. In order to do these books I ignored the myth propagated through apartheid and some political activists who said that there are differences between people."

The award-winning *Not So Fast, Songololo* explores South African themes from a South African viewpoint. Young Songololo guides his grandmother on and off the bus as the pair goes to town to buy the boy some new shoes. A *Kirkus Reviews* critic called the book an "evocative depiction of a young black boy in South Africa and his warm relationship with his grandmother." Karla Kuskin noted in the *New York Times Book Review* that there "is a sweet spirit in this simple, neatly constructed story." Kuskin went on to remark that Daly's "easy watercolors over loose pencil sketching pick up bright patterns and make sensitive studies of individual black faces."

In *Papa Lucky's Shadow,* Papa Lucky dusts off his dancing shoes and shows why he was a dancing champion in his younger days—much to the delight of his granddaughter, Sugar. "The peppy bebop quality of Sugar's narrative might inspire some impromptu toe-tapping," noted a reviewer for *Publishers Weekly.* Ilene Cooper commented in *Booklist* that the "exuberant artwork" adds "spice to a story that might otherwise have been too sweet." Sian Griffiths observed in a review in *Times Educational Supplement* that "Daly is at the forefront of

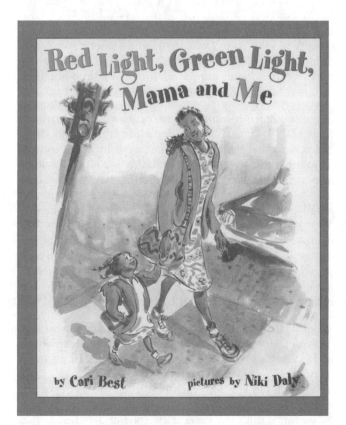

Daly's work as an illustrator includes creating artwork for Cari Best's picture book Red Light, Green Light, Mama, and Me. (Illustration copyright © 1995 by Niki Daly. Reproduced by permission of Orchard Books, an imprint of Scholastic, Inc.)

a wave of South African writers and illustrators . . . who have made their mark abroad."

In the late 1980s Daly established Songololo Books, a children's book imprint of David Philip Publishers in South Africa. As an editor he promoted children's literature for all South African children, cultivating not only stories *about* black South Africans, but *by* them as well. In addition to publishing his own texts, Daly illustrated several books by other authors, including Reviva Schermbrucker's *Charlie's House* and Wendy Hartmann's *All the Magic in the World.* In the former title, a small boy watches his elders build a makeshift hut of corrugated iron in his shanty town and then attempts to do the same with his own materials. Set in the wheat lands of the Cape, *All the Magic in the World* tells of the games of a group of farm laborers' children. Fortunately, South Africa made the transition from apartheid in 1994.

In *Why the Sun and Moon Live in the Sky,* Daly retells a Nigerian mythic tale, while his story *My Dad* harkens back to the difficulties the author/illustrator confronted as a child living with an alcoholic father. Reviewing *Why the Sun and Moon Live in the Sky,* a *Publishers Weekly* contributor noted that Daly's "witty illustrations" invest the tale with "offbeat charm." The reviewer also applauded the book's "wonderful balance of high energy and refined aesthetics," while Nancy B. Cardozo commented in the *New York Times Book Review* that the youngest children "are likely to be hooked by the lovely pictures; the older ones will respond to the characters and themes; parents may end up having the most fun of all as they watch their children fill the wild and hopeful spaces in this fine book with their own wild hope."

A young boy on a South African beach provided the inspiration for Daly's picture book *The Boy on the Beach.* According to a reviewer for *Publishers Weekly,* the book "summons the sights and sounds of a summertime outing through sun-drenched watercolors and keenly tuned language." When the boy on the beach becomes separated from his parents, a lifeguard takes him to Lost and Found where he is reunited with them. "Daly maintains a rigorous visual pace by varying broad vistas of busy seashore activity with close-ups," commented the *Publishers Weekly* reviewer. Kate McClelland observed in *School Library Journal* that the author/illustrator's "watercolor illustrations are cheerfully energetic in depicting the vibrant colors of the busy beach, the sprightliness of little Joe . . . and his parents' carefree enjoyment of the day."

Daly's ability to capture the texture of everyday life in his native Africa is exhibited in the pages of *Welcome to Zanzibar Road.* A chapter book, this self-illustrated story features a cast of quirkily named animals in human roles. A leopard named Louie-Louie runs the local store, and when Mama Jumbo the elephant arrives in town and starts to build a house under a pawpaw tree, the leopard is one of many neighbors to lend a hand. Ultimately, Mama Jumbo is joined by Little Chico, a chicken that proves to be a loyal friend. Cast in a story that *Booklist* critic Abby Nolan dubbed "bright and airy," Daly's animal characters "are kind, full of music, and perfectly satisfied with their unhurried lives." "South African culture flows joyfully in this vibrant tale," wrote *School Library Journal* critic Michele Shaw, the critic predicting that *Welcome to Zanzibar Road* is "sure to be a hit as a read-aloud or as a beginning reader."

Daly introduces one of his most popular characters in *Jamela's Dress.* Fun-loving, playful Jamela adores the fabric her mother has bought to make herself a dress for a friend's wedding. The girl wraps herself in the soft colorful material and parades through town like royalty, luxuriating in the chants of "Kwela Jamela African Queen!" Unfortunately, Jamela does not notice that her royal garb has suffered the indignities of bicycle grease and chicken pecking; the fabric is now stained and torn. Everyone is angry with her until a photographer, who has captured the girl's royal exploits on film, wins a prize for his photograph and shares the award money with his young subject, allowing her to replace the damaged textile. Joan Zaleski commented in *School Library Journal* that *Jamela's Dress* "is filled with the musical language of South Africa. Daly's illustrations are vibrant and colorful and impart a child's eye view of the world." Zaleski dubbed the book a "delightful read-aloud that will be enjoyed by a wide audience," while a *Publishers Weekly* writer remarked of the work that "Daly splashes luminous watercolors across the pages of this. . . . sympathetic and light-hearted slice of life."

Jamela wins more young fans in *What's Cooking, Jamela?, Where's Jamela?,* and *Happy Birthday, Jamela!* When her mother asks her to take care of the chicken the family plans to serve for Christmas dinner, Jamela balks when the discussion turns to the chicken's unpleasant destiny, and in *What's Cooking, Jamela?* she decides to set the ill-fated fowl free. After the chicken causes chaos in a local hair salon, the girl is able to convince her mother to let the bird continue to be a pet instead of becoming the main course. According to a *Horn Book* reviewer, Daly's "lively illustrations . . . capture Jamela's spirit." A *Kirkus Reviews* contributor called Jamela "a charmer and so is her story," while a critic in *School Library Journal* considered *What's Cooking, Jamela?* "an enjoyable read." Writing in *Booklist,* Hazel Rochman praised the work, noting that Daly's "words and pictures capture Jamela's dynamic world."

Jamela's mother gets a new job and the family moves to a bigger house in *Where's Jamela?* As Daly's young readers will relate, the girl is unhappy about having to leave her home behind, and when she climbs into a large box to avoid the chaos of the move no one is aware of her hiding place. Eventually, she is discov-

ered, and when she looks out her window at the new house and finds it sheltered by the same sky, Jamela feels more confident about the change. A *Kirkus Reviews* contributor noted that *Where's Jamela?* "will captivate young readers with its engaging protagonist and warm portrayals of close family," while *Horn Book* contributor Lauren Adams commended the author/illustrator for capturing "the child's perspective with immediacy of experience and lots of sensory details." A visit to the city to shop for a special birthday dress is the focus of *Happy Birthday, Jamela!,* in which Daly's "exuberant watercolor pictures show the girl in a vibrant multiracial neighborhood, and kids everywhere will relate to the joyful birthday story," according to Rochman.

Daly turns from his present-day heroine to a well-known character from storybook history in *Pretty Salma.* Based on the story of Little Red Riding Hood, this tale is set in Ghana, West Africa, where a naive young girl is tricked out of her purchases by a wily dog while on her way home from market. Although Mr. Dog is less threatening than the traditional wolf character, his trickster ways are still a threat to Salma's grandmother. When he finds the elderly woman home alone, however, the girl's quick-thinking ultimately results in a timely rescue. Daly's "cartoon-style paintings capture the sights and flavor of the setting," wrote *School Library Journal* critic Genevieve Gallagher, the reviewer adding that the author/illustrator adds "humorous details to this modern version of a timeless tale." Rochman noted Daly's decision to mix modern and traditional elements in his ink-and-watercolor illustrations for *Pretty Salma,* writing that his "lively version" of the story ranks beside "other comic retellings" of time-honored folk and fairy tales.

Set in eighteenth-century Venice, *Bravo, Zan Angelo!* finds Daly taking a bit of a departure from South African scenes and themes. In this story a little boy wants to join his rather grumpy grandfather's commedia dell' arte street theater group. Grandfather, a once-famous clown, reluctantly gives in, allowing Angelo to play a small part as a rooster. Mary Simons, writing in the *New York Times Book Review,* observed that Daly's "illustrations, exquisitely drawn and illuminated with Venetian light, carry the story farther than the words." *Booklist* critic Michael Cart wrote that "Daly's good-natured story about an unusual subject . . . is greatly enhanced by his beautiful illustrations."

While Daly has gained international acclaim, he continues to make his home in South Africa. As he explained to Michael Thorne in an interview for the Illustrators Portfolio Web site, "Originally, we returned to Cape Town with our son Joe when he was a baby because we wanted to surround him with my large, unruly family. However, during the process of staying and seeing the changes taking place in the country, I felt that, as a South African, I didn't want to miss the experience of transformation. As a writer I [have] benefited from being close to my South African roots. I also feel that I would not have developed as independently as an artist living in the UK where one is forced to confront competition and the yearly swing of trends and financial dips that take place in publishing overseas. Isolation is not a bad thing provided one is a perfectionist and sets standards beyond one's known abilities."

Daly's themes and motifs continue to surprise. His picture books range from the sublime to the silly, and in between they subtly challenge social prejudices without being didactic. Daly summed up his achievement in an essay for *Something about the Author Autobiography Series:* "My motivation—a love for drawing pictures and a wish to be famous for something I do well—has remained with me since I was a kid. . . . What has emerged though, after . . . years of illustrating and writing children's books, is my position on the ideological battleground. I've discovered that I'm a banner-carrying subversive. Emblazoned on my banner is the message 'STRUT YOUR STUFF!'"

Biographical and Critical Sources

BOOKS

Children's Literature Review, Volume 41, Gale (Detroit, MI), 1997.
St. James Guide to Children's Writers, 5th edition, edited by Sara Pendergast and Tom Pendergast, St. James Press (Detroit, MI), 1999.
Something about the Author Autobiography Series, Volume 21, Gale (Detroit, MI), 1996.

PERIODICALS

Black Issues Book Review, March, 2000, review of *Jamela's Dress,* p. 60.
Booklinks, November, 2004, Jennifer Mattson, review of *Where's Jamela?,* p. 42.
Booklist, July, 1982, review of *Joseph's Other Red Sock,* p. 1442; September 15, 1992, Ilene Cooper, review of *Papa Lucky's Shadow,* p. 145; August, 1998, Michael Cart, review of *Bravo, Zan Angelo!,* p. 2014; March 15, 2000, review of *Jamela's Dress,* p. 1342; November 1, 2001, Hazel Rochman, review of *What's Cooking, Jamela?,* p. 482; November 15, 2001, Hazel Rochman, review of *Daddy Island,* p. 585; February, 2003, Julie Cummins, review of *Once upon a Time,* p. 311; September 1, 2004, Jennifer Mattson, review of *Where's Jamela?,* p. 122; April 15, 2005, Gillian Engberg, review of *Ruby Sings the Blues,* p. 1459; May 1, 2006, Abby Nolan, review of *Welcome to Zanzibar Road,* p. 88; August 1, 2006, Hazel Rochman, review of *Happy Birthday, Jamela!,* p. 84; February 1, 2007, Hazel Rochman, review of *Pretty Salma: A Little Red Riding Hood Story from Africa,* p. 60.
Bulletin of the Center for Children's Books, January, 2002, review of *What's Cooking, Jamela?,* p. 168.

Growing Point, November, 1983, Margery Fisher, review of *Leo's Christmas Surprise,* p. 4168.
Horn Book, September, 2001, review of *What's Cooking, Jamela,* p. 572; May-June, 2005, Susan Dove Lempke, review of *Ruby Sings the Blues,* p. 306; September-October, 2006, Susan Dove Lempke, review of *Happy Birthday, Jamela!,* p. 564; September-October, 2007, Robin Smith, review of *Sallie Gal and the Wall-a-kee Man,* p. 583.
Junior Bookshelf, June, 1978, review of *The Little Girl Who Lived down the Road,* p. 134; December, 1983, G. Bott, review of *Leo's Christmas Surprise,* p. 234.
Kirkus Reviews, March 15, 1986, review of *Not So Fast, Songololo,* pp. 468-469; September 15, 2001, review of *What's Cooking, Jamela?,* p. 1356; July 15, 2004, review of *Where's Jamela?,* p. 682; May 1, 2007, review of *A Family for Old Mill Farm.*
Library Media Connection, August-September, 2003, review of *Once upon a Time,* p. 70.
New York Times Book Review, June 1, 1986, Karla Kuskin, review of *Not So Fast, Songololo,* p. 48; November 5, 1995, Nancy B. Cardozo, review of *Why the Sun and Moon Live in the Sky,* p. 31; December 6, 1998, Mary Simons, review of *Bravo, Zan Angelo!,* p. 78.
Publishers Weekly, July 29, 1979, review of *Vim the Rag Mouse,* p. 105; June 29, 1992, review of *Papa Lucky's Shadow,* pp. 62-63; May 15, 1995, review of *Why the Sun and Moon Live in the Sky,* p. 72; May 10, 1999, reviews of *The Boy on the Beach* and *Jamela's Dress,* pp. 66-67; July 18, 2005, review of *Ruby Sings the Blues,* p. 205; April 15, 2007, review of *Pretty Salma,* p. 50.
School Librarian, February, 1992, Nansi Taylor, review of *Charlie's House,* pp. 17-18; summer, 2000, review of *Pa's Perfect Pizza,* p. 79; winter, 2001, review of *What's Cooking, Jamela?,* p. 186; spring, 2002, review of *Old Bob's Brown Bear,* p. 17, and review of *Not So Fast, Songolo,* p. 73; autumn, 2003, review of *Once upon a Time,* p. 129.
School Library Journal, December, 1979, review of *Vim the Rag Mouse,* pp. 72, 74; June, 1999, Kate McClelland, review of *The Boy on the Beach,* p. 42; August, 1999, Joan Zaleski, review of *Jamela's Dress,* p. 132; October, 2001, review of *What's Cooking, Jamela?,* p. 64; September, 2004, Kathy Krasniewicz, review of *Where's Jamela?,* p. 157; July, 2006, Michele Shaw, review of *Welcome to Zanzibar Road,* p. 71; August, 2006, Mary Hazelton, review of *Happy Birthday, Jamela!,* p. 78; April, 2007, Genevieve Gallagher, review of *Pretty Salma,* p. 121; June, 2007, Linda L. Walkins, review of *A Family for Old Mill Farm,* p. 96; September, 2007, Kathryn Kosiorek, review of *Sallie Gal and the Wall-a-kee Man,* p. 172.
Teacher Librarian, February, 2003, review of *Old Bob's Brown Bear,* p. 42.
Times Educational Supplement, June 23, 1978, Carolyn O'Grady, "Paradise Lost and Found," p. 21; July 2, 1993, Sian Griffiths, "Mum and Dad and Gran," p. 10.
Times Literary Supplement, October 25, 1985, Lucy Ellmann, "Childhood's Image," p. 1218.
Tribune Books (Chicago, IL), September 22, 2002, review of *Old Bob's Brown Bear,* p. 4; June 8, 2003, review of *Once upon a Time,* p. 5.

ONLINE

Childlit.org, http://www.childlit.org.za/ (February 14, 2009), "Niki Daly."
Illustrators Portfolio Web site, http://www.illustrators.co.za/ (September 17, 2005), interview with Daly.*

* * *

de SÉVE, Randall

Personal

Married Peter de Séve (an illustrator); children: Paulina, Fia.

Addresses

Home—Brooklyn, NY.

Career

Writer and educator.

Writings

The Toy Boat, illustrated by Loren Long, Philomel (New York, NY), 2007.

Sidelights

As a parent and educator, Randall de Séve explained in an online interview for Powell's Books that she wanted "to write stories children and adults will want to read over and over again; to me, that's the sign of a great kids' book." Inspired by a toy boat that de Séve and her daughter Paulina made from a can, a cork, and a toothpick, her picture book *The Toy Boat* describes a child's search for freedom and letting go. In the story, a boy sails his boat on a lake, controlling it with a string. When a storm causes the toy boat to become loose, it encounters several adventures before a friendly breeze sends it back to shore. A reviewer for *Kirkus* called *The Toy Boat* "a must for little sailors," while a *Publishers Weekly* reviewer called de Séve's story "a resonant tale with wide appeal." In *Booklist,* Julie Cummins commented that, "with plenty of buoyant charm and imaginative artwork [by Loren Long], this contemporary *Little Toot* has an abundance of child appeal."

Biographical and Critical Sources

PERIODICALS

Booklist, August, 2007, Julie Cummins, review of *The Toy Boat,* p. 71.
Kirkus Reviews, August 1, 2007, review of *The Toy Boat.*
Publishers Weekly, August 20, 2007, review of *The Toy Boat,* p. 66.
School Library Journal, September, 2007, Susan Moorhead, review of *The Toy Boat,* p. 161.

ONLINE

Powell's Books Web site, http://www.powells.com/ (March 8, 2009), interview with de Séve.*

E-F

EDWARDS, David 1962-

Personal
Born December 29, 1962; married; children: four. *Hobbies and other interests:* Visiting living history museums, collecting children's books.

Addresses
Home—Tucson, AZ.

Career
Children's author.

Writings
The Pen That Pa Built, illustrated by Ashley Wolff, Ten Speed Press (Berkeley, CA), 2007.

Sidelights
An avid collector of children's books, David Edwards added one more title to the genre with his picture book *The Pen That Pa Built.* Using the traditional nursery rhyme "This Is the House That Jack Built," Edwards creates a new version of the tale, this time describing the processes involved in creating a homespun wool blanket. Brought to life in Ashley Wolff's vivid illustrations, *The Pen That Pa Built* starts as the father of the family builds an enclosure for his herd of sheep. As they turn the pages, readers follow the family's work shearing, carding, dyeing, spinning and eventually weaving the flock's bountiful wool. In addition to learning how raw wool is processed into usable fiber, Edwards also provides information about farm life in the early nineteenth century, depicting how most families of that era made the majority of the goods they required for everyday life.

Writing in *Kirkus Reviews,* a critic noted of *The Pen That Pa Built* that "the ending neatly ties all the strands together," with the family's cooperative effort resulting in a fluffy blanket for the expected arrival of a new baby. *Booklist* critic Jesse Karp believed that Edwards' book offers young readers "a simple, step-by-step rundown of the process of refining wool," going on to describe the narrative as "pleasant and the rhymes clever."

Biographical and Critical Sources

PERIODICALS

Booklist, November 15, 2007, Jesse Karp, review of *The Pen That Pa Built,* p. 50.
Kirkus Reviews, September 15, 2007, review of *The Pen That Pa Built.**

* * *

ESEKI, Bruno
See MPHAHLELE, Es'kia

* * *

ESEKIE, Bruno
See MPHAHLELE, Es'kia

* * *

FELLOWES, Julian 1950-

Personal
Born August 17, 1950, in Cairo, Egypt; son of diplomats; married; wife's name Emma; children: Peregrine. *Education:* Attended Cambridge University and Webber Douglas School of Drama.

Addresses
Home—Dorchester, England.

Career

Actor, 1981—; screenwriter, producer, and director. Film roles include: (as Nigel Jenkins) *Baby: Secret of the Lost Legend,* 1985; (as Noel Coward) *Goldeneye: The Secret Life of Ian Fleming,* 1989; (as Desmond Arding) *Shadowlands,* 1993; (as Colonel Dent) *Jane Eyre,* 1996; (as Bishop) *Savage Hearts,* 1997; (as Timmons) *Regeneration,* 1997; and (as minister of defense) *Tomorrow Never Dies,* 1997. Television roles include (as Hugo) *Knights of God* (series); (as Major Dunnett) *Sharpe's Rifles* (series), 1993; (as Dr. Jobling) *Martin Chuzzlewit* (miniseries) 1994; (as Wuden) *Little Lord Fauntleroy* (miniseries), 1995; (as Queen's counsel for the prosecution) *Killing Me Softly,* 1995; (as Sir Henry Posonby) *The Final Cut,* 1995; (as Prince Regent) *Sharpe's Regiment* (series), 1996; (as Claud Seabrook, Member of Parliament) *Our Friends in the North* (miniseries), 1996; (as Lord Richmond) *Aristocrats* (miniseries), 1999; (as Lord Angus Errol Sharon Kilwillie) *Monarch of the Glen* (series), 2000-05; (as prosecution counsel) *Dirty Tricks,* 2000; and (as presenter) *A Most Mysterious Murder: The Case of Charles Bravo,* 2004. Also teacher of script-writing master classes.

Awards, Honors

Emmy Award, Academy of Television Arts and Sciences, for *Little Lord Fauntleroy;* Screenwriter of the Year designation, National Association of Theater Owners, Academy Award, Academy of Motion Picture Arts and Sciences, Golden Globe Award nomination, Hollywood Foreign Press Association, and New York Film Critics Circle Award, all 2002, all for *Gosford Park.*

Writings

Little Lord Fauntleroy (television miniseries), British Broadcasting Corporation, 1995.
The Prince and the Pauper (teleplay; based on Mark Twain's novel of the same title), 1996.
(And author of afterword) *Gosford Park* (screenplay; produce by USA Films, 2001), with introduction by Robert Altman, Newmarket Press (New York, NY), 2002.
Piccadilly Jim (screenplay), 2004.
(With Matthew Faulk and Mark Skeet) *Vanity Fair* (screenplay; produced 2004), journals and correspondence by Mira Nair, Newmarket Press (New York, NY), 2004.
Snobs (novel), Weidenfeld & Nicolson (London, England), 2004, St. Martin's Press (New York, NY), 2005.
(And director) *Separate Lies* (screenplay; adapted from Nigel Balchin's novel *A Way through the Wood*), Fox Searchlight Pictures, 2005.
(Author of book) *Mary Poppins* (musical; based on the book by P.L. Travers), produced in London, England, 2006.
The Curious Adventures of the Abandoned Toys (picture book), illustrated by S.D. Schindler, Henry Holt (New York, NY), 2007.

(Author of introduction) Isabel Colegate, *The Shooting Party,* Penguin (London, England), 2007.

Author of English dialogue for film *Deux frères,* 2004; author, with Tina Pepler, of teleplays for BBC TV miniseries *Julian Fellowes Investigates: A Most Mysterious Murder,* including *The Case of Charles Bravo,* 2004, *The Case of Rose Harsent,* 2005, *The Case of George Harry Storrs,* 2005, and *The Case of the Earl of Erroll,* 2005.

Sidelights

Julian Fellowes started his career as an actor in plays and has performed roles in nearly fifty films and television programs. He added writing to his repertoire in 1994 with the Emmy Award-winning television miniseries *Little Lord Fauntleroy,* and his film work includes the screenplays for the period dramas *Gosford Park* and *Vanity Fair.* His work on *Gosford Park* earned Fellowes an Academy award, a Golden Globe award nomination, and a New York Film Critics Circle award. He was also named screenwriter of the year by the National Association of Theater Owners in 2002.

Fellowes' adult novel *Snobs* reflects its author's familiarity with the English class system. In the story a gold digger marries a wealthy earl, only to leave him for an actor. The plot is made more complex by a cast of characters that includes an upper-class and titled mother-in-law, a distinctly not-so-upper-class mother, a stately mansion, and all the accoutrements of a formulaic period piece. A *Kirkus Reviews* contributor described *Snobs* as "a wonderful commonplace book of wit and wisdom" that is "disguised as a novel." Andrew Barrow, writing in the British *Spectator,* called Fellowes' story "provocative, titillating and seductive," adding that the book "never loses momentum."

While much of Fellowes' work has been geared for adults, his stage dramatization of P.L. Travers' *Mary Poppins* and his picture book *The Curious Adventures of the Abandoned Toys* are decidedly child-friendly. Featuring artwork by S.D. Schindler, *The Curious Adventures of the Abandoned Toys* follows a stuffed bear named Doc, who cheers up young patients at a hospital. When the hospital is renovated, the well-worn Doc is tossed away, but when he is rescued by the men driving the garbage truck, the bear ultimately finds a new home with other discarded toys at the local dump. In a series of adventures, Doc helps various toys find their way home or back into the arms of a beloved child. "Doc's story will appeal to those with a fondness for old-fashioned storybooks," according to *School Library Journal* contributor Jayne Damron, while a *Kirkus Reviews* writer cited Fellowes' ability to combine "sophisticated language" with "touches of humor," while also "giving each of the toys a simple but distinct personality." "Fellowes exhibits a wonderful flair for both dialogue and characterization," concluded *Booklist* critic Shelle Rosenfeld, the reviewer adding that *The Curious Adventures of the Abandoned Toys* "echoes . . . the drama and poignancy of classic animal tales."

Biographical and Critical Sources

PERIODICALS

Booklist, October 1, 2007, Shelle Rosenfeld, review of *The Curious Adventures of the Abandoned Toys,* p. 56.

Encore, July, 2006, Bob Ellis, review of *Separate Lies,* p. 14.

Entertainment Weekly, April 5, 2002, Julian Fellowes, "My Oscar Diary: What's It Like to Be Served up an Oscar?" p. 78.

Kirkus Reviews, December 15, 2004, review of *Snobs,* p. 1156; August 15, 2007, review of *The Curious Adventures of the Abandoned Toys.*

New Republic, Stanley Kauffmann, "Promises, Promises," p. 24.

New York, December 24, 2001, Peter Rainer, "Magical Mystery," p. 104.

New York Times Book Review, December 2, 2007, Krystyna Poray Goddu, review of *The Curious Adventures of the Abandoned Toys.*

Publishers Weekly, October 29, 2007, review of *The Curious Adventures of the Abandoned Toys,* p. 55.

School Library Review, January, 2008, Jayne Damron, review of *The Curious Adventures of the Abandoned Toys,* p. 86.

Spectator, April 3, 2004, Andrew Barrow, review of *Snobs,* p. 52.

ONLINE

British Broadcasting Corporation Web site, http://www.bbc.co.uk/ (February 2, 2009), "Julian Fellowes."

Sundance Channel Web site, http://www.sundancechannel.com/ (August 28, 2002), "Julian Fellowes."

Writers Guild of America Web site, http://www.wga.org/ (July 19, 2002), Richard Stayton, "The Butler Didn't Write It: Julian Fellowes on *Gosford Park.*"*

*   *   *

FITZGERALD, Joanne 1956-

Personal

Born 1956, in Canada.

Addresses

Home—Georgetown, Ontario, Canada.

Career

Illustrator.

Awards, Honors

Governor General's Award, 1991, for *Doctor Kiss Says Yes* by Teddy Jam; Mr. Christie's Book Award, 2001, for *The Little Rooster and the Diamond Button* by Celia Barker Lottridge; *Quill & Quire* Best Picture Book designation, 2007, for *Yum! Yum!*

Writings

SELF-ILLUSTRATED

This Is Me and Where I Am, Fitzhenry & Whiteside (Markham, Ontario, Canada), 2004.

Yum! Yum!: Delicious Nursery Rhymes, Fitzhenry & Whiteside (Markham, Ontario, Canada), 2007.

ILLUSTRATOR

Gail Chislett, *Pardon Me, Mom,* Annick Press (Toronto, Ontario, Canada), 1986.

Susan Green, *In the Woods,* Gage Educational (Toronto, Ontario, Canada), 1987.

Betty Waterton, *Plain Noodles,* Douglas & McIntyre (Toronto, Ontario, Canada), 1989, published as *Baby Boat,* Knopf (New York, NY), 1989.

Niko Scharer, *Emily's House,* Douglas & McIntyre (Toronto, Ontario, Canada), 1990.

Teddy Jam, *Doctor Kiss Says Yes,* Douglas & McIntyre (Toronto, Ontario, Canada), 1991.

Celia Barker Lottridge, reteller, *Ten Small Tales: Stories from around the World,* Douglas & McIntyre (Toronto, Ontario, Canada), 1993, Margaret K. McElderry Books (New York, NY), 1994.

Teddy Jam, *Jacob's Best Sisters,* Douglas & McIntyre (Toronto, Ontario, Canada), 1996.

Celia Barker Lottridge, reteller, *The Little Rooster and the Diamond Button: A Hungarian Folktale,* Douglas & McIntyre (Toronto, Ontario, Canada), 2001.

Sharon Jennings, *When You Get a Baby,* Fitzhenry & Whiteside (Markham, Ontario, Canada), 2002.

Anne Laurel Carter, *Circus Play,* Orca Book Publishers (Custer, WA), 2002.

Phoebe Gilman, *The Blue Hippopotamus,* North Winds Press (Toronto, Ontario, Canada), 2007.

Works featuring Fitzgerald's illustrations have been translated into French and adapted for Braille.

Sidelights

Joanne Fitzgerald is an illustrator whose use of bright colors and detail have made her self-illustrated picture books such a success in her native Canada and elsewhere. Her contributions to picture books by other writers have also earned Fitzgerald several awards: she won the coveted Governor General's Award for her artwork in *Doctor Kiss Says Yes* by Teddy Jam, and her illustrations for Celia Barker Lottridge's *The Little Rooster and the Diamond Button: A Hungarian Folktale* were awarded the Mr. Christie's Book Award. Fitzgerald's pen-and-ink and watercolor images use detailed borders to reflect the Hungarian roots of Lottridge's story, noted a *Kirkus Reviews* writer in a review of *The Little Rooster and the Diamond Button,* and she incorporates "just enough detail to highlight the tale's absurdity." Praising the images Fitzgerald contributes to another book by Lottridge, the folktale collection *Ten*

Small Tales: Stories from around the World, a *Publishers Weekly* contributor wrote that the artist "attractively interprets the tales with serene watercolors in which calm tones capture the fun of the plots while leaving most of the sparkle for the narrative."

Fitzgerald's original self-illustrated picture books include *This Is Me and Where I Am* and *Yum! Yum!: Delicious Nursery Rhymes.* In *This Is Me and Where I Am* helps young readers learn to understand their unique place within the wider world, such as their house or apartment number, the name of their street, town or city, and country, and also appreciate the private space they have within their own home, such as their bedroom. Praising *This Is Me and Where I Am* in *Booklist,* Carolyn Phelan dubbed the work "a winner for reading aloud individually as well as for school units on community or global awareness," and in *School Library Journal* Anne L. Tormohlen praised Fitzgerald's detailed cartoon art as a "perfect . . . match [for] the text." Writing in *Resource Links,* Lori Lavallee noted that *This Is Me and Where I Am* is likely to inspire "dialogue and imaginative storytelling between child and adult."

In *Yum! Yum!* Fitzgerald presents thirteen traditional nursery rhymes—such as Jack Sprat, Little Jack Horner,

Higgledy Piggledy, and Hey Diddle Diddle—and creates illustrations for each one that sets the action at a farmer's market, where delicious food of all types abounds. Each nursery-rhyme character is an animal dressed in human clothing, and in Fitzgerald's "beautifully detailed" illustrations "the animals are well defined by their expressive faces," according to *School Library Journal* critic Ieva Bates. "Subtle humor abounds" in the author/illustrator's interpretation, Bates added, and in *Kirkus Reviews* a contributor described *Yum! Yum!* as a "delightful compilation" featuring pastel-toned illustrations that will "put children's powers of observation to good use." Writing that the book's "illustrations in soft pastels are a real pleasure to discover," Rachelle Gooden concluded in *Resource Links* that *Yum! Yum!* is sugared with small details that "are clever and sure to get a chuckle out of readers young and old."

Biographical and Critical Sources

PERIODICALS

Booklist, September 1, 2001, Marta Segal, review of *The Little Rooster and the Diamond Button: A Hungarian Folktale,* p. 112; December 1, 2002, Diane Foote, re-

Joanne Fitzgerald created the artwork for Celia Barker Lottridge's multicultural story collection Ten Small Tales: Stories from around the World.
(Illustration copyright © 1993 by Joanne Fitzgerald. Reproduced by permission of Groundwood Books, Ltd.)

Fitzgerald's stylized cartoons add a comical air to Lottridge's folktale adaptation **The Little Rooster and the Diamond Button.** (Illustration copyright © 2001 by Joanne Fitzgerald. Reproduced by permission of Groundwood Books, Ltd.)

view of *Circus Play,* p. 672; October 1, 2004, Carolyn Phelan, review of *This Is Me and Where I Am,* p. 334; December 1, 2007, Carolyn Phelan, review of *Yum! Yum! Delicious Nursery Rhymes,* p. 47.

Horn Book, January-February, 1994, Sarah Ellis, review of *Ten Small Tales: Stories from around the World,* p. 112.

Kirkus Reviews, September 15, 2001, review of *The Little Rooster and the Diamond Button,* p. 1361; September 15, 2002, review of *Circus Play;* October 15, 2007, review of *Yum! Yum!*

Publishers Weekly, February 28, 1994, review of *Ten Small Tales,* p. 88; December 13, 2004, review of *This Is Me and Where I Am,* p. 66; December 10, 2007, review of *Yum! Yum!,* p. 54.

Quill & Quire, November, 1996, Teresa Toten, review of *Jacob's Best Sisters;* September, 2001, Jeffrey Canton, review of *The Little Rooster and the Diamond Button;* November, 2002, Nathan Whitlock, review of *Circus Play;* July, 2004, Ciabh McEvenue, review of *This Is Me and Where I Am;* October, 2007, Philippa Sheppard, review of *The Blue Hippopotamus;* November, 2007, Carlyn Zwarenstein, review of *Yum! Yum!.*

Resource Links, February, 1997, review of *Jacob's Best Sisters,* p. 112; December, 2001, Linda Ludke, review

of *The Little Rooster and the Diamond Button,* p. 7; December, 2002, Sandra Tee, review of *Circus Play,* p. 3, and Denise Parrott, review of *When You Get a Baby,* p. 7; December, 2004, Lori Lavallee, review of *This Is Me and Where I Am,* p. 2; December, 2007, Linda Berezowski, review of *The Blue Hippopotamus,* p. 3; February, 2008, Rachelle Gooden, review of *Yum! Yum!,* p. 2.

School Library Journal, January, 2002, Be Astengo, review of *The Little Rooster and the Diamond Button,* p. 120; November, 2004, Anne L. Tormohlen, review of *This Is Me and Where I Am,* p. 103; December, 2007, Ieva Bates, review of *Yum! Yum!,* p. 108.

*   *   *

FLINN, Alex 1966-

Personal

Born October 23, 1966, in Glen Cove, NY; daughter of Nicholas (a ship chandler), and Manya (a homemaker) Kissanis; married Eugene Flinn, Jr. (an attorney), May 23, 1992; children: Katherine, Meredith. *Education:* University of Miami, bachelor of music, 1988; Nova

Alex Flinn (Reproduced by permission.)

Southeastern University Law School, J.D., 1992. *Religion:* Greek Orthodox. *Hobbies and other interests:* Volunteer work, theater, opera.

Addresses

Home—Miami, FL. *E-mail*—Alixwrites@aol.com.

Career

Writer and attorney. Miami-Dade State Attorney's Office, Miami, FL, intern; Martinez & Gutierrez, Miami, practicing attorney, 2001.

Member

Society of Children's Book Writers and Illustrators.

Awards, Honors

American Library Association (ALA) Best Book for Young Adults and Quick Picks for Reluctant Young Adult Readers, both 2001, American Booksellers Association Pick of the Lists, *Book Sense* 76 list, New York Public Library Books for the Teen Age designation, Tayshas (TX) State List, Iowa Educational Media Association High School Book Award Master List, Rhode Island Teen Book Award Master List, Popular Paperbacks for Young Adults List nomination, and Children's Literature Choices List, all 2002, Oklahoma Sequoia Young Adult Master List, 2003-04, and Maryland Black-eyed Susan Award, 2004, all for *Breathing Underwater;* ALA Quick Picks and Young Adults Books nomination, both 2002, both for *Breaking Point;* International Reading Association Young-Adult Choice designation, for *Breathing Underwater, Noting to Lose,* and *Fade to Black;* Lone Star State Award nomination, 2009, for *Beastly;* numerous other state awards.

Writings

Breathing Underwater, HarperCollins (New York, NY), 2001.
Breaking Point, HarperCollins (New York, NY), 2002.
Nothing to Lose, HarperCollins (New York, NY), 2004.
Fade to Black, HarperCollins (New York, NY), 2005.
Diva, HarperTempest (New York, NY), 2007.
Beastly, HarperTeen (New York, NY), 2007.
A Kiss in Time, HarperTeen (New York, NY), 2009.

Flinn's works have been translated into Spanish, Catalan, and Slovenian.

Adaptations

Flinn's novels have been adapted for audiocassette by Listening Library. *Beastly* was adapted for a television film by CBS.

Sidelights

"I write for teens because I never finished being one," Alex Flinn told an online interviewer for *Embracing the Child.* Despite her own fond memories of growing up, Flinn's young-adult novels, which include *Breathing Underwater, Breaking Point, Fade to Black,* and *Diva,* have been praised for their edgy realism. Using the point of view of a male teen in each of her books, she tells about an abusive relationship and dating violence in *Breathing Underwater,* while *Breaking Point* addresses school violence and peer pressure. *Fade to Black* follows a high schooler who must confront discrimination and fear when he is publicly announced to be HIV positive, while in *Diva* Flinn turns the tables on the narrator of *Breathing Underwater* by recounting that novel's events from another character's point of view. As Paula Rohrlick noted in a *Kliatt* review of another Flinn novel, *Nothing to Lose,* the author "doesn't hesitate to tackle disturbing topics and succeeds in making the experiences and emotions of her protagonists realistic and gripping."

Born in New York state, Flinn grew up with a love of reading, and favorite authors include Astrid Lindgren, Beverly Cleary, Judy Blume, Marilyn Sachs, and Laura Ingalls Wilder. She decided to be a writer at an early age; when her mother suggested that the five year old should be an author, Flinn recalled on her home page that "I guess I must have nodded or something because from that point on, every poem I ever wrote in school was submitted to *Highlights* or *Cricket* magazine. I was collecting rejection slips at age seven."

By the time Flinn was in high school, her artistic aspirations had expanded to include the performing arts. While attending the University of Miami she studied opera, singing as a coloratura. Following graduation, she enrolled in law school and then interned with the Miami-Dade State Attorney's Office in a misdemeanor court and volunteering with battered women. As an intern, she became involved with domestic violence cases, and she eventually drew on this experience in her novel *Breathing Underwater.* Establishing a private practice, and marriage to a fellow attorney followed, but while on leave for a pregnancy, Flinn returned to her first love and decided to devote her full time to writing.

Along with Flinn's legal work and volunteer work with battered women, a startling statistic influenced her first novel: over a quarter of high-school and college women reported having been in an abusive relationship. Also, a client in the battered women's shelter where she volunteered was murdered by her husband in front of the woman's children. To research *Breathing Underwater,* Flinn read several books on abuse counseling and interviewed other women working in domestic-violence programs. Flinn also began reading young-adult novels, for she saw her tale as one dealing with teenagers. The work of author Richard Peck particularly impressed her, and a workshop presented by Peck was another inspiration.

Told via the journal entries of Nick Andreas, *Breathing Underwater* examines an abusive relationship from the viewpoint of the abuser. As Flinn discovered in her research, it is the troubled home life of the abuser that fu-

Cover of Flinn's young-adult novel Nothing to Lose. (Jacket art copyright © 2004 by Dennis Clouse Cyclone Design. Reproduced by permission HarperCollins Children's Books, a division of HarperCollins.)

els the cycle of abuse, and through Nick readers could better understand the root of this cycle. At age sixteen, Nick has long been considered one of the cool kids in school. He is wealthy, good looking, popular, intelligent, a charmer, a football player, and drives a classic Mustang. That is his public face, however. Behind closed doors is revealed a different Nick, one tainted by the abuse of a divorced father who continually labels his son a loser. When he meets Caitlin McCourt, a pretty but overweight girl who exudes little self-confidence, he recreates the only relationship he knows, transforming his controlling relationship with Caitlin into a verbally abusive and ultimately physically abusive one.

Breathing Underwater opens with Nick in court, facing a restraining order from Caitlin. The court finds him guilty and sentences him to six months of counseling. He must also keep a weekly journal that tracks his relationship with Caitlin beginning with the first time he met her. Flinn's dual narrative aligns Nick's journal entries with his post-court return to the affluent Key Biscayne High School where everybody now knows his secret. At first Nick resists taking responsibility for what he has done, and he resists participating in counseling. However, a wake-up call comes in the form of a tragedy involving one of Nick's friends.

Critical response to *Breathing Underwater* was overwhelmingly positive, a *Publishers Weekly* reviewing writing that the "correlation between Nick's controlling behavior and his father's abuse is subtle but effective." Joel Shoemaker, writing in *School Library Journal,* called Flinn's narrative an "open and honest portrayal of an all-too-common problem" while a critic for *Booklist* dubbed *Breathing Underwater* "a quick and absorbing read." In *Voice of Youth Advocates,* Beth Anderson found Flinn's novel "almost too painful to read," but added that the book serves teens by providing a "road map to warning signs" of abuse.

Caitlin tells her story in *Diva,* and her narrative explores the emotions of a young woman who obsesses about her weight while dreaming of a career in opera and dealing with the random visits of Nick and the tawdry drama of her mom's affair with a married man. In *Diva* Flinn adopts the blog format in creating part of Caitlin's narrative, and the format provides readers with a fast-paced story in which "Flinn turns a fine eye on the seemingly never-ending mother-daughter dance," according to *Booklist* critic Ilene Cooper. According to Tina Zubak, reviewing the novel for *School Library Journal,* in *Diva* Flinn treats readers to "a solid story, full of self-deprecating humor, snappy dialogue, and well-developed characters and situations." In *Kirkus Reviews* a critic dubbed the novel "realistic and thoughtful."

Flinn tackles another serious juvenile problem—school violence—in *Breaking Point.* Here fifteen-year-old narrator Paul is at a crossroad. Since his parents' divorce, Paul's dad has wanted no part of his son, while his

Cover of Flinn's novel Diva, *featuring cover art by Gina Triplett.* (Cover art copyright © 2006 by Gina Triplett. Reproduced by permission of HarperCollins Publishers.)

mom uses the teen as an emotional crutch. Formerly home-schooled, nerdish Paul now enters exclusive Gate-Brickell Christian School, where his mother works to qualify her son for reduced tuition. Mother and son also live in a small apartment, making Paul an easy target of the snobby, affluent clique at Gate-Brickell. At first made the subject of practical jokes, Paul is surprised when he is eventually befriended by a popular fellow student. Charlie Good has plans for Paul, however, and he tests the teen by convincing him to destroy mailboxes, steal, and drink alcohol. Desperate to fit in, Paul complies, even gaining access to the school computer and changing one of Charlie's grades in order to gain the approval of his new friend. Ultimately, things escalate into tragedy.

Kimberly L. Paone, writing in *Voice of Youth Advocates,* compared *Breaking Point* to Robert Cormier's *The Chocolate War,* while Francisca Goldsmith described Flinn's novel in *Booklist* as "grim and emotional, . . . cathartic reading for teens." Janet Hilburn, writing in *School Library Journal,* concluding that the novelist "has succeeded in her goal" of understanding what can make teens angry and isolated, and added:

"Despite his actions, Paul comes across as a likable, although misguided, teen in a book that is well worth reading." Paone predicted of *Breaking Point* that Flinn's "timely, engaging book is certain to grab the interest of teens."

Nothing to Lose focuses on seventeen-year-old Michael Daye, who lives with his mother and stepfather in Miami. When the family violence escalates to the point of no return, Michael's mother fights back, and her ultra-wealthy attorney husband winds up dead. With his mother now charged with murder, Michael adopts the assumed name of Robert Frost and joins a traveling carnival. Here he is working the Whack-a-Mole game and hopes to escape police interrogation, the trauma of his family's situation, and his feelings of guilt over not being able to protect his mother. When the carnival winds up in his Miami hometown, Michael is forced to stick it out or lose his job, and once again he finds himself embroiled in his mother's high-profile murder trial and questions surrounding his stepfather's death.

The narrative of *Nothing to Lose* alternates between an account of the events leading up to the stepfather's murder and Michael's ultimate decision to come forth and aid his mother in her legal battles. Flinn presents readers with what a *Publishers Weekly* contributor described as a "compelling premise and format" that combine to produce a "juicy story and edgy narration [that] will likely hook readers. Praising the novel as a "heartrending, unforgettable book," *School Library Journal* reviewer Lynn Evarts added that Flinn presents an accurate portrait of the aftereffects of abuse as well as exploring "the legal implications of 'self-defense.'" *Nothing to Lose* serves up a "fast-paced, readable mystery," wrote *Booklist* reviewer Michael Cart, and the secondary story about Michael's life as a carney and his romance with a coworker named Kirstie "add[s] gritty texture and a layer of emotional richness to the already intriguing plot."

One of Flinn's most popular novels due to its exploration of issues ranging from bullying and racism to physical disability and homophobia, *Fade to Black* finds an HIV-positive sixteen year old in the hospital following a brutal attack with a baseball bat. A Latino, Alejandro Crusan has been bullied by racist and outspoken school jock Clinton Cole ever since he moved to his rural Florida hometown, and now the evidence points to Cole as the prime suspect. The only witness to the attack, Daria Bickel, has Down syndrome, and her testimony—and perspective—is questioned by some. The mystery surrounding the attack unfurls through three intertwined narratives: that of Alex, Clinton, and Daria, the last which Flinn relates in free verse. According to *Booklist* critic Cindy Dobrex, *Fade to Black* allows readers the chance to "ferret . . . out the reality from the conflicting narratives" and highlights "the sensitive issues raised along the way." In *Kliatt* Paula Rohrlick called Flinn's novel "worthy and thought-provoking."

Flinn takes a break from hard-hitting realism in *Beastly,* in which she retells the classic story of Beauty and the Beast. She resets the time-honored tale in modern-day Brooklyn and introduces sixteen-year-old Kyle Kingsbury, a snobby teen from a wealthy family. When Kyle plans a prank designed to humiliate an unpopular girl in his ninth-grade class, his victim taps into her secret powers as a witch and retaliates by transforming Kyle into a furry, long-clawed beast. Hidden by his father in the garden behind an abandoned mansion, Kyle now has a challenge: to break the spell he has two years to find true love. When a house burglar creeps into Kyle's garden, the monstrous teen strikes a deal with the man: send the beast his teenage daughter, Lindy, and Kyle will not report the burglar to the police. Although the remainder of the story progresses in typical fairy-tale fashion, as Jennifer Mattson observed in *Booklist,* "Flinn . . . address[s] some larger, painful truths about male adolescence" in *Beastly,* giving her story "equally strong appeal for boys and girls." Calling the novel "eminently satisfying," a *Publishers Weekly* contributor added that Flinn's "happily-ever-after ending is rewarding," and *Kliatt* writer Paula Rohrlick wrote that "YAs will appreciate [Flinn's] . . . storytelling skills and her flawed but ultimately sympathetic main character."

Despite her focus on serious themes, Flinn considers herself first and foremost a storyteller. "The story has to come first," she commented in her online interview for *Embracing the Child.* A successful young-adult novel combines "a good story with characters [readers] . . . really care about, and the 'S' word: Suspense." Flinn finds the business of writing and publishing exciting in its own right. As she told Kathie Bergquist in a *Publishers Weekly* interview, "Sometimes I feel like I should be the one paying [my publishers]. It's just been so exciting!" She passed along some advice to budding writers in an interview with *Teacher Librarian* contributor Teri S. Lesesne: "Don't write to trends. Try, instead, to write something that no one but you could write. It is this freshness that will get you published."

Biographical and Critical Sources

PERIODICALS

Book, July-August, 2003, Kathleen Odean, "Unanimous Verdict: For These Lawyers the Decision's In: Kids Are a More Rewarding Audience than Jurors," p. 31.
Booklist, August, 2001, review of *Breathing Underwater,* p. 2106; September 1, 2002, Francisca Goldsmith, review of *Breaking Point,* p. 16; March 15, 2004, Michael Cart, review of *Nothing to Lose,* p. 1299; April 15, 2005, Cindy Dobrez, review of *Fade to Black,* p. 1448; October 1, 2006, Ilene Cooper, review of *Diva,* p. 48; February 1, 2008, Jennifer Mattson, review of *Beastly,* p. 39.
Horn Book, May-June, 2004, Peter D. Sieruta, review of *Nothing to Lose,* p. 327.

Kirkus Reviews, April 1, 2002, review of *Breaking Point,* pp. 490-491; February 15, 2004, review of *Nothing to Lose,* p. 177; March 15, 2005, review of *Fade to Black,* p. 351; September 15, 2006, review of *Diva,* p. 952.
Kliatt, November, 2002, Jean Palmer, review of *Breathing Underwater,* p. 19; July, 2003, Paula Rohrlick, review of *Breaking Point,* p. 21; March, 2004, Paula Rohrlick, review of *Nothing to Lose,* p. 10; May, 2005, Paula Rohrlick, review of *Fade to Black,* p. 10; September, 2007, Paula Rohrlick, review of *Beastly,* p. 11.
Publishers Weekly, April 23, 2001, review of *Breathing Underwater,* p. 79; June 25, 2001, Kathie Bergquist, interview with Flinn, p. 26; May 20, 2002, review of *Breaking Point,* p. 68; March 29, 2004, review of *Nothing to Lose,* p. 64; October 29, 2007, review of *Beastly,* p. 58.
School Library Journal, May, 2001, Joel Shoemaker, review of *Breathing Underwater,* p. 149; May, 2002, Janet Hilburn, review of *Breaking Point,* p. 152; May, 2005, Hillias J. Martin, review of *Fade to Black,* p. 126; November, 2006, Tina Zubak, review of *Diva,* p. 135; November, 2007, Donna Rosenblum, review of *Beastly,* p. 122.
Teacher Librarian, June, 2005, Teri S. Lesesne, interview with Flinn.
Voice of Youth Advocates, June, 2001, Beth Anderson, review of *Breathing Underwater;* June, 2002, Kimberly L. Paone, review of *Breaking Point,* pp. 117-118; October, 2002, Barbara S. Wysocki, review of *Breaking Point,* p. 84; March, 2004, Lynn Evarts, review of *Nothing to Lose,* p. 210.

ONLINE

Alex Flinn Web log, http://alixwrite.livejournal.com (February 2, 2009).
Cynthia Leitich Smith Web site, http://www.cynthialeitich smith.com/ (November 7, 2002), Cynthia Leitich Smith, interview with Flinn.
Embracing the Child Web site, http://www.eyeontomorrow. com/embracingthechild/ (August 27, 2002), interview with Flinn.*

*   *   *

FOSTER, Gerald L.

Personal

Male; children: Mark.

Addresses

Home—Lincoln, MA.

Career

Author, artist, and architect. Architects Collaborative, former vice president and partner; former instructor at Harvard Graduate School of Design, Boston Architectural Center, and University of Massachusetts—Amherst. *Exhibitions:* Work exhibited at galleries and at DeCordova Museum.

Writings

SELF-ILLUSTRATED

(Coauthor with M.R. Montgomery) *A Field Guide to Airplanes of North America,* Houghton Mifflin (Boston, MA), 1984, third edition, 2006.

A Field Guide to Trains of North America, Houghton Mifflin (Boston, MA), 1996.

American Houses: A Field Guide to the Architecture of the Home, Houghton Mifflin (Boston, MA), 2004.

OTHER

(Illustrator) Mark Foster, *Whale Port: A History of Tuckanucket,* Houghton Mifflin (Boston, MA), 2007.

Sidelights

In addition to publishing several well-received books about airplanes, trains, and American homes for general readers, Gerald L. Foster has also contributed the artwork to *Whale Port: A History of Tuckanucket,* a picture book written by Foster's son, Mark Foster. Set in the fictional town of Tuckanucket, located along the entire New England coast, the book presents a history of the whaling industry while following the changes Tuckanucket experiences after its founding in 1683 through to its evolution into a popular destination for tourists interested in whale-sighting expeditions. Despite encountering setbacks throughout the years, including

Gerald L. Foster creates the artwork for son Mark Foster's picture book **Whale Port.** (Illustration copyright © 2007 by Gerald Foster. All rights reserved. Reproduced by permission of Houghton Mifflin Harcourt Publishing Company.)

natural disasters and the demise of the whaling industry in the early twentieth century, Tuckanucket perseveres, and its evolution mirrors that of the New England region.

Several critics commended the efforts of the Fosters in *Whale Port.* Reviewing the book in *Horn Book,* Roger Sutton claimed that both author and illustrator "have elegantly synthesized a tremendous amount of information into a beguiling format." A *Kirkus Reviews* critic held a similar view, writing that "the appealing format of this volume . . . blends large-scale colorful art and an abundance of information." The *Kirkus Reviews* writer also favorably compared *Whale Port* to books by Arthur Geisert and David Macaulay. Describing *Whale Port* as a "handsome title," *School Library Journal* contributor Lynne Mattern singled out Gerald Foster's pictures for particular praise, noting that his "fine pen-and-watercolor scenes are perfectly suited to the subject matter and successfully depict each era."

Biographical and Critical Sources

PERIODICALS

Booklist, December 1, 2007, Kristen McKluski, review of *Whale Port: A History of Tuckanucket,* p. 38.

Horn Book, November-December, 2007, Roger Sutton, review of *Whale Port,* p. 696.

Kirkus Reviews, September 1, 2007, review of *Whale Port.*

Library Journal, February 15, 2004, Valerie Nye, review of *American Houses: A Field Guide to the Architecture of the Home,* p. 121.

Model Railroader, October, 1996, Jim Hediger, review of *A Field Guide to Trains of North America,* p. 52.

Publishers Weekly, February 9, 2004, review of *American Houses,* p. 72.

School Library Journal, November, 2007, Lynne Mattern, review of *Whale Port,* p. 146.*

*   *   *

FRAZIER, Sundee T. 1968-
(Sundee Tucker Frazier)

Personal

Born 1968; married; children: two. *Education:* University of Southern California, B.A.; Vermont College, M.F.A.

Addresses

Home—Renton, WA. *E-mail*—sundeefrazier@yahoo. com.

Career

Author.

Awards, Honors

Coretta Scott King/John Steptoe New Talent Author Award, American Library Association, 2008, for *Brendan Buckley's Universe and Everything in It.*

Writings

(As Sundee Tucker Frazier) *Check All That Apply: Finding Wholeness as a Multiracial Person,* InterVarsity Press (Downers Grove, IL), 2002.

(As Sundee Tucker Frazier) *Worship, His Love Endures Forever: Eight Studies for Individuals or Groups,* InterVarsity Press (Downers Grove, IL), 2004.

Brendan Buckley's Universe and Everything in It (for children), Delacorte (New York, NY), 2007.

The Other Half of My Heart (for children), Delacorte (New York, NY) 2010.

Contributor to *Just Don't Marry One: Interracial Dating, Marriage, and Parenting,* edited by George A. Yancey and Sherelyn Whittum Yancey, Judson Press (Valley Forge, PA), 2002.

Cover of Sundee T. Frazier's young-adult novel Brendan Buckley's Universe and Everything in It, *featuring artwork by Robert Papp.* (Illustration copyright © 2007 by Robert Papp. All rights reserved. Used by permission of Delacorte Press, an imprint of Random House Children's Books, a division of Random House, Inc.)

Sidelights

In her award-winning first effort for young readers, *Brendan Buckley's Universe and Everything in It,* author Sundee T. Frazier explores issues faced by children of mixed-race heritage. A budding scientist, ten-year-old Brendan Buckley is extremely inquisitive and asks questions about everything. The one question he knows not to ask regards the whereabouts of his maternal grandfather, who the boy has never met and his mom refuses to talk about. When Brendan unexpectedly meets his grandfather, named Ed, at a rock and mineral show, he is compelled to find out more about the man. Brendan initiates a relationship with his grandfather, eventually learning from his parents how Ed's prejudice against mixed-race couples divided the family. After a critical incident, however, Ed begins to see his daughter's family from a different perspective and sheds his earlier hostility towards interracial relationships.

Biracial herself, Frazier earned favorable reviews in her book about the tensions mixed-race marriages may cause in families. In his *Booklist* review of *Brendan Buckley's Universe and Everything in It,* Todd Morning singled out the author's main character for particular praise, describing Brendan as well rounded and "not just a placard for the author's central message." A *Kirkus Reviews* contributor offered a similar comment about Brendan, calling the novel's young protagonist "an appealing character with a sense of honor." The *Kirkus Reviews* contributor went on to recommend *Brendan Buckley's Universe and Everything in It* as an "accessible selection to inspire discussion of racism and prejudice."

"Though there were signs from an early age that I was meant to be a creative writer, I didn't seriously begin pursuing the craft of fiction writing until I was in my late twenties," Frazier told *SATA.* "I gave myself the goal of publishing a children's novel by the time I turned forty. I thought I was giving myself plenty of time. *Brendan Buckley's Universe and Everything in It* came out days before my thirty-ninth birthday! But now I am living my dream of writing for children (I can think of no greater calling to which to commit my professional life), and I encourage everyone—including all the children I meet—to consider what they really want to do with their lives and go for it. You never know what will happen until you try!"

Biographical and Critical Sources

PERIODICALS

Booklist, January 1, 2008, Todd Morning, review of *Brendan Buckley's Universe and Everything in It,* p. 74.
Kirkus Reviews, September 15, 2007, review of *Brendan Buckley's Universe and Everything in It.*

ONLINE

Sundee Tucker Frazier Home Page, http://www.sundee frazier.com (January 24, 2009).

*   *   *

FRAZIER, Sundee Tucker
See FRAZIER, Sundee T.

G

GARCIA, Emma 1969-

Personal
Born 1969, in England.

Addresses
Home—London, England.

Career
Writer and school inspector working in London, England.

Writings

SELF-ILLUSTRATED

Tip Tip Dig Dig, Boxer Books (London, England), 2007.
Toot Toot Beep Beep, Boxer Books (London, England), 2008.

Biographical and Critical Sources

PERIODICALS

Kirkus Reviews, October 15, 2007, review of *Tip Tip Dig Dig.*
School Library Journal, November, 2007, Gay Lynn Van Vleck, review of *Tip Tip Dig Dig,* p. 92.*

*   *   *

GIBBONS, Alan 1953-

Personal
Born August 14, 1953, in Warrington, Cheshire, England; son of Albert (a laborer) and Phyllis Gibbons; married March, 1983; wife's name Pauline (a social

Alan Gibbons (Reproduced by permission.)

worker); children: Joseph, Robbie, Rachel, Megan. *Education:* Warwick University, B.A. (with honors; French and European literature); Liverpool University, P.G.C.E. (primary education). *Politics:* "Socialist." *Hobbies and other interests:* Music, sport.

Addresses
Home—Liverpool, England. *E-mail*—contact@alan gibbons.com.

Career

Writer and educator. Process worker in Middlewich, Cheshire, England, 1975-78, and Crewe, Cheshire, 1978-82; case worker for welfare agency, Liverpool, England, 1982-88; taught primary and secondary school in Liverpool for eighteen years. Judge, Blue Peter Book Award, 2001.

Member

National Union of Teachers (president, Knowsley Division, 1996), National Association of Writers in Education.

Awards, Honors

Carnegie Medal shortlist, and Blue Peter Book Award, both 2000, both for *Shadow of the Minotaur;* Carnegie Medal shortlist, 2003, for *The Edge;* Booktrust Teenage Prize shortlist, 2003, for *Caught in the Crossfire,* and 2004, for *The Dark Beneath;* Leicester Book of the Year; Angus Book of the Year; Stockport Book Award; Catalyst Award; Salford Librarians Special Award; Salford Young-Adult Book Award; Birmingham Chills Award.

Writings

JUVENILE FICTION

Our Peculiar Neighbour, illustrated by Toni Goffe, Dent (London, England), 1990.
Pig, illustrated by Diana Catchpole, Dent (London, England), 1990.
Whose Side Are You On?, Orion (London, England), 1991.
The Jaws of the Dragon, Dent (London, England), 1991, Lerner Publishing (Minneapolis, MN), 1994.
Dagger in the Sky, Dent (London, England), 1992.
S.O.S. Save Our Santa, illustrated by Caroline Church, Dent (London, England), 1992.
Chicken, Orion (London, England), 1994.
Grandad's Ears, Collins (London, England), 1994.
Hattie Hates Hats, illustrated by Bethan Matthews, Collins (London, England), 1994.
Not Yeti, illustrated by Anthony Lewis, Orion (London, England), 1994.
Ganging Up, Orion (London, England), 1995.
The Climbing Boys, Collins (London, England), 1995.
City of Fire, Collins (London, England), 1995.
Playing with Fire, Orion (London, England), 1996.
When My Ship Came In, illustrated by Joe Rice, Collins (London, England), 1996.
Street of Tall People, Orion (London, England), 1996.
A Fight to Belong, Save the Children, 1999.
Julie and Me . . . and Michael Owen Makes Three, Orion (London, England), 2001.
Julie and Me: Treble Trouble, Orion (London, England), 2002.

The Cold Heart of Summer, Barrington Stoke (Edinburgh, Scotland), 2002.
The Edge, Dolphin (London, England), 2002.
Deathriders, Heinemann Educational (Oxford, England), 2003.
Caught in the Crossfire, Orion (London, England), 2003.
The Dark Beneath, Dolphin (London, England), 2003.
The Lost Boys' Appreciation Society, Dolphin (London, England), 2004.
The Defender, Orion (London, England), 2004.
Hold On, Orion (London, England), 2005.
Blood Pressure, Orion (London, England), 2005.
The Greatest, illustrated by Dylan Gibson, Barrington Stoke (Edinburgh, Scotland), 2006.
The Number Seven Shirt, Barrington Stoke (Edinburgh, Scotland), 2008.
Night Hunger, Barrington Stoke (Edinburgh, Scotland), 2008.
Charles Darwin: Discover the World of Darwin through the Diary of a Ship's Boy, illustrated by Leo Brown, Kingfisher (New York, NY), 2008.

"TOTAL FOOTBALL" SERIES

Some You Win, Orion (London, England), 1997.
Under Pressure, Orion (London, England), 1997.
Divided We Fall, Orion (London, England), 1998.
Injury Time, Orion (London, England), 1998.
Last Man Standing, Orion (London, England), 1998.
Power Play, Orion (London, England), 1998.
Twin Strikers, Orion (London, England), 1999.
Final Countdown, Orion (London, England), 1999.

"LEGENDEER" TRILOGY

Shadow of the Minotaur, Orion (London, England), 2000.
Vampyr Legion, Orion (London, England), 2000.
Warriors of the Raven, Orion (London, England), 2001.

"LOST SOULS" SERIES

Rise of the Blood Moon, Orion (London, England), 2006.
Setting of a Cruel Sun, Orion (London, England), 2006.
The Darkwing Omnibus, (contains *Rise of the Blood Moon* and *Setting of a Cruel Sun*), Orion (London, England), 2007.

"HELL'S UNDERGROUND" SERIES

Scared to Death, Orion (London, England), 2007.
The Demon Assassin, Orion (London, England), 2008.
Renegade, Orion (London, England), 2009.

OTHER

Columnist for *Liverpool Echo.* Contributor to periodicals, including *Times Educational Supplement, Junior Education, Carousel,* and *Books for Keeps.*

Sidelights

In gritty, realistic works such as *Ganging Up* and *Caught in the Crossfire,* British author Alan Gibbons examines difficult themes such as racism, bullying, and fundamentalism. Gibbons has also written a number of well-received fantasy tales, including *Shadow of the Minotaur* and *Rise of the Blood Moon.* "I write because I am driven by a love of story-telling, because I am thrilled by the rhythms and the cadences of memorable, resonant language," Gibbons stated in an essay on his home page.

Gibbons was born in Cheshire, England, in 1953, and grew up in the small country village of Whitegate. "I came from a family of farm laborers," he once explained to *SATA.* "For as long as I can remember I was listening to, reading about, re-telling, and illustrating all sorts of legends. Robin Hood, the Arthurian romance, the myths of ancient Rome and Greece, the tales of the Vikings: they were the stuff of my dreams." Gibbons elaborated, "A myth is a made up story, and as a writer of fiction, that's what I tell: made-up stories. But a myth is also a question of belief, so it has to be a made-up story that rings true. It communicates morality and values." Many of Gibbons' books, particularly his works for older readers, reflect the values he learned during his own childhood as a kid uprooted from a secure environment and forced to make it in a school where the rules were different and might made right, no matter what.

"In true stories, just as in myths, the way is rarely straight or easy," Gibbons continued. "When I was eight, my dad was involved in a bad accident. His leg was shattered and he had to take an indoor job." Mr. Gibbons' new job took the family to the town of Crewe, an industrial community, where Gibbons suddenly found himself "plunged into a very different kind of life from the small village where I grew up, having to fight bullying and learn to cope in a much tougher environment than I was used to." A good student and a quick study, Gibbons learned to navigate his new social landscape. As the years passed, he also developed a strong interest in athletics, and his heroes were men such as world heavyweight champion Muhammad Ali, soccer star Pelé, and George Best. "They weren't just great sportsmen," recalled Gibbons; "they were fighters. Against poverty, against racism."

Although he applied himself to his studies during grade school, Gibbons "found that the rigid grammar school system worked against creativity. I got to university, but had stopped writing my legends. As a result, I grew bored and lost interest in the academic world." After graduating with honors from Warwick University with degrees in French and European literature, he turned his back on intellectual pursuits and took a series of factory jobs, even working as an advice worker for five years. Married in 1983, Gibbons and his wife went on to have four children. In his thirties he was inspired to enroll at Liverpool University, where he earned the teaching qualification necessary to become a primary school teacher.

Teaching exposed Gibbons to the world of children's literature. "I discovered writers such as Robert Cormier, Robert Swindells, Robert Westall, Phillip Pullman, and Geoffrey Trease," he recalled. "Inspired by their work, in 1990 I started writing again: picture books, young readers, novels. I was staggered by the range and quality of children's literature and wanted to be part of that world." One of the earliest stories penned by Gibbons was the picture book *Pig.* In this 1990 work, a boy and his little sister on their daily trek home from school are suddenly swept up in what *Growing Point* reviewer Margery Fisher called "an agreeable rush and scurry" as a pig hoping to save its bacon leads a long line of pursuers through the English countryside. With the children's help, the pig on the lam goes into hiding and eventually finds its way to the care of the City Farm, where it becomes a community pet. Another book for the younger set, an imaginative romp titled *Not Yeti,* was described by *Books for Keeps* contributor George Hunt as "highly eventful and entertaining."

Gibbons' entire life changed after he made a commitment to writing. "After a day of teaching, I would plunge into my study, writing at least two hours a night, five days a week, pouring out my own mythologies," he recalled. Recollections from his childhood were reworked into the novels *Chicken* and *Ganging Up,* each of which deals with what Gibbons would call mythic themes about values and the choice between right and wrong. In *Chicken,* which was published in 1994, Davey and his family move to Liverpool, where Davey's older brother quickly makes friends with a gang of toughs, glad to fit in. The less-outgoing Davey soon draws the attention of his new school's bully population in what *Magpies* reviewer Melanie Guile called "a well-crafted short novel with unusually witty dialogue, convincing cameo characters, [and] a tough climax." London *Observer* contributor Naomi Lewis dubbed Davey's story of growing up "frequently funny . . . when not dire." While Davey goes it alone in *Chicken,* in Gibbons' novel *Ganging Up* best friends and soccer fans Gerry and John find their friendship threatened when John joins a local gang. Gerry quickly finds that John's choice has repercussions on his own life in an "action-packed book" that a *Junior Bookshelf* contributor believed would appeal to "that most elusive readership, boys whose interest seem entirely physical and outdoor."

History weaves its way into several of Gibbons' books, among them *Whose Side Are You On?* and *Dagger in the Sky.* In *Whose Side Are You On?* readers meet ten-year-old Mattie Jones, whose friendship with a Pakistani boy named Pravin prompts racist remarks from a couple of local school bullies. Unfortunately, Mattie opts to run rather than stay and defend his friendship. Cowardice leads him into an old abandoned house . . .

and back into the eighteenth century, where he helps a group of slaves rebel against their masters and thus finds the courage to take him back to the present. *Books for Keeps* contributor Chris Lutrario praised *Whose Side Are You On?* as "interesting and exciting," while *School Librarian* critic Marie Flay called the work an "enjoyable and at times compelling novel."

In addition to dealing with a period of English history—the rise of the Blackshirts under British fascist agitator Oswald Mosley during the 1930s—*Street of Tall People* reflects Gibbons' longtime interest in sports. In the novel, a young Londoner named Jimmy Priest runs up against Benny Silver in a boxing match and is impressed by the Jewish boy's determination. As the two become friends, Jimmy becomes aware of the rising tide of anti-Semitism that is growing among many in his poor East End neighborhood. Citing *Street of Tall People* as an "impressive" book about friendship, *Magpies* contributor Kevin Steinberger praised Gibbons for the "depth of research that has enabled him to charge the story with stunning verisimilitude and characterization and evocation of place and mood." Team sports also figure in Gibbons' eight-part "Total Football" series, as member of the Rough Diamonds soccer team—soccer is called "football" in Great Britain, where this story takes place—attempt to redeem their loser image with an attitude readjustment. Within the series, Gibbons focuses on the personal struggles of each of the team members in turn, as they deal with poverty, family concerns, and the temptation to cross the line into petty crime.

Domestic abuse is the subject of Gibbons' *The Edge.* This novel centers on Danny and his mother, who flee their bleak living circumstances only to discover they are not as secure as they had hoped. In the words of London *Guardian* contributor Lindsey Fraser, the work "shows a writer in confident and committed mode." In *The Dark Beneath,* a British teenager defies authorities after she becomes involved with a group of political refugees seeking asylum. "Gibbons doesn't trade in pat answers," Fraser stated, adding of *The Dark Beneath* that readers "won't close the novel without having added considerably to their palette of experience and knowledge."

Gibbons looks at social injustice in *Caught in the Crossfire,* a work triggered by a race riot in Oldham, England, and the terrorist attacks of September 11, 2001. The novel focuses on six teenagers, including a Muslim brother and sister who suffer at the hands of the thuggish Creed, a leader of the right-wing Patriotic League. "There's a slice of real life in this book," observed *Bookseller* critic Wendy Cooling. According to London *Guardian* reviewer Gillian Cross, *Caught in the Crossfire* "encourages readers to look critically at the society in which we live and the complicated ways in which individual behaviour interacts with economic and social pressures." The critic added that Gibbons "writes with

passionate conviction about the importance of community and the need for ordinary people to resist attempts to destroy it."

The Troubles, the decades-long conflict in Northern Ireland, is at the heart of *The Defender.* Living in a quiet English village, fourteen-year-old Ian Moore encounters two men seeking revenge on his father, a member of the Loyal Ulster Defenders who left Northern Ireland after the murder of Ian's mother. As Ian runs for his life, readers learn about his father's decision to join the violent nationalist group. "Sides are never taken; there is no specific condemnation of who did what to whom, because Gibbons is more interested in exploring the outside forces that contrive to make someone make certain irrevocable choices," Keith Gray remarked in the London *Guardian.* In the thriller *Blood Pressure,* fifteen-year-old Aidan must leave his comfortable suburban home to live with his ailing grandfather in a rough-and-tumble Liverpool neighborhood. Soon, Aidan learns of his mother's secret past, and he also discovers the truth about his biological father, a notorious gangster. Gibbons writes "with understanding and energy," a *Bookseller* critic noted of the novel.

In addition to his issue-oriented fiction, Gibbons has written a number of critically acclaimed fantasy tales. He received the Blue Peter Book Award for *Shadow of the Minotaur,* the first work in his "Legendeer" trilogy, which follows a teenager caught in an often dangerous virtual-reality game based on Greek myths and legends. The series concluded with *Vampyr Legion* and *Warriors of the Raven.* Gibbons' "Lost Souls" sequence includes *Rise of the Blood Moon* and its sequel, *Setting of a Cruel Sun.* Writing on the Orion Books Web site, Danuta Kean described *Rise of the Blood Moon* as "a rich, profound and powerful story of war, cruelty, tyranny, betrayal and love, set in a sumptuous world of spices and silks and gloriously Gothic monsters."

The success of Gibbons' fiction can be attributed to many things, including the respect he shows his audience. "The one thing I never do is try to get down with the kids," he remarked to Benedicte Page in the *Bookseller.* "There's nothing sadder than a 51-year-old man talking like Eminem. I think teenage themes are universal: yearning, love, betrayal. Teenagers connect with strong themes."

Biographical and Critical Sources

PERIODICALS

Bookseller, November 15, 2002, Wendy Cooling, review of *Caught in the Crossfire,* p. 36; February 18, 2005, Benedicte Page, "Never Try to Sound like Eminem: Alan Gibbons Shares His Secrets for Successful Writing for Teenage Boys," p. 34, and review of *Blood Pressure,* p. 36.

Books for Keeps, September, 1992, Chris Lutrario, review of *Whose Side Are You On?,* p. 25; September, 1995, George Hunt, reviews of *Not Yeti,* p. 11; September, 1996, George Hunt, review of *Street of Tall People* and *Ganging Up,* p. 12.

Daily Post (Liverpool, England), February 5, 2004, "Teenage Fiction with a Gritty Tone," p. 12.

Evening Chronicle (Newcastle, England), January 5, 2006, review of *Shadow of the Minotaur,* p. 40.

Growing Point, September, 1991, Margery Fisher, review of *Pig,* p. 5574; January, 1992, Margery Fisher, review of *The Jaws of the Dragon,* p. 5630.

Guardian (London, England), September 11, 2001, Lindsey Fraser, review of *Julie and Me and Michael Owen Makes Three,* p. 67; September 24, 2002, Lindsey Fraser, review of *The Edge,* p. 51; April 12, 2003, Gillian Cross, review of *Caught in the Crossfire,* p. 33; November 18, 2003, Lindsey Fraser, review of *The Dark Beneath,* p. 13; October 23, 2004, Keith Gray, review of *The Defender;* December 6, 2005, Kate Agnew, review of *Hold On,* p. 7.

Junior Bookshelf, June, 1992, review of *The Jaws of the Dragon,* pp. 120-121; October, 1995, review of *Ganging Up,* pp. 183-184.

Liverpool Echo (Liverpool, England), August 8, 2006, review of *Rise of the Blood Moon,* p. 18; January 13, 2003, Rachael Tinniswood, interview with Gibbons, p. 6; July 10, 2007, Janet Tansley, review of *Scared to Death,* p. 23.

Magpies, November, 1994, Melanie Guile, review of *Chicken,* p. 30; March, 1996, Kevin Steinberger, review of *Street of Tall People,* pp. 35-36.

Observer (London, England), August 22, 1993, Naomi Lewis, review of *Chicken,* p. 48; July 21, 1996, Jennifer Selway, review of *Street of Tall People,* p. 17.

School Librarian, August, 1991, Marie Flay, review of *Whose Side Are You On?,* pp. 113-114; May, 1992, Robert Protherough, review of *The Jaws of the Dragon,* p. 71; summer, 1998, Michael Kirby, review of *Some You Win* and *Under Pressure,* p. 78; winter, 1999, Chris Brown, review of *Final Countdown,* p. 191.

Scotsman, January 29, 2003, Leila Farrah, "Alan Gibbons: Discover Your Hidden Value," p. 18.

ONLINE

Alan Gibbons Home Page, http://www.alangibbons.com (March 1, 2009).

Alan Gibbons Web log, www.alangibbons.net (March 1, 2009).

Bookseller Web site, http://www.thebookseller.com/ (January 22, 2009), Caroline Horn, interview with Gibbons.

Contemporary Writers in the UK Web site, http://www.contemporarywriters.com/ (March 1, 2009), "Alan Gibbons."

Orion Books Web site, http://www.orionbooks.co.uk/ (March 1, 2009), Danuta Kean, interview with Gibbons.

GIFFORD, Clive 1966-

Personal

Born 1966, in England. *Education:* Southampton University, degree.

Addresses

Home—Manchester, England. *E-mail*—clivegiff@aol.com.

Career

Journalist and author. Usborne (publisher), London, England, former senior editor; MikroLeisure (computer games company), founder and former owner. Worked variously as a security guard, road-line painter, and radio disc jockey.

Awards, Honors

Times Education Supplement Information Book of the Year Award.

Writings

FOR CHILDREN

The Usborne Book of Planes and Helicopters, illustrated by Mark Franklin, Usborne (London, England), 1993.

Racing Cars, illustrated by Chris Lyon, Usborne (London, England), 1993.

The Usborne Book of Cutaway Planes, Usborne (London, England), 1995.

The Usborne Book of Juggling, Usborne (London, England), 1995.

The Really Useless Spy School, illustrated by Guy Parker-Rees, Hodder (London, England), 1996.

Uncle Alf and the Time Travel Detectives, illustrated by Robin Lawrie, Hodder (London, England), 1996.

The Cosmic Toaster illustrated by Vince Reid, Hodder (London, England), 1996.

Mindmaster (based on an original idea by Tony Allen), Usborne (London, England), 1996.

Time Warp Virus, illustrated by Geo Parkin, Usborne (London, England), 1996.

The Flask of Doom, illustrated by Geo Parkin, Usborne (London, England), 1996.

Tactics, illustrated by Bob Bond, Usborne (London, England), 1997.

Football, illustrated by Tony Kerins, Hodder (London, England), 1998.

Cycling, illustrated by Nick Dewar, Hodder (London, England), 1998.

Swimming, Hodder (London, England), 1998.

Media, Dorling Kindersley (London, England), 1999, published as *Media and Communications,* Knopf (New York, NY), 1999.

Basketball, Hodder (London, England), 1999.

How the Future Began: Machines, Kingfisher (New York, NY), 1999.

Golf, Hodder (London, England), 2000.

(With Anthony Wilson) *The Kingfisher Encyclopedia of the Future,* Kingfisher (London, England), 2000, Kingfisher (New York, NY), 2001.

Juggling, Hodder (London, England), 2000.

Athletics, Hodder (London, England), 2000.

Room Makeover, Hodder (London, England), 2000.

Cricket, Hodder (London, England), 2000.

Quiz Kids, cartoons by Mark Davis, Miles Kelly (Great Bardfield, England), 2000.

Live on Mars, illustrated by Scoular Anderson, Oxford University Press (Oxford, England), 2000, published as *How to Live on Mars,* Franklin Watts (New York, NY), 2001.

How the Future Began: Everyday Life, Kingfisher (New York, NY), 2000.

How to Build a Robot, illustrated by Tim Benton, Oxford University Press (Oxford, England), 2000, Franklin Watts (New York, NY), 2001.

How to Meet Aliens, illustrated by Scoular Anderson, Franklin Watts (New York, NY), 2001.

Yuk! The Gruesome File of Foul Facts, Funfax (London, England), 2001.

The Kingfisher Facts and Records Book of Space, Kingfisher (New York, NY), 2001.

The Water Puppets: A Story from Vietnam, Hodder (London, England) 2001, published as *The Water Puppets: A Story from the War in Vietnam,* Barron's (Hauppauge, NY) 2002.

The Kingfisher Young People's Book of Living Worlds, Kingfisher (New York, NY), 2002, published as *The Kingfisher Book of Living Worlds,* Kingfisher (London, England), 2002.

So You Think You Know The Lord of the Rings?, Hodder (London, England), 2002.

World War I, Hodder (London, England), 2002.

World War II: True Stories, illustrated by John Yates, Hodder (London, England), 2002.

Geography: Over 2,000 Questions and Answers, Miles Kelly (Great Bardfield, England), 2002.

Refugees, Thameside Press (North Mankato, MN), 2002.

Soccer: The Ultimate Guide to the Beautiful Game, Kingfisher (New York, NY), 2002, published as *Football: The Ultimate Guide to the Beautiful Game,* Kingfisher (London, England), 2002.

The Kingfisher Geography Encyclopedia, Kingfisher (Boston, MA), 2003.

Racism, Chrysalis Education (North Mankato, MN), 2003.

Drugs and Sports, Heinemann Library (Oxford, England), 2003, Raintree (Chicago, IL), 2004.

So You Think You Know David Beckham?, Hodder (London, England), 2003.

So You Think You Know Harry Potter?, Hodder (London, England), 2003.

Robots, Kingfisher (Boston, MA), 2003.

So You Think You Know the Simpsons?, Hodder (London, England), 2003.

Euthanasia, Chrysalis Education (London, England), 2004.

A World-Class Sprinter, Heinemann Library (Chicago, IL), 2004.

Diary of a Kickboxing Freak, Heinemann Library (Oxford, England), 2004.

The Arms Trade, Chrysalis Education (North Mankato, MN), 2004.

So You Think You Know Lemony Snicket?, Hodder (London, England), 2004.

So You Think You Know Premier League Football?, Hodder (London, England), 2004.

So You Think You Know the '80s?, Hodder (London, England), 2004.

So You Think You Know the '60s?, Hodder (London, England), 2004.

So You Think You Know TV Soaps?, Hodder (London, England), 2004.

So You Think You Know London?, Hodder (London, England), 2004.

The Fair of Fear?, Letts (London, England), 2004.

Pants Attack!, illustrated by Gemma Silcox, Letts (London, England), 2004.

Ratman and the Big Cat, illustrated by Rikki O'Neill, Letts (London, England), 2004.

A Big Hit for Kit, illustrated by Elke Zinsmeister, Letts (London, England), 2004.

There's a Slug in My Mug, illustrated by Karen Sapp, Letts (London, England), 2004.

Food Technology, Chrysalis Education (North Mankato, MN), 2004.

Spies, Kingfisher (Boston, MA), 2004.

Summer Olympics: The Definite Guide to the World's Greatest Sports Celebration, Kingfisher (Boston, MA), 2004, published as *Olympics: The Definite Guide to the Greatest Sports Celebration in the World,* Kingfisher (London, England), 2004.

Sustainable Development, Raintree (Chicago, IL), 2004.

The Concise Geography Encyclopedia, Kingfisher (Boston, MA), 2005.

Flooding and Drought, Smart Apple Media (North Mankato, MN), 2005.

(With James Harrison and Eleanor Van Zandt) *The Kingfisher Student Atlas of North America,* Kingfisher (Boston, MA), 2005.

Robots, Franklin Watts (London, England), 2005, Smart Apple Media (North Mankato, MN), 2006.

Materials, Kingfisher (Boston, MA), 2005.

Bus Stop Bob, illustrated by Louise Gardner, Letts (London, England), 2005.

The Phony Phantom Gopher, illustrated by Janet Samuel, Letts (London, England), 2005.

Soccer Skills, Kingfisher (Boston, MA), 2005, published as *Football Skills,* Kingfisher (London, England), 2005.

Space Exploration, Franklin Watts (London, England), 2005, Chrysalis Education (North Mankato, MN), 2006.

Mountain Biking, Chrysalis Education (London, England), 2005, Chrysalis Education (North Mankato, MN), 2006.

Skateboarding, Chrysalis Education (London, England), 2005, Chrysalis Education (North Mankato, MN), 2006.

Espionage and Disinformation, Heinemann Library (Oxford, England), 2005, Heinemann Library (Chicago, IL), 2006.

The Vietnam War, Lucent (Farmington Hills, MI), 2005.

Advertising and Marketing: Developing the Marketplace, Heinemann Library (Oxford, England), 2005, Heinemann Library (Chicago, IL), 2006.

So You Think You Know Test Cricket?, Hodder (London, England), 2005.

So You Think You Know Narnia?, Hodder (London, England), 2005.

So You Think You Know The Da Vinci Code?, Hodder (London, England), 2005.

So You Think You Know Roald Dahl?, Hodder (London, England), 2005.

So You Think You Know Dr. Who?, Hodder (London, England), 2005.

Weathering and Erosion, Smart Apple Media (North Mankato, MN), 2005.

Waste, Heinemann Library (Chicago, IL), 2006.

Pollution, Heinemann Library (Chicago, IL), 2006.

Skateboarding, DK (New York, NY), 2006.

Fantastic Football, Oxford University Press (Oxford, England), 2006.

Snowboarding, Chrysalis Education (North Mankato, MN), 2006.

Crimebusters, Oxford University Press (Oxford, England), 2006, Barron's (Hauppauge, NY), 2007.

So You Think You Know James Bond?, Hodder (London, England), 2006.

So You Think You Know Man Utd.?, Hodder (London, England), 2006.

Rugby, Franklin Watts (London, England), 2006.

Football, Franklin Watts (London, England), 2006.

(With others) *The Kingfisher Science Encyclopedia,* Kingfisher (Boston, MA), 2006.

Energy, Heinemann Library (Chicago, IL), 2006.

Racing: The Ultimate Motorsports Encyclopedia, Kingfisher (Boston, MA), 2006, published as *The Kingfisher Motorsports Encyclopedia,* Kingfisher (London, England), 2006.

Track Athletics, Franklin Watts (London, England), 2006, Sea to Sea (North Mankato, MN), 2009.

Striker, Franklin Watts (London, England), 2006, Sea to Sea (North Mankato, MN), 2007.

The Kingfisher Soccer Encyclopedia, Kingfisher (Boston, MA), 2006, published as *The Kingfisher Football Encyclopedia,* Kingfisher (London, England), 2006.

Violence on the Screen, Evans (London, England), 2006, Smart Apple Media (North Mankato, MN), 2007.

So You Think You Know His Dark Materials?, Hodder (London, England), 2006.

So You Think You Know Discworld?, Hodder (London, England), 2006.

So You Think You Know the World Cup?, Hodder (London, England), 2006.

Gangs, Evans (London, England), 2006, Smart Apple Media (North Mankato, MN), 2007.

Badminton, Franklin Watts (London, England), 2007.

Tennis, Franklin Watts (London, England), 2007.

Netball, Franklin Watts (London, England), 2007.

Millionaires, Wayland (London, England), 2007.

Goalkeeper, Sea to Sea (North Mankato, MN), 2007.

Snowboarding, illustrated by Des Higgins, photographs by Mark C. Hopkins, Kingfisher (Boston, MA), 2007.

Tomb Hunters, Running Press (Philadelphia, PA), 2007.

Honda, Franklin Watts (London, England), 2007, Sea to Sea (North Mankato, MN), 2009.

So You Think You Know Shakespeare?, Hodder (London, England), 2007.

Linked Lives: Ten Explorers Who Changed the World, Kingfisher (Boston, MA), 2008.

Linked Lives: Ten Leaders Who Changed the World, Kingfisher (Boston, MA), 2008.

Robots, illustrated by Frank Picini, Atheneum (New York, NY), 2008.

Tennis, Wayland (London, England), 2008.

Cricket, Wayland (London, England), 2008.

(With Mike Goldsmith and Sean Callery) *Explore,* Kingfisher (Boston, MA), 2008.

Track and Field, PowerKids Press (New York, NY), 2009.

Basketball, PowerKids Press (New York, NY), 2009.

Ducati, Sea to Sea (North Mankato, MN), 2009.

Soccer, Sea to Sea (North Mankato, MN), 2009.

Swimming, PowerKids Press (New York, NY), 2009.

Contributor of short stories to anthologies.

OTHER

Making the Most of Your Dragon 32, Interface (London, England), 1983.

Dynamic Games for Your ORIC, Interface (London, England), 1983.

Dynamic Games for Your Amstrad, Interface (London, England), 1984.

Adventures for Your ZX Spectrum, Virgin (London, England), 1984.

(With Tim Hartnell) *The Amstrad Programmer's Guide,* Pitman (London, England), 1985.

The Script, Marillion: An Illustrated Biography, Omnibus (London, England), 1987.

Author of column in *Surrey Herald.* Contributor to periodicals, including *TNT, PC Ace, Men's Health, Trailfinders, National Student,* and *SX* magazine.

Sidelights

English author Clive Gifford has penned numerous books for children, his topics ranging from sports, to current events, to science and nature. Soccer is the focus of several titles, including *Soccer: The Ultimate Guide to the Beautiful Game,* a 2002 work covering one of the world's most popular sports. Here, Gifford not only traces the history of the game, but also offers tips on improving a player's technique and strategy. As well, the author provides short biographies of several famous players and provides readers with information about important soccer venues around the world. "This attractive book covers the history, skills, and strategy of soccer," wrote *Booklist* critic Todd Morning, in a review of *Soccer.* Gifford offers more facts about the game in *The Kingfisher Soccer Encyclopedia.* In this book, the author covers some of the more significant rules, international championships, and career opportunities for youths interested in soccer. *Booklist* reviewer Kathleen McBroom thought that the "deceptively slim volume packs a considerable amount of information," going on to suggest "the international coverage will appeal to a wide audience."

Gifford covers a range of sporting events in *Summer Olympics: The Definite Guide to the World's Greatest Sports Celebration.* Opening his book with a short history of the Olympics, he then focuses on other aspects of the event, which is held every four years, including previous host cities, events in which athletes compete, and famous figures from previous competitions. Writing in *School Library Journal,* Andrew Medlar called the 2004 volume "strong, ambitious, and useful."

For readers looking for material about issues widely discussed at the beginning of the twenty-first-century, Gifford has written several titles focusing on contemporary problems. In *Pollution,* the author details different forms of pollution as well as ways each impact the health of individuals, while in *Gangs,* Gifford explains the attraction such groups offer to troubled teens. Tackling another pressing concern, *The Arms Trade* explores the sale of weapons around the world and the effects these armaments have on civilian populations. "This book packs in copious information from a well-rounded perspective," claimed *Booklist* contributor Roger Leslie. *Violence on the Screen* encourages readers to reexamine entertainment available to youths, asking them to consider the effects of violence found in popular movies, television programs, and video games. "The points Gifford raises will engage teens and spark argument," predicted *Booklist* critic Hazel Rochman.

Reference books covering a variety of themes have been a large part of Gifford's focus, many of them written for the publisher Kingfisher. For readers interested in learning more about the world around them, *The Kingfisher Young People's Book of Living Worlds* presents a wealth of knowledge about ecology in "a fact-filled, lavishly illustrated compendium of earth-science information," noted Eva Elisabeth VonAncken in *School Library Journal.* Published in 2003, *The Kingfisher Geography Encyclopedia* gives interested students more knowledge about countries and continents. Briefly, Gifford supplies facts about a country's landscape, gives statistics about different nations, and provides material about the earth's physical characteristics. Reviewing the title in *School Library Journal,* Barbara Auerbach predicted that the work would "likely . . . inspire further research." A *Booklist* critic similarly wrote that *The Kingfisher Geography Encyclopedia* "promises to spark the interest of users."

Biographical and Critical Sources

PERIODICALS

Booklist, December 15, 2000, John Peters, review of *How the Future Began: Everyday Life,* p. 813; July, 2002,

Todd Morning, review of *Soccer: The Ultimate Guide to the Beautiful Game,* p. 1835; March 1, 2004, review of *The Kingfisher Geography Encyclopedia,* p. 1237; January 1, 2005, Roger Leslie, review of *The Arms Trade,* p. 840; June 1, 2006, Kathleen McBroom, review of *The Kingfisher Soccer Encyclopedia,* p. 135; December 15, 2006, Hazel Rochman, review of *Violence on the Screen,* p. 41; March 15, 2007, John Peters, review of *Gangs,* p. 44.

Kirkus Reviews, September 15, 2008, review of *Linked Lives: Ten Explorers Who Changed the World.*

Publishers Weekly, May 19, 2003, review of *So You Think You Know Harry Potter?,* p. 76; November 3, 2003, review of *The Kingfisher Geography Encyclopedia,* p. 76.

Reading Today, October-November, 2001, Lynne T. Burke, review of *The Kingfisher Encyclopedia of the Future,* p. 31.

School Library Journal, December, 2000, Mary R. Hofmann, review of *How the Future Began,* p. 160; September, 2000, Eldon Younce, review of *How the Future Began: Machines,* p. 245; December 2001, Linda Wadleigh, review of *The Kingfisher Facts and Records Book of Space,* p. 160; April, 2002, Jean Lowery, review of *How to Live on Mars,* p. 172; June, 2002, Michael McCullough, review of *How to Build a Robot,* p. 158; July, 2002, Blair Christolon, review of *Soccer: The Ultimate Guide to the Beautiful Game,* p. 134; December, 2002, Eva Elisabeth VonAncken, review of *The Kingfisher Young People's Book of Living Worlds,* p. 160; April, 2004, Barbara Auerbach, review of *The Kingfisher Geography Encyclopedia,* p. 93; August, 2004, Andrew Medlar, review of *Summer Olympics: The Definite Guide to the World's Greatest Sports Celebration,* p. 137; May, 2005, Lynn Evarts, review of *Spies,* p. 150; October 15, 2006, Mary Ellen Quinn, review of *The Kingfisher Science Encyclopedia,* p. 93; December, 2005, Peg Glisson, review of *The Kingfisher Student Atlas of North America,* p. 90; February, 2006, Blair Christolon, review of *Soccer Skills,* p. 118; May, 2006, Blair Christolon, review of *The Kingfisher Soccer Encyclopedia,* p. 146; June, 2006, Caroline Geck, review of *Pollution,* p. 174; May, 2007, Jeffrey A. French, review of *Racing: The Ultimate Motorsports Encyclopedia,* p. 154.

ONLINE

Clive Gifford Home Page, http://www.clivegifford.co.uk (January 25, 2009).*

*   *   *

GRAFE, Max

Personal

Born in LA.

Addresses

Home—Brooklyn, NY. *Agent*—Levy Creative Management, 300 E. 46th St., Ste. 4G, New York, NY 10017.

Career

Printmaker, painter, and illustrator.

Illustrator

Daniel Pennac, *Eye of the Wolf* (originally published, 1982), translated from the French by Sarah Adams, Candlewick Press (Cambridge, MA), 2002.

Nancy C. Wood, *Old Coyote,* Candlewick Press (Cambridge, MA), 2004.

Ruth Sawyer, *The Wee Christmas Cabin of Carn-na-ween,* Candlewick Press (Cambridge, MA), 2005.

Laura Amy Schlitz, reteller, *The Bearskinner: A Tale of the Brothers Grimm,* Candlewick Press (Cambridge, MA), 2007.

David Elliott, *What the Grizzly Knows,* Candlewick Press (Cambridge, MA), 2008.

Sidelights

A printmaker and painter, artist Max Grafe joined the world of children's books by providing the illustrations to the English edition of *Eye of the Wolf.* Written by French author Daniel Pennac, the picture book explores the special relationship that develops between a boy named Africa and a one-eyed wolf. Living in a zoo enclosure, Blue Wolf dreads his confined life and dislikes the humans who stole him away from his pack. When a young boy visits his cage repeatedly, the wolf is at first irritated, but after Africa closes one eye and stares at the animal, the wolf senses the connection and recounts his life story to his new human friend. Via his locked gaze with Blue Wolf, Africa in turn shares his past experiences as a neglected child. According to *Booklist* contributor Ed Sullivan, Grafe's "haunting black-and-white illustrations" for *Eye of the Wolf* help reinforce the book's themes of "fellowship, healing, and meaningful relationships," while a *Publishers Weekly* reviewer thought the "dreamlike mixed-media illustrations . . . reinforce the graceful mingling of real and surreal events."

In 2004, Grafe teamed up with author Nancy Wood to create a moving story about the cycle of life in *Old Coyote.* A grayed and tired creature, Old Coyote realizes his time on earth has come to an end, so in preparation, he takes one final walk through the desert landscape, thanking the saguaro cactus for its shade, reminiscing next to the den he and his mate once shared, and saying goodbye to the rabbits he once hunted for food. Locating a special rock high atop a mountain, Old Coyote lies down for one final rest, dreaming of a new life where he can once again outrun any creature. Several reviewers suggested that the picture book would be a good choice to introduce young readers to the topic of death, finding Grafe's artwork well suited to that theme. Describing the illustrations as "somewhat impressionistic, mimicking what might be seen by Old Coyote's aging eyes," *School Library Journal* critic Roxanne Burg

called *Old Coyote* a "suitable" work for a sensitive topic. *Booklist* contributor Terry Glover also offered warm words for Grafe's pictures, claiming that the artist's "mixed-media, earth-toned illustrations beautifully capture the essence of it all."

In *The Wee Christmas Cabin of Carn-na-ween,* Grafe provides new illustrations for a story by Ruth Sawyer that was originally published in 1941. Giving help to others in need for all her life, a poor woman named Oona has few material goods to her name and desperately wishes to own a small house of her own. One snowy Christmas Eve, a tired, hungry, and homeless Oona receives an impressive gift from the bog fairies of the Carn-na-ween, a small cabin of her very own. In return, however, the woman must continue to provide comfort for others in times of trouble, making her a protector of the needy. Grafe's pictures for the book "balance an enchanting folk-art-like simplicity with an

★ "Vividly portrays the impact of Ireland's potato famine."
—*Booklist,* Starred

the Grave

JAMES HENEGHAN

Cover of James Heneghan's young-adult novel The Grave, *which features Max Grafe's detailed artwork.* (Laurel-Leaf Books, 2002. Used by permission of Laurel-Leaf, an imprint of Random House Children's Books, a division of Random House, Inc.)

edge of realism," proclaimed *Horn Book* commentator Alison M. Amato, while *Booklist* critic Julie Cummins thought the "mixed-media artwork" in *The Wee Christmas Cabin of Carn-na-ween* "invests the tale with an appealing mystical quality."

Grafe has also created artwork for Laura Amy Schlitz's adaptation of *The Bearskinner: A Tale of the Brothers Grimm*. A story from the Brothers Grimm cannon that is not often retold, *The Bearskinner* shares with readers the tale about a despondent soldier who makes a deal with the devil. For seven years, the soldier must not bathe or pray to God, kill himself or tell anyone of his situation. He must also, instead of clothes, wear a ragged bearskin hide. If the soldier can endure, the devil will reward him with untold riches, a bargain the determined man eventually wins. Through his use of light and dark in the illustrations, themes of good and evil are revealed, observed *School Library Journal* contributor Kirsten Cutler, the critic adding that the artist thereby creates an "interplay of light and shadow that is very atmospheric, effectively reflecting the content of the story." Writing in *Kirkus Reviews,* a critic suggested that Grafe's "textured" pictures "ably extend the dark mood and dramatic themes of soul bargaining and personal torment."

Biographical and Critical Sources

PERIODICALS

Booklist, March 1, 2003, Ed Sullivan, review of *Eye of the Wolf,* p. 1199; December 1, 2004, Terry Glover, review of *Old Coyote,* p. 664; November 15, 2005, Julie Cummins, review of *The Wee Christmas Cabin of Carn-na-ween,* p. 47; November 15, 2007, Gillian Engberg, review of *The Bearskinner: A Tale of the Brothers Grimm,* p. 40.

Horn Book, November-December, 2005, Alison M. Amato, review of *The Wee Christmas Cabin of Carn-na-ween,* p. 697; January-February, 2008, review of *The Bearskinner,* p. 12.

Kirkus Reviews, December 15, 2002, review of *Eye of the Wolf,* p. 1855; July 15, 2004, review of *Old Coyote,* p. 695; October 15, 2007, review of *The Bearskinner;* September 15, 2008, review of *What the Grizzly Knows.*

Publishers Weekly, January 13, 2003, review of *Eye of the Wolf,* p. 61; September 26, 2005, review of *The Wee Christmas Cabin of Carn-na-ween,* p. 89.

School Library Journal, February, 2003, Susan Oliver, review of *Eye of the Wolf,* p. 146; October, 2004, Roxanne Burg, review of *Old Coyote,* p. 137; December, 2007, Kirsten Cutler, review of *The Bearskinner,* p. 157.*

H

HALPERN, Julie 1975-

Personal

Born January 14, 1975, in suburban Chicago, IL; daughter of two teachers; married Matthew Cordell (an illustrator), 2003; children: Romy Bess. *Education:* University of Wisconsin—Madison, B.A. (film and women's studies; M.L.S. *Hobbies and other interests:* Reading, travel, board games.

Addresses

Home and office—P.O. Box 8583, Gurnee, IL 60031-7018. *E-mail*—julie@juliehalpern.com.

Career

Writer and middle-school librarian in Illinois.

Member

American Library Association.

Awards, Honors

Quick Picks for Reluctant Young-Adult Readers citation, American Library Association—Young Adult Library Services Association, and Ken Book Award for literary contribution to understanding mental illness, National Alliance on Mental Illness NYC-Metro, both 2008, both for *Get Well Soon.*

Writings

Toby and the Snowflakes (picture book). illustrated by husband Matthew Cordell, Houghton Mifflin (Boston, MA), 2004.
Get Well Soon (young-adult novel), Feiwel & Friends (New York, NY), 2007.

Into the Wild Nerd Yonder (young-adult novel), Feiwel & Friends (New York, NY), 2009.

Sidelights

While growing up in the Chicago suburbs, author and librarian Julie Halpern recalled on her home page: "I never really considered myself a writer or a reader." However, Halpern spent hours writing, often creatively. In addition to composing letters to pen pals, she wrote "stories for my friends . . . in which my friends' crushes actually liked them." She took a creative writing class in college, and following graduation she continued writing for fun by producing her own "zines": self-published magazines covering a single topic. Through one of her zines, Halpern met her husband, illustrator Matthew Cordell.

Halpern's first book, *Toby and the Snowflakes,* grew out of the desire to work with her artist husband and was inspired by her fondness for winter. In this picture book, young Toby is sad when his best friend moves away. Playing outside one day, he discovers he can talk to snowflakes. He suddenly has dozens of new companions, until spring comes and they melt away. Luckily, another boy soon moves into the neighborhood, giving Toby a chance to discover another friend. "The narrative has a natural flow, told in clear language," Margaret R. Tassia observed in *School Library Journal.* Halpern's "story seems to stretch," a *Publishers Weekly* reviewer noted, the critic adding that the author's text "conveys a genial directness." "Although the storyline is a bit disjointed, its message should appeal to kids with both real and imaginary friends," a *Kirkus Reviews* critic concluded.

Halpern's first novel, *Get Well Soon,* "is based on my own hospitalization for depression in high school, although throughout the editing process a lot of the de tails have become fictionalized," as she told Jessica Burkhart in a online interview. "I always thought the experience would make a great book, filled with inter esting characters and bizarre situations. And since I read so much [young-adult literature], and so much of it is dark and depressing, I thought it would be nice to write a funny book about a not so funny topic." In the novel, sixteen-year-old Anna Bloom is suffering from panic attacks and begins cutting school, so her frustrated parents have her committed to a mental hospital. *Get Well Soon* collects the letters that the witty, sarcastic Anna writes to her friend during her three-week stay.

Although *Get Well Soon* deals with a serious subject, "Anna's voice, filled with spot-on musings, sarcasm, slang, and swearing, is uproariously funny and authentic," Gillian Engberg remarked in a *Booklist* review. "At the heart of her story, though, is a never-didactic message about emotional growth and psychic healing," a *Kirkus Reviews* writer maintained, and a *Publishers Weekly* critic concluded that in *Get Well Soon* "readers will get a kick out of Anna's snarky sense of humor and her capacity for self-renewal."

"It is with my first novel that I think I can finally recognize that I am, and have always been, a writer," Halpern revealed on her home page. She has followed *Get Well Soon* with a second young-adult novel titled *Into the Wild Nerd Yonder,* and she has plans to write more. "I don't think I relate to anyone more than I do to thirteen year-olds," the novelist admitted. "It's the combination of their honesty, confusion, and drama. And we have the same sense of humor."

Biographical and Critical Sources

PERIODICALS

Booklist, October 15, 2007, Gillian Engberg, review of *Get Well Soon,* pp. 41-42.
Kirkus Reviews, July 1, 2004, review of *Toby and the Snowflakes,* p. 630; September 15, 2007, review of *Get Well Soon.*
Publishers Weekly, November 12, 2007, review of *Get Well Soon,* p. 57.
School Library Journal, October, 2004, Margaret R. Tassia, review of *Toby and the Snowflakes,* p. 114.
Voice of Youth Advocates, August, 2007, Erin Wyatt, review of *Get Well Soon,* p. 241; February, 2008, Melissa Moore, review of *Get Well Soon,* p. 524.

ONLINE

Jessica Burkhart Web Log, http://jessicaburkhart.blogspot.com (January 25, 2008), Jessica Burkhart, interview with Halpern.
Julie Halpern Home Page, http://www.juliehalpern.com (January 21, 2009).*

HILLERMAN, Anthony Grove
See HILLERMAN, Tony

*   *   *

HILLERMAN, Tony 1925-2008
(Anthony Grove Hillerman)

OBITUARY NOTICE—

See index for *SATA* sketch: Born May 27, 1925, in Sacred Heart, OK; died of pulmonary failure, October 26, 2008, in Albuquerque, NM. Journalist, educator, editor, novelist, memoirist, and author. Hillerman was named a Special Friend of the Dineh (Navajo people) by the Navajo Nation in 1987. The honor commemorated the sharing of deep mutual respect between the people who live at the dusty intersection of the Four Corners (Utah, Colorado, New Mexico, and Arizona) and the outsider who came to love the people, their land, and their culture. After a successful but unexciting fifteen-year career as a newspaper journalist, Hillerman changed his course. He earned a graduate degree at the University of New Mexico (where he later taught for twenty years) and began a new career as a novelist. Thirty-five years and thirty books later, Hillerman had won the hearts of millions of readers. He accumulated many prominent awards, including the Edgar Allan Poe Award, the Grandmaster Award of the Mystery Writers of America, and the Golden Spur Award of the Western Writers of the America. Most of Hillerman's books are mystery novels. Eighteen of these novels chronicle the adventures of two officers of the Navajo Tribal Police: Lieutenant Joe Leaphorn, a cynical veteran near the end of his career, who spends much of his life outside the Navajo culture; and Officer Jim Chee, a younger man attempting to assimilate his life in law enforcement with his spiritual quest to become a shaman to his people. Hillerman's novels succeed on many levels, and his crime stories have been rated as top-notch in their genre. His sensitive treatment of Navajo culture earned him the highest regard from the Dineh, and many readers mistakenly believed that Hillerman had himself been born into the Navajo Nation. His masterful development of character, setting, and theme drew millions of mainstream readers into his fold. Hillerman's police officers were complicated men who struggled to balance life in two worlds, dealing with the tug of war between tradition and technology, the maturing process of men in a cultural landscape that is also threatened by age, and the conflict between public service and personal obligation. His attention to place left readers with a deep appreciation for the desert in all its manifestations: the beauty, the danger, and the eternity of the land. Hillerman's people were the Dineh, but his themes were universal. From Leaphorn's debut in *The Blessing Way* (1970) to Chee's introduction in *People of Darkness* (1978) to the last novel, featuring both officers, *The Shape Shifter* (2006), Hillerman's admirers remained loyal. Not all of his books were crime novels. *Hillerman's Country: A Journey through the Southwest with Tony Hillerman* (1991) is a collection of photographs by the author's brother, Barney, with commentary by the author. *Finding Moon* (1995) is a novel set in Cambodia. Hillerman also wrote essays, a children's story, and an autobiography. He also edited collections of fiction, photographs, and essays, but he will be remembered for his haunting tales of the Navajos and their world.

OBITUARIES AND OTHER SOURCES:

BOOKS

Bulow, Ernie, and Tony Hillerman, *Talking Mysteries: A Conversation with Tony Hillerman,* University of New Mexico Press (Albuquerque, NM), 1991.

Erisman, Fred, *Tony Hillerman,* Boise State University (Boise, ID), 1989.

Greenberg, Martin, editor, *The Tony Hillerman Companion: A Comprehensive Guide to His Life and Work,* HarperCollins (New York, NY), 1994.

Hillerman, Tony, *Seldom Disappointed: A Memoir,* HarperCollins (New York, NY), 2001.

Sobol, John, *Tony Hillerman: A Public Life,* ECW Press (Toronto, Ontario, Canada), 1994.

St. James Encyclopedia of Popular Culture, St. James Press (Detroit, MI), 2000.

PERIODICALS

Chicago Tribune, October 28, 2008, sec. 1, p. 28.
Los Angeles Times, October 28, 2008, pp. A1, A18.
New York Times, October 28, 2008, p. B17.
Times (London, England), October 29, 2008, p. 58.

*   *   *

HODGMAN, Ann 1956-

Personal

Born 1956; married David Owen; children: two. *Education:* Harvard College, graduate.

Addresses

Home—Washington, CT.

Career

Writer.

Writings

Stella's Story: The Last, HarperCollins (New York, NY), 1976.

Skystars: The History of Women in Aviation, illustrated by Rudy Djabbaroff, Atheneum (New York, NY), 1981.

True Tiny Tales of Terror, illustrated by Derek Pell, Putnam (New York, NY), 1982.

Attack of the Mutants: A Thundercats Adventure (based on *Thundercats* television series), illustrated by Mones, Random House (New York, NY), 1985.

Galaxy High School, Yearling (New York, NY), 1987.

Seaside Mystery ("Choose Your Own Adventure" series), illustrated by Judith Mitchell, Bantam (New York, NY), 1987.

A Day in the Life of a Fashion Designer, illustrated by Gayle Jann, Troll Associates (Mahwah, NJ), 1988.

A Day in the Life of a Theater Set Designer, illustrated by Gayle Jann, Troll Associates (Mahwah, NJ), 1988.

There's a Batwing in My Lunchbox, illustrated by John Pierard, Avon (New York, NY), 1988.

Hard Times for Cats, Abbeville (New York, NY), 1992.

(With Jennifer Daniel and Ann Whitman) *My First Book of Questions: Easy Answers to Hard Questions,* illustrated by Robin Brickman, Scholastic (New York, NY), 1992.

Stinky Stanley, illustrated by John Cymerman, Pocket Books (New York, NY), 1993.

Addams Family Values (based on the movie), Aladdin (New York, NY), 1993.

Stinky Stanley Stinks Again, Pocket Books (New York, NY), 1993.

(With Patty Marx) *How to Survive Junior High,* illustrated by Mena Dolobowsky, Troll Associates (Mahwah, NJ), 1994.

I Saw Mommy Kicking Santa Claus: The Ultimate Holiday Survival Guide, Perigee (New York, NY), 2004.

(With Patti Marx) *You Know You're 40 When—,* illustrated by Taylor Lee, Broadway Books (New York, NY), 2004.

The House of a Million Pets, illustrated by Eugene Yelchin, Henry Holt (New York, NY), 2007.

Food columnist for *Spy.*

"LUNCHROOM" SERIES; FOR CHILDREN

Night of a Thousand Pizzas, illustrated by Roger Leyonmark, Berkley (New York, NY), 1990.

Frog Punch, Berkley (New York, NY), 1990.

The Cookie Caper, Berkley (East Rutherford, NJ), 1990.

French Fried Aliens, Berkley (East Rutherford, NJ), 1990.

Rubberband Stew, Berkley (East Rutherford, NJ), 1990.

The Flying Popcorn Experiment, Berkley (East Rutherford, NJ), 1990.

Invasion of the Fast Food, illustrated by Roger Leyonmark, Berkley (New York, NY), 1990.

Space Food, Berkley (New York, NY), 1990.

Day of the Monster Plant, Berkley (New York, NY), 1991.

Mutant Garbage, Berkley (New York, NY), 1991.

"MY BABYSITTER IS A VAMPIRE" SERIES; FOR CHILDREN

My Babysitter Is a Vampire, illustrated by John Pierard, Pocket Books (New York, NY), 1991.

My Babysitter Has Fangs, Pocket Books (New York, NY), 1992.

My Babysitter Bites Again, illustrated by John Pierard, Pocket Books (New York, NY), 1993.

My Babysitter Bites Back, Pocket Books (New York, NY), 1993.

My Babysitter Flies by Night, Pocket Books (New York, NY), 1994.

My Babysitter Goes Bats, Pocket Books (New York, NY), 1994.

My Babysitter Is a Movie Monster, Pocket Books (New York, NY), 1995.

"CHILDREN OF THE NIGHT" SERIES; FOR CHILDREN

Dark Dreams, Puffin (New York, NY), 1993.
Dark Music, Puffin (New York, NY), 1994.
Dark Triumph, Puffin (New York, NY), 1994.

COOKBOOKS

Beat This: Cookbook, illustrated by Robin Zingone, Chapters (Shelburne, VT), 1993.

Beat That: Cookbook, illustrated by Robin Zingone, Chapters (Shelburne, VT), 1995.

One Bite Won't Kill You: More than 200 Recipes to Tempt Even the Pickiest Kids on Earth, and the Rest of the Family Too, illustrated by Roz Chast, Houghton Mifflin (Boston, MA), 1999.

"1,003 THINGS" SERIES

(With Lisa Birnbach and Patricia Marx) *1,003 Great Things about Kids,* Andrews McMeel (Kansas City, MO), 1998.

(With Lisa Birnbach and Patricia Marx) *1,003 Great Things about Friends,* Andrews McMeel (Kansas City, MO), 1999.

(With Lisa Birnbach and Patricia Marx) *1,003 Great Things about Teachers,* Andrews McMeel (Kansas City, MO), 2000.

(With Lisa Birnbach and Patricia Marx) *1,003 Great Things about America,* Andrews McMeel (Kansas City, MO), 2002.

(With Lisa Birnbach and Patricia Marx) *1,003 Great Things about Moms,* Andrews McMeel (Kansas City, MO), 2002.

(With Lisa Birnbach and Patricia Marx) *1,003 Great Things to Smile About,* Andrews McMeel (Kansas City, MO), 2004.

(With Lisa Birnbach and Patricia Marx) *1,003 Great Things about Being a Woman,* Andrews McMeel (Kansas City, MO), 2005.

(With Lisa Birnbach and Patricia Marx) *1,003 Great Things about Being Jewish,* Andrews McMeel (Kansas City, MO), 2006.

1,003 Ways to Stay Young, Andrews McMeel (Kansas City, MO), 2007.

Sidelights

A mother of two, Ann Hodgman is a former food columnist for the magazine *Spy,* and the proud owner of twenty pets. In addition to writing cookbooks such as *One Bite Won't Kill You: More than 200 Recipes to Tempt Even the Pickiest Kids on Earth, and the Rest of the Family Too,* Hodgman has turned her wry humor to younger readers through her work writing children's books, including the "My Babysitter Is a Vampire" and "Lunchroom" series. Along with Lisa Birnbach and Patricia Marx, she has also coauthored the humorous "1,003 Things" books, which contain a wealth of comedic anecdotes, clichés, and truisms.

Hodgman is an inveterate animal lover, and her affection for her many pets—including cats, dachshunds, rabbits, a prairie dog, pygmy mice, canaries, owls, and raccoons—inspired *The House of a Million Pets.* Offering care tips, humorous anecdotes, and general advice for pet owners, the book also features illustrations by Eugene Yelchin. Tanya D. Auger, writing in *Horn Book,* wrote that "Hodgman's breezy tone and silly sense of humor will keep most [readers] hooked," while in *School Library Journal* Patricia Manning noted that *The House of a Million Pets* "speaks directly to readers, inviting them to be part of the total experience, even when the going gets gross." A *Kirkus Reviews* writer concluded of Hodgman's book that "her tales are equally engaging, truthful and funny to readers of all ages."

Biographical and Critical Sources

PERIODICALS

Booklist, September 1, 2007, Debbie Carton, review of *The House of a Million Pets,* p. 110.

Horn Book, January-February, 2008, Tanya D. Auger, review of *The House of a Million Pets,* p. 111.

Kirkus Reviews, August 1, 2007, review of *The House of a Million Pets.*

New York Times Book Review, October 14, 2007, J.D. Biersdorfer, "Animals Everywhere," p. 21.

Publishers Weekly, September 3, 2007, review of *The House of a Million Pets,* p. 59.

School Library Journal, December, 2007, Patricia Manning, review of *The House of a Million Pets,* p. 152.

ONLINE

Houghton Mifflin Web site, http://www.houghtonmifflin books.com/ (March 9, 2009), profile of Hodgman.*

J

JARMAN, Julia 1946-

Personal

Born March 28, 1946, near Peterborough, Cambridgeshire, England; married Peter Jarman (an engineer); children: three. *Education:* Attended University of Manchester. *Hobbies and other interests:* Gardening, theater, computers, literature.

Addresses

Home—Bedfordshire, England. *Agent*—Caroline Walsh, David Higham Associates, 5-8 Lower John St., Golden Sq., London W1F 9HA, England. *E-mail*—juliajarman@ btopenworld.com.

Career

Author, 1983—. Worked previously as a teacher of English and drama.

Awards, Honors

Stockport Schools Book Award, for *Big Red Bath, Ghost Writer,* and *Class Two at the Zoo;* NASEN Highly Commended Award, and West Sussex Book Award shortlist, both for *Ghost Writer;* North East Teenage Book Award shortlist, for *Peace Weavers;* Lancashire Children's Book of the Year shortlist, and Lanarkshire Schools Book Award, both for *Hangman.*

Writings

When Poppy Ran Away, illustrated by Karen Elliott, Andersen (London, England), 1985.
Ollie and the Bogle, illustrated by Katariina Lempinen, Andersen (London, England), 1987.
Poppy and the Vicarage Ghost, illustrated by Lazlo Acs, Andersen (London, England), 1988.
Squonk, illustrated by Jean Baylis, Heinemann (London, England), 1989.

The Ghost of Tantony Pig, illustrated by Lazlo Acs, Andersen (London, England), 1990.
(With Damon Burnard) *Georgie and the Dragon,* A & C Black (London, England), 1991.
Plays (contains *Pirates!, Tim and Tara's Magic Tricks,* and *Toby and the Kidnapped Kittens*), illustrated by Kareen Taylerson, Ginn (Aylesbury, England), 1991.
(With Damon Burnard) *Georgie and the Planet Raider,* illustrated by T. Burnard, A & C Black (London, England), 1993.
Will There Be Polar Bears?, illustrated by Priscilla Lamont, Heinemann (London, England), 1993, Artists & Writers Guild (New York, NY), 1994.
The Jessame Stories, illustrated by Duncan Smith, Heinemann (London, England), 1994.
(With Damon Burnard) *Georgie and the Computer Bugs,* A & C Black (London, England), 1995.
Return of Squonk, illustrated by Jean Baylis, Heinemann (London, England), 1995.
(With Julie Anderson) *Gertie and the Bloop,* A & C Black (London, England), 1996.
The Crow Haunting, Andersen (London, England), 1996.
More Jessame Stories, illustrated by Duncan Smith, Mammoth (London, England), 1997.
Little Mouse Grandma, illustrated by Alex de Wolf, Mammoth (London, England), 1997.
Convict: A Tale of Criminals Sent to Australia, Watts (London, England), 1997.
The Sewer Sleuth: A Tale of Victorian Cholera, Watts (London, England), 1997.
Chillers: The Haunting of Nadia, Puffin (London, England), 1998.
Hangman, Andersen (London, England), 1999.
The Revenge of Tommy Bones, Collins (London, England), 2001.
Ghost Writer, Andersen (London, England), 2002.
Peace Weavers, Andersen (London, England), 2004, with a new afterword, Scholastic (London, England), 2006.
Jack in a Box, illustrated by Marjolein Pottie, Collins (London, England), 2004.
Big Red Bath, illustrated by Adrian Reynolds, Orchard (London, England), 2004, published as *Big Red Tub,* Orchard (New York, NY), 2004.

The Magic Backpack, illustrated by Adriano Gon, Crabtree (New York, NY), 2004.

The Not-so-Nice Victorians, Franklin Watts (London, England), 2005.

Kangaroo's Cancan Café, illustrated by Lynne Chapman, Orchard (London, England), 2005.

Grandma's Seaside Bloomers, illustrated by Roger Fereday, Franklin Watts (London, England), 2007.

Class Two at the Zoo, Carolrhoda Books (Minneapolis, MN), 2007.

Class Three by the Sea, Carolrhoda Books (Minneapolis, MN), 2007.

Also author of *Bully Bear, Rabbit's Surprise Birthday,* and *Terrible Tiger,* all for Rigby; *Harry and the Clever Spider* and *Harry and the Clever Spider at School,* both for Collins; and *Molly and the Giant* for Oxford University Press.

"UPSTARTS" SERIES; READERS

Pippa and the Witch, illustrated by Alexa Rutherford, Ginn (Aylesbury, England), 1990.

Toby and the Space Cats, illustrated by Nick Ward, Ginn (Aylesbury, England), 1990.

Not-So-Silly Billy, illustrated by Jacqui Thomas, Ginn (Aylesbury, England), 1990.

The Magic Carrot, illustrated by David Mostyn, Ginn (Aylesbury, England), 1990.

Emily the Spy, illustrated by Robert Geary, Ginn (Aylesbury, England), 1990.

Aunt Horrible and the Very Good Idea, illustrated by Linda Birch, Ginn (Aylesbury, England), 1990.

James and the Dragon, illustrated by Tony Ross, Ginn (Aylesbury, England), 1990.

The Rabbit Said Miaow, illustrated by Paula Martys, Ginn (Aylesbury, England), 1990.

The Goat Is Eating Debbie!, illustrated by Paula Martys, Ginn (Aylesbury, England), 1990.

Naughty Norman, illustrated by Terry McKenna, Ginn (Aylesbury, England), 1990.

Fat Cat, illustrated by Anna Llinares, Ginn (Aylesbury, England), 1990.

Lucy Calls the Fire Brigade, illustrated by Paula Martys, Ginn (Aylesbury, England), 1990.

Babies Are Yuck!, illustrated by Paula Martys, Ginn (Aylesbury, England), 1990.

There's a Monster, illustrated by Paula Martys, Ginn (Aylesbury, England), 1990.

Paul and the Robber, illustrated by Paula Martys, Ginn (Aylesbury, England), 1990.

Look at My Spots, illustrated by Paula Martys, Ginn (Aylesbury, England), 1990.

Lucy the Tiger, illustrated by Paula Martyr, Ginn (Aylesbury, England), 1990.

"ALL ABOARD" SERIES; READERS

Sam and the Tadpoles, illustrated by Julie Park, Ginn (Aylesbury, England), 1994.

You Can't Scare Me, illustrated by Julie Park, Ginn (Aylesbury, England), 1994.

Detective Tilak, illustrated by Julie Park, Ginn (Aylesbury, England), 1994.

Mountain Rescue, illustrated by Julie Park, Ginn (Aylesbury, England), 1994.

The Great Lorenzo, illustrated by Julie Park, Ginn (Aylesbury, England), 1994.

Speedy's Day Out, illustrated by Julie Park, Ginn (Aylesbury, England), 1994.

Hiccups!, illustrated by Julie Park, Ginn (Aylesbury, England), 1994.

Big Sister Rosie, illustrated by Julie Park, Ginn (Aylesbury, England), 1994.

Clumsy Clara, illustrated by Andrew Cooke, Ginn (Aylesbury, England), 1994.

Little Monster, illustrated by Caroline Ewen, Ginn (Aylesbury, England), 1994.

Clouds, illustrated by Caroline Ewen, Ginn (Aylesbury, England), 1994.

No, Sam!, illustrated by Julie Park, Ginn (Aylesbury, England), 1994.

The Terrible Fright, illustrated by Julie Park, Ginn (Aylesbury, England), 1994.

Computer Kate, illustrated by Robert Geary, Ginn (Aylesbury, England), 1994.

Bobby's Bad Day, illustrated by Julie Park, Ginn (Aylesbury, England), 1994.

The Magic Smell, illustrated by Julie Park, Ginn (Aylesbury, England), 1994.

Rosie and the Dinosaurs, illustrated by Julie Park, Ginn (Aylesbury, England), 1994.

Nog's Dinner, illustrated by Julie Park, Ginn (Aylesbury, England), 1994.

Jabeen and the New Moon, illustrated by Julie Park, Ginn (Aylesbury, England), 1994.

Pancakes, illustrated by Julie Park, Ginn (Aylesbury, England), 1994.

Grandad's Balloon, illustrated by Julie Park, Ginn (Aylesbury, England), 1994.

Pandora and the Pirates, illustrated by Rowan Barnes-Murphy, Ginn (Aylesbury, England), 1994.

The Hot Pepper Queen and the Mango Babies, illustrated by Sophie Allsopp, Ginn (Aylesbury, England), 1994.

Fussy Frieda, illustrated by Andy Hammond, Ginn (Aylesbury, England), 1994.

(Reteller) *The Ghost Next Door,* illustrated by Gwyneth Williamson, Ginn (Aylesbury, England), 1994.

Swan Rescue, illustrated by Julie Park, Ginn (Aylesbury, England), 1994.

The Parrot, illustrated by Julie Park, Ginn (Aylesbury, England), 1994.

(With Miriam Simon) *All Aboard: Extended Stories for Reading Aloud,* Ginn (Aylesbury, England), 1994.

Something in the Fridge, illustrated by Tony Ross, Ginn (Aylesbury, England), 1994.

The Giant Sandwich, illustrated by Jonathan Longley, Ginn (Aylesbury, England), 1994.

The Ghost in the Castle, illustrated by Julie Park, Ginn (Aylesbury, England), 1994.

The Greedy Guinea-Pig, illustrated by Julie Park, Ginn (Aylesbury, England), 1994.

Lizzie and the Car Wash, illustrated by Julie Park, Ginn (Aylesbury, England), 1994.

Scat Cat!, illustrated by Julie Park, Ginn (Aylesbury, England), 1994.

A Guinea-Pig for Rosie, illustrated by Julie Park, Ginn (Aylesbury, England), 1994.

(With Miriam Simon) *Sam and Rosie's ABC,* illustrated by Julie Park, Ginn (Aylesbury, England), 1994.

The Wizard, illustrated by Amelia Rosato, Ginn (Aylesbury, England), 1995.

Dognapped? and Other Stories from Mulberry Green, Ginn (Aylesbury, England), 1995.

Rosie's Photo Album, illustrated by Julie Park, Ginn (Aylesbury, England), 1996.

"TALES FROM THE WHISPERY WOODS" SERIES; READERS

Flying Friends, illustrated by Guy Parker-Rees, Scholastic (London, England), 2002.

Mole's Useful Day, illustrated by Guy Parker-Rees, Scholastic (London, England), 2002.

Owl's Big Mistake, illustrated by Guy Parker-Rees, Scholastic (London, England), 2003.

Always There, illustrated by Guy Parker-Rees, Scholastic (London, England), 2003.

Rabbit Helps Out, illustrated by Guy Parker-Rees, Scholastic (London, England), 2003.

"TIME-TRAVELLING CAT" SERIES

Topher and the Time-Travelling Cat, illustrated by David Atack, Andersen (London, England), 1992, published as *The Time-Travelling Cat and the Egyptian Goddess,* Collins (London, England), 2001.

A Test for the Time-Travelling Cat, Andersen (London, England), 1997, published as *The Time-Travelling Cat and the Tudor Treasure,* Collins (London, England), 2001.

The Time-Travelling Cat and the Roman Eagle, Collins (London, England), 2001.

The Time-Travelling Cat and the Aztec Sacrifice, Andersen (London, England), 2006.

The Time-Travelling Cat and the Viking Terror, Andersen (London, England), 2008.

Adaptations

The Jessame Stories and *More Jessame Stories* were recorded on audiocassette, read by Adjoah Andoh, Mammoth, 2001. *The Time-Travelling Cat and the Egyptian Goddess* and *The Time-Travelling Cat and the Tudor Treasure* were adapted as audiobooks, Chivers Children's Audio.

Sidelights

British children's writer Julia Jarman is the author of more than one hundred books for young people. Known for her mysteries, time-travel fantasies, and books for newly independent readers, the prolific Jarman is often commended for her ability to create well-developed characters. In *Writing,* Anita Rowe called Jarman "one of the most versatile young people's authors writing today."

Jarman's first novel, *When Poppy Ran Away,* was inspired by a childhood prank. While playing with a friend, the author recalled to a contributor in the *Peterborough Evening Telegraph,* "I gave her a potion made from water and soot. She drank it and I enjoyed it at the time, but after I came home, my conscience got the better of me and I was convinced I had murdered her." In *When Poppy Ran Away,* young Poppy Field grows tired of her perfectly organized life of music lessons, ballet classes, and babysitting. Forced to spend time with the seemingly ideal Virginia Creeber, the girl decides to play a joke on her friend. When Poppy realizes what she has done, she fears her parents' reaction and decides to run away, dramatically altering her boring everyday routine. *School Librarian* critic Sue May called young Poppy an "assertive and adventurous" character in a book that "certainly represents a move towards girls taking the initiative."

Poppy returns in *Poppy and the Vicarage Ghost,* where the young protagonist discovers a young boy hiding in the ex-vicarage she is hired to watch for the summer. Running away from his father, who wants to take him to South America, the boy and Poppy explore the haunted house. They find not only a secret passage, but also the ghost—and skeleton—of Alice Cookeson, a girl who hid beneath the residence during the English Civil War. Writing in *Growing Point,* a critic praised Jarman's use of "triumphs and quests" as well as her ability "to mingle humour, affection and atmosphere in an ingenious tale."

Called "a most unusual story" by *Junior Bookshelf* reviewer Marcus Crouch, *The Ghost of Tantony Pig* follows Laurie Gell as he tries to discover the source of the noise emanating from Hogsbottom Field. After a wealthy tycoon decides to build a mansion on the sight, much to the distress of villagers, witnesses claim they hear strange, pig-like grunts coming from Hogsbottom. Learning of an old tale concerning the sacred pig of St. Antony's Church, Laurie begins to wonder if he is the descendant of a boy who, during the Black Plague, received a warning from a pig of the danger to his village. "Traditional and modern elements are mixed with cheerful confidence in an immensely exciting and pointed fantasy-adventure," claimed a *Growing Point* critic, while Margaret Mallett wrote in *School Librarian* that Jarman's "story . . . moves swiftly to an exciting and satisfying end."

Fantasy again is featured in *Topher and the Time-Travelling Cat,* a book for older readers "who are likely to enjoy the mix of fantasy and family life," suggested Frances Ball in a *School Librarian* review. Living a quiet life with his father in London after the death of his mother, Topher Hope unexpectedly receives a guest one day, a cat that resembles a statue his mother once brought back from Egypt. Naming the foundling Ka, Topher finds the cat typing a word on his computer, "Bubastis." After Ka fails to return to the Hope house for several days, Topher decides to investigate more about "Bubastis" in the British Museum. Ultimately, the boy finds himself going back in time to Egypt where he searches for his pet cat. Describing the book as "an easy-paced read into which the reader is gradually drawn," a *Junior Bookshelf* critic noted that *Topher and the Time-Travelling Cat* "has the feel of a fern slowly unfurling."

Jarman has also authored several books for the beginning-to-read audience, including *The Jessame Stories* and *More Jessame Stories*. In the first work, readers are introduced to Jessame, a young girl of Ghanaian heritage who lives in the London neighborhood of Bethnal Green. Through this collection of tales, children learn about the everyday life of another young girl as Jessame visits a nearby museum, listens to the tales of her sea-faring uncle, and attends school, all of which, according to *Books for Keeps* reviewer Chris Powling, appeal to a child's desire to learn more about the lives of others. Powling went on to remark on Jarman's ability to record Jessame's activities "so exactly you feel you're inside her head sharing them." Also considering the tales in *The Jessame Stories* "witty and well written," *School Librarian* critic Irene Babsky found that Jessame's experiences mirror "a good range of the hopes, fears, and incidents that punctuate the lives of most children."

The girl's further adventures are served up in *More Jessame Stories*. Here, Jarman shows the young girl as she enjoys other events, such as a picnic, family wedding, and helping a new girl adjust to her school. While the things Jessame does are common to many readers, a *Books for Keeps* reviewer noted that the appeal of *More Jessame Stories* lies in Jarman's ability to "convey a vivid sense of life freshly experienced." The critic went on to describe the volume as "delightful in a literal sense," recording many aspects of London life not regularly found in children's books.

Peace Weavers, a young-adult work, centers on Hilde, a pacifist who lives with her parents on an air force base. During an archaeological dig, workers unearth the skeleton of a woman that dates from the sixth century. After Hilde finds some gold jewelry at the same site, she begins having strange dreams about a girl named Mathilde who served as an envoy between two warring tribes. Writing in the *Bookseller,* Claudia Mody called *Peace Weavers* "a timely novel about peace in our world."

Jarman received the Stockport Schools Book Award for her lively picture book *Big Red Bath*. At bath time one evening, young Stella and Stan are joined by a host of animals, including a duck, a giraffe, and a lion, creating a bubbly mess. When a hippo hops into the crowded tub, though, it careens down the stairs, out of the house,

and into space. A contributor in *Publishers Weekly* described the tale as "a frothy flight of fancy," and a *Kirkus Reviews* critic noted that the author "has created an imaginative tale of good clean fun!" Carolyn Phelan, writing in *Booklist,* praised the combination of Jarman's text and Adrian Reynolds' illustrations, remarking: "Bright and bouncy like the rhyming text, the large, cleanly defined drawings glow with warm washes."

In *Class Two at the Zoo,* a humorous tale told in verse, a group of excited schoolchildren ignore their teacher's warnings about wandering off and soon find themselves swallowed by a huge anaconda. It is up to young Molly, who first spots the dilemma, to devise a clever solution to her classmates' problem. *Class Two at the Zoo* received solid reviews: a contributor in *Kirkus Reviews* described the work as a "bouncy cautionary tale," and Gay Lynn Van Vleck, writing in *School Library Journal,* observed that Jarman's story "will surely tickle the fancy of most field-trip participants."

Biographical and Critical Sources

PERIODICALS

Booklist, January 1, 2005, Carolyn Phelan, review of *Big Red Tub,* p. 869.
Bookseller, January 16, 2004, Claudi Mody, review of *Peace Weavers,* p. 37.
Books for Keeps, July, 1994, Chris Powling, review of *The Jessame Stories,* p. 28; September, 1997, review of *Little Mouse Grandma,* p. 23; May, 1998, review of *More Jessame Stories,* p. 25.
Books for Your Children, autumn-winter, 1987, review of *Ollie and the Bogle,* p. 17; autumn, 1988, V. Taylor, review of *Poppy and the Vicarage Ghost,* p. 32.
Growing Point, July, 1987, review of *Ollie and the Bogle,* pp. 4818-4819; November, 1988, review of *Poppy and the Vicarage Ghost,* pp. 5076-5077; March, 1991, review of *The Ghost of Tantony Pig,* pp. 5491-5492.
Junior Bookshelf, October, 1988, review of *Poppy and the Vicarage Ghost,* p. 249; February, 1991, Marcus Crouch, review of *The Ghost of Tantony Pig,* p. 33; August, 1993, review of *Topher and the Time-Travelling Cat,* p. 136; October, 1994, review of *The Jessame Stories,* p. 174; August, 1996, review of *The Crow Haunting,* pp. 157-158.
Kirkus Reviews, December 15, 2004, review of *Big Red Tub,* p. 1203; July 15, 2005, review of *Jack in a Box,* p. 791; August 15, 2007, review of *Class Two at the Zoo.*
Peterborough Evening Telegraph (Peterborough, England), September 28, 2006, "How Childhood Prank Sparked Writing Career."
Publishers Weekly, January 17, 2005, review of *Big Red Tub,* p. 54; October 8, 2007, review of *Class Two at the Zoo,* p. 53.
School Librarian, September, 1986, Sue May, review of *When Poppy Ran Away,* pp. 250-253; February, 1991, Margaret Mallett, review of *The Ghost of Tantony*

Pig, p. 23; May, 1993, Frances Ball, review of *Topher and the Time-Travelling Cat,* p. 61; November, 1994, Irene Babsky, review of *The Jessame Stories,* p. 151; November, 1997, Marie Imeson, review of *More Jessame Stories,* p. 192; autumn, 1999, Sandra Bennett, review of *Hangman,* p. 99.

School Library Journal, December, 2004, Julie Roach, review of *Big Red Tub,* p. 110; September, 2007, Gay Lynn Van Vleck, review of *Class Two at the Zoo,* p. 166.

Writing, February, 2008, Anita Rowe, interview with Jarman.

ONLINE

David Higham Associates Web site, http://www.david higham.co.uk/ (March 1, 2009), "Julia Jarman."

Julia Jarman Home Page, http://www.juliajarman.com (March 1, 2009).

*   *   *

JOCELYN, Marthe 1956-

Personal

Born 1956, in Toronto, Ontario, Canada; married Tom Slaughter (an artist; separated); children: Hannah, Nell.

Addresses

Home—New York; (summers) Stratford, Ontario, Canada. *E-mail*—marthe@marthejocelyn.com.

Career

Writer and illustrator. Jesse Design (toy and clothing design firm), owner for fifteen years; worked variously as a cookie seller, waitress, sailor, and photo stylist.

Member

PEN International, International Board on Books for Young People, Authors Guild, Writer's Union of Canada, Society of Children's Book Writers and Illustrators, Canadian Society of Children's Authors, Illustrators, and Performers.

Awards, Honors

Canadian Governor General's Award finalist, for *Hannah's Collections;* Book of the Year for Children Award finalist, Canadian Library Association (CLA), 2001, and Hackmatack Award finalist and Red Cedar Award finalist, both 2002-03, all for *Earthly Astonishments;* Best Books for Young Adults selection, American Library Association, Book of the Year for Children shortlist, CLA, and TD Canadian Children's Literature Award, Canadian Children's Book Centre, all 2005, all for *Mable Riley;* Norma Fleck Award shortlist, 2005, for *A Home for Foundlings;* Top Ten Young Adult Fiction

Marthe Jocelyn (Reproduced by permission.)

Books of the Year designation, Ontario Library Association, 2007, for *How It Happened in Peach Hill;* Book of the Year for Young Adults Award finalist, CLA, 2009, for *Would You.*

Writings

EARLY CHAPTER BOOKS

The Invisible Day, illustrated by Abby Carter, Dutton (New York, NY), 1997.

The Invisible Harry, illustrated by Abby Carter, Dutton (New York, NY), 1998.

The Invisible Enemy, illustrated by Abby Carter, Dutton (New York, NY), 2002.

SELF-ILLUSTRATED PICTURE BOOKS

Hannah and the Seven Dresses, Dutton (New York, NY), 1999.

Hannah's Collections, Dutton (New York, NY), 2000.

A Day with Nellie, Tundra Books (Toronto, Ontario, Canada), 2002.

Mayfly, Tundra Books (Toronto, Ontario, Canada), 2004.

Ready for Spring, Tundra Books (Toronto, Ontario, Canada), 2008.

Ready for Summer, Tundra Books (Toronto, Ontario, Canada), 2008.

Ready for Autumn, Tundra Books (Toronto, Ontario, Canada), 2008.

Ready for Winter, Tundra Books (Toronto, Ontario, Canada), 2008.

PICTURE BOOKS

One Some Many, illustrated by husband, Tom Slaughter, Tundra Books (Toronto, Ontario, Canada), 2004.

Over Under, illustrated by Tom Slaughter, Tundra Books (Toronto, Ontario, Canada), 2005.

ABC x 3: English, Español, Français, illustrated by Tom Slaughter, Tundra Books (Toronto, Ontario, Canada), 2005.

Eats, illustrated by Tom Slaughter, Tundra Books (Toronto, Ontario, Canada), 2007.

Same Same, illustrated by Tom Slaughter, Tundra Books (Toronto, Ontario, Canada), 2009.

Jocelyn achieves a folk-art style in her collage art for the self-illustrated picture book Hannah and the Seven Dresses. (Dutton Children's Books, 1999. Reproduced by permission of the illustrator.)

YOUNG-ADULT NOVELS

Earthly Astonishments, Dutton (New York, NY), 2000.

Mable Riley: A Reliable Record of Humdrum, Peril, and Romance, Candlewick Press (Cambridge, MA), 2004.

How It Happened in Peach Hill, Wendy Lamb Books (New York, NY), 2005.

Would You, Wendy Lamb Books (New York, NY), 2007.

OTHER

A Home for Foundlings (nonfiction), Tundra Books (Toronto, Ontario, Canada), 2005.

(Editor) *Secrets* (short stories), Tundra Books (Toronto, Ontario, Canada), 2005.

(Editor) *First Times* (short stories), Tundra Books (Toronto, Ontario, Canada), 2007.

(Illustrator) Beth Gleick, *Time Is When,* Tundra Books (Toronto, Ontario, Canada), 2008.

Contributor of short stories to anthologies, including *On Her Way: Stories and Poems about Growing up Girl.*

Sidelights

Marthe Jocelyn, a Canadian-born author of picture books, short stories, and novels for young adults, has written such award-winning works as *Mable Riley: A Reliable Record of Humdrum, Peril, and Romance* and *How It Happened in Peach Hill.* Discussing her fictional pursuits in an essay on the Random House Web site, Jocelyn remarked that "exploring alternate realities began as a game in childhood and eventually became a consuming pastime, otherwise known as research. I *love* doing research. I depend on what I learn not only for flavor and accuracy of details, but also for the occasional serendipitous discovery that alters the plot of a story."

Jocelyn came to writing relatively late in life, after working at a variety of other occupations. Raised in Toronto, Ontario, Canada, and spending summers in nearby Stratford, where her family has roots stretching back several generations, Jocelyn left Canada in tenth grade to attend boarding school in Great Britain. She has since lived in many different places and sampled many different jobs, even selling cookies, before settling down in New York City and opening her own company designing children's toys and clothing. While raising her two daughters, and reading children's books to them, Jocelyn was inspired to try her hand at adding "children's book author and illustrator" to her resume.

Jocelyn's chapter book *The Invisible Day* centers on ten-year-old Billie, a girl who is frustrated by the lack of privacy in the tiny loft apartment she shares with her mother, a librarian at Billie's school. When Billie discovers a jar of powder that makes her invisible, she finally gets to experience life out of her mother's sight. Calling *The Invisible Day* "a fun book," Mary Thomas added in the *Canadian Review of Materials* that Jocelyn's tale boasts "a strong female protagonist and an interesting, without being harrowing, storyline." A *Publishers Weekly* critic also praised the book, predicting that Jocelyn's "whimsical, high-spirited novel" will be "a sure-fire crowd-pleaser."

Jocelyn followed her first book with two related ones, *The Invisible Harry,* in which Billie uses the invisibility powder to try to adopt a puppy without her mother finding out, and *The Invisible Enemy,* about what happens when a mean classmate steals some of Billie's powder out of her backpack. As Jocelyn explained, *The Invisible Harry* was inspired by her younger daughter, Nell, who begged to be allowed to have a pet even though Jocelyn declared it unfair to coop a dog up in their small New York apartment. In fact, Jocelyn has never had a pet dog, so she researched the work by observing dogs in her neighborhood.

Mable Riley was inspired by a diary kept by Jocelyn's grandmother, Mable Rose. The author discovered the diary while poking around in the attic of a house her family has owned in Stratford for over a century. Most of the journal was filled with dry recollections, but "hidden on the back pages were a few lines of dreadful romantic poetry," Jocelyn noted on *Kidsreads.com.* "Just enough to reveal a character to me, a yearning and curious girl, at odds with the docility expected of her. That's when Mable Riley was born."

Like the real-life Mable Rose, the fictional Mable Riley records her experiences as a teacher in a turn-of-the-twentieth-century one-room school near Stratford, where she sometimes entertains herself by writing about love. Along the way, Mable Riley also gets caught up in the budding suffragist and labor movements through her eccentric, feminist neighbor, Mrs. Rattle. Although Jocelyn's book clearly has a message, it "is never strident," commented *Booklist* contributor Hazel Rochman, "because the funny, poignant diary entries show family and neighbors without reverence." *Horn Book* contributor Anita L. Burkam wrote of the novel that "social issues are given a realistic shades-of-gray treatment, the diary format is handled adroitly, and the diarist herself is engaging and many-faceted." *Mable Riley* received the first annual TD Canadian Children's Literature Award for the most distinguished book of the year.

The nonfiction *A Home for Foundlings* also has roots in Jocelyn's ancestors' experiences; in this case, those of her grandfather. As a child he lived in London's Foundling Hospital, a place where women who became pregnant and could not afford to support their babies abandoned them. However, the hospital had limited resources, and many of the "rescued" foundlings still perished. Jocelyn records the appalling conditions of the foundling home through brief biographies of several actual residents, as well as through her archival finds, such as photographs and official documents. Including detailed information helps "create drama in this history," Rochman commented, while Lori Walker concluded in *Canadian Review of Materials* that *A Home*

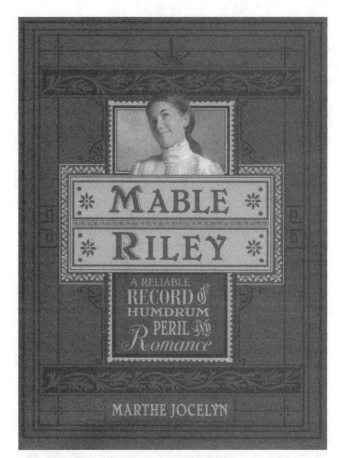

Cover of Jocelyn's middle-grade novel Mable Riley, *featuring artwork by Michael Koelsch.* (Candlewick Press 2004. Text copyright © 2004 Marthe Jocelyn. Jacket illustration copyright © 2004 Michael Koelsch. Reproduced by permission of the publisher Candlewick Press, Inc., Somerville, MA.)

for Foundlings "provides a rich opportunity to explore poverty and the plight of children throughout the ages and the continents."

Jocelyn is also the author of several self-illustrated picture books for young listeners, including *Hannah and the Seven Dresses* and *Mayfly,* that are illustrated with unique mixed-media collages. For *Hannah and the Seven Dresses,* about a little girl who cannot decide what to wear on her birthday, Jocelyn created not only dresses but entire rooms out of scraps of fabric. "Wallpaper, carpets, accouterments, and Hannah herself all have an eye-popping three-dimensional quality," Ilene Cooper noted in *Booklist. Mayfly,* a simple story about children spending time at their family's summer cabin, features spreads that *Resource Links* reviewer Carolyn Cutt called "whimsical . . . bright, colorful and imaginative." *School Library Journal* contributor Shelley B. Sutherland further commented that the author's "interesting multidimensional collages . . . capture the exuberance of the narrative."

Jocelyn has collaborated with her husband, artist Tom Slaughter, on a number of works for young readers. In *ABC x 3: English, Español, Français,* the duo offers an alphabet book in which each term is presented in three languages. Writing in *Booklist,* Jennifer Mattson observed that "this introduction to basic cognates may help children build confidence before undertaking further study," and *School Library Journal* critic Mary Hazelton described the work as "a stimulating and interesting approach to learning about languages." Slaughter's cut-paper illustrations can also be found in *Eats,* which describes the feeding habits of such animals as giraffes, anteaters, and pandas. In *School Library Journal,* Nancy Menaldi-Scanlan called Jocelyn's story here "a good choice from both an artistic and scientific point of view."

Set in New York during the 1920s, *How It Happened in Peach Hill,* a young-adult novel, centers on fifteen-year-old Annie and her mother, Madame Caterina, a self-proclaimed clairvoyant. The pair travels from town to town, with Annie pretending to be a dim-witted fool in order to gather the information about local residents that her mother will use in her act. When they arrive in Peach Hill, however, Annie decides to end the charade, which upsets her scheming, narcissistic parent. According to *Booklist* critic Heather Booth, Jocelyn's "blend of coming-of-age, adventure, and intrigue . . . will appeal to fans of spunky female characters," and a *Publishers Weekly* reviewer observed that "the story will engage young readers as they root for Annie to break free and become her own person." In *Resource Links,* Claire Hazzard wrote that *How It Happened in Peach Hill* "is well researched, and Jocelyn has an excellent eye for period details."

Would You is based on a tragic incident from the author's own life in which her sister was severely injured in an automobile accident. The work focuses on the relationship between Natalie, a high school student, and her older sister, Claire, a relationship that is dramatically altered when Claire is hit by a car and suffers massive brain trauma. "Natalie reacts honestly, neither beautifully nor nobly," wrote a contributor in *Publishers Weekly,* and a *Kirkus Reviews* critic described Jocelyn's novel as "a realistic and very credible account of how one family's life is inexplicably and unexpectedly shattered." "Readers will fly through the pages of this book, crying, laughing, and crying some more," stated Heather E. Miller in a *School Library Journal* review of *Would You.*

Biographical and Critical Sources

PERIODICALS

Booklinks, March, 2005, Gwenyth Swain, review of *Mable Riley: A Reliable Record of Humdrum, Peril, and Romance,* p. 16.

Booklist, January 1, 1998, Hazel Rochman, review of *The Invisible Day,* p. 813; November 15, 1998, Ilene Cooper, review of *The Invisible Harry,* p. 590; July, 1999, Ilene Cooper, review of *Hannah and the Seven Dresses,* p. 1951; September 15, 2000, Denise Wilms, review of *Hannah's Collections,* p. 236; June 1, 2002, Gillian Engberg, review of *The Invisible Enemy,* p. 1723; December 1, 2002, Ilene Cooper, review of *A Day with Nellie,* p. 675; March 1, 2004, Hazel Rochman, review of *Mable Riley,* p. 1201; April 1, 2004, Carolyn Phelan, review of *One Some Many,* p. 1366; August, 2004, Carolyn Phelan, review of *Mayfly,* p. 1943; March 1, 2005, Hazel Rochman, review of *A Home for Foundlings,* p. 1151; December 15, 2005, Jennifer Mattson, review of *ABC x 3: English, Español, Français,* p. 48; January 1, 2007, Heather Booth, review of *How It Happened in Peach Hill,* p. 104; July 1, 2008, Ilene Cooper, review of *Would You,* p. 65.

Canadian Review of Materials, March 27, 1998, Mary Thomas, review of *The Invisible Day;* March 3, 2000, Jo-Anne Mary Benson, review of *The Invisible Day;* February 4, 2005, Lori Walker, review of *A Home for Foundlings.*

Horn Book, May-June, 2004, Anita L. Burkam, review of *Mable Riley,* p. 329; March-April, 2007, Betty Carter, review of *How It Happened in Peach Hill,* p. 194; July-August, 2008, Christine M. Heppermann, review of *Would You,* p. 449.

Kirkus Reviews, September 15, 2002, review of *A Day with Nellie,* p. 1392; February 15, 2004, review of *Mable Riley,* p. 180; June 15, 2004, review of *One Some Many,* p. 578; March 1, 2005, review of *Over Under,* p. 288; August 15, 2007, review of *Eats;* June 1, 2008, review of *Would You.*

Kliatt, March, 2007, Claire Rosser, review of *How It Happened in Peach Hill,* p. 15; May, 2007, Stephanie Squicciarini, review of *Mable Riley,* p. 25; July, 2008, Claire Rosser, review of *Would You,* p. 16.

Publishers Weekly, October 27, 1997, review of *The Invisible Day,* p. 76; June 21, 1999, review of *Hannah and the Seven Dresses,* p. 66; February 28, 2000, review of *Earthly Astonishments,* p. 80; February 23, 2004, review of *Mable Riley,* p. 77; March 19, 2007, review of *How It Happened in Peach Hill,* p. 64; June 2, 2008, review of *Would You,* p. 47.

Resource Links, June, 1998, review of *The Invisible Day,* p. 7; February, 1999, review of *The Invisible Harry,* p. 9; October, 1999, review of *Hannah and the Seven Dresses,* p. 4; October, 2000, review of *Hannah's Collections,* pp. 2-3; April, 2002, Joanne de Groof, review of *The Invisible Enemy,* p. 23; April, 2004, Carolyn Cutt, review of *Mayfly,* p. 4; April, 2005, Gail de Vos, review of *Over Under,* p. 4; October, 2005, Kathyrn McNaughton, review of *ABC x 3,* p. 4; December, 2005, Rachel Steen, review of *Secrets,* p. 13; February, 2007, Claire Hazzard, review of *How It Happened in Peach Hill,* p. 37; October, 2007, Linda Berezowski, review of *Eats,* p. 5; December, 2007, Myra Junyk, review of *First Times,* p. 39; April, 2008, Susan Miller, reviews of *Ready for Spring, Ready for Summer, Ready for Autumn,* and *Ready for Winter,* p. 3.

School Library Journal, April, 2000, Carrie Schadle, review of *Earthly Astonishments,* p. 138; October, 2000, Meghan R. Malone, review of *Hannah's Collections,* p. 128; May, 2002, Alison Grant, review of *The Invisible Enemy,* p. 154; January, 2003, Be Astengo, review of *A Day with Nellie,* p. 97; March, 2004, Kimberly Monaghan, review of *Mable Riley,* p. 213; May, 2004, Shelley B. Sutherland, review of *Mayfly,* p. 116; June, 2004, Rachel G. Payne, review of *One Some*

Many, p. 128; October, 2005, Mary Hazelton, review of *ABC x 3*, p. 116; February, 2006, Alison Grant, review of *Secrets*, p. 132; April, 2007, Kim Dare, review of *How It Happened in Peach Hill*, p. 138; November, 2007, Robyn Zaneski, review of *First Times*, p. 126; December, 2007, Nancy Menaldi-Scanlan, review of *Eats*, p. 92; July, 2008, Amelia Jenkins, reviews of *Ready for Spring, Ready for Summer, Ready for Autumn,* and *Ready for Winter*, p. 76, and Heather E. Miller, review of *Would You*, p. 100.

Teaching Children Mathematics, March, 2000, Betsy J. Liebmann, review of *Hannah and the Seven Dresses*, p. 470.

Voice of Youth Advocates, June, 2005, review of *A Home for Foundlings*, p. 159.

ONLINE

Kidsreads.com, http://www.kidsreads.com/ (March 1, 2009), "Marthe Jocelyn."

Marthe Jocelyn Home Page, http://www.marthejocelyn.com (March 1, 2009).

Random House Web site, http://www.randomhouse.com/ (March 1, 2009), "Marthe Jocelyn."

Tundra Books Web site, http://www.tundrabooks.com/ (March 1, 2009), "Marthe Jocelyn."

*   *   *

JOSEPHSON, Judith Pinkerton 1943-

Personal

Born 1943; children: two daughters. *Hobbies and other interests:* Playing the violin, singing, reading, cooking, swimming, biking, walking, sewing, knitting.

Addresses

Home—CA.

Career

Writer.

Writings

The Monarch Butterfly, Crestwood House (Mankato, MN), 1988.

The Loon, Crestwood House (Mankato, MN), 1988.

(With Pat Dorff and Edith Fine) *File—Don't Pile!: For People Who Write: Handling the Paper Flow in the Workplace or Home Office,* St. Martins (New York, NY), 1994.

Umbrellas, Carolrhoda (Minneapolis, MN), 1998.

(With Edith Fine) *Nitty-Gritty Grammar: A Not-So-Serious Guide to Clear Communication,* Ten Speed Press (Berkley, CA), 1998.

(With Edith Fine) *More Nitty-Gritty Grammar: Another Not-So-Serious Guide to Clear Communication,* Ten Speed Press (Berkley, CA), 2001.

Growing up in World War II, 1941-1945, Lerner (Minneapolis, MN), 2003.

Growing up in Pioneer America, 1800-1890, Lerner (Minneapolis, MN), 2003.

Growing up in a New Century, 1890-1914, Lerner (Minneapolis, MN), 2003.

(With Edith Hope Fine) *Armando and the Blue Tarp School,* illustrated by Hernan Sosa, Lee & Low Books (New York, NY), 2007.

BIOGRAPHIES; FOR CHILDREN

Allan Pinkerton: The Original Private Eye, Lerner (Minneapolis, MN), 1996.

Jesse Owens, Track and Field Legend, Enslow (Springfield, NJ), 1997.

Mother Jones: Fierce Fighter for Workers' Rights, Lerner (Minneapolis, MN), 1997.

Nikki Giovanni: Poet of the People, Enslow (Berkeley Heights, NJ), 2000.

Walt Disney, Genius of Entertainment, Enslow (Berkeley Heights, NJ), 2006.

Bold Composer: A Story about Ludwig van Beethoven, illustrated by Barbara Kiwak, Millbrook Press (Minneapolis, MN), 2007.

Louis Armstrong, Lerner (Minneapolis, MN), 2008.

Nelson Mandela, Lerner (Minneapolis, MN), 2009.

Sidelights

Judith Pinkerton Josephson has taught middle school, elementary, and pre-school, as well as leading adult writing seminars. Her lifelong habit of writing has also led her to produce a number of books for young readers, including biographies revolving around men and women who stood up to adversity. In *Jesse Owens, Track and Field Legend,* she profiles the first American to win four gold medals in the 1936 Berlin Olympics, while in *Mother Jones: Fierce Fighter for Workers' Rights* she profiles a labor organizer who fought for workers' rights at the turn of the twentieth century. Hazel Rochman, writing in *Booklist,* wrote of *Mother Jones* that "readers will be caught by the fierce personality of this brave woman." Reviewing another Josephson biography, *Allan Pinkerton: The Original Private Eye,* Susan Dove Lempke noted in *Booklist* that the author "has unearthed much interesting information."

Josephson has contributed several books to the "Our America" series, which chronicles life and childhood from the years 1800 through 1945. Of *Growing up in a New Century: 1890-1914,* Elaine Weischedel wrote in *School Library Journal* that "Josephson gives an informative account of life in city tenements and child labor as well as other topics."

Primarily an author of nonfiction, Josephson has also dabbled in fiction, cowriting *Armando and the Blue Tarp School* with Edith Hope Fine. The book follows the story of a Mexican boy who scours the local dump for items of value and also struggles to obtain an education. A *Kirkus Reviews* critic wrote of the picture book that "the simplicity of the story is what lets it run deep" and effectively reflect a "bite of realism."

Judith Pinkerton Josephson teams up with fellow writer Edith Hope Fine for Armando and the Blue Tarp School, *featuring artwork by Hernan Sosa.* (llustration copyright © 2007 by Hernan Sosa. All rights reserved. Reproduced by permission of Lee & Low Books, Inc.)

Biographical and Critical Sources

PERIODICALS

Booklist, October 15, 1996, Susan Dove Lempke, review of *Allan Pinkerton: The Original Private Eye,* p. 417; February 1, 1997, Hazel Rochman, review of *Mother Jones: Fierce Fighter for Workers' Rights,* p. 931; February 1, 2003, Ilene Cooper, review of *Growing up in a New Century: 1890-1914,* p. 992.

Kirkus Reviews, September 15, 2007, review of *Armando and the Blue Tarp School.*

School Library Journal, October, 1996, Pat Katka, review of *Allan Pinkerton,* p. 156; April, 1997, Ruth K. Mac-

Donald, review of *Mother Jones,* p. 150; January, 1998, Todd Morning, review of *Jesse Owens, Track and Field Legend,* p. 125; February, 2003, Marion F. Gallivan, review of *Growing up in Pioneer America: 1800-1890,* p. 157; July, 2003, Elaine Fort Weischedel, review of *Growing up in a New Century,* p. 142.

Voice of Youth Advocates, August, 2003, review of *Growing up in Pioneer America,* p. 188.

ONLINE

Judith Pinkerton Josephson Home Page, http://www. judithjosephson.com (March 11, 2009).*

K

KANER, Etta 1947-

Personal

Born October 17, 1947; daughter of Meilech (a furrier) and Sally (a homemaker) Kaner; married David Nitkin (an ethicist), 1970; children: two daughters. *Education:* University of Toronto, B.A. (honors); University of Wisconsin, M.A. *Hobbies and other interests:* Gardening, reading, dancing.

Addresses

Home—Toronto, Ontario, Canada.

Career

Writer and educator. Elementary school teacher in Mississauga, Ontario, Canada, 1972—; teacher of gifted children and those with learning disabilities. Presents workshops based on her books to school and library groups.

Awards, Honors

Science in Society Award, Canadian Science Writers' Association, *Scientific American* Young Readers Book Award, and Silver Birch Award, Ontario Library Association (OLA), both 1994, for *Bridges;* Silver Birch Award, 1995, for *Towers and Tunnels;* Our Choice selection, Canadian Children's Book Centre (CCBC), 1999, and Silver Birch Award, OLA, 2000, both for *Animal Defenses;* Our Choice selection, CCBC, Henry Bergh Children's Book Award, American Society for the Prevention of Cruelty to Animals, both 2002, and Outstanding Children's Book Award, Animal Behavior Society, 2003, all for *Animal Talk;* Outstanding Children's Book Award, Animal Behavior Society, 2005, for *Animal Groups;* Louis J. Battan Author's Award, 2007, for *Who Likes the Wind?*

Writings

Balloon Science, illustrated by Louise Phillips, Addison-Wesley (Reading, MA), 1989.

Etta Kaner (Reproduced by permission.)

I Am Not Jenny, Groundwood Press (Toronto, Ontario, Canada), 1991.

Sound Science, illustrated by Louise Phillips, Addison-Wesley (Reading, MA), 1991.

Bridges, illustrated by Pat Cupples, Kids Can Press (Toronto, Ontario, Canada), 1994.

Towers and Tunnels, illustrated by Pat Cupples, Kids Can Press (Toronto, Ontario, Canada), 1995.

Animal Defenses: How Animals Protect Themselves, illustrated by Pat Stephens, Kids Can Press (Toronto, Ontario, Canada), 1999, revised edition published as *How Animals Defend Themselves,* 2006.

Animals at Work: How Animals Build, Dig, Fish, and Trap, illustrated by Pat Stephens, Kids Can Press (Toronto, Ontario, Canada), 2001.

Animal Talk: How Animals Communicate through Sight, Sound, and Smell, illustrated by Pat Stephens, Kids Can Press (Toronto, Ontario, Canada), 2002.

Animal Groups: How Animals Live Together, illustrated by Pat Stephens, Kids Can Press (Toronto, Ontario, Canada), 2004.

Word Catchers! for Reading and Spelling, LinguiSystems (East Moline, IL), 2004.

More Word Catchers! for Reading and Spelling, LinguiSystems (East Moline, IL), 2004.

Animals Migrating: How, When, Where, and Why Animals Migrate, illustrated by Pat Stephens, Kids Can Press (Toronto, Ontario, Canada), 2005.

Have You Ever Seen a Duck in a Raincoat?, illustrated by Jeff Szuc, Kids Can Press (Toronto, Ontario, Canada), 2009.

Contributor of book reviews to *Quill & Quire.*

"EXPLORING THE ELEMENTS" SERIES

Who Likes the Wind?, illustrated by Marie Lafrance, Kids Can Press (Toronto, Ontario, Canada), 2006.

Who Likes the Snow?, illustrated by Marie Lafrance, Kids Can Press (Toronto, Ontario, Canada), 2006.

Who Likes the Sun?, illustrated by Marie Lafrance, Kids Can Press (Toronto, Ontario, Canada), 2007.

Who Likes the Rain?, illustrated by Marie Lafrance, Kids Can Press (Toronto, Ontario, Canada), 2007.

Sidelights

Canadian author Etta Kaner is an elementary school teacher with a knack for introducing young people to the role science plays in everyday life. Kaner's books, which include *Towers and Tunnels, Animal Groups: How Animals Live Together,* and *Who Likes the Wind?,* feature riddles, hands-on activities, easy-to-do experiments, and interesting facts with which readers can amaze and impress their teachers, parents, and friends. The recipient of the Henry Bergh Children's Book Award, among other honors, Kaner especially enjoys the investigative phase of writing. "Since most of my books are nonfiction and about topics that I know very little about, I need to do a lot of research," she remarked on her home page. "I love to talk to experts in various fields and love to find out about things I don't know."

Born in 1947, Kaner developed an early love for literature. "I guess that I've always enjoyed words in one form or another," she once told *SATA,* "whether it was listening to my father tell humorous stories about members of our family or participating in speech contests and plays in school or voraciously reading books from the local library." Among her favorite writers while growing up during the 1950s and early 1960s were C.S. Lewis, E.B. White, Hugh Lofting, and Laura Ingalls Wilder. Reading was one thing, but writing was something else, according to Kaner. "Although I often got A's on my stories in school, writing them was pure torture. I used to write stories with a lot of descriptive language . . . adjectives describing trees, water, mountains, and plants in different seasons. I always felt I had to find the perfect word to describe these various elements of nature and I went through agony trying to think of it. I finally took the advice of my grade-eight teacher and bought a thesaurus."

After high school, Kaner attended the University of Toronto and then moved to the United States briefly to earn a master's degree at the University of Wisconsin. "Once I graduated from university . . . my creative energies went into making planters, curtains, and wall hangings out of macramé, acting in community theaters in Toronto, and teaching," the author explained. "Being a teacher is very similar to being a writer. Teachers are generally creative, curious, good problem solvers, and enjoy learning and being with children. I think that's what writers of children's books are too."

It was only after her oldest daughter had started school and Kaner's days at home were more relaxed, with only her four year old to care for, that she was inspired to began writing again. "One day, my younger daughter and I were mucking about with balloons," she recalled. "We were painting faces on them and attaching paper springs for arms and legs. I wondered what else could be done with balloons, and since I didn't know much about them, I started to do some research. Part of that research was going to the library and part of it was go-

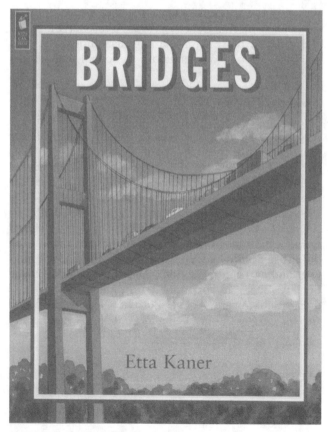

Cover of Kaner's book **Bridges,** *featuring cover art by Pat Cupples.* (Illustration copyright © 1994 by Pat Cupples. Reproduced by permission.)

ing on a fascinating but smelly tour of a balloon factory. (The smell came from the ammonia used in the manufacturing process.) I soon realized that I had enough material for a book, and that's how *Balloon Science* was born."

For a year, Kaner developed more than forty experiments using balloons, repeating each one many times to be sure it worked. She also interviewed people, composed the text, and then went back and edited her work. Another year would pass while *Balloon Science* was designed, illustrations were drawn, and it was printed. Finally, in 1989, Kaner became a published author.

Although Kaner has written some fiction, most of her books since *Balloon Science* have been nonfiction works that explore the world of science. Interviews are her favorite part of the writing process. "Sometimes I get strange but interesting information that I wasn't looking for," Kaner explained. "I once interviewed a train engineer about train whistles for my book *Sound Science.* He told me about the time he worked in northern Ontario. He said that when moose heard a train coming, they would run onto the track because they thought the train whistle was the love call of another moose. To avoid further accidents, train whistles were changed to a higher pitch."

Bridges came about when Kaner grew interested in all the different types of bridges in the world and wondered how different bridge designs came about. Soon her mind was filled with questions. Why do many bridges use arches? What makes a bridge strong enough to support cars, trucks, and people? Why do bridges come in so many different shapes? Answering these questions with the help of experts, and then organizing all she had learned into a book that children could understand took Kaner nearly twelve months. When *Bridges* was published in 1994, it earned its author critical recognition, including the Science in Society Award. Citing the book's "essentially technical but also interesting and easy-to-grasp style" in his review for *Quill & Quire,* Martin Dowding also poked fun at Kaner's inclusion of what he deemed "dreadfully droll jokes, no doubt included to take the sting out of 'too much science,' [but that] add to the fun." Brenda Partridge also had praise for *Bridges* in her *Canadian Materials* review, calling the work "very non-threatening" because its technical subject matter is balanced by colorful illustrations and Kaner's "easy-to-understand language."

Researching *Towers and Tunnels* allowed Kaner to learn more about famous places she knew of but had never before studied, including the Eiffel Tower of Paris, France; Toronto's C.N. Tower; and the Eurotunnel linking Great Britain and France under the English Channel. Each of these engineering feats was accomplished through the work of designers, engineers, workmen, and visionaries. Talking with engineers, Kaner was able to design experiments that allow her readers to better

Cover of Kaner's nonfiction picture book Animal Defenses, *featuring artwork by Pam Stephens.* (Illustration copyright © 1999 by Pat Stephens. Reproduced by permission.)

understand the building techniques used and the physical science in play in each construction project. Calling the book "highly informative, readable, and very brightly illustrated," *Quill & Quire* contributor Phyllis Simon praised *Towers and Tunnels* for the depth of its research and its discussion of how a skyscraper is made: from studying the earth on which it is to be built to designing the building to the materials used in its construction.

Researching her book *Animal Defenses: How Animals Protect Themselves* required Kaner to sift through dozens of books to learn how different animals—everything from porcupines to dolphins, butterflies to armadillos—safeguard themselves. "I found it fascinating that animals, unlike people, rarely fight to get out of a tight spot," Kaner explained to *SATA.* "They only fight if all the other ways they've tried to get rid of their enemy have failed." Kaner's book includes a section titled "Strange but True" in which she explains a number of eye-opening defenses animals have developed: "from playing tricks to pretending to be a snake or some other scary creature to using special protective gear. I was especially interested in the way animals form partnerships with other species to help each other out. I could hardly believe that a tiny fish like the Luther's goby could act as a guide to a blind shrimp while the shrimp could warn the goby of danger." Praised by critics for its organization and breadth of coverage, *Animal Defenses* presents information "in a particularly accessible way" according to *Booklist* contributor Carolyn Phelan.

Kaner has produced a number of other well-received works about animal behavior, including *Animals at Work: How Animals Build, Dig, Fish, and Trap*. This book explores the survival techniques, storage methods, and mating habits of such creatures as the honeybee, weaverbird, and otter. According to *School Library Journal* critic Cathie E. Bashaw, "Kaner piques readers' curiosity with catchy section headings and by asking questions." In *Animal Talk: How Animals Communicate through Sight, Sound, and Smell*, the author examines the ways animals use body language and signals, sound, and smell to send messages about territory and sources of food. *Booklist* contributor Hazel Rochman praised Kaner's "lively, informal text," and Catherine Threadgill, writing in *School Library Journal*, noted that the author "delivers interesting facts on an assortment of mammals, insects, fish, and birds."

Kaner looks at the social behavior of wild creatures in *Animal Groups*, which describes the ways animals play, protect their young, and groom each other, among other topics. *School Library Journal* reviewer Nancy Call observed that the book "will widen young browsers' understanding of the subject." The amazing journeys of army ants, Arctic terns, sea turtles, and a host of other creatures are the subject of *Animals Migrating: How, When, Where, and Why Animals Migrate*. Here Kaner's "style is engaging and personal," commented Rochman.

In her "Exploring the Elements" series for beginning readers, Kaner examines common weather conditions. In each of the four titles, including *Who Likes the Sun?* and *Who Likes the Snow?*, she employs a lift-the-flap format and offers succinct explanations of scientific concepts. In *Who Likes the Wind?*, for instance, a youngster wonders why her soap bubble bursts; the answer appears when the reader opens a gatefold page. Kaner's "Exploring the Elements" series earned solid reviews. *Who Likes the Snow?* "is packed with fascinating information," remarked Mary Hazelton in *School Library Journal*, and a *Kirkus Reviews* contributor described *Who Likes the Rain?* as "a winner with nature lovers, puddle jumpers, curious young scientists and teachers." Critiquing *Who Likes the Wind?*, Phelan called the work "a user-friendly introduction to the science behind everyday occurrences."

In addition to being a writer and a teacher, Kaner is devoted to her husband and two daughters, and the family's summers used to be spent at a country cottage, swimming, hiking, picking wild blueberries, and enjoying the Canadian wildlife. "I liked to take advantage of these trips to pick my family's brains for riddles for whatever book I happen to be working on," Kaner admitted. "To paraphrase a well-known expression, I find that four heads are better than one. Family trips also give me ideas for new books. I always enjoy meeting people and learning about new things, since I never know what might turn into a book!"

Biographical and Critical Sources

PERIODICALS

Booklist, April 15, 1999, Carolyn Phelan, review of *Animal Defenses: How Animals Protect Themselves,* p. 1533; April 15, 2002, Hazel Rochman, review of *Animal Talk: How Animals Communicate through Sight, Sound, and Smell,* p. 1397; April 15, 2005, Hazel Rochman, review of *Animals Migrating: How, When, Where, and Why Animals Migrate,* p. 1452; April 1, 2006, Carolyn Phelan, review of *Who Likes the Wind?,* p. 67; March 1, 2007, Carolyn Phelan, review of *Who Likes the Sun?,* p. 86; January 1, 2008, Carolyn Phelan, review of *Who Likes the Rain?,* p. 66.

Canadian Review of Materials, March, 1990, Eve Williams, review of *Balloon Science,* p. 70; September, 1994, Brenda Partridge, review of *Bridges,* pp. 136-137.

Horn Book, July-August, 2006, Betty Carter, review of *Who Likes the Wind?,* pp. 463.

Hungry Mind Review, summer, 1999, Ralph Blythe, review of *Animal Defenses,* p. 44.

Kirkus Reviews, September 1, 201, review of *Animals at Work: How Animals Build, Dig, Fish, and Trap,* p. 1293; March 15, 2005, review of *Animals Migrating,* p. 354; August 15, 2007, review of *Who Likes the Rain?*

Quill & Quire, May, 1994, Martin Dowding, review of *Bridges,* p. 36; May, 1995, Phyllis Simon, review of *Towers and Tunnels,* p. 50.

Resource Links, October, 2001, Shannon Danylko, review of *Animals at Work,* p. 25; April, 2002, Karen McKinnon, review of *Animal Talk,* p. 35; April, 2004, Karen MacKinnon, review of *Animal Groups: How Animals Live Together,* p. 30; June, 2005, Karen MacKinnon, review of *Animals Migrating,* p. 25; February, 2007, Karen McKinnon, review of *How Animals Defend Themselves,* p. 4, and Tanya Boudreau, review of *Who Likes the Snow?,* p. 23; June, 2007, Tanya Boudreau, review of *Who Likes the Sun?,* p. 21.

School Library Journal, June, 1992, Tina Smith Entwistle, review of *Sound Science,* p. 133; June, 1999, Arwen Marshall, review of *Animal Defenses,* p. 116; October, 2001, Cathie E. Bashaw, review of *Animals at Work,* p. 142; July, 2002, Catherine Threadgill, review of *Animal Talk,* p. 108; May, 2004, Nancy Call, review of *Animal Groups,* p. 133; September, 2005, Patricia Manning, review of *Animals Migrating,* p. 225; December, 2006, Mary Hazelton, review of *Who Likes the Snow?,* p. 124.

ONLINE

Kids Can Press Web site, http://www.kidscanpress.com/ (March 1, 2009), "Etta Kaner."*

KENNEDY, Anne 1955-
(Anne Vittur Kennedy)

Personal

Born July 25, 1955; daughter of Art Vittur; married; husband's name Jack.

Addresses

Home—Lewis Center, OH.

Career

Children's book author and illustrator. Formerly worked as a music teacher.

Writings

(As Anne Vittur Kennedy) *One Shining Star: A Christmas Counting Book,* Zondervan (Grand Rapids, MI), 2006.

ILLUSTRATOR

Michael J. Pellowski, *Copycat Dog,* Troll (Mahwah, NJ), 1986.

Michael J. Pellowski, *Maxwell Finds a Friend,* Troll (Mahwah, NJ), 1986.

Elspeth Campbell Murphy, *Where's My Lamb?,* Chariot Books (Elgin, IL), 1987.

Elspeth Campbell Murphy, *The Littlest One,* Chariot Books (Elgin, IL), 1987.

Elspeth Campbell Murphy, *Too Many Bunnies,* Chariot Books (Elgin, IL), 1987.

Elspeth Campbell Murphy, *Who Lost a Mitten?,* Chariot Books (Elgin, IL), 1987.

Laura Damon, *Funny Fingers, Funny Toes,* Troll (Mahwah, NJ), 1988.

Laura Damon, *Secret Valentine,* Troll (Mahwah, NJ), 1988.

Morgan Matthews, *What's It Like to Be a Farmer,* Troll (Mahwah, NJ), 1990.

Elspeth Campbell Murphy, *The Big Red Truck,* Chariot Books (Elgin, IL), 1990.

I'm a Little Teapot, and Other Movement Songs, Scholastic (New York, NY), 1994.

Jesse Cohen, designer, *My First Toolbox: A Handy Board Book Set,* Dutton (New York, NY), 1995.

Margo Lundell, *A Visit to the Doctor,* Western Publishing (Racine, WI), 1996.

Grace Maccarone, *The Silly Story of Goldie Locks and the Three Squares,* Scholastic (New York, NY), 1996.

Chris Angelilli, *The Christmas Snowman,* Golden Books (New York, NY), 1997.

(With others) Sandra Fisher, *365 Phonics Activities,* Publications International (Lincolnwood, IL), 1998.

JoAnne Hammer, *My Little Flap Book of Letters,* Ideal, 1998.

JoAnne Hammer, *My Little Flap Book of Colors,* Ideal, 1998.

Mary Manz Simon, *What Did Jesus Do? Stories about Honesty and Forgiveness,* Thomas Nelson (Nashville, TN), 1998.

Mary Manz Simon, *What Did Jesus Do? Stories about Obedience and Friendship,* Thomas Nelson (Nashville, TN), 1998.

Maria Birmingham, Karen E. Bledsoe, and Kelly Milner Halls, *365 Outdoor Activities,* Publications International (Lincolnwood, IL), 2000.

Kirsten Hall, *The Magical World of Ballet,* Scholastic (New York, NY), 2001.

Kirsten Hall, *The Magical World of Fairies,* Scholastic (New York, NY), 2001.

Justine Korman Fontes, *The Day the TV Broke,* Troll (Mahwah, NJ), 2002.

Matt Mitter, *The 100th Day of School!,* Reader's Digest (Pleasantville, NY), 2003.

Kirsten Hall, *Ballerina Girl,* Children's Press (New York, NY), 2003.

Matt Ringler, *One Little, Two Little, Three Little Apples,* Scholastic (New York, NY), 2005.

Eileen Spinelli, *Callie Cat, Ice Skater,* Albert Whitman (Morton Grove, IL), 2007.

Jane Clarke, *The Best of Both Nests,* Albert Whitman (Morton Grove, IL), 2007.

Ann Dixon, *When Posey Peeked at Christmas,* Albert Whitman (Morton Grove, IL), 2008.

Eileen Spinelli, *Peace Week in Miss Fox's Class,* Albert Whitman (Morton Grove, IL), 2009.

Sidelights

The grand-and great-grand daughter of artists known for their mural work in churches throughout the United States, Anne Kennedy continues her family's artistic tradition in a different way: she creates illustrations for a variety of children's picture books. Originally working as a music instructor, Kennedy changed her line of work in the early 1980s by providing the artwork for Michael J. Pellowski's picture book *Copycat Dog.* Since then, she has contributed pictures to numerous titles, including books by Eileen Spinelli, Ann Dixon, and Kirsten Hall.

One collaboration between Spinelli and Kennedy, *Callie Cat, Ice Skater* shares with young readers the joy a small feline feels whenever she takes to the ice. While her friends might prefer other activities, Callie would rather be in her backyard, gliding across a frozen pond. One day, her friends May and Liza learn of a local skating competition in which the winner earns a ride in a limousine, ice time at a local skating rink, and new clothes. When Callie learns about this upcoming challenge, she begins to focus all of her energy on winning the contest, encouraged by her friends and their new-found interest in the sport. In the end, although the graceful feline does not win the skating event, she does learn a valuable lesson: that personal fulfillment often means more than being the best.

Kennedy earned special attention from reviewers for her work in *Callie Cat, Ice Skater.* Writing in *Kirkus Reviews,* a critic noted that her artwork captures "the spins, the details and expressions of all types of animals." Describing *Callie Cat, Ice Skater* as "a rewarding picture book," *Booklist* contributor Carolyn Phelan added that Kennedy's illustrations not only complement the text's humor, but also "express Callie's deeper feelings." Recommending the work in particular for young girls, *School Library Journal* commentator Kristen Frey wrote that Kennedy's "charmingly personified animals and icy landscapes pair nicely with [Spinelli's] . . . warmhearted wintertime story line."

Biographical and Critical Sources

PERIODICALS

Booklist, October 15, 2007, Carolyn Phelan, review of *Callie Cat, Ice Skater,* p. 50.
Bulletin of the Center for Children's Books, December, 2007, Deborah Stevenson, review of *Callie Cat, Ice Skater,* p. 190.
Kirkus Reviews, September 15, 2007, review of *Callie Cat, Ice Skater.*
Lima News (Lima, OH), August 13, 2008, Bart Mills, "Bringing Art to the Masses: Generations of Vittur Family Continue to Be Artists."
School Library Journal, March, 2007, Jane Clarke, review of *The Best of Both Nests,* p. 156; December, 2007, Kristen Frey, review of *Callie Cat, Ice Skater,* p. 101.*

*   *   *

KENNEDY, Anne Vittur
See KENNEDY, Anne

*   *   *

KIRWAN, Wednesday

Personal

Female. *Education:* Kansas City Art Institute, B.F.A., 2002.

Addresses

Home—San Francisco, CA. *E-mail*—wkirwan@wednesdaykirwan.com.

Career

Author, illustrator, and fine artist. Elementary school art teacher; educator, Bay Area Discovery Museum, Sausalito, CA.

Wednesday Kirwan (Photograph courtesy of Wednesday Kirwan.)

Writings

SELF-ILLUSTRATED

Nobody Notices Minerva, Sterling (New York, NY), 2007.
Minerva the Monster, Sterling (New York, NY), 2008.

Sidelights

Wednesday Kirwan grew up in Duluth, Minnesota, the middle child of three. After earning a fine arts degree in painting and art history at Kansas City Art Institute, Kirwan made her way to California where she started working with children as an art educator. Taking inspiration from the preschoolers she taught, as well as from her own days spent as a mischievous child, she wrote and illustrated a story about a rascally yet lovable little Boston terrier named Minerva as a special Christmas gift for her always-patient father.

In *Nobody Notices Minerva* readers are introduced to Minerva, the middle child-dog in a busy family. In an effort to gain the attention of her distracted mother and father, Minerva begins behaving badly. She tears up wallpaper, plucks leaves from a houseplant, and even pokes her brother with a fork. Blessed with understanding parents, the plucky pup eventually learns from her father that positive actions earn greater rewards than negative ones. In *Minerva the Monster* the pup pretends to be a monster for the day, ignoring the responsibilities of cleaning up her crayons, helping mom with the mail, and raking the leaves. Again, Minerva's wise parents carefully guide their offspring into better behavior by pointing out all the fun activities that monsters cannot do. Minerva learns a lesson, although the story ends with a mischievous twist.

Calling _Nobody Notices Minerva_ a "wryly funny tale," a _Kirkus Reviews_ critic thought young children would likely appreciate how Kirwan uses "humor rather than laborious preaching to get a timely message across." Similarly, _Booklist_ reviewer Ilene Cooper predicted that "little ones will understand just where she's coming from." Referring to _Minerva the Monster,_ another _Kirkus Reviews_ contributor believed that "little ones will understand the many moods of Minerva," moods that are captured by Kirwan in the girl's "many expressive faces."

Biographical and Critical Sources

PERIODICALS

Booklist, October 15, 2007, Ilene Cooper, review of _Nobody Notices Minerva,_ p. 52.

Kirkus Reviews, August 15, 2007, review of _Nobody Notices Minerva;_ August 15, 2008, review of _Minerva the Monster._

ONLINE

Wednesday Kirwin Home Page, http://www.wednesday kirwan.com (January 25, 2009).

Kirwan's self-illustrated picture books include **Minerva the Monster,** _which follows the antics of a feisty Boston terrier._ (Illustration copyright © 2008 by Wednesday Kirwan. All rights reserved. Reproduced by permission of Sterling Publishing Co., Inc.)

KOJA, Stephan

Personal

Male.

Career

Writer and museum curator. Österreichische Galerie Belvedere, Vienna, Austria, curator.

Writings

Claude Monet, translated from the German by John Brownjohn, Prestel (New York, NY), 1996.

(With Katja Miksovsky) _Claude Monet: The Magician of Colour,_ translated from the German by Andrea P.A. Belloli, Prestel (New York, NY), 1997.

(Editor) _America: The New World in Nineteenth-Century Painting,_ translated from the German, Prestel (New York, NY), 1999.

(Editor) _Nordic Dawn: Modernism's Awakening in Finland, 1890-1920,_ translated by the German, Prestel (New York, NY), 2001.

(Editor) _Gustav Klimt: Landscapes,_ translated from the German by John Gabriel, Prestel (New York, NY), 2002.

(Editor) _Gustav Klimt: The Beethoven Frieze and the Controversy over the Freedom of Art,_ translated from the German, Prestel (New York, NY), 2006.

Gustav Klimt: A Painted Fairy Tale translated from the German, Prestel (New York, NY), 2007.

Author of other books published in German.

Biographical and Critical Sources

PERIODICALS

Booklist, November 1, 2005, Ray Olson, review of _Nordic Dawn: Modernism's Awakening in Finland, 1890-1920,_ p. 22.

Kirkus Reviews, August 1, 2007, review of _Gustav Klimt: The Beethoven Frieze and the Controversy over the Freedom of Art._

Library Journal, October 1, 1999, Jack Perry Brown, review of _America: The New World in Nineteenth-Century Painting,_ p. 84; June 15, 2007, Katherine C. Adams, review of _Gustav Klimt,_ p. 64.

New York Times Book Review, December 8, 2002, Christopher Benfey, review of _Gustav Klimt: Landscapes,_ p. 20.

School Library Journal, September, 2007, Carol Schene, review of _Gustav Klimt: A Painted Fairy Tale,_ p. 218.*

L

LACOMBE, Benjamin 1982-

Personal
Born 1982, in Paris, France. *Education:* Graduated from École Nationale Supérieure des Arts Décoratifs (EN-SAD), 2006.

Addresses
Home—Paris, France. *E-mail*—contact@benjamin lacombe.com.

Career
Author and illustrator. *Exhibitions:* Works included in international exhibitions in Paris, France; Tokyo, Japan; Rome, Italy; and New York, NY.

Writings

SELF-ILLUSTRATED

(Reteller) Charles Perrault, *Le petit chaperone rouge,* Seuil Jeunesse (Toulon, France), 2003.
Cerise griotte, Seuil Jeunesse (Paris, France), 2006, published as *Cherry and Olive,* Walker Books (New York, NY), 2007.
Longs cheveux, Talents Hauts (Paris, France), 2006.
Les amants papillons, Seuil Jeunesse (Paris, France), 2007.
(Coauthor with Sebastien Perez) *La funeste nuit d'Ernest,* Sarbacane (Paris, France), 2007.
(Coauthor with Sebastien Perez) *La petite sorciere,* Seuil Jeunesse (Paris, France), 2008.
(Coauthor with Sebastien Perez) *Le grimoire sorcieres,* Seuil Jeunesse (Paris, France), 2008.
La mélodie des Tuyaux, Seuil Jeunesse (Paris, France), 2009.

ILLUSTRATOR

Charles Perrault, *Le maître chât,* Hatier (Paris, France), 2006.

Mimi Barthelemy, *Pourquoi la carapace de la tortue?,* Seuil Jeunesse (Paris, France), 2006.
Sebastien Perez, *Destins de chiens,* Max Milo (Paris, France), 2007.
Cecile Roumiguere, *L'enfant silence,* Seuil Jeunesse (Paris, France), 2008.
Brenda Williams, *Lin Yi's Lantern: A Moon Festival Tale,* Barefoot Books (Cambridge, MA), 2009.
Edgar Allan Poe, *Les contes macabres,* Soleil/Métamorphose (Toulons, France), 2009.

Contributor of illustrations to *Raconte moi encore un conte,* Tourbillon, 2007.

OTHER

Blues Bayou, illustrated by Daniela Cytryn, Milan Jeunesse (Paris, France), 2009.
Le carnet rouge, illustrated by Agata Kawa, Seuil Jeunesse (Paris, France), 2009.

Sidelights
The author and illustrator of several books for children in his native France, Benjamin Lacombe reached English audiences with *Cherry and Olive,* a 2007 translation of his work about a solitary young girl. Originally published as *Cerise griotte, Cherry and Olive* follows the story of Cherry, a child who is teased by her classmates in the school playground. Consequently, the sensitive girl escapes into the world of books, although she really would enjoy the companionship of a friend. One day, such a friend appears in the form of a stray dog the girl names Olive. For a short time, the pair enjoy taking walks together, and Cherry even gains enough confidence to confront the children at school who have made unkind comments about Olive. Even though the pup's true owner eventually surfaces, he turns out to be a classmate of Cherry's. Angelo appreciates the care Cherry took of his dog, and his gratitude plants the seeds for a new friendship.

Several critics responded favorably to *Cherry and Olive,* suggesting that Lacombe's book might connect with those readers who are shy and lonely themselves. Writing in *School Library Journal,* Joan Kindig thought that *Cherry and Olive* would be useful in situations "where lonely children might need some help fitting in with others." A *Kirkus Reviews* contributor similarly predicted that Lacombe's story "may make heartening reading for sensitive children." The author's artwork also earned special attention, with *Booklist* critic Michael Cart noting that the French author/illustrator's "moody, highly stylized pictures . . . add emotional weight" to an engaging tale.

Biographical and Critical Sources

PERIODICALS

Booklist, November 1, 2007, Michael Cart, review of *Cherry and Olive,* p. 54.
Kirkus Reviews, October 15, 2007, review of *Cherry and Olive.*
School Library Journal, December, 2007, Joan Kindig, review of *Cherry and Olive,* p. 92.

ONLINE

Benjamin Lacombe Home Page, http://benjaminlacombe. com (January 30, 2009).
Benjamin Lacombe Web log, http://benjaminlacombe. hautefort.com (January 30, 2009).

*   *   *

LIN, Grace 1974-

Personal

Born May 17, 1974; daughter of Jer-shang (a doctor) and Lin-Lin Lin; married Robert Mercer (an architect; deceased 2007). *Education:* Rhode Island School of Design, B.F.A. (illustration), 1996.

Addresses

Home—Somerville, MA. *Office*—P.O. Box 401036, North Cambridge, MA 02140. *E-mail*—gracelin@ concentric.com.

Career

Freelance illustrator and author, beginning 1997. Formerly worked in a children's bookstore.

Member

Society of Children's Book Writers and Illustrators.

Grace Lin (Reproduced by permission.)

Writings

SELF-ILLUSTRATED PICTURE BOOKS

The Ugly Vegetables, Charlesbridge (Watertown, MA), 1999.
Dim Sum for Everyone!, Alfred A. Knopf (New York, NY), 2001.
Kite Flying, Alfred A. Knopf (New York, NY), 2002.
Okie-dokie, Artichokie!, Viking (New York, NY), 2003.
Olvina Flies, Henry Holt (New York, NY), 2003.
Robert's Snow, Penguin (New York, NY), 2004.
Jingle Bells, Little, Brown (New York, NY), 2004.
Fortune Cookie Fortunes, Alfred A. Knopf (New York, NY), 2004.
Deck the Halls, Little, Brown (New York, NY), 2004.
The Twelve Days of Christmas, Little, Brown (New York, NY), 2004.
Merry Christmas! Let's All Sing! (three board books; with sing-along CD), Little, Brown (New York, NY), 2005.
Our Seasons, Charlesbridge (Watertown, MA), 2006.
Olvina Swims, Henry Holt (New York, NY), 2007.
The Red Thread: An Adoption Fairy Tale, Albert Whitman (Morton Grove, IL), 2007.
Lissy's Friends, Viking (New York, NY), 2007.
Bringing in the New Year, Alfred A. Knopf (New York, NY), 2008.

JUVENILE NOVELS

The Year of the Dog (novel), Little, Brown (New York, NY), 2006.

The Year of the Rat (novel), Little, Brown (New York, NY) 2007.

Where the Mountains Meet the Moon, Little, Brown (New York, NY), 2009.

ILLUSTRATOR

Shelley Gill and Deborah Tobola, *The Big Buck Adventure,* Charlesbridge (Watertown, MA), 1999.

Roseanne Thong, *Round Is a Mooncake: A Book of Shapes,* Chronicle Books (San Francisco, CA), 2000.

Paul Yee, *The Jade Necklace,* Crocodile Books (New York, NY), 2001.

Roseanne Thong, *Red Is a Dragon: A Book of Colors,* Chonicle Books (San Francisco, CA), 2001.

Dana Meachen Rau, *My Favorite Foods,* Compass Point Books (Minneapolis, MN), 2001.

Frances Park and Ginger Park, *Where on Earth Is My Bagel?,* Lee & Low (New York, NY), 2001.

Cari Meister, *A New Roof,* Children's Press (New York, NY), 2002.

C.C. Cameron, *One for Me, One for You,* Roaring Brook Press (Brookfield, CT), 2003.

Kathy Tucker, *The Seven Chinese Sisters,* Albert Whitman (Morton Grove, IL), 2003.

Roseanne Thong, *One Is a Drummer,* Chronicle Books (San Francisco, CA), 2004.

Xiaohong Wang, *One Year in Beijing,* China Sprout, 2006.

Ranida McKneally, *Our Seasons,* Charlesbridge (Watertown, MA), 2006.

OTHER

(Compiler, with husband Robert Mercer) *Robert's Snowflakes: Artists' Snowflakes for Cancer Cure,* Viking (New York, NY), 2005.

Sidelights

Boston-based illustrator and author Grace Lin shares her Asian-American heritage in the colorful artwork she creates for both original picture-book stories such as *Robert's Snow, Bringing in the New Year,* and *The Red Thread: An Adoption Fairy Tale* and texts by other writers. In addition, she has written several novels that echo her picture-book themes, among them *The Year of the Dog, The Year of the Rat,* and *Where the Mountains Meet the Moon.*

Praising the illustrations in Lin's self-illustrated picture-book debut, *The Ugly Vegetables,* in which a young girl shares her first impressions of her family's Chinese vegetable garden, a *Horn Book* contributor praised the author/illustrator's "lively, color-saturated paintings." "With slightly distorted, flattened perspectives and rounded, comforting shapes," the critic added, "Lin's style borders on the naive with a fresh folklike quality."

Dim Sum for Everyone! follows three sisters and their parents as the family visits a Chinatown restaurant to enjoy the traditional meal in which diners feast on small portions from many dishes. In *Booklist* Carolyn Phelan dubbed the work a "simple, well-designed picture book." The family from *Dim Sum for Everyone!* returns in several more books by Lin, dining in another Chinese restaurant in *Fortune Cookie Fortunes,* engaging in a traditional sport in *Kite Flying,* and celebrate Chinese New Year in *Bringing in the New Year.* In *Kite Flying,* Ma-Ma makes the kite frame, Ba-Ba attaches the paper body, and the three sisters add eyes, whiskers, and paint to create the colorful dragon kite that ultimately takes to the air. Citing Lin's appropriately "spare" text in *Fortune Cookies Fortunes,* Julie Cummins wrote in *Booklist* that the book's "overall simplicity is effective and appealing." "Bright, lively colors and scenes presented from unusual perspectives are hallmarks of Lin's art," noted *Booklist* reviewer Ilene Cooper, the critic adding that the pen and watercolor artwork in *Fortune Cookie Fortunes* is "no exception."

The preparation of special dumplings, new haircuts for everyone, and other festivities that include happiness poems and a dragon puppet all combine in *Bringing in the New Year,* which *Booklist* critic Gillian Engberg wrote will "create a mood that will resonate strongly with many children." In *School Library Journal* Kirsten Cutler noted that Lin's "lustrous gouache illustrations are saturated with bold primary colors and deftly convey the joyousness" of the traditional Chinese celebration.

A young hen takes center stage in Lin's picture books *Olvina Flies* and *Olvina Swims.* Hawaii is too far away to reach on chicken-wing-power, the bird realizes in *Olvina Flies.* However, she wants to join her feathered friends at the island's bird conference, so Olvina boards an airplane and meets Halley, a penguin in a similar situation. *Olvina Swims* finds the two birds still on vacation in Hawaii, where the lure of the warm, sunny beaches prompts the timid Olvina to overcome her fear of the water. Lin's "reassuring story gets a madcap twist" from the author/illustrator's "jelly bean-colored" gouache paintings, noted Cooper of *Olvina Flies,* while a *Publishers Weekly* reviewer praised the author/illustrator's use of "comical details" and use of "boldly hued patterns" on walls, clothes, and picture borders. In *Olvina Swims* "Lin's straightforward story will reassure nervous young swimmers," according to *School Library Journal* Rachel G. Payne, and a *Kirkus Reviews* writer dubbed the book "a refreshing dive into a common anxiety with an uplifting message."

Animals also take center stage in *Robert's Snow,* a book that holds a special place in Lin's heart. Written while her husband, Robert Mercer, was undergoing treatment for cancer, *Robert's Snow* became a fund-raiser for Boston's Dana Farber Cancer Institute and inspired an auction featuring wooden snowflakes crafted by hundreds of artists and illustrators. Sadly, Lin's husband lost his fight with cancer in 2007. In Lin's picture book, readers meet a young mouse named Robert. Robert's mouse family makes its home in an old shoe, which the playful young mouse thinks is fine, whatever the weather. When the snows begin to fall, others in the shoe start to grumble, but Robert remains unconcerned until he plays outside too long during a storm and cannot find his way home. Noting that young children will share Robert's fear of becoming lost when his home is buried by snow, Cooper wrote that "Lin's bright water-colors combine sweetness and humor," while in *Publishers Weekly* a critic praised the book's "fetching, rotund mice," which "beam with familial closeness."

Other picture books by Lin include *The Red Thread* and *Lissy's Friends,* both which feature the author's brightly colored art. Described by *Booklist* critic Shelle Rosenfeld as a "heartfelt story-within-a-story about destiny, love, and what really makes a family," *The Red Thread* finds a young Asian girl listening to a story told by her adopted Caucasian parents. The story tells of a childless couple who, with the help of a wise peddler, discover the invisible thread that leads them across the seas to the baby destined to steal their hearts. In *Lissy's Friend* a new girl at school uses her skill with origami to make new friends. The "bright illustrations and vivid language" in *The Red Thread* "will likely appeal even to preschoolers," according to *School Library Journal* contributor Deborah Vose, and a *Kirkus Reviews* critic deemed the book "a splendid addition to the adoption [book] category." Young children "will find the artwork compelling and the story of making friends of interest," concluded Teresa Pfeifer in her *School Library Journal* review of *Lissy's Friends,* while in *Kirkus Reviews* a critic described the picture book as a "tender story" that shows how a child can deal with change and achieve "a successful and creative outcome."

In *The Year of the Dog* readers meet Pacy, a likeable Taiwanese-American girl who enjoys spending time with her new best friend while also deciding what to be when she grows up. While mulling over the life of a scientist, an actress, and an author, Pacy also busies herself with school activities and family life, introducing readers to both "authentic Taiwanese-American and universal childhood experiences," according to *Horn Book* critic Roxanne Hsu Feldman. Pacy returns in *The Year of the Rat,* as she anticipates a new year that, according to the Chinese horoscope, holds much promise. However, after her best friend moves away, Pacy becomes the only Asian student left in her school and she begins to feel like an outsider. Another challenge comes when her father shows little enthusiasm for her decision to become a writer when she grows up. According to Feldman, in *The Year of the Dog* Lin's "appealing, childlike" drawings "add a delightful flavor to a gentle tale full of humor," while *School Library Journal* critic Diane Eddington dubbed the book "a lighthearted coming-of-age novel with a cultural twist." "Lin deftly handles Pacy's dilemmas and internals struggles [in *The Year of the Rat*] with sensitivity and tenderness," Feld-

man also concluded, and Marilyn Taniguchi wrote in *School Library Journal* that the "heartwarming" novel "will leave readers hoping for more about this engaging heroine and her family." Comparing the "Pacy" series to beloved books by Carolyn Hayward and Maud Hart Lovelace, Cooper maintained that Lin mixes "the soul and the spirit" of girl-friendly stories with "charming ink drawings."

Lin once told *SATA:* "My most vivid memory of childhood is lying on the living room floor reading a book. I would sprawl next to my mother's banana plant (big plant!) and read. My mother would call throughout the house, 'Grace, where are you? Clean your room!' I would cozy up closer to the banana plant, which hid me from view, and continue reading.

"It's this love of books that has been a constant in my life. When I became old enough to think about the future, I wanted to be either an Olympic figure-skater or a book illustrator. When I realized that I fell down every time I tried to lift one foot off the ice, my direction became clear.

"Now I write and illustrate books that I wish I could have had when I was younger. As a child, I was hungry for books with an Asian-American character. I wanted the main character to be someone just like me. Back then, the few books with Asian characters were folktales, not something that fit into my contemporary life. It's much better now, but I don't forget the desire I had.

"I hope my books bring some joy into the world and, maybe, make someone smile and think: 'This book is about me.'"

Biographical and Critical Sources

PERIODICALS

Booklist, June 1, 2001, Carolyn Phelan, review of *Dim Sum for Everyone!,* p. 1880; February 1, 2003, Ilene Cooper, review of *Olvina Flies,* p. 1001; September 1, 2003, Diane Foote, review of *Okie-dokie, Artichokie!,* p. 135; February 15, 2004, Ilene Cooper, review of *Fortune Cookie Fortunes,* p. 1063; October 15, 2004, Ilene Cooper, review of *Robert's Snow,* p. 411; November 15, 2005, Ilene Cooper, review of *Robert's Snowflakes: Artists' Snowflakes for Cancer's Cure,* p. 50; January 1, 2006, Ilene Cooper, review of *The Year of the Dog,* p. 92; July 1, 2006, Jennifer Mattson, review of *Our Seasons,* p. 62; October 15, 2006, Linda Perkins, review of *One Year in Beijing,* p. 55; May 15, 2007, Gillian Engberg, review of *Lissy's Friends,* p. 52; October 15, 2007, Shelle Rosenfeld, review of *The Red Thread: An Adoption Fairy Tale,* p. 53; November 15, 2007, Ilene Cooper, review of *The Year of the Rat,* p. 45; December 15, 2007, Gillian Engberg, review of *Bringing in the New Year,* p. 48.

Horn Book, September, 1999, review of *The Ugly Vegetables,* p. 595; May-June, 2003, Susan Dove Lempke, review of *Olvina Flies,* p. 329; March-April, 2006, Roxanne H. Feldman, review of *The Year of the Dog,* p. 190; May-June, 2008, Roxanne Hsu Feldman, review of *The Year of the Rat,* p. 319.

Kirkus Reviews, June 15, 1999, p. 966; June 1, 2002, review of *Kite Flying,* p. 806; March 1, 2003, review of *Olvina Flies,* p. 390; September 1, 2003, review of *Okie-dokie, Artichokie!,* p. 1127; April 15, 2004, review of *Fortune Cookie Fortunes,* p. 397; November 1, 2004, review of *Robert's Snow,* p. 1052; December 15, 2005, review of *The Year of the Dog,* p. 1324; June 15, 2006, review of *Our Seasons,* p. 635; May 1, 2007, reviews of *Olvina Swims* and *Lissy's Friends;* August 15, 2007, review of *The Red Thread;* December 1, 2007, reviews of *The Year of the Rat* and *Bringing in the New Year.*

Publishers Weekly, July 5, 1999, p. 69; March 10, 2003, review of *Olvina Flies,* p. 71; October 6, 2003, review of *Okie-dokie, Artichokie!,* p. 83; September 27, 2004, Shannon Maughan, "Children's Artists Help Fund Cancer Research," p. 30; November 29, 2004, review of *Robert's Snow,* p. 39; January 2, 2006, review of *The Year of the Dog,* p. 62; September 10, 2007, review of *The Red Thread,* p. 59.

School Library Journal, July, 2001, Genevieve Ceraldi, review of *Dim Sum for Everyone!,* p. 84.; July, 2002, Marianne Saccardi, review of *Kite Flying,* p. 108; April, 2003, Marianne Saccardi, review of *Olvina Flies,* p. 132; June, 2004, Bina Williams, review of *Fortune Cookie Fortunes,* p. 114; November, 2005, Angela J. Reynolds, review of *Robert's Snowflakes,* p. 118; March, 2006, Diane Eddington, review of *The Year of the Dog,* p. 196; August, 2006, Jill Heritage Maza, review of *Our Seasons,* p. 106; March, 2007, Barbara Scotto, review of *One Year in Beijing,* p. 189; June, 2007, Rachel G. Payne, review of *Olvina Swims,* p. 112; July, 2007, Teresa Pfeifer, review of *Lissy's Friends,* p. 80; September, 2007, Deborah Vose, review of *The Red Thread,* p. 169; March, 2008, Marilyn Taniguchi, review of *The Year of the Rat,* and Kirsten Cutler, review of *Bringing in the New Year,* both p. 170.

ONLINE

Grace Lin Home Page, http://www.gracelin.com (February 2, 2009).

Grace Lin Web log, http://outergrace.blogspot.com (February 2, 2009).*

*   *   *

LIPSYTE, Robert 1938-

Personal

Born January 16, 1938, in New York, NY; son of Sidney I. (a principal) and Fanny (a teacher) Lipsyte; children: Sam, Susannah. *Education:* Columbia University, B.A., 1957, M.S., 1959.

Robert Lipsyte (Photograph by Neilson Barnard/Getty Images.)

Addresses

Home—New York, NY. *E-mail*—robert@robertlipsyte. com.

Career

Journalist and author. *New York Times,* New York, NY, copyboy, 1957-59, sports reporter, 1959-67, sports columnist, 1967-71, 1991-2002; *New York Post,* New York, NY, columnist, 1977; Columbia Broadcasting System, Inc. (CBS-TV), New York, NY, sports essayist for program *Sunday Morning,* 1982-86; National Broadcasting Company, Inc. (NBC-TV), New York, NY, correspondent, 1986-88; Public Broadcasting Service (PBS-TV), New York, NY, host of program *The Eleventh Hour,* 1989-90; Twin Cities Public Television (TPT-TV), Minneapolis, MN, host of program *Life (Part Two).* Has also worked as a journalism teacher and radio commentator. *Military service:* U.S. Army, 1961.

Awards, Honors

Dutton Best Sports Stories Award, E.P. Dutton, 1964, for "The Long Road to Broken Dreams," 1965, for "The Incredible Cassius," 1967, for "Where the Stars of Tomorrow Shine Tonight," 1971, for "Dempsey in the

Window," and 1976, for "Pride of the Tiger"; Mike Berger Award, Columbia University Graduate School of Journalism, 1966; Wel-Met Children's Book Award, Child Study Children's Book Committee at Bank Street College of Education, 1967, and American Library Association (ALA) Notable Book for Children 1940-70 includee, all for *The Contender; One Fat Summer* named a *New York Times* Outstanding Children's Book, and selected among ALA Best Young-Adult Books, both 1977; New Jersey Author citation, New Jersey Institute of Technology, 1978; Emmy Award for on-camera achievement, Academy of Television Arts and Sciences, 1990, for hosting *The Eleventh Hour;* Pulitzer Prize finalist for commentary, 1992; Meyer Berger Award for Distinguished Reporting, Columbia University, 1996; ALAN Award, Assembly on Literature for Adolescents/ NCTE, 1999; Margaret A. Edwards Award, ALA, 2001, for lifetime contribution to young adult literature.

Writings

FOR YOUNG ADULTS; FICTION

The Contender, Harper (New York, NY), 1967.
One Fat Summer, Harper (New York, NY), 1977.
Summer Rules, Harper (New York, NY), 1981.
Jock and Jill, Harper (New York, NY), 1982.
The Summerboy, Harper (New York, NY), 1982.
The Brave, Harper (New York, NY), 1991.
The Chemo Kid, Harper (New York, NY), 1992.
The Chief, Harper (New York, NY), 1993.
Warrior Angel, HarperCollins (New York, NY), 2003.
Raiders Night, HarperTempest (New York, NY), 2006.
Yellow Flag, HarperTempest (New York, NY), 2007.

NONFICTION; FOR CHILDREN

Assignment: Sports, Harper (New York, NY), 1970, revised edition, 1984.
Free to Be Muhammad Ali, Harper (New York, NY), 1978.
Arnold Schwarzenegger: American Hercules, Harper (New York, NY), 1993.
Jim Thorpe: Twentieth-Century Jock, Harper (New York, NY), 1993.
Michael Jordan: A Life above the Rim, HarperCollins (New York, NY), 1994.
Joe Louis: A Champ for All America, HarperCollins (New York, NY), 1994.
Heroes of Baseball: The Men Who Made It America's Favorite, Atheneum (New York, NY), 2005.

FICTION; FOR ADULTS

(With Steve Cady) *Something Going,* Dutton (New York, NY), 1973.
Liberty Two, Simon & Schuster (New York, NY), 1974.

SCREENPLAYS

Shining Star, United Artists, 1975.
The Act, 1982.

Scriptwriter for *Saturday Night with Howard Cosell.*

NONFICTION; FOR ADULTS

(With Dick Gregory) *Nigger,* Dutton (New York, NY), 1964.
The Masculine Mystique, illustrated by Tim Lewis, New American Library (New York, NY), 1966.
SportsWorld: An American Dreamland, Quadrangle (New York, NY), 1975.
(With Peter Levine) *Idols of the Game: A Sporting History of the Twentieth Century,* Turner Publications, 1995.
In the Country of Illness: Comfort and Advice for the Journey, Knopf (New York, NY), 1998.

Contributor to periodicals, including *TV Guide, Harper's, Nation, New York Times, New York Times Book*

Cover of Lipsyte's popular and hard-hitting novel **The Contender,** *featuring artwork by Ed Acuna.* (Jacket copyright © 1987 by Ed Acuna. Cover © 1987 by HarperCollins Publishers. Used by permission of HarperCollins Children's Books, a division of HarperCollins Publishers.)

Review, and *New York Times Sports Magazine.* Correspondent for TomDispatch.com and ESPN.com.

Lipsyte's works are housed in the De Grummond Collection, University of Southern Mississippi, and the Kerlan Collection, University of Minnesota.

Sidelights

Robert Lipsyte, a reporter and columnist who has covered sports for the *New York Times, USA Today,* and ESPN.com, is the author of such acclaimed young-adult novels as *The Contender, One Fat Summer,* and *Raiders Night.* "I've always had two writing lives, one as a journalist and one as a fiction writer," Lipsyte stated on his home page. "They've complemented each other. I love them both."

Lipsyte is part of what has since been recognized as a revolution in young-adult literature; his first novel, *The Contender,* maintains a place in the YA canon alongside S.E. Hinton's groundbreaking *The Outsiders* and Paul Zindel's *The Pigman.* Lipsyte transformed the sports novel from its action-oriented model with predictable plot and one-dimensional characters into "a realistic, coming-of-age story with sports serving as a metaphor for the real action in the novel: coping with life," according to Jack Forman in the *St. James Guide to Young-Adult Writers.* *The Contender* started a trend in sports books for younger readers in its focus on characters who experience a transformation through a combination of hard work and adherence to ethics. Lipsyte's efforts have not gone unrecognized; in 2001, he received the Margaret A. Edwards Award for his lifetime contribution to young adult literature.

Not surprisingly, the majority of Lipsyte's books involve aspects of athletics. Because of his experience as a sportswriter, he is considered an authority in the field of children's sports stories: A typical Lipsyte hero learns somewhere along the line that winning is not the only goal. This theme is announced early in *The Contender,* when Harlem high school dropout Albert Brooks wanders into a local gym and is challenged by the words of its owner, Donatelli: "Everyone wants to be a champion. That's not enough. You have to start by wanting to be a contender. It's the climbing that makes the man. Getting to the top is an extra reward."

Lipsyte's boxing series, begun in 1967 with *The Contender,* was extended with *The Brave* in 1991, *The Chief* in 1993, and *Warrior Angel* in 2003. He has also penned a three-book series of "breezily funny novels," according to Forman that feature the teenager Bobby Marks: *One Fat Summer, Summer Rules,* and *The Summerboy.* Additionally, Lipsyte has authored something of a romantic fantasy in *Jock and Jill* and a multi-layered novel about illness and ecology in *The Chemo Kid,* the latter a book that owes much to Lipsyte's own battles with cancer.

Cover of Lipsyte's young-adult novel Warrior Angel, *featuring a photograph by Chris Rogers.* (Photograph © 2003 by Chris Rogers. Cover copyright © 2004 by HarperCollins Publishers. Used by permission of HarperCollins Children's Books, a division of HarperCollins Publishers.)

Lipsyte has also created a number of sports biographies for younger readers, including works on Muhammad Ali, Jim Thorpe, Michael Jordan, and Joe Louis. For adults, he has written novels and several sports books, as well as penning *In the Country of Illness: Comfort and Advice for the Journey,* "a witty guide to the planet of pain which we must sometimes orbit or visit," as a *Kirkus Reviews* writer characterized the work. Beyond his writing and journalism career, Lipsyte has also been involved in television as a commentator and program host.

Lipsyte believes in providing realistic portraits of athletes who do not lead perfect lives solely because of their physical abilities, but must contend with ordinary problems in other areas of their lives. He also feels the importance of success in sports should be downplayed because many people—especially youngsters who have not had the time to develop skills in other areas—may be humiliated when they are unable to display athletic prowess. In an article for *Children's Literature in Edu-*

cation, Lipsyte commented: "Sports is, or should be, just one of the things people do—an integral part of life, but only one aspect of it. Sports is a good experience. It's fun. It ought to be inexpensive and accessible to everybody." He added, "In our society, sports is a negative experience for most boys and almost all girls. . . . They're required to define themselves on the basis of competitive physical ability." According to Lipsyte, many sports programs are not fair because individuals with only average ability are quickly weeded out of the system. In short, he contends that America's fixation on sports—what he terms "SportsWorld"—has created a nation of spectators rather than participants.

Apparently, no precedent of athletic participation existed in Lipsyte's family. Instead, intellectual pursuits were stressed due to the fact that both of his parents were teachers. Because the family's house contained many books, the young Lipsyte spent hours reading and decided early on to become a writer. He received an undergraduate degree in English from Columbia University in New York, and he planned to continue his education by attending graduate school. Yet, unpredictably, his career as a sports reporter began. In 1957, a few days after graduation from Columbia, he answered a classified ad for a copyboy at the *New York Times,* taking the job to help pay for graduate school. However, this job led to a sports-writing position with the paper, one that he held—with a short intermission for military service—until 1971.

Lipsyte began covering the boxing beat for the *New York Times* in 1964 and followed Muhammad Ali's career for more than three years. In his biography of the boxer titled *Free to Be Muhammad Ali,* the author categorizes Ali as "far and away the most interesting character in that mythical kingdom I call SportsWorld." Ali's outspokenness—manifested in snappy, original sayings—also offered the author plenty of material with which to write stories. In *Free to Be Muhammad Ali* Lipsyte recounts episodes from the fighter's life and supplies illustrations of his charismatic nature. Mel Watkins, writing in the *New York Times Book Review,* categorized the work as "a thoughtful, complex portrait of one of America's greatest athletes" and added that the reader derives a sense of Ali's personality and "the affection and respect the author feels for him as an athlete and as a man."

Lipsyte drew upon his experiences as a boxing writer to produce his first novel for young readers, *The Contender.* The protagonist, Alfred Brooks, is an orphaned seventeen-year-old boy living in Harlem. A recent high-school dropout, Alfred lives with his aunt and works as a stock boy in a grocery store. The work chronicles the metamorphosis of the aimless Alfred into a disciplined young man with long-term goals. He achieves this change by applying principles he learns while training to be a boxer. After months of training, Alfred enters the ring and wins several matches as an amateur. His trainer, Donatelli, sensing that Alfred does not have the killer instinct required to be a top boxer, advises him to quit fighting competitively. Alfred insists on fighting once more against a worthy opponent to see if he has the requisite courage to be a contender. Although ultimately losing the contest, Alfred discovers an inner resolve that will help him in everyday life.

The recipient of several awards, *The Contender* was also generally well received by critics. John S. Simmons, writing in *Elementary English,* noted that "Lipsyte has a done a masterful job of reconciling 'controversial' issues with the realities of censorship" in the sometimes violent novel. The critic praised the author's realistic approach, in which the protagonist's gains are "modest and his successes frequently tainted with fear, reproach, and self-deprecation." Susan O'Neal commented in *School Library Journal* that, "admirably, the author tries to portray Alfred's world through the boy's own eyes," and concluded that, as a sports story, *The Contender* "is a superior, engrossing, insider's book." Saul Bachner, reviewing Lipsyte's debut novel in the *Journal of Reading,* felt that for the classroom teacher, the novel "is invaluable. More than one Alfred Brooks sits in our classes."

In the fall of 1967, Lipsyte left the boxing beat to begin writing a general sports column for the *New York Times.* In his part-memoir, part-sports history, *SportsWorld* he remarked: "It was an exciting time to be writing a column, to be freed from the day-to-day responsibility for a single subject or the whims of the assignment desk." Despite the acclaim his columns received, Lipsyte left the *New York Times* in the fall of 1971. During the next few years he taught journalism at the college level, visited schools to talk about his books, wrote jokes for a television show called *Saturday Night with Howard Cosell,* and spent nine months at the *New York Post* writing a column about the people of that city.

By the late 1970s Lipsyte had returned to YA fiction with a trilogy consisting of *One Fat Summer, Summer Rules,* and *The Summerboy.* The author shares similarities with his trilogy's fictional protagonist, Bobby Marks, who also comes of age in the 1950s and conquers an adolescent weight problem. Each book is set in a resort town in upstate New York called Rumson Lake, where Bobby's family spends each summer. Lipsyte presents the maturation process of his protagonist from the age of fourteen to eighteen. In the trilogy, Bobby faces problems, but overcomes them by relying on determination, hard work, and positive values. Critics have endorsed the novels for tackling adolescent dilemmas in a realistic manner and for offering believable first-person narration.

In *One Fat Summer* fourteen-year-old Bobby jumps off the scales when the 200-pound mark rolls by. But one summer, he takes a job at the resort mowing lawns and loses enough weight to make him feel better about himself. Along the way he battles a snide employer and a gang of local hoodlums. Jane Abramson, writing in

School Library Journal, felt that Bobby's "self-deprecating delivery where every joke is at his own expense is awfully funny," while Stephen Krensky commented in the *New York Times Book Review* that "the dramatic movement of Bobby's metamorphosis is effectively rendered."

The writing of this trilogy was interrupted when Lipsyte was forced to battle his own problems: in the summer of 1978 he was diagnosed with cancer. Fortunately, treatment proved effective, and he returned to a normal routine, publishing *Summer Rules* in 1981 and the final book of the "Bobby Marks" trilogy, *The Summerboy,* in 1982. Bobby is sixteen in *Summer Rules* and working as a summer camp counselor at Rumson Lake. There is a budding romance and a matter of conscience for Bobby to deal with in this "sophisticated . . . provocative and perceptive" story, according to Zena Sutherland in *Bulletin of the Center for Children's Books.* Gail Tansill Lambert had high praise for the title in *Best Sellers:* "My enthusiasm for this book is boundless. Robert Lipsyte is the adolescent male's answer to Judy Blume. . . . He is a heavyweight in the field of children's literature. . . . *Summer Rules* leaves you feeling good about families, and about kids growing up."

In *The Summerboy* Bobby is eighteen and once again at the summer resort, this time working at a local laundry where co-workers dismiss him as a rich summer kid. He finally finds a place after he calls on his fellow workers to protest their unsafe working conditions and loses his job for his troubles. Norma Klein, reviewing *The Summerboy* in the *Nation,* noted that Lipsyte adds a fresh, urban, and Jewish perspective to the YA genre. Dubbing Bobby Marks a "wry, introspective" protagonist, Klein went on to conclude that "Lipsyte writes books that teen-agers who loved *Catcher in the Rye* and don't know where to turn next will appreciate."

In the early 1980s Lipsyte took a break from writing books and worked as a television correspondent. His return to writing was marked by 1991's *The Brave,* a sequel to *The Contender.* In *The Brave,* Sonny Bear, a seventeen-year-old, half-Native runaway, meets Alfred Brooks in New York City. Alfred is now a forty-year-old police sergeant who seeks to curtail drug trafficking in the city. Unwittingly becoming a pawn in the drug war, Sonny is rescued by Alfred, who also teaches him how to box. His boxing partner is Martin Witherspoon, a young African American with dreams of writing. Indeed it is Martin who is the putative author of *The Brave.* However, in the course of the action, Alfred is shot and paralyzed, and Sonny is stripped of his amateur status when it is revealed that he was paid for previous fights. A contributor to *Kirkus Reviews* called *The Brave* "a gritty tale of a young man who learns to replace his anger with pride," while a *Horn Book* reviewer noted that the "boxing sequences in this powerful story hammer at our senses until we, too, feel Sonny's pain and rage and his strength."

Lipsyte again successfully fought cancer in 1991, and he writes about the experience in *The Chemo Kid,* the story of a teen with cancer. Instead of a book that teaches young people to accept death, Lipsyte's novel is an uplifting and often humorous take on illness. Fred Bauer is treated for a rare form of cancer and recovers, only to be left with superhuman powers as a result of the experimental chemotherapy he has undergone. He deals out justice to drug dealers, polluters, and bullies alike. He removes the problem of steroid drug dealing among athletes and corrects the local toxic waste problem his girlfriend Mara has been battling. Sutherland noted Lipsyte's "resilient" writing style in his *Bulletin of the Center for Children's Books* review, and also commented on the "convincingly juvenile" nature of Fred, the "interesting" medical material, and "cheering" family support.

Lipsyte revisits Sonny Bear and Marty Witherspoon in *The Chief,* "an easy-to-read sports story about Sonny's bid for the heavyweight championship," according to Betsy Hearne in *Bulletin of the Center for Children's Books.* Sonny has not yet won any championships and is ekeing out a living on the professional boxing circuit. Acting as his publicist is Witherspoon, a fledgling novelist who cuts a great deal for him with Hollywood: the chance to be a Native-American actor. Just as fame and fortune are awaiting him in Hollywood, though, his reservation in New York is facing serious decisions about their gambling casino and he must decide whether to go to New York or Hollywood. "Lipsyte is a dynamic sports writer, with an ability to grip readers to the knockout," remarked Hearne. *Kirkus Reviews* dubbed the book "memorable sports fiction," with "pulse-pounding action scenes."

In *Warrior Angel,* a sequel to *The Chief,* Sonny Bear has become the youngest heavyweight champion ever, but he is dissatisfied with the achievement. His promoter is cheating him, he is surrounded by hangers-on, and Bear feels like his career has been a failure. Then he receives strange e-mail messages from someone calling himself Warrior Angel. The messages, which encourage him to continue fighting and claim that Warrior Angel has been sent by God to help him, are really from troubled teen Richard Starkey. who has delusions and lives in a group home. When the boy runs away from the home and travels to see his hero, Bear signs him on as assistant trainer. Richard helps Bear prepare for his next title fight in unexpected ways.

Michael McCullough, reviewing *Warrior Angel* for *School Library Journal,* maintained that Lipsyte "pulls no punches with the raw, real-life language." A critic for *Kirkus Reviews* praised Lipsyte's "muscular prose and vivid detail." Reviewing the book for *Kliatt,* Paula Rohrlick called it "a fierce, gripping tale," while *Horn Book* critic Peter D. Sieruta cited "the intriguely enigmatic lead characters and hard-edged prose."

In his controversial novel *Raiders Night,* Lipsyte examines the dangers of hazing and steroid use. The work

Cover of Lipsyte's provocative novel **Raider's Night,** *which focuses on the aftermath of a school hazing.* (Cover art © 2006 by Modern Dog Design Co. Reproduced by permission.)

concerns Matt Rydek, the popular co-captain of Nearmont High School's football team, a contender for the state title. With a college scholarship on the line, and feeling pressured by the win-at-all-costs attitude of his father, Matt begins taking injections of an illegal steroid from an unscrupulous gym owner. Then, during a preseason training camp, Matt witnesses his sadistic co-captain, Ramp, sexually assault a talented younger player who threatens to win Ramp's starting position. When his teammates and coaches attempt to cover up the incident, Matt must decide if he wants to risk everything he has worked for by revealing the truth. "Lipsyte's careful rendering of the world in which Matt moves gives his story an awful and terrifying ring of truth," observed a critic in *Publishers Weekly,* and Ed Sullivan, writing in *Booklist,* noted that teens "will feel Matt's pain as he struggles between turning his back on his team and listening to his conscience." According to *School Library Journal* contributor Diane P. Tuccillo, with *Raiders Night* Lipsyte "has added to his repertoire a remarkable, tough, important story exposing various negative elements that are far too common in today's world of sports."

After the publication of *Raiders Night,* Lipsyte noticed a disturbing trend while preparing for school visits. "I

have been invited to school by librarians and English teachers and then uninvited by the coaches, athletic directors, and principals," he told *ALAN Review* contributor Chris Goering. "It is not the language. It is not the sex and drugs. . . . It is seen as a negative look at jock culture that these guys are really invested in. That has been different and interesting to me."

The world of stock car racing is the setting for *Yellow Flag,* a work inspired by Lipsyte's years of covering NASCAR events. Seventeen-year-old Kyle Hildebrand, a skilled trumpet player who walked away from the sport years earlier, feels compelled to return to the racetrack after his brother, Kris, is injured in a crash. Once behind the wheel, Kyle rediscovers his love of racing and performs admirably, landing several important sponsors for his team. His success, however, threatens the future of his jazz quintet, which is poised to break into the limelight. "Lipsyte maintains a good level of tension, leaving it unclear throughout most of the book which road Kyle will choose," commented Jeffrey A. French in *School Library Journal.* Paula Rohrlick, writing in *Kliatt,* praised the book's action, remarking that "the race scenes are exhilarating, conveyed with great detail and an insider's knowledge."

In addition to novels, Lipsyte has also penned a number of biographies for young readers. In *Arnold Schwarzenegger: American Hercules* he paints a picture of the actor, strong man, and eventual politician, comparing Schwarzenegger to singer Elvis Presley and boxer Muhammad Ali. A *Kirkus Reviews* critic called this biography a "revealing, fluidly written picture of a charming, manipulative, driven man." More sports oriented is Lipsyte's *Jim Thorpe: Twentieth-Century Jock,* a biography of "perhaps the greatest all-round male athlete in American history," as Lipsyte styled this Native-American superstar. Michael Jordan also gets the Lipsyte treatment in a "spectacular biography," according to a *Kirkus* reviewer, as does African-American boxer Joe Louis. More sports profiles for readers of all ages are presented in *Idols of the Game: A Sporting History of the American Century,* which looks at sixteen athletes whose careers had a significant impact on twentieth-century U.S. culture. Gene Lyons in *Entertainment Weekly* called the book a "very lively and anecdotal . . . popular history." In *Heroes of Baseball: The Men Who Made It America's Favorite,* a collective biography, Lipsyte offers profiles of such baseball luminaries as Babe Ruth, Ty Cobb, Mickey Mantle, Jackie Robinson, and Ichiro Suzuki. He also examines the career of Curt Flood, whose challenge of the "reserve clause" helped further the economic rights of ballplayers. According to *School Library Journal* contributor Marilyn Taniguchi, "the author's own opinions are perhaps what make this book notable: his arguments are lively, readable, and well documented," and a *Publishers Weekly* reviewer described *Heroes of Baseball* as "engaging social history of 20th-century America, with bite-size sidebars about baseball cards, funny nicknames, wackiest mascots, Yogisms and a nifty timeline."

On the strength of his decades-long writing career, Lipsyte has become a staunch advocate of providing teenagers with quality reading material. As he remarked to Goering, young-adult literature "has a great responsibility to not lie to the youth. It is a real responsibility of young adult literature to tell kids the truth no matter how complex and painful it might be to get the truth in a book. We can't lie to them. There is a teaching element to these books. There is kind of a reaching out from one generation to another telling people that you can survive."

Biographical and Critical Sources

BOOKS

Cart, Michael, *Presenting Robert Lipsyte,* Twayne (New York, NY), 1995.

Drew, Bernard, *The One Hundred Most Popular Young-Adult Authors,* Libraries Unlimited, 1996.

Lipsyte, Robert, *The Contender,* Harper (New York, NY), 1967.

Lipsyte, Robert, *SportsWorld: An American Dreamland,* Quadrangle (New York, NY), 1975.

Lipsyte, Robert, *Free to Be Muhammad Ali,* Harper (New York, NY), 1978.

Lipsyte, Robert, *Assignment: Sports,* revised edition, Harper (New York, NY), 1984.

Lipsyte, Robert, *Jim Thorpe: Twentieth-Century Jock,* Harper (New York, NY), 1993.

St. James Guide to Young-Adult Writers, St. James Press (Detroit, MI), 1999.

PERIODICALS

ALAN Review, fall, 1983, Earl Lomax, review of *Jock and Jill,* p. 27; winter, 2007, Chris Goering, interview with Lipsyte.

Best Sellers, May, 1981, Gail Tansill Lambert, review of *Summer Rules,* pp. 79-80.

Booklist, January 1, 2003, Ed Sullivan, review of *Warrior Angel,* p. 871; February 15, 2006, GraceAnne A. DeCandido, review of *Heroes of Baseball: The Men Who Made It America's Favorite Game,* p. 94; May 15, 2006, Ed Sullivan, review of *Raiders Night,* p. 46.

Bulletin of the Center for Children's Books, April, 1981, Zena Sutherland, review of *Summer Rules,* p. 156; February, 1992, Zena Sutherland, review of *The Chemo Kid,* p. 162; July-August, 1993, Betsy Hearne, review of *The Chief,* p. 351.

Children's Literature in Education, spring, 1980, "Robert Lipsyte on Kids/Sports/Books," pp. 43, 44, 45, 47.

Elementary English, January, 1972, John S. Simmons, "Lipsyte's *Contender:* Another Look at the Junior Novel," p. 117.

English Journal, April, 1971, John N. Conner, review of *Assignment: Sports,* p. 529.

Entertainment Weekly, December 8, 1995, Gene Lyons, review of *Idols of the Game,* p. 62.

Horn Book, March-April, 1992, review of *The Brave,* p. 209; March-April, 2003, Peter D. Sieruta, review of *Warrior Angel,* p. 213; January-February, 2008, Lauren Adams, review of *Yellow Flag,* p. 90.

Journal of Adolescent and Adult Literacy, February, 2004, James Blasingame, review of *Warrior Angel* and interview with Lipsyte, p. 426.

Journal of Reading, May, 1981, Saul Bachner, "Three Junior Novels on the Black Experience," pp. 692-695.

Kirkus Reviews, September 15, 1991, review of *The Brave,* p. 1225; May 15, 1993, review of *The Chief,* p. 664; November 15, 1993, review of *Arnold Schwarzenegger: American Hercules,* p. 1463; November 15, 1994, review of *Michael Jordan: A Life above the Rim,* p. 1535; February 1, 1998, review of *In the Country of Illness: Comfort and Advice for the Journey,* p. 175; December 15, 2002, review of *Warrior Angel,* p. 1853; June 1, 2006, review of *Raiders Night,* p. 576; August 15, 2007, review of *Yellow Flag.*

Kliatt, March, 2003, Paula Rohrlick, review of *Warrior Angel,* p. 13; July, 2006, Paula Rohrlick, review of *Raiders Night,* p. 10; September, 2007, Paula Rohrlick, review of *Yellow Flag,* p. 15.

Nation, November 12, 1983, Norma Klein, "Not for Teens Only," pp. 312-314.

New York Times Book Review, May 31, 1970, Sam Elkin, review of *Assignment: Sports,* p. 14; July 10, 1977, Stephen Krensky, review of *One Fat Summer,* p. 20; March 4, 1979, Mel Watkins, review of *Free to Be Muhammad Ali,* p. 32.

New York Times Magazine, November 30, 1986, Robert Lipsyte, "The Athlete's Losing Game," p. 59.

Publishers Weekly, September 25, 1995, review of *Idols of the Game,* p. 40; March 20, 2006, review of *Heroes of Baseball,* p. 57; July 24, 2006, review of *Raiders Night,* p. 59.

School Library Journal, November, 1967, Susan O'Neal, review of *The Contender,* p. 78; March 7, 1977, Jane Abramson, review of *One Fat Summer,* p. 152; June, 2001, Walter Dean Myers, "Pulling No Punches," p. 44; March, 2003, Michael McCullough, review of *Warrior Angel,* p. 235; April, 2006, Marilyn Taniguchi, review of *Heroes of Baseball,* p. 158; July, 2006, Diane P. Tuccillo, review of *Raiders Night,* p. 106; September, 2007, Jeffrey A. French, review of *Yellow Flag,* p. 202.

Teacher Librarian, October, 2003, Rosemary Chance, "The Contender Returns," p. 49.

Voice of Youth Advocates, April, 1992, Colleen Macklin, review of *The Chemo Kid,* p. 32.

ONLINE

Robert Lipsyte Home Page, http://robertlipsyte.com (March 1, 2009).

*   *   *

LISSIAT, Amy
See THOMPSON, Colin

LÓPEZ, Rafael 1961-

Personal

Born August 8, 1961, in Mexico City, Mexico; son of two architects; married; wife's name Candice (a professor of graphic arts); children: Santiago. *Education:* Arts Center (Pasadena, CA), studied illustration.

Addresses

Home—San Diego, CA; and San Miguel de Allende, Mexico. *Office*—Rafael López Studio, 843 10th Ave., Studio C, San Diego, CA 92101. *E-mail*—rafael@ rafaellopez.com.

Career

Artist and illustrator. Urban Art Trail Project, San Diego, CA, creator and contributor. Graphic artist; creator of campaign poster and two stamps for the U.S. Postal Service.

Awards, Honors

Américas Award, Consortium of Latin American Studies Programs, 2005, for *My Name Is Celia,* and 2008, for *Yum! ¡Mmmm! ¡Qué rico!;* Pura Belpré Illustrator Honor Book, American Library Association, 2006, for *My Name Is Celia/Me llamo Celia.*

Illustrator

Monica Brown, *My Name Is Celia: The Life of Celia Cruz/Me llamo Celia: la vida de Celia Cruz,* Rising Moon (Flagstaff, AZ), 2004.

Pat Mora, *¡Yum! ¡Mmmm! ¡Qué rico!: America's Sproutings,* Lee & Low Books (New York, NY), 2007.

Pam Muñoz Ryan, *Our California,* Charlesbridge (Watertown, MA), 2008.

Pat Mora, *Book Fiesta! Celebrate Children's Day/Book Day; Celebremos el día de los niños, el día de los libros,* HarperCollins (New York, NY), 2008.

Sidelights

Artist and illustrator Rafael López draws inspiration from his Mexican heritage, as well as from the people and places around him. López began studying art in his adopted home of California, but he only found his own unique style while traveling with his wife around Mexico." I immediately was inspired by the textures on the walls of Mexico's houses, by the warm Mexican colors, by the popular culture that surrounded me,"the illustrator explained on the La Prensa San Diego Web site. His art, which he calls"very ethnic, with lots of icons from Mexican and Latino popular culture,"has found an audience throughout the United States. López has also designed two stamps for the U.S. Postal Service, and created posters for the "Artists for Obama" campaign during the 2008 presidential campaign.

"Intimidated by the drawings of my now 6-year-old son Santiago, I decided to venture into children's books," López revealed in his Web log. He enjoyed success with his first set of illustrations, for Monica Brown's bilingual *My Name Is Celia: The Life of Celia Cruz/Me llamo Celia: la vida de Celia Cruz.* López's paintings for this biography of the famous salsa singer "are alive with motion, lush with brilliantly layered colors, and informed with verve and symbolism," wrote Ann Welton in *School Library Journal.* The book earned López both an Américas award and a Pura Belpré Illustration Honor citation.

For Pat Mora's *¡Yum! ¡Mmmm! ¡Qué rico!: America's Sproutings,* a collection of haiku about native-grown American foods, "I wanted to use bold hues to express the spirit of the poetry and connect the viewer to the taste of the food," López explained on his Web log. Throughout the book, his "acrylic-on-wood-panel illustrations burst with vivid colors and stylized Mexican flair," Julie Cummins noted in *Booklist.* In *School Library Journal* Marilyn Taniguchi praised the illustrator's "artful compositions and brilliant complementary colors," adding that "the art conveys an infectious sense of fun." As a *Kirkus Reviews* critic concluded of *¡Yum! ¡Mmmm! ¡Qué rico!* "López's vibrant, folklorish illustrations make the book a visual feast."

López has also illustrated Pam Muñoz Ryan's *Our California,* a rhyming tour through America's most populous state. According to Ilene Cooper in *Booklist,* the artist contributes "pictures that demand a second look" because his acrylic-on-wood technique "make[s] the visuals seem almost three-dimensional." Using differing

Rafael López created the colorful art that brings to life Pam Muñoz Ryan's picture book Our California. (Illustration copyright © 2008 by Rafael López. All rights reserved. Used by permission of Charlesbridge Publishing, Inc.)

styles, López's pictures"remain fresh and surprising as he finds ways to express wonder and affection," a *Publishers Weekly* critic noted. The art "is so colorful, evocative, and eye-filling that it is tempting to review the title solely as a book of pictures," Marian Drabkin remarked in her *School Library Journal* review of *Our California.*

López reteams with Mora for *Book Fiesta! Celebrate Children's Day/Book Day; Celebremos el día de los niños, el día de los libros.* This tribute to reading is "beautifully illustrated in bright, bold, acrylic paintings that integrate books and letters into timeless scenes," Andrew Medlar commented in *Booklist.* A *Kirkus Reviews* writer similarly remarked that "a festival atmosphere [is] brilliantly expressed in López's luminous full-page montages of a world of reading opportunities."

Although López spends much of his time creating public art works in the San Diego area, he finds children's books both challenging and rewarding. "It requires an initial vision, tons of enthusiasm, lots of patience and willingness to work as a team and to compromise," the artist explained on PaperTigers.org. "And, of course, the discipline to carry that enthusiasm all the way to the finish line. But the results can be incredibly fulfilling: knowing that many kids will be able to enjoy the pictures and stories. What a fun way to help kids learn!"

Biographical and Critical Sources

PERIODICALS

Booklist, December 1, 2007, Julie Cummins, review of *¡Yum! ¡Mmmm! ¡Qué rico!: America's Sproutings,* p. 45; December 15, 2007, Ilene Cooper, review of *Our California,* p. 48; January 1, 2009, Andrew Medlar, review of *Book Fiesta! Celebrate Children's Day/ Book Day; Celebremos el día de los niños, el día de los libros,* p. 90.

Kirkus Reviews, September 15, 2007, review of *¡Yum! ¡Mmmm! ¡Qué rico!;* December 15, 2007, review of *Our California;* February 1, 2009, review of *Book Fiesta!*

Publishers Weekly, December 17, 2007, review of *Our California,* pp. 50-51.

San Diego Business Journal, September 26, 2005, Pat Broderick, "Public Art Pits Dollars vs. Decorations," p. 1.

School Library Journal, January, 2005, Ann Welton, review of *My Name Is Celia: The Life of Celia Cruz/Me llamo Celia: la vida de Celia Cruz.* p. 120; September, 2007, Marilyn Taniguchi, review of *¡Yum! ¡Mmmm! ¡Qué rico!,* p. 185; June, 2008, Marian Drabkin, review of *Our California,* p. 130.

ONLINE

La Prenza San Diego Web site, http://www.laprensa-san diego.org/ (September 16, 2005), "Local Artist Adds Rhythm and Heritage to Your Stamps."

PaperTigers.org, http://www.papertigers.org/ (March 1, 2008), "Gallery: Rafael López."

Rafael López Home Page, http://www.rafaellopez.com (February 2, 2009).

Rafael López Studio Web Log, http://rafaellopezstudio.blog spot.com (September 28, 2008).*

M

MacLACHLAN, Emily
See CHAREST, Emily MacLachlan

* * *

MALLEY, Gemma
(G.R. Malley)

Personal
Born in England; married; husband's name Mark (an educator); children: one son. *Education:* University of Reading, bachelor's degree (philosophy).

Addresses
Home—South London, England.

Career
Journalist and novelist. Formerly worked as an editor of business periodicals; Office for Standards in Education, Children's Services, and Skills, London, England, former senior staff member in communications department.

Writings

YOUNG-ADULT NOVELS

The Declaration, Bloomsbury (New York, NY), 2007.
The Resistance, Bloomsbury (New York, NY), 2008.

Contributor to periodicals, including *Company,* London *Sunday Telegraph,* and London *Guardian,* sometimes under name G.R. Malley.

Sidelights
Gemma Malley worked as a journalist for several major British publications, as well as in a civil-service job, before turning to a career as a novelist. "I think work-

ing with young people and getting them excited in a book, a subject, or the world around them is about the most rewarding thing you can do," Malley noted in an

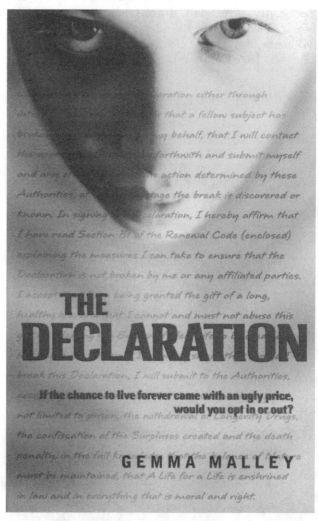

Cover of Gemma Malley's novel **The Declaration**, *which imagines a world in which ageing has been halted.* (Bloomsbury U.S.A. Children's Books, 2007. Cover photograph © Ghislain & Marie David de Lossy/The Image Bank/Getty Images.)

interview for the Bloomsbury Web site. Her futuristic novels *The Declaration* and *The Resistance* are set in a world in which ageing no longer exists and young people must now be warehoused due to lack of space. Within this grim setting, Malley sets about exploring what would happen if modern science was able to cure the many infirmities of old age and mankind ever achieved its goal of eternal life.

In *The Declaration* the year is 2140 and pharmaceuticals now stop people from growing old. Children are the new threat to the species due to their demands on food, space, and jobs, and pregnancy is now outlawed. For those infants accidently born, life in a Surplus hall is their destiny after they are discovered by the Catchers and their parents are condemned for their selfishness. Fourteen-year-old Anna Covey is one such "accident": as a Surplus, she lives in grim captivity at Grange Hall. When a new Surplus named Peter arrives, he inspires Anna with the desire to escape from the hall and locate her parents. Against the efforts of Peter and Anna to escape from their prison and make their way in a hostile world, Malley weaves the story of Grange Hall and its evil house matron. *The Declaration* "will appeal to any teens who have ever felt their age is held against them,"

concluded *School Library Journal* reviewer Eric Norton, and a *Kirkus Reviews* writer described Malley's novel as "well worth reading." Most intriguing is Anna's misplaced loyalty to Grange Hall; her "faith in her tormentors is thought-provoking and deeply sad," the critic added. While noting that Malley sometimes tends toward telling rather than showing in her dystopian narrative, London *Guardian* reviewer Diane Samuels praised *The Declaration* as "a crafted story with a desire to tackle serious contemporary issues about humanity's relationship with death, nature, science and personal and social responsibility."

Described by a *Kirkus Reviews* writer as an "unsubtle but worthwhile and tension-packed sequel" to *The Declaration, The Resistance* finds Anna and Peter now a few years older and successfully living as Legals. Although they hope to live quietly and raise a family under the radar, Peter's connections with the corporation that manufactures the age-defying drug Longevity+ (his grandfather is company chairman) have made him useful to the Surplus underground. Hoping to gain the trust of his grandfather and gain important information about a second generation of the powerful drug, Peter ultimately discovers a horrible secret: the active ingredient in Longevity+ is one that can only be harvested from the young humans being held in Surplus halls.

Biographical and Critical Sources

PERIODICALS

Booklist, November 15, 2007, Jennifer Mattson, review of *The Declaration,* p. 53.
Bookseller, June 29, 2007, Caroline Horn, "Imagine Never Growing Older," p. 26.
Guardian (London, England), October 20, 2007, Diane Samuels, review of *The Declaration,* p. 20.
Kirkus Reviews, September 15, 2007, review of *The Declaration;* July 15, 2008, review of *The Resistance.*
Publishers Weekly, November 19, 2007, review of *The Declaration,* p. 58.
School Library Journal, February, 2008, Eric Norton, review of *The Declaration,* p. 120.
Sunday Times (London, England), September 20, 2008, Nicolette Jones, review of *The Declaration,* p. 56.

ONLINE

Bloomsbury Web site, http://www.bloomsbury.com/ (February 9, 2009), "Gemma Malley."*

Malley continues her science-fiction premise about a world gone awry in **The Resistance.** (Bloomsbury U.S.A. Children's Books, 2008. Jacket photograph © by Nicole Hill/Rubberball Productions/Getty Images.)

*   *   *

MALLEY, G.R.
See MALLEY, Gemma

MAZER, Norma Fox 1931-

Personal

Born May 15, 1931, in New York, NY; daughter of Michael and Jean Fox; married Harry Mazer (a novelist), February 12, 1950; children: Anne, Joseph, Susan, Gina. *Education:* Briefly attended Antioch College; attended night classes at Syracuse University.

Addresses

Home and office—644 North St., Montpelier, VT 05602. *E-mail*—norma@foxmazer.com.

Career

Writer, 1964—.

Awards, Honors

National Book Award nomination, 1973, for *A Figure of Speech;* Lewis Carroll Shelf Award, University of Wisconsin, 1975, for *Saturday the Twelfth of October,* 1976, for *Dear Bill, Remember Me?;* American Library Association (ALA) Notable Book citation, 1976, for *Dear Bill, Remember Me? and Other Stories,* and 1988, for *After the Rain;* Christopher Award, 1976, for *Dear Bill, Remember Me?; New York Times* Outstanding Books of the Year listee, 1976, for *Dear Bill, Remember Me?,* 1984, for *Downtown; School Library Journal* Best Books of the Year listee, 1976, for *Dear Bill, Remember Me?,* 1997, for *When She Was Good,* 1979, for *Up in Seth's Room,* 1988, for *After the Rain;* ALA Best Books for Young Adults listee, 1976, for *Dear Bill, Remember Me?,* 1977, (with Harry Mazer) for *The Solid Gold Kid,* 1979, for *Up in Seth's Room,* 1983, for *Someone to Love,* 1984, for *Downtown,* 1988, for *After the Rain,* 1989, for *Silver,* 1993, for *Out of Control,* 1998, for *When She Was Good;* Children's Book Council/ International Reading Association (IRA) Children's Choice, 1978, for *The Solid Gold Kid,* 1986, for *A, My Name Is Ami,* 1989, for *Heartbeat;* ALA Best of the Best Books listee, 1970-83, for *Up in Seth's Room;* Austrian Children's Books honor designation, and German Children's Literature prize, both 1982, both for *Mrs. Fish, Ape, and Me, the Dump Queen;* Edgar Allan Poe Award, Mystery Writers of America, 1982, and California Young Readers Medal, 1985, both for *Taking Terri Mueller;* New York Public Library Books for the Teen Age listee, 1984, for *Downtown,* 1989, for *Silver,* 1990, for *Heartbeat* and *Waltzing on Water,* 1991, for *Babyface,* 1994, for *Out of Control,* 1995, for *Missing Pieces,* 2002, for *Girlhearts;* Iowa Teen Award, 1985-86, for *When We First Met,* and 1989, for *Silver;* Association of Booksellers for Children Choice designation, Canadian Children's Books Council Choice designation, *Horn Book* Fanfare Book, and Newbery Honor Book designation, all 1988, all for *After the Rain;* ALA One Hundred Best of the Best Books designation, 1968-93, for *Silver* and *The Solid Gold Kid;* German Literature Prize, 1989, for *Heartbeat;* American Booksellers Pick

Norma Fox Mazer (Reproduced by permission.)

of the Lists designation, 1990, for *Babyface,* 1992, for *Bright Days, Stupid Nights,* 1993, for *Out of Control,* and 1994, for *Missing Pieces;* IRA Teacher's Choice designation, for *Babyface, Bright Days, Stupid Nights, Out of Control,* and *Missing Pieces;* Editor's Choice, *Booklist,* 1997, for *When She Was Good;* YALSA Best Book for Young Adults designation, 1998, for *When She Was Good,* 2008, for *The Missing Girl; Los Angeles Times* Book Prize finalist, and *Smithsonian* magazine Notable Book designation, 2002, and IRA Young-Adult Choice designation, 2003, all for *Girlhearts.;* honorary M.F.A., Vermont College.

Writings

YOUNG-ADULT FICTION

I, Trissy, Delacorte (New York, NY), 1971, reprinted, Dell (New York, NY), 1986.

A Figure of Speech, Delacorte (New York, NY), 1973.

Saturday the Twelfth of October, Delacorte (New York, NY), 1975.

Dear Bill, Remember Me? and Other Stories, Delacorte (New York, NY), 1976.

(With husband, Harry Mazer) *The Solid Gold Kid,* Delacorte (New York, NY), 1977.

Up in Seth's Room, Delacorte (New York, NY), 1979.

Mrs. Fish, Ape, and Me, the Dump Queen, Dutton (New York, NY), 1980.

Taking Terri Mueller, Avon/Morrow (New York, NY), 1981.

Summer Girls, Love Boys, and Other Short Stories, Delacorte (New York, NY), 1982.

When We First Met, Four Winds (New York, NY), 1982.

Downtown, Avon/Morrow (New York, NY), 1983.

Someone to Love, Delacorte (New York, NY), 1983.

Supergirl (screenplay novelization), Warner Books (New York, NY), 1984.

A, My Name Is Ami, Scholastic (New York, NY), 1986.

Three Sisters, Scholastic (New York, NY), 1986.

After the Rain, Morrow (New York, NY), 1987.

B, My Name Is Bunny, Scholastic (New York, NY), 1987.

Silver, Morrow (New York, NY), 1988.

(With Harry Mazer) *Heartbeat,* Bantam (New York, NY), 1989.

Babyface, Morrow (New York, NY), 1990.

C, My Name Is Cal, Scholastic (New York, NY), 1990.

D, My Name Is Danita, Scholastic (New York, NY), 1991.

E, My Name Is Emily, Scholastic (New York, NY), 1991.

(With Harry Mazer) *Bright Days, Stupid Nights,* Morrow (New York, NY), 1992.

Out of Control, Morrow (New York, NY), 1993.

Missing Pieces, Morrow (New York, NY), 1995.

When She Was Good, Arthur A. Levine Books (New York, NY), 1997.

Crazy Fish, Morrow (New York, NY), 1998.

Good Night, Maman, Harcourt Brace (San Diego, CA), 1999.

Girlhearts, HarperCollins (New York, NY), 2001.

What I Believe, Harcourt (Orlando, FL), 2005.

Ten Ways to Make My Sister Disappear, Arthur A. Levine Books (New York, NY), 2007.

The Missing Girl, HarperTeen (New York, NY), 2008.

OTHER

(Editor, with Margery Lewis) *Waltzing on Water: Poetry by Women,* Dell (New York, NY), 1989.

(Editor, with Jacqueline Woodson) *Just a Writer's Thing: A Collection of Prose and Poetry from the National Book Foundation's 1995 Summer Writing Camp,* National Book Foundation (New York, NY), 1996.

(With Nathan Aaseng, Myra C. Livingston, and others) *Courage: How We Face Challenges,* Troll Communications (Mahwah, NJ), 1997.

Has Anyone Seen My Emily Greene? (picture book), illustrated by Christine Davenier, Candlewick Press (Cambridge, MA), 2007.

Stories and essays anthologized in *Sixteen . . . Short Stories by Outstanding Writers for Young Adults,* edited by Donald R. Gallo, Delacorte (New York, NY), 1984; *Short Takes,* by Elizabeth Segal, Lothrop (New York, NY), 1986; *Visions: Nineteen Short Stories by Outstanding Writers for Young Adults,* edited by Gallo, Delacorte, 1987; *Authors' Insights: Turning Teenagers into Readers and Writers,* edited by Gallo, Boynton/Cook (Portsmouth, NH), 1992; *Leaving Home,* edited by Hazel Rochman and Darlene Z. McCampbell, HarperCollins (New York, NY), 1997; *Stay True: Short Sto-*ries about Strong Girls, edited by Marilyn Singer, 1998; *Places I Never Meant to Be: Original Short Stories by Censored Writers,* edited by Judy Blume, Simon & Schuster (New York, NY), 1999; *The Year We Missed My Birthday: Eleven Birthday Stories,* edited by Lois Metzger, Scholastic (New York, NY), 2005; *Hot Flashes: Women Writers on the Change of Life,* edited by Lynne Taetzsch; *Ultimate Sports,* edited by Gallo; and *Night Terrors,* edited by Lois Duncan. Contributor of stories, articles, and essays to magazines, including *ALAN Review, Boys and Girls, Calling All Girls, Child Life, English Journal, Ingenue, Jack and Jill, Redbook, Signal, Top of the News,* and *Voice of Youth Advocates.*

Adaptations

Mazer's novels recorded on audio cassette and released by Listening Library include *Taking Terri Mueller,* 1986, *Dear Bill, Remember Me? and Other Stories,* 1987, and *After the Rain,* 1988. *When We First Met* was adapted for television by Home Box Office, 1984.

Sidelights

"It's not hard to see why Norma Fox Mazer has found a place among the most popular writers for young adults these days," observed Suzanne Freeman in the *Washington Post Book World.* "At her best, Mazer can cut right to the bone of teenage troubles and then show us how the wounds will heal. She can set down the everyday scenes of her characters' lives in images that are scalpel sharp," the critic continued, adding that "what's apparent throughout all of this is that Mazer has taken great care to get to know the world she writes about. She delves into the very heart of it with a sure and practiced hand." Mazer's many acclaimed books for teen readers include *After the Rain, A Figure of Speech, Silver,* and *Missing Pieces.*

New York Times Book Review contributor Barbara Wersba described Mazer as "a dazzling writer" who "brings to her work a literacy that would be admirable in any type of fiction." In her National Book Award-nominated *A Figure of Speech,* Mazer tells the story of an elderly man who is neglected by all of his family except his granddaughter. "The fine definition of all characters, the plausibility of the situations and the variety of insights into motivation make [the novel] almost too good to be true," Tom Heffernan asserted in *Children's Literature.* "There is no point at which it passes into an area of depiction or explanation that would exceed the experience of a young adolescent," the critic added. "But there is also no point at which the psychological perceptiveness and narrative control would disappoint an adult reader."

Mazer grew up in Glens Falls, New York, the middle daughter in a family of three girls. Her father was a route driver, delivering such things as milk and bread, and the family lived in a succession of apartments and houses. School, reading, and boys were her childhood loves. During her teen years, a job with her school newspaper gave Mazer her first opportunity to write for publication, and writing soon became the focus of her existence at school. When she was fifteen years old, Mazer met her future husband, Harry Mazer. He was a friend of her older sister, and at the age of twenty-one, he seemed ancient. Two years later, they met again, and a much-more-confident Mazer was determined that Harry should fall in love with her. Harry thought that Mazer was too young, though, and she had to work at making him notice her. The couple fell in and out of love and quarreled many times before finally getting married.

During the early part of their marriage, the Mazers worked at various jobs and tried to learn how to cook. Three children soon became part of the family, and Mazer took on the role of Mom. In between caring for her children, she began to question what she would do in life, and in a serious talk with her husband both Mazers revealed a desire to be a writer. They decided that if they were really serious about writing, they had to do at least a little every day. So, for three years, the Mazers spent an hour at the end of each day writing. Money from an insurance settlement finally enabled them to write full-time.

To support the family, the Mazers wrote for the women's true confessions market. These stories, while presented as the first-person confessions of women who had made serious mistakes in their lives, were actually the work of professional writers. During the following years, they each wrote one of these 5,000-to-8,000-word stories every week, leaving little time to devote to the writing of novels. In 1970 Mazer managed to find the time to pen her novel *I, Trissy,* and it was published the following year. *A Figure of Speech* came two years later and received a National Book Award nomination. As Mazer recalled in an essay for *Something about the Author Autobiography Series* (SAAS), "I remember meeting a member of the National Book Award committee some time after *A Figure of Speech* had received a . . . nomination and hearing him say to me, '. . . and you just came out of nowhere.' I laughed. My 'nowhere' had been the ten years I'd spent writing full time and learning the craft."

Mazer has earned special acclaim for her young-adult novels, some of which she has written with her husband. Although her fictional characters are not always likable, they are believable young people struggling with challenges while teetering on the verge of adulthood. Her novel *Taking Terri Mueller* earned Mazer an Edgar Allan Poe award from the Mystery Writers of America although she had not intended it as a mystery. The book follows Terri Mueller and her father as they wander from town to town, never staying in one place for more than a year. Although Terri is happy with her father, she is old enough to wonder why he will never talk about her mother, who supposedly died ten years ago. An overheard discussion leads Terri to discover that she

Cover of Mazer's novel **When She Was Good,** *featuring artwork by S. Saelig Gallagher.* (Jacket art © 1997 by S. Saelig Gallagher. Reproduced by permission of Scholastic, Inc.)

had been kidnaped by her father after a bitter custody battle. "The unfolding and the solution of the mystery [of the truth about Terri's mother] are effectively worked," remarked a *Horn Book* reviewer; "filled with tension and with strong characterization, the book makes compelling reading." Freeman similarly observed that, despite the potential for simplifying Terri's conflict, "Mazer does not take the easy way out in this book. There are no good guys or bad guys. There are no easy answers." The critic concluded, "We believe in just about everything Terri does, because Mazer's writing makes us willing to believe. She wins us completely with this finely wrought and moving book."

In her Newbery Honor Book *After the Rain* Mazer returns to the subject of a elderly man dying; but in this instance, grandfather Izzy rebuffs his loving family, and granddaughter Rachel must exert herself to build a relationship with him. As it becomes clear to her that Izzy is dying and needs companionship, Rachel decides to regularly spend her free time with him. "It's surprising that she should make such a decision," claimed *Washington Post Book World* contributor Cynthia Samuels, "but once the reader accepts her choice and begins to join her on her daily visits with the crotchety old man, the story becomes both moving and wise." The result, continued the critic, is a book that "deals with death and loss in an original and sensitive way." Carolyn Meyer, however, felt that there is a lack of tension in the story, "You never really worry that Rachel won't do the right thing," she wrote in the *Los Angeles Times Book Review*. In contrast, a *Kirkus Reviews* critic suggested that "what distinguishes this book, making it linger in the heart, are the realistic portrayals of the tensions, guilt, and sudden, painfully moving moments involved in Rachel's and Izzy's situations." As a *Horn Book* reviewer concluded, Izzy's "harsh, rough personality [is] so realistic and recognizable that we feel we have known him and can understand the sorrow that overcomes Rachel. [*After the Rain* is] . . . a powerful book, dealing with death and dying and the strength of family affection."

With *Good Night, Maman* Mazer ventures into historical fiction. The young-adult novel centers around twelve-year-old Karin, who, amid World War II, must struggle to find freedom and begin a new life without her beloved mother. The Nazi invaders have sent Karin's father to a prison in Poland and Karin, her brother, and her mother are in hiding in an attic. When they are told they must leave, the children head south. Karin and her brother eventually board a ship headed to America, leaving their ill-stricken mother behind. "This moving World War II story is neither highly dramatic nor politically charged. It is the very personal and immediate experience of a young girl grappling with the loss of her old life and a new life that changes daily," explained Lauren Adams in *Horn Book*. A *Publishers Weekly* reviewer concluded that "the strength of this novel lies in its intimate recognition of the way adolescents think and feel." Mazer explained in a *Teen Reads* online interview that writing historical fiction is difficult because a writer must fit a fictional character into an actual event. "I had to write this novel over completely four times, and this was because I was working out how to balance fiction and history," she remarked. To prepare to write *Good Night, Maman,* Mazer noted, "I read a fair number of books, most of them memoirs of people who had lived through the Holocaust. What struck me was that despite the numbing universality of that murderous time, each person's story, each survivor's story, was unique, distinct. . . . my intention in writing this book was not to write history, but to write the unique history of an individual, albeit a fictional one."

Like *Good Night, Maman, Girlhearts* deals with a young girl's loss of a parent. Sarabeth Silver is devastated by the death of her mother, the only parent and family member she has ever known. With no one to turn to, Sarabeth decides to track down the extended family members who had turned their back on her mother after she became pregnant with Sarah at age sixteen. "With a pitch-perfect intensity, Mazer captures the fractured sense of loss, of self, of time, that comes with a death in the family," explained GraceAnn A. De-

Candido in *Booklist*. Writing in *School Library Journal*, Susie Paige noted that "the theme of death and renewal is not a new one, but Mazer's characters deal with the process in a realistic, heartrending manner." In *Publishers Weekly* a reviewer praised the novel for conveying its author's "intimate recognition" of teen emotions, adding that Mazer "conveys the heroine's feelings of shock, numbness, loneliness and powerlessness with her usual authenticity."

Mazer melds prose with poetry in *What I Believe*. The book tracks middle-schooler Vickie Marnet's changing world after her middle-aged father is laid off from his corporate job and the Marnet family falls from affluence into depression and struggling financial circumstances. Moving from the family's comfortable suburban home to a crowded city apartment, Vickie must now deal with a new school while her mother heads off to work and a renter moves into the spare bedroom to help pay the rent. Consisting of diary entries, e-mails, and Vickie's poetry, Mazer's text reflects the girl's "struggles to master the dramatic changes in her life," according to *Booklist* reviewer Holly Koelling. A *Kirkus Reviews* writer praised "Mazer's ear for teen language," while in *School Library Journal* Denise Moore asserted that readers will be "drawn into the girl's struggle" and "taken with the novel's free-flowing style and revelations." Calling *What I Believe* an "emotionally taut" narrative, a *Publishers Weekly* concluded that Vicki's "often poignant journal entries add up to a candid portrayal of how a teen's life can change overnight."

In *Ten Ways to Make My Sister Disappear* Mazer focuses on preteen narrator Sprig, whose frustration with her older sister, Dakota, has reached epic proportions. With their architect father away in Afghanistan building schools, twelve-year-old Dakota has begun behaving like a mother as well as an annoying older sister, and she now combines her usual teasing with suggestions on how the ten year old should behave. As if Dakota's behavior is not annoying enough, Sprig's best friend has a crush on a boy in their class, and this has put a new strain on their relationship. Commenting on Mazer's ability to convey "the dynamics of friendship and sisterhood" within her often lighthearted story, *School Library Journal* critic Erin Schirota added that *Ten Ways to Make My Sister Disappear* provides "an excellent introduction to the world of boys, sibling rivalry, and loyalty." "Sprig's generally sunny disposition . . . helps keep the novel fresh and funny despite her woes," asserted Susan Dove Lempke in *Horn Book*, the critic adding that Mazer's conclusion in the novel "rings completely true." Praising the "small but well-defined moments" in which Sprig gains maturity and understanding, *Booklist* critic Ilene Cooper deemed *Ten Ways to Make My Sister Disappear* "a solid choice for an underserved age group."

Five sisters and a secret stalker are at the center of the drama in *The Missing Girl*. Seventeen-year-old Beauty,

as well as Mim, Stevie, Fancy, and eleven-year-old Autumn Herbert, live in the poor part of town, and each sister has a special quality that makes her unique. As the girls go about their lives, spending time with friends, walking to school, arguing, and doing all the things average girls do, they are secretly being studied by a neighbor. A disturbed man, the neighbor seeks the perfect girl to put among his other possessions and he hopes to find her among the Herbert sisters. Narrated in turn by Beauty, Fancy, and Autumn and by their nameless stalker, *The Missing Girl* tells a frightening story about how evil can exist stealthy, undetected, and close to home. "Scenes between the child and her abductor are chilling," wrote *School Library Journal* critic Carolyn Lehman, while Rachel L. Smith described the novel in *Horn Book* as "a skillful psychological examination of a disturbed, dangerous predator and of a family that experiences trauma." Although Mazer's thrilling story contains "creepy" elements, it "ends on a hopeful note with a theme of self-empowerment," according to *Kliatt* critic Myrna Marler, and Lehman described it as a "well-crafted thriller with mythic undertones." "Sharply delineated characters, engrossing narrative and Mazer's keen insight . . . keep the tension ratcheted way, way up," concluded a *Publishers Weekly* critic in a review of *The Missing Girl.*

Like her novels, Mazer's short-story collections, which include *Dear Bill, Remember Me? and Other Stories* and *Summer Girls, Love Boys, and Other Short Stories,* have also won her many readers. "Clearly, Mazer appreciates the short-story form, with its narrow focus and spotlit moments," commented a *Kirkus Reviews* writer about *Dear, Bill, Remember Me? and Other Stories.* The eight short stories in the collection deal with young girls going through a period of crisis: In "Up on Fong Mountain," Jessie strives to be accepted as something other than an extension of her boyfriend, while eighteen-year-old Louise in "Guess Whose Friendly Hands" knows she is dying of cancer and wishes her mother and sister would accept her reality. Mazer's tales "are clearly broadcast on a young teenager's wavelength, with the signal unobtrusively amplified as in good YA novels," contended a *Kirkus Reviews* contributor.

Bruce Bennett, writing in the *Nation,* noted that *Summer Girls, Love Boys and Other Short Stories* "is accessible to teenagers as well as adults. Most of the characters are young people," the critic elaborated, "but Mazer writes about them with an affectionate irony that older readers will appreciate." Because Mazer "has the skill to reveal the human qualities in both ordinary and extraordinary situations as young people mature," stated *New York Times Book Review* contributor Ruth I. Gordon, ". . . it would be a shame to limit their reading to young people, since they can show an adult reader much about the sometimes painful rite of adolescent passage into adulthood." Strengthening the effect of Mazer's collections is the fact that they are "written specifically

as a book, a fact which gives the stories an unusual unity and connectedness," related Bennett.

As Mazer noted in *SAAS,* there is "a kind of mystery" in all of her books. "I write and my readers read to find out the answers to questions, secrets, problems," she explained, "to be drawn into the deepest mystery of all—someone else's life." Freeman asserted that, "in its sharpest moments, Mazer's writing can etch a place in our hearts," and in her *Top of the News* essay, Mazer declared: "I love stories. I'm convinced that everyone does, and whether we recognize it or not, each of us tells stories. A day doesn't pass when we don't put our lives into story. Most often these stories are . . . of the moment. They are the recognition, the highlighting of . . . our daily lives. . . . In my own life, it seems that events are never finished until I've either told them or written them."

Biographical and Critical Sources

BOOKS

Butler, Francelia, editor, *Children's Literature: Annual of the Modern Language Association Seminar on Children's Literature and the Children's Literature Association,* Volume 4, Temple University Press (Philadelphia, PA), 1975.
Children's Literature Review, Volume 23, Gale (Detroit, MI), 1991.
Contemporary Literary Criticism, Volume 26, Gale (Detroit, MI), 1983.
Holtze, Sally Holmes, *Presenting Norma Fox Mazer,* Twayne (New York, NY), 1987.
St. James Guide to Young-Adult Writers, 2nd edition, St. James Press (Detroit, MI), 1999.
Something about the Author Autobiography Series, Volume 1, Gale (Detroit, MI), 1986, pp. 185-202.

PERIODICALS

Booklist, June 1-15, 1993, review of *Out of Control,* p. 1804; April 1, 1995, Merri Monks, review of *Missing Pieces,* p. 1388; September, 1997, Stephanie Zvirin, review of *When She Was Good,* p. 118; April 15, 1998, Stephanie Zvirin, "What Grandparents Teach," p. 1445; August, 1999, Hazel Rochman, review of *Good Night, Maman,* p. 2053; November 15, 1999, Stephanie Zvirin review of *When She Was Good,* p. 613; July, 2001, GraceAnne A. DeCandido, review of *Girlhearts,* p. 2000; September 15, 2005, Holly Koelling, review of *What I Believe,* p. 67; September 1, 2007, Ilene Cooper, review of *Ten Ways to Make My Sister Disappear,* p. 113.
Book Report, January-February, 1998, Marilyn Heath, review of *When She Was Good,* p. 35; November, 1999, Sherry York, "Child Sexual Abuse: A Bibliography of Young Adult Fiction," p. 30; November-December, 2001, Catherine M. Andronik, review of *Girlhearts,* p. 61.

Bulletin of the Center for Children's Books, October, 1997, Deborah Stevenson, review of *When She Was Good,* p. 61; December, 1999, review of *Good Night, Maman,* p. 53; April, 2001, review of *Girlhearts,* p. 310.

Children's Book and Play Review, March, 2002, review of *Girlhearts,* p. 12.

Emergency Librarian, January, 1998, review of *When She Was Good,* p. 50.

Horn Book, April, 1983, review of *Taking Terri Mueller,* pp. 172-173; November 1999, Lauren Adams, review of *Good Night, Maman,* p. 743; November-December, 2007, Susan Dove Lempke, review of *Ten Ways to Make My Sister Disappear,* p. 684; May-June, 2008, Rachel L. Smith, review of *The Missing Girl,* p. 321.

Kirkus Reviews, October 1, 1976, review of *Dear Bill, Remember Me?,* pp. 1101-1102; May 1, 1987, review of *After the Rain,* p. 723; October 15, 1999, review of *Good Night, Maman,* p. 1647; April 1, 2001, review of *Girlhearts,* p. 502; October 1, 2005, review of *What I Believe,* p. 1083; May 15, 2007, review of *Has Anyone Seen My Emily Greene?*

Kliatt, September, 1999, review of *Good Night, Maman,* p. 10; July, 2001, review of *Girlhearts,* p. 12; September, 2005, Claire Rosser, review of *What I Believe,* p. 11; January, 2008, Myrna Marler, review of *The Missing Girl,* p. 10.

New York Times Book Review, March 17, 1974, Jill Paton Walsh, review of *A Figure of Speech,* p. 8; March 13, 1983, Ruth I. Gordon, review of *Summer Girls, Love Boys, and Other Stories,* p. 29; June 17, 2001, Emily-Greta Tabourin, review of *Girlhearts,* p. 25.

Publishers Weekly, July 27, 1990, review of *Babyface,* p. 235; November 8, 1991, review of *E, My Name Is Emily,* p. 64; June, 22, 1992, review of *Bright Days, Stupid Nights,* p. 63; April 5, 1993, review of *Out of Control,* p. 79; July 21, 1997, review of *When She Was Good,* p. 202; June 12 1995, review of *Missing Pieces,* p. 62; November 8, 1999, review of *Good Night, Maman,* p. 69; April 23, 2001, review of *Girlhearts,* p. 79; October 17, 2005, review of *What I Believe,* p. 68; June 25, 2007, review of *Has Anyone Seen My Emily Greene?,* p. 59; December 17, 2007, review of *The Missing Girl,* p. 52.

School Library Journal, March, 1991, Judith Porter, review of *C, My Name Is Cal,* p. 193; March, 1991, Connie Tyrrell Burns, review of *D, My Name Is Danita,* p. 193; November, 1991, Susan Oliver, review of *E, My Name Is Emily,* p. 120; July, 1992, Cindy Darling Codell, review of *Bright Days, Stupid Nights,* p. 90; January, 1998, review of *When She Was Good,* p. 43; December, 1999, Amy Lilien-Harper, review of *Good Night, Maman,* p. 137; May, 2001, Susie Paige, review of *Girlhearts,* p. 156; October, 2005, Denise Moore, review of *What I Believe,* p. 166; June, 2007, Mary Jean Smith, review of *Has Anyone Seen My Emily Greene?,* p. 115; November, 2007, Erin Schirota, review of *Ten Ways to Make My Sister Disappear,* p. 130; February, 2008, Carolyn Lehman, review of *The Missing Girl,* p. 120.

Teacher Librarian, December, 2001, Rosemary Chance, review of *Young Women Speak Out,* p. 23.

Tribune Books (Chicago, IL), June 17 2001, review of *Girlhearts,* p. 4.

Voice of Youth Advocates, August, 1993, review of *Out of Control,* p. 154; April, 1998, review of *When She Was Good,* p. 38; August, 2001, review of *Girlhearts,* p. 204.

Washington Post Book World, April 10, 1983, Suzanne Freeman, "The Truth about the Teens," p. 10; May 10, 1987, Cynthia Samuels, review of *After the Rain,* p. 19.

ONLINE

Norma Fox Mazer Home Page, http://normafoxmazer.net (February 2, 2009).

TeenReads, http: www.teenreads.com/ (August 25, 2000), interview with Mazer.

*   *   *

McARDLE, Paula 1971-

Personal

Born 1971, in Newcastle-under-Lyme, Staffordshire, England. *Education:* University of Brighton, degree (illustration), 1994

Addresses

Home—England.

Career

Illustrator and fine-art painter. Formerly worked for a greeting-card company. *Exhibitions:* Work exhibited at Potteries Museum and Art Gallery, 1997; Art Multiple Gallery, Düsseldorf, Germany, 1997; Harrods, London, England, 1998; New York Art Expo, 1998-2004; and in Japan and the United States.

Illustrator

Anne Shelby, *The Adventures of Molly Whuppie, and Other Appalachian Folktales* University of North Carolina Press (Chapel Hill, NC), 2007.

Biographical and Critical Sources

PERIODICALS

Kirkus Reviews, September 15, 2007, review of *The Adventures of Molly Whuppie, and Other Appalachian Folktales.*

School Library Journal, November, 2007, Mary Jean Smith, review of *The Adventures of Molly Whuppie, and Other Appalachian Folktales,* p. 152.

ONLINE

West End Publishing Web site, http://www.wepart.com/ (February 9, 2009), "Paula McArdle."*

McELMURRY, Jill

Personal

Born in CA; daughter of illustrators; married Eric Webster. *Education:* Attended State University of New York at Purchase and School of Visual Arts. *Hobbies and other interests:* House renovation, working on her farm.

Addresses

Home—NM. *Agent*—Marcia Wernick, Sheldon Fogelman, Inc., 10 E. 40th St., New York, NY 10016. *E-mail*—jillmcelmurry@yahoo.com.

Career

Writer and illustrator.

Awards, Honors

Oppenheim Toy Portfolio Platinum Award, 2002, for *The Kettles Get New Clothes;* Notable Book designation, Association of Jewish Libraries, 2003, for *It's a Miracle!; Child* magazine Best Picture Book designation, 2004, for *Where's Stretch?*

Writings

SELF-ILLUSTRATED

Mad about Plaid!, Morrow Junior Books (New York, NY), 2000.
Mess Pets, SeaStar Books (New York, NY), 2002.
I'm Not a Baby!, Atheneum Books for Young Readers (New York, NY), 2005.

ILLUSTRATOR

Lilian Moore, *I'm Small and Other Verses,* Candlewick Press (Cambridge, MA), 2001.
Dayle Ann Dodds, *The Kettles Get New Clothes,* Candlewick Press (Cambridge, MA), 2002.
Stephanie Spinner, *It's a Miracle!: A Hanukkah Storybook,* Atheneum Books for Young Readers (New York, NY), 2003.
Reeve Lindbergh, *Our Nest,* Candlewick Press (Cambridge, MA), 2004.
Karen Pandell, *Where's Stretch?,* Candlewick Press (Cambridge, MA), 2004.
Karen Pandell, *Peekaboo, Stretch!,* Candlewick Press (Cambridge, MA), 2006.
Jessica Swaim, *The Hound from the Pound,* Candlewick Press (Cambridge, MA), 2007.
Alice Schertle, *Little Blue Truck,* Harcourt (Orlando, FL), 2008.
Florence Parry Heide, *The One and Only Marigold,* Schwartz & Wade (New York, NY), 2009.

Jill McElmurry (Photograph courtesy of Jill McElmurry.)

Alice Schertle, *Little Blue Truck Leads the Way,* Harcourt (Orlando, FL), 2009.

Sidelights

California-born author and illustrator Jill McElmurry has followed her family's tradition in the arts by becoming an illustrator. Although she attended both the State University of New New and the School of Visual Arts in New York City, McElmurry is predominately self-taught, and she has been drawing and painting since she was a child. In addition to creating award-winning illustrations for books by writers such as Dayle Ann Dodds, Stephanie Spinner, and Alice Shertle, among others, McElmurry has also penned several self-illustrated picture-books, among them *Mess Pets, Mad about Plaid!,* and *I'm Not a Baby!* McElmurry's "rich gouache illustrations capture the old-fashioned feel of the book well," concluded *Horn Book* critic Robin Smith in a review of the illustrator's work for Jessica Swaim's picture book *The Hound from the Pound.* Discussing the artist's contribution to Lindberg's bedtime story *Our Nest, Booklist* contributor Jennifer Mattson noted that McElmurry channels her characteristic focus on color and pattern into gentle images that capture the colorful "folk-art simplicity" of Lindberg's story and exude an appropriate "vibrancy and charm."

McElmurry began her writing career with *Mad about Plaid!,* in which Madison Pratt finds an abandoned plaid handbag while walking her dog in a neighborhood park. Picking up the purse, the unwitting girl suddenly finds that the plaid on the purse is contagious; soon, everything everywhere is plaid, even Madison's tears! Fortunately, the savvy girl turns the purse inside out, replacing all the crazy-making plaid with a soothing blue the same color as the handbag's lining. Praising *Mad about Plaid!* as a "whimsical adventure," a *Publishers Weekly* reviewer also cited McElmerry's "highly energetic illustrations," with their "accomplished, retro feel." In *Booklist* Catherine Andronik wrote that *Mad about Plain!* will "fit nicely into a story hour" and make a jumping-off point for a discussion of the affect of color on people's moods.

In McElmurry's *Mess Pets* twin sisters Hilary—the tidy one—and Hannah—the sloppy one—share a room. Both sisters are content with the line-down-the-middle arrangement they have devised, until one day when a new creature emerges from the piled-up jumble littering Hannah's side of the bedroom. Hilary soon wants a mess pet of her own, so she borrows enough of her sister's clutter—which she places in a tidy pile—to cause the appearance of a second creature. "Young readers may find the illustrations of the clutter, trash, and dirty laundry amusing and will identify with the siblings' rivalry," predicted *School Library Journal* contributor Shara Alpern in her review of *Mess Pets*. A *Kirkus Reviews* critic noted that, although McElmurry's "partially rhyming text is unevenly paced," "the glories of this messy realm shouldn't be missed."

Featuring what a *Publishers Weekly* critic described as "witty, Victorian dialogue and droll illustrations," *I'm Not a Baby!* finds a boy frustrated that his parents refuse to acknowledge that he ever grows up. Even when Leo Leotardi is old enough to graduate from school, perform a significant role in a challenging stage play, and even start work in a busy office, his Edwardian-era parents and his loving Nanny Fanni continue to view him the way McElmurry's illustrations reveal: as a bouncy, bonneted bambino. Young readers "will be deeply amused by the premise" of *I'm Not a Baby!*, noted Mattson, "and wholly sympathetic to the frustrations of being labeled, patronized, or willfully misunderstood." In *School Library Journal*, Kate McClelland wrote that McElmurry's "wonderfully silly treatment will elicit giggles of recognition" at story time, while a *Kirkus Reviews* writer praised *I'm Not a Baby!* for its "comic gouache illustrations" featuring a humorous pairing of past and present.

Biographical and Critical Sources

PERIODICALS

Booklist, April 1, 2000, Catherine Andronik, review of *Mad about Plaid!,* p. 1469; December 15, 2002, Julie Cummins, review of *The Kettles Get New Clothes,* p. 766; April 15, 2004, Jennifer Mattson, review of *Our Nest,* p. 1441; June 1, 2006, Jennifer Mattson, review of *I'm Not a Baby!,* p. 75; October 1, 2007, Kristen McKulski, review of *The Hound from the Pound,* p. 61; April 1, 2008, John Mattson, review of *Little Blue Truck,* p. 55.

Horn Book, May, 2001, review of *I'm Small and Other Verses,* p. 344; January-February, 2008, Robin Smith, review of *The Hound from the Pound,* p. 79; May-June, 2008, Kitty Flynn, review of *Little Blue Truck,* p. 299.

Kirkus Reviews, September 15, 2002, review of *Mess Pets,* p. 1395; November 1, 2003, review of *It's a Miracle!: A Hanukkah Storybook,* p. 1320; April 1, 2004, review of *Our Nest,* p. 332; June 1, 2006, review of *I'm Not a Baby!,* p. 576; August 15, 2007, review of *The Hound from the Pound.*

Publishers Weekly, April 10, 2000, review of *Mad about Plaid!,* p. 99; March 26, 2001, review of *I'm Small, and Other Verses* p. 91; July 22, 2002, review of *The Kettles Get New Clothes,* p. 177; September 22, 2003, review of *It's a Miracle!,* p. 66; March 22, 2004, review of *Our Nest,* p. 84; June 26, 2006, review of *I'm Not a Baby!,* p. 50; April 28, 2008, review of *Little Blue Truck,* p. 137.

School Library Journal, May, 2000, Rosalyn Pierini, review of *Mad about Plaid!,* p. 148; May, 2001, Ellen A. Greever, review of *I'm Small, and Other Verses,* p. 145; October, 2002, Shara Alpern, review of *Mess Pets,* p. 120; December, 2002, Shelley B. Sutherland, review of *The Kettles Get New Clothes,* p. 93; October, 2003, Mara Alpert, review of *It's a Miracle!,* p. 68; May, 2004, Roxanne Burg, review of *Our Nest,* p. 117; July, 2006, Kate McClelland, review of *I'm Not a Baby!,* p. 83; July, 2008, Rachael Vilmar, review of *Little Blue Truck,* p. 81.

ONLINE

Jill McElmurry Web site, http://jillmcelmurry.com (February 2, 2009).

*   *   *

MELANSON, Luc

Personal

Born in Canada; married. *Education:* Université du Québec, bachelor's degree (graphic design).

Addresses

Home—Laval, Quebec, Canada. *E-mail*—luc@lucmelanson.com.

Career

Children's author and illustrator. Graphic artist; clients include Banque de France, Bank of Canada, *Harvard Business Review,* and *Reader's Digest.*

Awards, Honors

Governor General's Literary Award for best Canadian picture book, Canada Council for the Arts, 2002, for *Le grand voyage de monsieur;* awards from Society of Illustrators.

Writings

SELF-ILLUSTRATED

Ma drôle de ville, Dominique & Cie. (Saint-Lambert, Quebec, Canada), 2004.

ILLUSTRATOR

Chantale Landry, *Sa majestedé gouttières,* Boréal (Montreal, Quebec, Canada), 1992.

Josée Ouimet, *Une photo dans la valise,* Hurtubise (Ville LaSalle, Quebec, Canada), 1995.

Jean Provencher, *Un citadin a la campagne: quatre saisons a Sainte-Anastasie,* Boréal (Montreal, Quebec, Canada), 1995.

Laurent Chabin, *Le rêveur polaire,* Boréal (Montreal, Quebec, Canada), 1996.

Kim Yaroshevskaya, *La petite Kim,* Boréal (Montreal, Quebec, Canada), 1998, published as *Little Kim's Doll,* Douglas & McIntyre (Toronto, Ontario, Canada), 1999.

Lucie Papineau, reteller, *Hansel et Gretel,* Les 400 Coups (Laval, Quebec, Canada), 1998.

Gilles Tibo, *Le grand voyage de Monsieur*), Dominique (Saint-Lambert, Quebec, Canada), 2001, translated by Sheila Fischman as *The Grand Journey of Mr. Man,* 2001.

Bill Luttrell, *Redheaded Robbie's Christmas Story,* Sleeping Bear Press (Chelsea, MI), 2003.

Claudio Ricignuolo, *La grande musique à la portée de tous: les compositeurs,* Fides (Montreal, Quebec, Canada), 2004.

Burton P. Brodt, *Four Little Old Men: A (Mostly) True Tale from a Small Cajun Town,* Sterling (New York, NY), 2005.

Nancy Montour, *Journal d'un petit héros,* Dominique & Cie. (Saint-Lambert, Quebec, Canada), 2006.

Agnès Grimaud, *Effroyable mémère, incroyable sorcière,* Dominique & Cie. (Saint-Lambert, Quebec, Canada), 2006.

Carole Tremblay, *Le petit robot extra poutine,* Dominique & Cie. (Saint-Lambert, Quebec, Canada), 2006.

Pierrette Dubé, *Comment devenir une parfaite princesse en 5 jours,* Editions Imagine (Montreal, Quebec, Canada), 2006.

Nan Gregory, *Pink,* Groundwood Books (Toronto, Ontario, Canada), 2007.

Agnès Grimaud, *Effroyable mémère et le seigneur des noeuds,* Dominique & Cie. (Saint-Lambert, Quebec, Canada), 2007.

(With Steve Adams) Pierrette Dubé, *Le merveilleux de A à Z,* Editions Imagine (Montreal, Quebec, Canada), 2007.

Olivier Ka, *My Great Big Mama,* Groundwood Books (Toronto, Ontario, Canada), 2009.

Sidelights

Canadian artist Luc Melanson has provided the illustrations for a variety of works published both in Canada and the United States. In 2001, Melanson created the pictures to Gilles Tibo's *The Grand Journey of Mr. Man,* the French version of which earned a Governor General's Literary Award for best Canadian picture book from the Canada Council for the Arts. *The Grand Journey of Mr. Man* follows the path of a despondent father who recently lost his son. After traveling to the ends of the earth, the man finds an orphaned boy and, together, the two set out, each no longer alone.

In 1998, Melanson teamed up with Kim Yaroshevskaya, a Canadian author born in Moscow, to produce *La petite Kim,* published in English as *Little Kim's Doll.* Set in the 1930s, following the Russian Revolution, *Little Kim's Doll* shares the story of a little girl who desperately wants a doll of her own. Unfortunately, her parents think she needs toys that will make her strong, of-

Luc Melanson's work as an illustrator includes creating cover art for Arthur Slade's novel **Dust.** (Reproduced by permission of HarperCollins Ltd. (Canada).)

fering instead books, toy guns, and building blocks. Kim's desire for a doll, however, remains unsatisfied, and she eventually dresses up a kitchen spoon to substitute for a real baby doll. Seeing her daughter's determination to have a doll convinces Kim's mother that her daughter is indeed a strong little girl, and for her next birthday, Kim finally receives a doll of her own. "The dark jewel-toned illustrations are colourful and ably evoke that far away time and place," remarked *Resource Links* critic Isobel Lang. Though finding the pictures ill-matched to the target audience, *Canadian Review of Materials* contributor Carol McDougall nonetheless considered Melanson's artwork appealing, remarking that Melanson's "the stylized and sophisticated illustration[s].. make this visually a very handsome book."

Melanson illustrates a child's obsession with the color pink in *Pink,* a picture book written by Nan Gregory. Little Vivi loves pink, a color also enjoyed by a clique of popular girls at school. In her desire to belong to the group, Vivi wishes to have something of her very own that is completely pink. While passing a shop window, she spots the object of her heart's desire, a bride-doll dressed entirely in pink. As her parents cannot afford to purchase the toy, Vivi takes on chores for the other residents of her apartment building, slowly saving enough money for her dream. One spring day, Vivi's mother treats her daughter to a pink picnic, carefully preparing a thoughtful spread of all pink foods. After the delightful outing with her parents, Vivi passes the store selling the long-sought-after doll, but to her disappointment, someone else has purchased it. Although she is sad, the young girl realizes that the most important things in life, such as the love of her family, cannot be bought.

According to *Canadian Review of Materials* contributor Jeannette Timmerman, Melanson's illustrations in *Pink* "brilliantly catch the emotions shown by all of the characters with the colours used often reflecting the emotion by being dull or bright." *Resource Links* reviewer Susan Prior wrote that Melanson "does a wonderful job of bringing Vivi and the other characters in the book to life," while Carolyn Phelan wrote in *Booklist* that Melanson's "angular, pink-hued digital drawings strike an emotional chord of their own."

Biographical and Critical Sources

PERIODICALS

Booklist, October 1, 2007, Carolyn Phelan, review of *Pink,* p. 57.
Canadian Review of Materials, December 10, 1999, Carol McDougall, review of *Little Kim's Doll;* August 31, 2007, Jeannette Timmerman, review of *Pink.*
Kirkus Reviews, November 1, 2003, review of *Redheaded Robbie's Christmas Story,* p. 1318; July 15, 2007, review of *Pink.*

Nan Gregory's picture book Pink *features brightly colored, stylized artwork by Melanson.* (Illustration copyright © 2007 by Luc Melanson. Reproduced by permission.)

Publishers Weekly, April 12, 1999, review of *Little Kim's Doll,* p. 73; July 16, 2007, review of *Pink,* p. 163.
Resource Links, April, 1999, Isobel Lang, review of *Little Kim's Doll,* p. 8; February, 2008, Susan Prior, review of *Pink,* p. 2.
School Library Journal, January, 2002, Rosalyn Pierini, review of *The Grand Journey of Mr. Man,* p. 111; October, 2003, Eva Mitnick, review of *Redheaded Robbie's Christmas Story,* p. 65; January, 2006, Judith Constantinides, review of *Four Little Old Men: A (Mostly) True Tale from a Small Cajun Town,* p. 92; November, 2007, Ieva Bates, review of *Pink,* p. 92.

ONLINE

Luc Melanson Home Page, http://www.lucmelanson.com (January 30, 2009).
Luc Melanson Web Log, http://lucmelanson.blogspot.com (January 31, 2009).*

*　　*　　*

MESSINGER, Carla

Personal

Married Alan Messinger.

Addresses

Home and office—Allentown, PA.

Career

Educator and author. Substitute teacher in PA, 1971-82. Lenni Lenape Historical Society and Museum of Indian Culture, founder and executive director, 1978-2002; Native American Heritage Programs, founder and director, 2002—; Speaker at schools; lecturer at schools, including Cedar Crest College, Kutztown University, Lehigh University, Moravian College, Muhlenberg College, Temple University, University of Massachusetts, Amherst, Göttingen University (Germany), Glasgow University (Scotland), and Trondheim University (Norway).

Awards, Honors

President's Volunteer Action Award Citation, 1985; Jefferson Award, KYW-TV3, 1987; Allentown (PA) Human Relations Commission Award, 1989; Smithsonian Institution Award for Museum Leadership, 1991; U.S. Department of the Interior scholarship, 1991; Smithsonian Institution scholarships, 1994, 2000; Yakima Nation scholarships, 1997, 1998; Pennsylvania Council on the Arts scholarship, 1998; National Trust for Historic Preservation Conference scholarship, 1999; Pennsylvania Federation of Museums and Historical Societies Conference scholarship, 2000; National Museum of the American Indian scholarship, 2002.

Writings

(With Susan Katz) *When the Shadbush Blooms,* illustrated by David Kenietakeron Fadden, Tricycle (Berkeley, CA), 2007.

Sidelights

Carla Messinger, a member of the Turtle Clan Lenape, is the founder and director of the Native American Heritage Programs. Active in Native American projects, she also founded the Lenni Lenape Historical Society and Museum of Indian Culture as a way of teaching the public about the Lenape tribe's cultures and traditions. Messinger has expanded this mission through her work as a teacher and lecturer as well as through her picture book *When the Shadbush Blooms.* "Children are learning about native people and they get one paragraph" about this subject in their textbooks, Messinger said in an online interview in the *Northeast Times.* "We want to help reduce prejudices and make people aware of [Native American] contributions."

In *When the Shadbush Blooms,* Messinger joins with fellow writer Susan Katz to introduce Lenni Lenape traditions and customs to grade-school readers. Featuring the daily activities of a Lenni Lenape girl from the past and a contemporary Lenni Lenape girl, the book illustrates the traditions that have remained the same throughout time. *When the Shadbush Blooms* depicts the modern girl and her family living in a contemporary

house with her family: Native Americans live like most other Americans rather than in the primitive fashion of their forbears. A *Kirkus Reviews* contributor called the picture book "a gentle introduction" to Native-American life, and Shawn Brommer wrote in *School Library Journal* that *When the Shadbush Blooms* would be valuable to "children of all backgrounds during celebrations of families, traditions, and seasons."

Biographical and Critical Sources

PERIODICALS

Kirkus Reviews, August 15, 2007, review of *When the Shadbush Blooms.*
School Library Journal, November, 2007, Shawn Brommer, review of *When the Shadbush Blooms,* p. 96.

ONLINE

Native American Heritage Programs Web site, http://www.lenapeprograms.info/ (March 9, 2009), profile of Messinger.
Northeast Times Online, http://www.northeasttimes.com/ (December 4, 2003), Elizabeth Steiber, "Tribal Study at Spruance."
Ten Speed Press Web site, http://www.tenspeed.com/ (March 9, 2009), profile of Messinger.*

*   *   *

MICHELSON, Richard

Personal

Born in Brooklyn, NY; son of a shopkeeper; married; wife's name Jennifer; children: Samuel, Marisa. *Religion:* Jewish. *Hobbies and other interests:* Biking.

Addresses

Office—R. Michelson Galleries, 132 Main St., Northampton, MA 01060. *E-mail*—RM@RMichelson.com.

Career

Poet, children's-book author, curator, speaker, and gallery owner. R. Michelson Galleries, Amherst and Northampton, MA, owner. National Yiddish Book Center, curator of exhibitions; guest speaker and lecturer throughout the United States and internationally.

Awards, Honors

New Yorker Best Book designation, 1993, for *Did You Say Ghosts?;* Children's Book Committee Book of the Year designation, 1996, for *Animals That Ought to Be;*

Richard Michelson (Photo by Seth Kaye. Courtesy of Richard Michelson.)

Jewish Book Council Book of the Month designation, 1999, for *Grandpa's Gamble; Skipping Stones* magazine Multicultural Honor Award, 2002, for *Too Young for Yiddish;* National Council for the Social Studies/Children's Book Council Notable Social Studies Trade Book for Young People designation, 2006, for *Happy Feet;* Felix Pollack Prize in Poetry; New Letters Literary Award; Pablo Neruda Prize finalist; three New York Public Library Best Children's Books for Reading and Sharing designations.

Writings

FOR CHILDREN

Did You Say Ghosts? (verse collection), illustrated by Leonard Baskin, Macmillan (New York, NY), 1993.
Animals That Ought to Be: Poems about Imaginary Pets, illustrated by Leonard Baskin, Simon & Schuster (New York, NY), 1996.
A Book of Flies Real or Otherwise (verse collection), illustrated by Leonard Baskin, Marshall Cavendish (New York, NY), 1999.
Grandpa's Gamble (picture book), illustrated by Barry Moser, Marshall Cavendish (New York, NY), 1999.

Ten Times Better (verse collection), illustrated by Leonard Baskin, Marshall Cavendish (New York, NY), 2000.
Too Young for Yiddish (picture book), illustrated by Neil Waldman, Talewinds (Watertown, MA), 2002.
Happy Feet: The Savoy Ballroom Lindy Hoppers and Me (picture book), illustrated by E.B. Lewis, Harcourt (Orlando, FL), 2005.
Across the Alley (picture book), illustrated by E.B. Lewis, Putnam (New York, NY), 2006.
Oh, No, Not Ghosts! (verse collection), illustrated by Adam McCauley, Harcourt (San Diego, CA), 2006.
Tuttle's Red Barn: The Story of America's Oldest Family Farm, illustrated by Mary Azarian, Putnam (New York, NY), 2007.
As Good as Anybody: Martin Luther King, Jr., and Abraham Joshua Heschel's Amazing March toward Freedom, illustrated by Raul Colón, Knopf (New York, NY), 2008.
Animals Anonymous (verse collection), illustrated by Scott Fischer, Simon & Schuster (New York, NY), 2008.
A Is for Abraham: A Jewish Family Alphabet, illustrated by Ron Mazzellan, Sleeping Bear Press (Chelsea, MI), 2008.

Contributor of essays and book reviews to *New York Times Book Review* and *Publishers Weekly.*

POEMS; FOR ADULTS

Tap Dancing for the Relatives, illustrated by Barry Moser, University of Central Florida Press (Orlando, FL), 1985.
Semblant, illustrated by Leonard Baskin, Gehenna Press (Rockport, ME), 1992.
Masks, illustrated by Leonard Baskin, Gehenna Press (Rockport, ME), 1999.
Battles and Lullabies, University of Illinois Press (Urbana, IL), 2006.

Poetry included in anthologies, such as *The Norton Introduction to Poetry;* contributor to periodicals, including *New Letters* and *Poetry Northwest.*

Sidelights

A prize-winning poet and writer for children, Richard Michelson is the author of the illustrated books *Across the Alley, Happy Feet: The Savoy Ballroom Lindy Hoppers and Me, As Good as Anybody: Martin Luther King, Jr., and Abraham Joshua Heschel's Amazing March toward Freedom,* and *Animals That Ought to Be: Poems about Imaginary Pets,* the last featuring illustrations by the late artist Leonard Baskin. Noted for his ability to craft witty verse ripe with intelligence as well as imagination, Michelson has earned the Felix Pollack Prize in Poetry as well as the New Letters Literary Award for his adult verse. In addition to writing, Michelson is the owner of the R. Michelson Gallery, which exhibits the works of numerous contemporary sculptors, painters, and printmakers in galleries located in Amherst and Northampton, Massachusetts. His galleries represent a wide range of illustration art, including original works by Jane Dyer, Mordicai Gerstein, Trina Schart Hyman, Maurice Sendak, Barry Moser, Theodore Geisel (Dr. Seuss), E.B. Lewis, Diane DeGroat, and Jules Feiffer.

Born in Brooklyn, New York, Michelson experienced personal tragedy early in life when his father, a shop-keeper, was killed during a robbery. The horrors of the Holocaust also figured strongly; Michelson's aunt, re-calling her years as a young Jew living in Europe, was haunted by memories of Hitler's Gestapo. While his po-etry for adults—published in the collections *Tap Dancing for the Relatives* and *Battles and Lullabies*—reflects the serious nature of his reflections on history, racism, and culture, his work for younger readers is inspired by his love and respect for family and culture.

In picture books such as *Grandpa's Gamble, Too Young for Yiddish,* and *Happy Feet* Michelson depicts close-knit family relationships. Reflecting its author's Jewish traditions, *Grandpa's Gamble* finds a young boy trying to understand why his elderly grandfather spends so much time in prayerful silence. When the boy's ques-tion is answered by Grandpa Sam, the boy learns about the persecution of Jews in Poland many years before, and about how his immigrant grandfather used the op-portunities available after arriving in America to be-come a wealthy man before the illness of a child humbled him and caused him to return to his faith. *Too Young for Yiddish* again finds a boy turning to his grand-father, or Zayde, for guidance, this time with the hope of learning Yiddish. Although the man dismisses the child's request due to the boy's youth, his library of Yiddish books creates a connection between the two generations as time passes. In *Booklist* Hazel Rochman deemed *Grandpa's Gamble* a "moving immigrant Pass-over story" that brings to life "the intimate bonds of love and faith across generations," while a *Publishers Weekly* critic wrote that *Too Young for Yiddish* "pos-sesses both power and pathos" and stands as an "ur-gent" reminder to readers that the Yiddish language is slowly being lost to time.

Although the family is African American, *Happy Feet* is similar in theme to Michelson's Jewish-themed pic-ture books because it centers on a strong family. Focus-ing on the parent-child relationship, the story is nar-rated by a young boy whose father runs a business across the street from Harlem's Savoy ballroom, where the family has a front-row seat to the parade of culture, swing music, dance, and celebrity that passes through the dance palace's doors. Showcasing the rich culture that flowered in that New York neighborhood during the early twentieth century, *Happy Feet* serves as "a valentine to the renowned Savoy" as well as a "tribute [that] will take young readers back to Harlem-as-it-was," according to a *Kirkus Reviews* writer. The "beau-tifully lit, expressive watercolor" illustrations by Cald-cott Medal-winning artist E.B. Lewis add to the book's magic, according to *Booklist* contributor Carolyn Phelan, and in *School Library Journal* Nina Lindsay deemed *Happy Feet* a "charming" story in which Mich-elson presents "a dramatic read-aloud introduction" to

the Jazz era. *Across the Alley,* which also features Lewis's illustrations, focuses on two boys—one Jewish and one African American—who become best friends despite their family's cultural differences.

Friendship spanning racial boundaries is the focus of *Across the Alley,* a picture book that reunites Michelson and Lewis in what a *Kirkus Reviews* writer dubbed "a beautiful blend of story and art." In this story, Abe is Jewish and Willie is black, and although they live in a community in which racial segregation is common the two boys become friends. Their comradeship is first confined to nighttime talks across the alley, where their bedroom windows are close enough that the boys can pass objects between them. Ultimately, their shared love of music and baseball allows their friendship to see the light of day, with help from their open-minded family members. Lewis's paintings have a "timeless feel," noted *Booklist* contributor John Peters, while in *School Library Journal* Alexa Sandmann observed that "the poignancy of two boys who can be friends only at night is revealed brilliantly in both text and rich water-color art."

Brought to life in illustrations by Raul Colón, *As Good as Anybody* takes readers back to the civil rights era of the mid-twentieth century. In his marches to promote racial equality, Martin Luther King, Jr., was often joined by Abraham Joshua Heschel, a Polish-born rabbi. He-schel lost many family members during the Holocaust, and after moving to the United States he devoted much of his life to fighting bigotry. In what Gillian Engberg described in *Booklist* as a "powerful, well-crafted story," Michelson describes the parallels in the lives of the two men and effectively illustrates what words such as "seg-regation" and "discrimination" mean in day-to-day life. "Stirring opening quotes and an appended page of . . . biographical facts" make *As Good as Anybody* an "ex-ceptional title for sharing and discussion," according to Engberg, and in *School Library Journal* Barbara Auer-bach deemed the book "an eloquent tribute to two great men and their surprising alliance." Praising Colón's "softly textured" pencil drawings, done in warm hues, a *Kirkus Reviews* writer hailed *As Good as Anybody* "gentle powerful, and healing."

Many of Michelson's picture books have paired him with award-winning illustrators, and *Tuttle's Red Barn: The Story of America's Oldest Family Farm* is no exception. Brought to life in woodcut images by Calde-cott Award-winning artist Mary Azarian, *Tuttle's Red Barn* recounts the history of a family that sailed from England and established a new home place in what would become Dover, New Hampshire during the sev-enteenth century. Over twelve generations and through changing times, the Tuttles continue to inhabit their land, members spreading out over the acreage and con-tinuing to make their living by farming. In Michelson's story readers see the effects of wars, the predations of hostile natives, the industrial revolution, the arrival of gasoline-powered automobiles and farm machinery, and the growth of the surrounding community on a life of agriculture. Noting that Azarian's tinted woodcuts "epitomize the characters' self-reliance, optimism, and work ethic," *Horn Book* critic Joanna Rudge Long added that *Tuttle's Red Barn* "offers a real sense of history" to young readers.

While many of Michelson's books are based in reality, several are more fanciful. Praised by a *Publishers Weekly* contributor as "both imaginative and colorful, nonsensical and clever," the poetry collection *Animals That Ought to Be* features the narration of a young animal lover who dreams of a herd of new creatures that could make life more interesting: the Talkback Bat, for instance, would voice the verbal comebacks people never utter aloud, while the Channel Changer would eliminate the need to fumble with the television remote control at commercial time. The *Publishers Weekly* critic also cited Michelson's "cheery, effervescent tone," while *Horn Book* reviewer Mary M. Burns praised the "imaginative reality" brought to life in Baskin's "brilliant expressionistic paintings."

A Book of Flies Real or Otherwise trolls the same waters as *Animals That Ought to Be,* presenting a "wonderfully outre" collection of poems which contain "more than a touch of whimsy and humor," according to a *Publishers Weekly* contributor. Another collaboration between Michelson and Baskin, the book features thirteen insects that are depicted based on their common name, then described factually. The Midas fly, fruit fly, coffin fly, and black fly are among those portrayed in both fanciful and realistic form, resulting in an "off-beat aggregate of facts and fiction," according to the *Publishers Weekly* critic. Citing Baskin's "painstakingly executed illustrations," Burns added in *Horn Book* that *A Book of Flies Real or Otherwise* will "entice" young readers with Michelson's "jaunty, rhythmic rhymes" and "conversational text."

Other unique verse collections by Michelson include *Ten Times Better,* which uses unusual animals to introduce the concept of multiplication by ten, and *Oh, No, Not Ghosts!,* a book featuring art by Adam McCauley. Geared for teen readers, *Animals Anonymous* pairs Michelson's verse with artwork by Scott Fischer and introduces a menagerie of sassy animals that share more than a few characteristics of the modern adolescent. Noting the hip-hop beat created in the book's text, a *Kirkus Reviews* writer added that *Animals Anonymous* will have special appeal among "adults who work with and love teens for what they are."

Biographical and Critical Sources

PERIODICALS

Booklist, September 1, 1993, Ilene Cooper, review of *Did You Say Ghosts?,* p. 69; October 15, 1996, Hazel Rochman, review of *Animals That Ought to Be: Poems about Imaginary Pets,* p. 427; March 15, 1999,

Hazel Rochman, review of *Grandpa's Gamble,* p. 1333; October 1, 2000, Michael Cart, review of *Ten Times Better,* p. 343; November 1, 2005, Carolyn Phelan, review of *Happy Feet: The Savoy Ballroom Lindy Hoppers and Me,* p. 60; September 1, 2006, John Peters, review of *Across the Alley,* p. 117; October 1, 2007, Gillian Engberg, review of *Tuttle's Red Barn: The Story of America's Oldest Farm,* p. 62; February 1, 2008, Gillian Engberg, review of *As Good as Anybody: Martin Luther King, Jr., and Abraham Joshua Heschel's Amazing March toward Freedom,* p. 55.

Daily Hampshire Gazette (Amherst, MA), May 3, 2006, Bonnie Wells, "Poetry That Speaks of Everyday Cruelties and Love."

Horn Book, March-April, 1994, Lolly Robinson, review of *Did You Say Ghosts?,* p. 192; November-December, 1996, Mary M. Burns, review of *Animals That Ought to Be,* p. 754; September, 1999, Mary M. Burns, review of *A Book of Flies Real or Otherwise,* p. 620; January-February, 2008, Joanna Rudge Long, review of *Tuttle's Red Barn,* p. 115.

Kirkus Reviews, January 15, 2002, review of *Too Young for Yiddish,* p. 106; November 1, 2005, review of *Happy Feet,* p. 1186; August 1, 2006, review of *Oh No, Not Ghosts!,* p. 792; September 1, 2006, review of *Across the Alley,* p. 909; August 15, 2007, review of *Tuttle's Red Barn;* April 15, 2008, review of *As Good as Anybody;* June 1, 2008, review of *Animals Anonymous.*

New Yorker, December 13, 1993, review of *Did You Say Ghosts?,* p. 117.

Publishers Weekly, August 2, 1993, review of *Did You Say Ghosts?,* p. 81; September 23, 1996, review of *Animals That Ought to Be,* p. 76; March 22, 1999, review of *Grandpa's Gamble,* p. 90; August 2, 1999, review of *A Book of Flies Real or Otherwise,* p. 82; July 31, 2000, review of *Ten Times Better,* p. 94; January 14, 2002, review of *Too Young for Yiddish,* p. 60; August 14, 2006, review of *Oh No, Not Ghosts!,* p. 204; July 23, 2007, review of *Tuttle's Red Barn,* p. 68.

School Library Journal, October, 2000, Nina Lindsay, review of *Ten Times Better,* p. 190; March, 2002, Linda R. Silver, review of *Too Young for Yiddish,* p. 198; November, 2005, Nina Lindsay, review of *Happy Feet,* p. 100; August, 2006, Linda Ludke, review of *Oh No, Not Ghosts!,* p. 93; October, 2006, Alexa Sandmann, review of *Across the Alley,* p. 118; May, 2008, Barbara Auerbach, review of *As Good as Anybody,* p. 116.

ONLINE

Richard Michelson Home Page, http://www.rmichelson. com (February 2, 2009).*

*   *   *

MORGAN, Clay 1950-

Personal

Born 1950, in Portland, OR; son of a physician; married Barbara Radding, (a teacher), 1978; children:

Adam, Ryan. *Education:* Stanford University, B.A. (English), 1972; University of Montana, M.F.A. (fiction writing).

Addresses
Home—Houston, TX.

Career
Writer. Writing instructor at universities, including Lewis & Clark State College, Boise State University, and University of Houston—Clear Lake. Formerly worked as a smoke jumper; former commentator for National Public Radio's *All Things Considered.*

Awards, Honors
Idaho Fiction Competition winner, 1984, for *Aura;* Idaho Commission on the Arts fellowship, 1986; Pacific Northwest Booksellers Award, 1992, for *Santiago and the Drinking Party.*

Writings

FICTION

Aura, Confluence Press (Lewiston, ID), 1983.
Santiago and the Drinking Party, Viking (New York, NY), 1992.
The Boy Who Spoke Dog, Dutton (New York, NY), 2003.
The Boy Who Returned from the Sea, Dutton (New York, NY), 2007.

NONFICTION

Boise: The City and the People, photographs by Steve Bly, American & World Geographic (Helena, MT), 1993.
Idaho Unbound: A Scrapbook and Guide, West Bound Books (Ketchum, ID), 1995.
Shuttle-Mir = Mir-shattle: The United States and Russia Share History's Highest Stage, National Aeronautics and Space Administration/Lyndon B. Johnson Space Center (Houston, TX), 2001.

Sidelights
Born and raised in Idaho, Clay Morgan has spent time in many parts of the world, and he draws from his travels in his novels for both adults and children. Publishing his first novel, *Aura,* in the early 1980s, Morgan has alternated fiction with nonfiction works that range from guidebooks to his native Idaho to a NASA-authorized history of the U.S./Russian space shuttle program. Praising the author's 1992 novel *Santiago and the Drinking Party,* which was inspired by Morgan's experiences in South America, a *Publishers Weekly* contributor deemed the romance-tinged story a "haunting tale of community and solitude in the Amazonian jungle" that "achieves the resonance of myth."

In his middle-grade novel *The Boy Who Spoke Dog* Morgan transports readers back to the 1800s, where they meet Jack, a cabin boy who finds himself washed ashore on a small island off the coast of New Zealand. Once the home of sheep herders, the island now has no human inhabitants. Instead, the sheep and dogs that were left behind have created a new society: the dogs are now split into two groups, the sheepdogs that protect the docile sheep and the wild fangos, which act on their natural predatory instincts. Rescued from the wild dogs by the sheep dogs shortly after his arrival, Jack soon learns to communicate with the animals that share his island. Noting that Morgan's novel is told from both the boy's perspective and through the eyes of a border collie named Moxie, *Booklist* contributor Todd Morning praised *The Boy Who Spoke Dog* as "an unusual, engrossing novel." "More than just an exciting adventure tale," according to *School Library Journal* contributor James K. Irwin, *The Boy Who Spoke Dog* "is an exploration of the hidden link between people and animals."

As Morgan recalled on the Penguin Web site, "I once spent three days on a meadow, on the Aleutian Peninsula, watching eighteen grizzly bears going about their business. Their lives had nothing to do with human beings, and I realized what a unique and rich society the bears had evolved. They were kind, greedy, grumpy, funny, popular, lonely, conniving, brave, timid, bossy, and cruel. But they were not like people. They were bears." Years later, Morgan's memories of these bears returned and wove themselves into the bedtime stories he told his two young sons. "They wanted wilderness stories about our dog Moxie," the author explained. "So I began to weave together everything I had ever experienced, imagined, or read about dogs and children in the wild. I used as my models my favorite adventure stories: *Treasure Island, Robinson Crusoe, Call of the Wild, The Jungle Book, My Side of the Mountain,* and others. *The Boy Who Spoke Dog* comes out of all that, and out of everything I've ever done."

Readers reunite with Jack in *The Boy Who Returned from the Sea,* as the boy returns to the island in the hopes that he will reunite with Moxie. Things have changed, however, and now the boy is not the only human: swashbuckling Blackburn Jukes has also come aground here in search of a hidden cache of amber, and the pirate now forces Jack to help in his search. Once again the alternating narrative voice between Jack and Moxie, Morgan again avoids anthropomorphizing the novel's canine characters, making *The Boy Who Returned to the Sea* a compelling sequel to his first exotic middle-grade adventure.

Biographical and Critical Sources

PERIODICALS

Booklist, December 1, 2007, Francisca Goldsmith, review of *The Boy Who Returned from the Sea,* p. 42; January 1, 2004, Todd Morning, review of *The Boy Who Spoke Dog,* p. 860.

Kirkus Reviews, November 15, 2003, review of *The Boy Who Spoke Dog,* p. 1361; September 1, 2007, review of *The Boy Who Returned from the Sea.*

Publishers Weekly, May 25, 1992, review of *Santiago and the Drinking Party,* p. 36; December 15, 2003, review of *The Boy Who Spoke Dog,* p. 74.

School Library Journal, January, 2004, James K. Irwin, review of *The Boy Who Spoke Dog,* p. 133.

ONLINE

Penguin Web site, http://us.penguingroup.com/ (January 29, 2009), "Clay Morgan."*

*   *   *

MPHAHLELE, Es'kia 1919-2008
(Bruno Eseki, Bruno Esekie, Ezekiel Mphahlele, Zeke Mphahlele)

OBITUARY NOTICE—

See index for *SATA* sketch: Born December 17, 1919, in Pretoria, South Africa; died October 27, 2008, in Lebowakgomo, South Africa. Educator, novelist, short-story writer, essayist, and author. Mphahlele was venerated as both a voice and a critic of South African literature. He told the story of his own life in fiction and memoir; in so doing, he spoke for the millions of black South Africans who were pushed into apartheid by the National Party of South Africa in the late 1940s. His books earned praise from critics around the world. Mphahlele spent his childhood in rural South Africa and his teen years in a slum township of the capital city of Pretoria. His first memoir, the best-seller *Down Second Avenue* (1959), evokes the violence, oppression, and injustice meted out to black South Africans in the segregated townships where they were forced to live. His fiction, first collected in *Man Must Live and Other Stories* (1947), explores similar themes through characters that he generally presents, not as victims, but as survivors. Mphahlele grew up with certain advantages. He received a university education and worked as a schoolteacher until his opposition to the separate-and-decidedly-unequal directive of the Bantu Education Act cost him his job. Banned from teaching in 1952, he pursued a writing career until 1957, when he decided to seek his fortune elsewhere. Mphahlele was permitted to leave the country if he promised not to return; thus, his twenty-year exile began. He worked his way northward through Africa to France and eventually to the United States, where he earned a doctorate and taught at the universities of Pittsburgh and Denver. He continued to write short stories, essays, nonfiction, and criticism. His novel *The Wanderers* (1971) depicts the life of an exile not unlike himself, and readers could discern that free-

dom from oppression does not necessarily lead to spiritual fulfillment. In 1977 Mphahlele changed his given name of Ezekiel to its African equivalent, Es'kia, and returned to South Africa, where the evils of apartheid had been somewhat reduced, at least on the surface. He became the first black professor at the University of the Witwatersrand in Johannesburg, where he taught African literature for several years. While there, he noted that political and social upheaval in his country, while necessary, had the unplanned effect of diluting the rich tribal traditions of the very people who were intended to benefit from the cataclysmic change. In 2002 he created the Es'kia Institute in hopes of preserving and nurturing the black cultural and artistic heritage of his people. Mphahlele was honored around the world for his contributions to African literature, but never more so than when the legendary South African leader Nelson Mandela presented him with the Order of the Southern Cross. Mphahlele wrote several books after his return to South Africa, including the novels *Chirundi* (1984) and *Father Come Home* (1984), and *Renewal Time* (1988), a collection of short stories and autobiographical vignettes.

OBITUARIES AND OTHER SOURCES:

BOOKS

Barnett, Ursula A., *Ezekiel Mphahlele,* Twayne (Boston, MA), 1976.

Mphahlele, Es'kia, *Down Second Avenue,* Faber & Faber (London, England), 1959.

Mphahlele, Es'kia, *Afrika My Music: An Autobiography, 1957-83,* Ravan Press (Johannesburg, South Africa), 1984.

Mphahlele, Es'kia, *Bury Me at the Marketplace: Selected Letters,* edited by N. Chabani Mangayani, Skotaville (Johannesburg, South Africa), 1984.

Mphahlele, Es'kia, *Renewal Time,* Readers International (London, England), 1988.

PERIODICALS

Los Angeles Times, October 29, 2008, p. B6.
New York Times, November 1, 2008, p. B10.
Times (London, England), October 31, 2008, p. 78.

*   *   *

MPHAHLELE, Ezekiel
See MPHAHLELE, Es'kia

*   *   *

MPHAHLELE, Zeke
See MPHAHLELE, Es'kia

N

NAZOA, Aquiles 1920-1976

Personal
Born May 17, 1920, in Caracas, Venezuela; died in a car crash April 25, 1976, in La Victoria, Venezuela.

Career
Journalist, author, and poet.

Awards, Honors
Américas Award Commended designation, 2008, for *A Small Nativity*.

Writings

El ruiseñor de catuche, Editorial Avila Gráfica (Caracas, Venezuela), 1950.

Marcos Manaure: idea para una película Venezolana, Editorial Avila Gráfica (Caracas, Venezuela), 1950.

Cuentos contemporáneos Hispanoamericanos, Ediciones Buriball (La Paz, Bolivia), 1957.

El burro falutista, Pensamiento Vivo (Caracas, Venezuela), 1959.

Aviso luminoso, liberto de televisión, Dirección de Cultura (Caracas, Venezuela), 1960.

Minetras el palo va y viene, Dirección de Cultura (Caracas, Venezuela), 1960.

Caballo de manteca, Pensamiento Vivo (Caracas, Venezuela), 1960.

Cuba: de martí a Fidel Castro, Pensamiento Vivo (Caracas, Venezuela), 1961.

(Editor) *Poesí as costumbristas, humorísticas y festivas,* Dirección de Cultura (Caracas, Venezuela), 1962.

Pan y circo, Editorial Arte (Caracas, Venezuela), 1965.

Caracas, física y espiritual, Círculo Musical (Caracas, Venezuela), 1967.

Humor y amor, E. Requeña Mira (Caracas, Venezuela), 1970.

Venezuela auya, Corporacíon Nacional de Turismo (Caracas, Venezuela), 1971.

Vida privada de las muñecas de trapo, Corporación Nacional de Turismo (Caracas, Venezuela), 1975, translated as *Once upon a Rag Doll,* 1975.

Genial e ingenioso, la obra literaria y gráfica del gran artista Caraqueño Leoncio Martínez, Litografía Tecnocolor (Caracas, Venezuela), 1976.

Raúl Santana con un pueblo en el Bolsillo, Concejo Municipal del Distrito Federal (Caracas, Venezuela), 1976.

Los últimos poemas de Aquiles Nazoa: amigos, jardines y recuerdos, Litografía Tecnocolor (Caracas, Venezuela), 1978.

Teatro, edited with an introduction by César Rengifo, Dirección de Cultura (Caracas, Venezuela), 1978.

Obras completas, Universidad Central de Venezuela (Caracas, Venezuela), 1978.

Papeles líricos, Dirección de Cultura (Caracas, Venezuela), 1979.

Prosa, introduction by Héctor Mujica, Dirección de Cultura (Caracas, Venezuela), 1983.

Poesí de amor y humor, edited with an introduction by José Prats Sariol, Casa de las Américas (Havana, Cuba), 1985.

Poemas populares, introduction by Ludovico Silva, Monte Avila Editores (Caracas, Venezuela), 1987.

Venezuela, photographs by Karl Weidmann, Todtmann (Caracas, Venezuela), 1995.

(With Carmen Sánchez) *Viaje de poesía y color por la navidad,* illustrated by Ana Palmero Caceres, Ministerio de Energía y Minas (Caracas, Venezuela), 2000, translated by Hugh Hazelton as *A Small Nativity,* Groundwood Books (Toronto, Ontario, Canada), 2007.

Sidelights
Venezuelan humorist, poet, and columnist Aquiles Nazoa grew up in the Guarataro neighborhood of Caracas. Because he was fluent in English, Nazoa found work as a guide for tourists, and after his father's death when he was eighteen years old, he and his family relocated to Puerto Cabello where he got a job as the director of a

local newspaper. His humor columns for the newspaper grew in popularity, and Nazoa's writing—including his poetry—eventually became known nationally. Known for his humor and his poetic language, and also as the host of a Venezuelan television program, Nazoa reflected the popular culture of his country through his death in the mid-1970s.

Despite his fame in Venezuela, very few of Nazoa's works found their way to the United States. However, one of his poems was adapted by Carmen Sanchez as the picture book *A Small Nativity*. Illustrated by Ana Palmero Caceres, the book relates the story of Christmas from a Venezuelan point of view, recounting the journey of Mary and Joseph (Maria and José) and the visit of the three kings, transporting the characters to rural Venezuela and featuring animals and plants native to that country. For instance, the angel Gabriel appears as a young country boy who leads the wandering couple to the outskirts of a small Venezuelan village. The tale's "respectful reach across cultures and centuries is wide," wrote Kitty Flynn in her *Horn Book* review of *A Small Nativity*, and *Booklist* critic Carolyn Phelan considered the picture book a "fresh interpretation of the familiar story."

Biographical and Critical Sources

PERIODICALS

Booklist, October 15, 2007, Carolyn Phelan, review of *A Small Nativity*, p. 53.

A popular poem by Venezuelan writer Aquiles Nazoa was adapted for younger readers as **A Small Nativity,** *a picture book featuring artwork by Ana Palmero Caceres.* (Illustration copyright © 2007 by Ana Palmero Caceres. All rights reserved. Reproduced by permission.)

Horn Book, November-December, 2007, Kitty Flynn, review of *A Small Nativity*, p. 634.
Resource Links, December, 2007, Linda Berezowski, review of *A Small Nativity*, p. 8.

ONLINE

Groundwood Books Web site, http://www.groundwood books.com/ (March 8, 2009), profile of Nazoa.*

*   *   *

NEWBIGGING, Martha

Personal

Born in Toronto, Ontario, Canada; daughter of art teachers. *Education:* Degree from Ontario College of Art and Sheridan College. *Hobbies and other interests:* Kayaking, playing hockey.

Addresses

Home—Prince Edward County, Ontario, Canada. *E-mail*—Martha.Newbigging@sympatico.ca.

Career

Illustrator, Web site designer, animator, educator, graphic designer, and database programmer. Conducts workshops in animation, illustration, and comix at public schools and community events. *Exhibitions:* Animation work has been screened internationally at lesbian and gay film festivals.

Member

Canadian Society of Children's Authors, Illustrators, and Performers, Canadian Filmmakers' Distribution Centre, Canadian Children's Book Centre, Toronto Animated Image Society.

Awards, Honors

Science in Society Children's Book Award, Canadian Science Writers' Association, 1997, for *Crime Science* by Vivien Bowers; Best Children's Books of the Year selection, Bank Street College of Education, 2004, for *Archers, Alchemists, and 98 Other Medieval Jobs You Might Have Loved or Loathed* by Priscilla Galloway.

Illustrator

Nyla Ahmad, *CyberSurfer: The Owl Internet Guide for Kids,* Owl Books (Toronto, Ontario, Canada), 1996.
Vivien Bowers, *Crime Science: How Investigators Use Science to Track Down the Bad Guys,* Owl Books (Toronto, Ontario, Canada), 1997, published as *Crime Scene: How Investigators Use Science to Track Down the Bad Guys,* Maple Tree Press (Toronto, Ontario, Canada), 2006.

Martha Newbigging (Photograph courtesy of Martha Newbigging.)

Jackie French, *The Little Book of Big Questions,* Annick Press (Toronto, Ontario, Canada), 2000.

Priscilla Galloway, *Archers, Alchemists, and 98 Other Medieval Jobs You Might Have Loved or Loathed,* Annick Press (Toronto, Ontario, Canada), 2003.

Mark Shulman and Hazlitt Krog, *Attack of the Killer Video Book: Tips and Tricks for Young Directors,* Annick Press (Toronto, Ontario, Canada), 2004.

Toronto Public Library, *Research Ate My Brain: The Panic-proof Guide to Surviving Homework,* Annick Press (Toronto, Ontario, Canada), 2005.

Tanya Lloyd Kyi, *Jared Lester, Fifth Grade Jester,* Annick Press (Toronto, Ontario, Canada), 2006.

Laurie Coulter, *Cowboys and Coffin Makers: One Hundred Nineteenth-Century Jobs You Might Have Feared or Fancied,* Annick Press (Toronto, Ontario, Canada), 2007.

Laurie Coulter, *Ballplayers and Bonesetters: One Hundred Ancient Aztec and Maya Jobs You Might Have Adored or Abhorred,* Annick Press (Toronto, Ontario, Canada), 2008.

Paulette Bourgeois, *The Dirt on Dirt,* Kids Can Press (Toronto, Ontario, Canada), 2008.

Kristin Butcher, *Pharaohs and Foot Soldiers: One Hundred Ancient Egyptian Jobs You Might Have Desired or Dreaded,* Annick Press (Toronto, Ontario, Canada), 2009.

Sidelights

Canadian illustrator Martha Newbigging provides the artwork for children's books aimed at middle-grade readers. In her work, Newbigging has earned favorable attention from critics for her cartoon-style illustrations, which often add humor and compliment explanations in the text. While she has provided the pictures for one fiction work, the illustrator mainly focuses on nonfic-

tion books, many with a science or history theme. In addition, she wrote and illustrated the graphic narratives appearing in *Research Ate My Brain: The Panic-proof Guide to Surviving Homework,* a nonfiction work produced by the staff of the Toronto, Canada, Public Library.

In 2000, Newbigging added artwork to Jackie French's *The Little Book of Big Questions,* a volume devoted to answering questions students often have. Providing information about topics ranging from how astronauts relieve themselves in space to what happens after people die, *The Little Book of Big Questions* features the illustrator's cartoons, drawn using black and blue ink. Several reviewers thought that Newbigging's contributions add a touch of levity, *School Library Journal* contributor Debbie Whitbeck observing that the "cartoon drawings . . . add a little comic relief to these weighty topics." Other critics offered similar opinions, *Psychology Today* reviewer Paul Chance suggesting that "Newbigging's cartoons amuse as they illustrate the ideas," and *Canadian Review of Materials* contributor Julie Chychota declaring that the illustrator's "skewed sense of humor provides much-needed comic respite from some of the bigger 'big questions.'"

Newbigging's work in animation inspired her illustrations for *Attack of the Killer Video Book: Tips and Tricks for Young Directors,* a nonfiction guide written by Mark Shulman and Hazlitt Krog. In this title, readers learn the basics about video production, such as lighting, scripting, and editing. Writing in *Resource Links,* Anne Hatcher noted that Newbigging's "modern style coloured cartoons and helpful illustrations . . . visually reinforce and extend the text." In the *Canadian Review of Materials* Grace Sheppard observed that the pictures, "in addition to adding colour and appeal to the book, often help to clarify the concept that is being explained in the text."

In 2003, Newbigging teamed up with Priscilla Galloway to create *Archers, Alchemists, and 98 Other Medieval Jobs You Might Have Loved or Loathed,* the first of several collaborations that feature information about occupations in earlier time periods. Divided into sections covering work available during the Middle Ages, such as positions held in castles, churches, and law enforcement, *Archers, Alchemists, and 98 Other Medieval Jobs You Might Have Loved or Loathed* includes material about how a individual's gender affected his or her occupation. Newbigging's pictures "heighten the informal, upbeat tone of the informative text," according to *Booklist* critic Carolyn Phelan, while *Canadian Review of Materials* critic Ian Stewart applauded the work by noting that "Galloway's text combines wit with scholarship, and Newbigging's many whimsical, colored illustrations complement the text."

Jumping ahead a few centuries, Newbigging added the artwork to *Cowboys and Coffin Makers: One Hundred Nineteenth-Century Jobs You Might Have Feared or*

Fancied, a book written by Laurie Coulter. While common jobs, such as farmer, blacksmith, and schoolteacher, are covered by the duo, more unusual positions are also covered, such as candy maker, cartographer, and sandhog, the last a colloquial term for the workers who mined underground in urban areas, usually for subways, sewers, and bridge foundations. "The illustrations are helpful in depicting some jobs with which children may be unfamiliar," observed *School Library Journal* critic Lucinda Snyder Whitehurst. In *Canadian Review of Materials,* Shannon Ozirny noted that the book does not shy from some of the ugly aspects of history, such as the widespread mistreatment of Chinese laborers, and commended Newbigging's treatment of these topics in pictures. "While the cartoons keep the general tone of the book light," Ozirny wrote, "they also show the darker side of the period."

Biographical and Critical Sources

PERIODICALS

Audubon, September-October, 2008, Julie Leibach, review of *The Dirt on Dirt,* p. 98.

Booklist, December 1, 1997, Stephanie Zvirin, review of *Crime Science: How Investigators Use Science to Track Down the Bad Guys,* p. 625; January 1, 2004, Carolyn Phelan, review of *Archers, Alchemists, and 98 Other Medieval Jobs You Might Have Loved or Loathed,* p. 850; May 15, 2004, GraceAnne A. De-Candido, review of *Attack of the Killer Video Book: Tips and Tricks for Young Directors,* p. 1618; March 1, 2008, Linda Perkins, review of *The Dirt on Dirt,* p. 61.

Canadian Review of Materials, February 15, 2002, Julie Chychota, review of *The Little Book of Big Questions;* October 31, 2003, Ian Stewart, review of *Archers, Alchemists, and 98 Other Medieval Jobs You Might Have Loved or Loathed;* June 18, 2004, Grace Sheppard, review of *Attack of the Killer Video Book;* March 30, 2007, Shannon Ozirny, review of *Cowboys and Coffin Makers: One Hundred Nineteenth-Century Jobs You Might Have Feared or Fancied.*

Kliatt, March, 2006, Mary Ellen Snodgrass, review of *Research Ate My Brain: The Panic-proof Guide to Surviving Homework,* p. 36.

Psychology Today, November, 2000, Paul Chance, review of *The Little Book of Big Questions,* p. 75.

Resource Links, June, 2004, Anne Hatcher, review of *Attack of the Killer Video Book,* p. 31; December, 2005, Joan Marshall, review of *Research Ate My Brain,* p. 44; December, 2006, Wendy L. Hogan, review of *Jared Lester, Fifth Grade Jester,* p. 20; June, 2007, Joanne de Groot, review of *Cowboys and Coffin Makers,* p. 15.

School Library Journal, November, 2000, Debbie Whitbeck, review of *The Little Book of Big Questions,* p. 140; January, 2004, Anne Chapman Callaghan, review of *Archers, Alchemists, and 98 Other Medieval Jobs*

You Might Have Loved or Loathed, p. 146; June, 2004, Jeffrey Hastings, review of *Attack of the Killer Video Book,* p. 174; May, 2006, H.H. Henderson, review of *Research Ate My Brain,* p. 156; June, 2007, Lucinda Snyder Whitehurst, review of *Cowboys and Coffin Makers,* p. 166; May, 2008, Patricia Manning, review of *The Dirt on Dirt,* p. 143.

ONLINE

Martha Newbigging Home Page, http://www.marthanew bigging.com (February 8, 2009).

*   *   *

NYE, Naomi Shihab 1952-

Personal

Maiden name pronounced "shee-hab"; born March 12, 1952, in St. Louis, MO; daughter of Aziz (a journalist) and Miriam (a Montessori teacher) Shihab; married Michael Nye (a photographer and lawyer), September 2, 1978; children: Madison Cloudfeather (son). *Education:* Trinity University, B.A. (summa cum laude), 1974. *Politics:* "Independent." *Hobbies and other interests:* Reading, cooking, bicycling, traveling, collecting old postcards.

Addresses

Home—San Antonio, TX. *Agent*—Steven Barclay Agency, 12 Western Ave., Petaluma, CA 94952.

Career

Poet, essayist, editor of poetry anthologies for teens, and writer of books for young readers. Lannan fellow; visiting writer and speaker in schools and other venues beginning 1974.

Member

National Endowment for the Humanities (National Council member), Texas Institute of Letters, Phi Beta Kappa, Friends of the Library in San Antonio, King William Downtown Neighborhood Association, Radius of Arab-American Writers, American Arab Anti-Discrimination Committee.

Awards, Honors

Voertman Poetry Prize, Texas Institute of Letters, 1980, for *Different Ways to Pray;* four Pushcart prizes; Voertman Prize, and Notable Book designation, American Library Association (ALA), both 1982, and National Poetry Series selection, all for *Hugging the Jukebox;* Lavan Award, Academy of American Poets, and cowinner, Charity Randall Citation for Spoken Poetry, International Poetry Forum, both 1988; Jane Addams Children's Book Award, and Honorary Book for Christians

Naomi Shihab Nye (Reproduced by permission.)

and Jews designation, National Association for Christians and Jews, both 1992, both for *This Same Sky;* Best Book citation, *School Library Journal,* and Pick of the List citation, American Booksellers Association, both 1994, and Notable Children's Trade Book in the Field of Social Studies citation, National Council for Social Studies/Children's Book Council (NCSS/CBC), and Jane Addams Children's Book Award for picture book, both 1995, all for *Sitti's Secrets;* Paterson Prize for Books for Young People, Paterson Poetry Center, Children's Book of Distinction designation, *Hungry Mind Review,* ALA Best Books for Young Adults designation, and Notable Children's Book in the Field of Social Studies designation, NCSS/CBC, all 1996, all for *The Tree Is Older Than You Ares;* Guggenheim fellowship, 1997-98; Jane Addams Children's Book Award, Judy Lopez Memorial Award for Children's Literature, National Women's Book Association, Best Book for Young People, Texas Institute of Letters, Best Books for Young Adults designation, and Notable Book for Young Readers designation, both ALA, and Best Books for the Teen Age designation, New York Public Library, all 1998, and Middle East Book Awards, 2000, all for *Habibi;* Best Books for Young Adults designation, and Notable Book for Young Readers designation, both ALA, both 1998, both for *The Space between Our Footsteps;* Witter Bynner fellow, Library of Congress, 2000; Lee Bennett Hopkins Poetry Award, 2000, for *What Have You Lost?; Horn Book* Fanfare Best Books listee, and National Book Award for Young People's Litera-

ture finalist, both 2002, both for *Nineteen Varieties of Gazelle;* ALA Notable Children's Book designation, and Books for the Teen Age selection, New York Public Library, both for *Is This Forever, or What?;* ALA Notable Children's Book designation, and Lee Bennett Hopkins Poetry Award, both 2006, both for *A Maze Me.*

Writings

FOR CHILDREN

Sitti's Secrets, illustrated by Nancy Carpenter, Four Winds Press (New York, NY), 1994.

Benito's Dream Bottle, illustrated by Yu Cha Pak, Simon & Schuster (New York, NY), 1995.

Lullaby Raft, illustrated by Vivienne Flesher, Simon & Schuster (New York, NY), 1997.

Habibi (young-adult novel), Simon & Schuster (New York, NY), 1997.

Come with Me: Poems for a Journey, illustrated by Dan Yaccarino, Greenwillow Books (New York, NY), 2000.

Nineteen Varieties of Gazelle: Poems of the Middle East, HarperCollins (New York, NY), 2002.

Baby Radar, illustrated by Nancy Carpenter, HarperCollins (New York, NY), 2003.

A Maze Me: Poems for Girls, illustrated by Terre Maher, Greenwillow Books (New York, NY), 2005.

Going Going (young-adult novel), Greenwillow Books (New York, NY), 2005.

I'll Ask You Three Times, Are You OK?: Tales of Driving and Being Driven, Greenwillow Books (New York, NY), 2007.

Honeybee: Poems and Short Prose, Greenwillow Books (New York, NY), 2008.

FOR CHILDREN; EDITOR

This Same Sky: A Collection of Poems from around the World, Four Winds Press (New York, NY), 1992.

The Tree Is Older than You Are: A Bilingual Gathering of Poems and Stories from Mexico with Paintings by Mexican Artists, Simon & Schuster (New York, NY), 1995.

(With Paul B. Janeczko) *I Feel a Little Jumpy around You: A Book of Her Poems and His Poems Collected in Pairs,* Simon & Schuster (New York, NY), 1996.

The Space between Our Footsteps: Poems and Paintings from the Middle East, Simon & Schuster (New York, NY), 1998, published as *The Flag of Childhood: Poems from the Middle East,* Aladdin Paperbacks (New York, NY), 2002.

What Have You Lost?, photographs by husband, Michael Nye, Greenwillow Books (New York, NY), 1999.

Salting the Ocean: One Hundred Poems by Young Poets, illustrated by Ashley Bryan, Greenwillow Books (New York, NY), 2000.

Is This Forever, or What?: Poems and Paintings from Texas, Greenwillow Books (New York, NY), 2004.

POETRY; FOR ADULTS

Tattooed Feet, Texas Portfolio (Texas City, TX), 1977.
Eye-to-Eye, Texas Portfolio (Texas City, TX), 1978.
Different Ways to Pray, Breitenbush Publications (Portland, OR), 1980.
On the Edge of the Sky, Iguana (Madison, WI), 1981.
Hugging the Jukebox, Dutton (New York, NY), 1982.
Yellow Glove, Breitenbush Books (Portland, OR), 1986.
Invisible, Trilobite Press (Denton, TX), 1987.
(Translator of poetry, with Salma Khadra Jayyusi) Fadwa Tuqan, *A Mountainous Journey: An Autobiography,* translated by Olive Kenny, edited by Jayyusi, Graywolf Press (St. Paul, MN), 1990.
(Translator, with May Jayyusi) Muhammad al-Maghut, *The Fan of Swords: Poems,* edited and introduced by Salma Khadra Jayyusi, Three Continents Press (Washington, DC), 1991.
Mint, State Street Press (Brockport, NY), 1991.
Travel Alarm, Wings Press (San Antonio, TX), 1992.
Red Suitcase, BOA Editions (Brockport, NY), 1994.
Words under the Words: Selected Poems, Far Corner Books/Eighth Mountain Press (Portland, OR), 1995.
Fuel, BOA Editions (Rochester, NY), 1998.
Mint Snowball, Anhinga Press (Tallahassee, FL), 2001.
You and Yours, BOA Editions (Rochester, NY), 2005.
(Editor) *Between Heaven and Texas,* University of Texas Press (Austin, TX), 2006.
Tender Spot, Bloodaxe Books (Northumberland, England), 2008.

Poetry editor for *Texas Observer.* Contributor to poetry anthologies, including *Texas Poets in Concert: A Quartet,* edited by Richard B. Sale, University of North Texas Press (Denton, TX), 1990, and *The Color of Absence: Twelve Stories about Loss and Hope,* edited by James Howe, Atheneum (New York, NY), 2001.

NONFICTION

Never in a Hurry: Essays on People and Places, University of South Carolina Press (Columbia, SC), 1996.

Columnist for *Organica.*

RECORDINGS

Rutabaga-Roo: I've Got a Song and It's for You (children's songs), Flying Cat (Dallas, TX), 1979.
Lullaby Raft (folk songs), Flying Cat (San Antonio, TX), 1981.
The Spoken Page (poetry), International Poetry Forum, 1988.
The Poet and the Poem, Library of Congress Archive of Recorded Poetry and Literature (Washington, DC), 2000.

Contributor to *Poetry in America: Favorite Poems,* Library of Congress Archive of Recorded Poetry and Literature (Washington, DC), 2000.

Sidelights

Naomi Shihab Nye is an award-winning poet who has turned her hand to works for young readers, including poetry anthologies, picture books, and novels which explore "the ways heritage and history contribute to personal identity," observed a contributor in *Writing.* Nye's poetry is also informed by her Palestinian-American background, as well as by other cultures. In her work, wrote Jane L. Tanner in an essay for the *Dictionary of Literary Biography,* "Nye observes the business of living and the continuity among all the world's inhabitants. . . . She is international in scope and internal in focus."

Nye's work is built on a bedrock of such simple connections as the everyday lives of people around the world, or of ancestry played out in primary daily tasks. She employs a "direct, unadorned vocabulary" that conveys both depth and mystery, according to Patricia Monaghan in a *Booklist* review of *Red Suitcase.* "Writing helps us understand everything," Nye stated in *Writing.* "And certainly, to describe our own perspective on anything gives a shape to our identity. Whether we feel like an 'insider' or an outsider or both, whether we feel cozy or alienated and strange, writing can help us see and connect what we feel."

The idea of connections between peoples is fundamental to Nye's own life. The daughter of a Palestinian immigrant and an American, she was brought up in two worlds. "I felt I had an ideal childhood," Nye once remarked. "I grew up in a mixed neighborhood in St. Louis, in a home very nurturing for self-expression. We didn't have much money, our parents didn't always get along, but life itself felt rich and fascinating. I had the sense of people speaking up for themselves very early on. My father was a spectacular teller of Middle-Eastern folktales. My brother and I always went to sleep with our father's folktales and mother's lullabies."

At age five, Nye encountered the works of poet Carl Sandburg. "What drew me to poetry is the sense that everything is precious, and everything is worth noticing," she told Robert Hirschfield in the *Progressive.* "It's important to notice the details that make up our world, that connect us. I think we need to encourage that kind of attitude in children, in the young people we meet." By the age of seven, Nye had published her first poem in *Wee Wisdom.* Throughout her school years, Nye continued publishing her works, first in children's magazines, then later in publications such as *Seventeen.*

Nye's family moved to Jerusalem when she was in high school, and there she met her father's family for the first time. The move was a revelation for her, a confirmation of what she had long suspected: that even separated by space and time, there is a real connection between all peoples. Her father was editing the *Jerusalem Times,* and Nye wrote a column on teen matters for that daily's English-language newspaper. The Six-Day War cut short the family's stay, and they returned to the United States, settling in San Antonio, Texas, where Nye still resides.

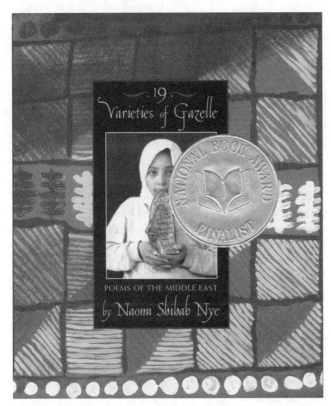

Cover of Nye's poetry collection Nineteen Varieties of Gazelle, *featuring a photograph by Michael Nye.* (Cover art copyright © by Michael Nye. Used by permission of HarperCollins Children's Books, a division of HarperCollins Publishers.)

Known as something of a renegade in high school, Nye was still devoted to reading and writing. "I passionately consumed the writings of [Henry David] Thoreau in high school," she once recalled. "In college, I was very attracted to the Beat writers like [Jack] Kerouac, [Gregory] Corso, and [Gary] Snyder. The writers of the 1920s were very appealing too, especially Gertrude Stein. But my strongest influence was, and is, William Stafford. I started reading him in high school but never formally studied under him. In fact, I didn't meet him until the late 1970s, but his work and life remain a powerful inspiration for me." Nye attended Trinity University in San Antonio, living at home all four years. She continued writing and publishing throughout her college years.

Upon graduation, Nye found work in the Texas Writers in the Schools project. Meanwhile, she was also establishing a name for herself as a poet with a distinctive voice, publishing chapbooks and collections of poetry. In 1982, her second full-length collection, *Hugging the Jukebox,* was chosen for the National Poetry Series and Nye gained national publication. Her poems deal with the everyday aspects of life as well as with the harsh realities of death and missed opportunities. Nye also garnered prestigious awards and was invited to teach at colleges and schools around the country.

Though Nye worked in a wide variety of writing forms, it was not until the early 1990s that she began to write for children. "I always felt that my poetry was for all ages," said Nye once, and indeed, some of her collections of poetry for children are used in high schools. "I've always been attracted to texts for children, whether poetry or prose," she once explained. "I think adults need them as much as children do sometimes, for clarity and focus." Questioning the "division between adult and children's literature," she has asserted that "we often underestimate what kids can understand."

Nye's travels served her well in compiling *This Same Sky: A Collection of Poems from around the World,* for she could solicit contributions from writers she had met all around the world. The contributions to *This Same Sky* celebrate the natural world and its human and animal inhabitants. "The book as a whole reflects the universality of human concerns across cultures," commented Jim Morgan in *Voice of Youth Advocates.* "The most striking aspect of this collection, and the book's greatest potential appeal to adolescents, is the sense of real human life behind the words." The poets speak directly, not in some idealized manner, and the work "would definitely be a strong multicultural contribution" to a school's poetry collection, Morgan concluded. Writing in *Horn Book,* Mary M. Burns deemed *This Same Sky* "invaluable for intercultural education as well as for pure pleasure."

Nye's second children's offering, the picture book *Sitti's Secrets,* was also written during the Gulf War. In the story, a young Arab-American girl, Mona, goes to visit her grandmother in Palestine. The child and grandmother do not speak the same language and at first must communicate through Mona's father, but soon they begin to use their own language as Mona watches her grandmother go through her daily routines of making flat bread and watching the men pick lentils. There are differences as well as commonalties between them, but Mona loves her sitti. Back in the United States, she writes to the U.S. president to ask for peace between people. Nye "writes a compassionate story in poetic, rich language," noted Maeve Visser Knoth in *Horn Book.* Knoth also commented on the use of illustration to further the effect of connections between cultures, as when Mona describes her grandmother's voice as "danc[ing] as high as the whistles of birds" and the Arabic letters on the page slowly turn into birds. This is a book, concluded Knoth, "about the love of a family separated by space but united in spirit."

Nye turns her poet's sensibilities to "capturing a stroller-bound toddler's delight in moving" in the picture book *Baby Radar,* according to a contributor for *Publishers Weekly.* Teaming up again with illustrator Nancy Carpenter, Nye tells "a beautiful story from a small child's viewpoint," as Rochman noted. The child in question is out for an airing in a stroller and delights in all the sights, sounds, and smells experienced from the perspective of the stroller. Pedestrians scurry by, birds peck at food on the sidewalk, a large dog with a wet nose approaches. At the park, she gets out of the stroller to feed the ducks, and by the time she returns home, her eyes are already closed. Diane S. Marton, writing in *School Library Journal,* called *Baby Radar* "sheer pleasure for storytime," while a critic for *Kirkus Reviews* commented that this humorous, child-centered view of the world would leave both parents and young readers "in stitches." The same contributor concluded that the book is a "tour de force for poet and artist both."

Nye returned to the anthology form, compiling poems, stories, and paintings from Mexico in the bilingual *The Tree Is Older than You Are: A Bilingual Gathering of Poems and Stories from Mexico with Paintings by Mexican Artists.* Delia A. Culbertson, writing in *Voice of Youth Advocates,* noted that this "bilingual anthology . . . brims over with a sense of wonder and playful exuberance, its themes as varied and inventive as a child's imagination." Writing in the *Bulletin of the Center for Children's Books,* Deborah Stevenson called Nye "a gifted poet and anthologist" and observed that the poems selected "are generally elegant and eloquent, often richly imaged and dreamy." *Horn Book* critic Nancy Vasilakis concluded of *The Tree Is Older than You Are* that "this bountiful, joyous collection offers much to appreciate."

The poems in *I Feel a Little Jumpy around You: A Book of Her Poems and His Poems Collected in Pairs*, which Nye coedited with Paul Janeczko, are arranged thematically and offer both a male and a female viewpoint. Described as "a wonder" by a critic for *Kirkus Reviews* and "a rich source for thought and discussion" by *School Library Journal* critic Kathleen Whalen, *I Feel a Little Jumpy around You* gathers some two hundred "rich, subtle poems," as a *Booklist* contributor noted, that detail the feelings of both genders on topics from politics to parenting. The anthology includes poets such as Emily Dickinson, Robert Bly, W.S. Merwin, and Rita Dove and supplies "visceral proof of how men and women perceive the world differently and what dreams and memories we hold in common," according to a *Horn Book* reviewer.

Habibi was Nye's first attempt at novel writing. The title comes from the Arabic word for "darling," which is what Liyana Abboud's father calls her. She is fourteen years old and would much rather stay in St. Louis, where she has a crush on a boy named Jackson. Once in Jerusalem, the Abbouds face racial prejudice and suspicion. The family must deal not only with the cultural differences between North America and the Middle East but also with the daily strife between Arabs and Jews. Israeli soldiers ransack her Arab grandmother's house; her doctor father is briefly arrested when he tries to protect a Palestinian youth who has been shot by soldiers. When Liyana befriends a Jewish boy, Omer, she tests her family's espoused belief in tolerance.

In *Publishers Weekly* a critic called *Habibi* "soul-stirring" and concluded that "Nye's climactic ending will leave readers pondering, long after the last page is turned, why Arabs, Jews, Greeks, and Armenians can no longer live in harmony the way they once did." *Horn Book* contributor Jennifer M. Brabander noted that the "leisurely progression of the narrative matches the slow and stately pace of daily life in this ancient land, and the text's poetic turns of phrase accurately reflect Liyana's passion for words and language." Writing in the *New York Times Book Review,* Karen Leggett concluded that *Habibi* "gives a reader all the sweet richness of a Mediterranean dessert, while leaving some of the historical complexities open to interpretation."

Nye further explores the "story behind the story" of the Middle East in *The Space between Our Footsteps.* The anthology contains work from more than one hundred poets and artists from nineteen countries, "a potluck of Middle Eastern tastes, and every dish is full of flavorful surprises," according to Angela J. Reynolds in *School Library Journal.* Susan P. Bloom, writing in *Horn Book,* compared the work with *This Same Sky,* observing that "Nye sets herself a smaller geographic landscape but as daunting a task—to capture in art and poetry the 'secrets [that] live in the spaces between our footsteps' in the multifarious cultures of the Middle East." A *Publishers Weekly* critic declared that Nye "amply achieves" that task, providing "a type of 'hors d'oeuvre' to stimulate further interest."

Other collections from Nye include *What Have You Lost?,* featuring photographs by her husband, and *Salting the Ocean: One Hundred Poems for Young Poets.* The former gathers the work of 140 contemporary poets, including Stafford and Lucille Clifton, in a volume that will prove "a great stimulus for students' personal writing," according to *Booklist* critic Hazel Rochman. Focusing on loss, regret, and failure, the book features poems dealing with petty and major losses, from gloves to spouses. *Salting the Ocean,* on the other hand, presents Nye's favorite student poems from her quarter-century of teaching poetry workshops. "Genuine, urgent, creative, and yearning, the accomplished voices in this excellent anthology's best entries will sweep up poetry fans and encourage young writers in their own search for a voice," wrote Gillian Engberg in *Booklist.* In *Is This Forever, or What?: Poems and Paintings from Texas* Nye showcases the work of more than one hundred artists with links to Texas, including Pat Mora, Sandra Cisneros, and Edward Hirsch. According to Susan P. Bloom in *Horn Book,* the contributors "address matters unique to the state and common to humanity," and Lindsay remarked in *School Library Journal* that the book demonstrates "how creative individuals who love their home and people can show strangers the beauty and oddity they see each day before them."

With *Come with Me: Poems for a Journey,* Nye returns to her own poetry roots, creating sixteen free-verse lyric poems that "make a unique contribution to original poetry for children," according to Lindsay. Lindsay also noted that Nye's voice "is direct and natural, but magical in its sensibility. . . . Each line exerts a pull like gravity." The poems in the collection are linked thematically, and all deal with journeys either inward or outward. A girl flies to the moon to escape her mother, an airplane pilot contrasts modern flight with traveling by covered wagon, and emotions are investigated in "this delightful, provocative collection," as *Booklist* critic Shelle Rosenfeld described it. *Come with Me,* Rosenfeld concluded, "beautifully depicts life and poetry as journeys filled with possibilities, discoveries, and rewards."

In *A Maze Me: Poems for Girls,* a collection of some seventy original poems, Nye examines a wide variety of familiar experiences, many of particular interest to female readers. Despite the diversity of topics the poems address, observed Lindsay in *School Library Journal,* "all are in Nye's unique voice: keenly detailed, empathetic, and humorous." According to a *Publishers Weekly* contributor, "the best poems take a detailed image and expose its wider application to daily life," as in "Rose," which celebrates the beauty of nature by examining a spider's web. "A wide age range will respond to these deeply felt poems," concluded Gillian Engberg in *Booklist.*

The eighty-two pieces in *Honeybee: Poems and Short Prose* "call for us to rediscover such beelike traits as interconnectedness, strong community, and honest communication," Jill Heritage Maza stated in *School Library Journal.* Nye began the work after hearing news reports about the loss of a large portion of the nation's honeybee population. "Filled with signs of warning and hope, the poems sing with an almost ecstatic appreciation for nature," wrote Engberg, and Brabander observed that "readers will sense the connections, and disconnections, between humans and honeybees without feeling they're being preached at."

With the renewed focus given to the Middle East after the September 11, 2001, terrorist attacks in New York City and Washington, DC, Nye's intercultural work gained renewed importance. Her earlier collection of Middle Eastern poetry, *The Space between Our Footsteps,* was reissued as *The Flag of Childhood: Poems from the Middle East.* That year, Nye also brought out a collection of original poems from the same region, *Nineteen Varieties of Gazelle: Poems of the Middle East.* The poems in the book explore Nye's feelings of being an Arab American at such a turbulent time, as well as investigate aspects of the current conflict between Arabs and Jews in Palestine and Israel. The first poem in the collection, titled "September 11, 2001," explores feelings inspired by that event. Rochman, writing in *Booklist,* praised this "small, timely collection" which brings the headlines down to the human level. Rochman also felt that the "drama of the present [Arab-Israeli] war . . . will most move young readers," and that Nye's "best poems bring big and small together." Tragedies are thus made very personal: Nye details how the fight between Israel and Palestine affects one small boy and girl, for example. A critic for *Kirkus Reviews* further commended the poems in this collection for be-

ing "as rich as the subject"; as the reviewer commented, "Poem after poem will elicit a gasp of surprise, a nod of the head. . . . There are no false steps here."

A young political activist attempts to rally support for her community's historic district in *Going Going,* a novel for teens. Set in San Antonio, the work centers on Florrie, an intelligent, energetic sixteen year old whose dislike of franchise establishments prompts her to start a campaign to promotes local, independent businesses, like her own family's Mexican diner. As she stages a number of protests, Florrie falls for Ramsey, whose father manages a corporate-owned hotel. "The novel conveys a strong message, but it belongs honestly to Florrie, who will engage readers with her vivid individualism," Lauren Adams commented in *Horn Book.* In *I'll Ask You Three Times, Are You OK?: Tales of Driving and Being Driven,* a collection of first-person fictional narratives, Nye describes several memorable encounters from her travels around the globe. The author "brings a keen curiosity and a poet's sensibility" to her tales, a *Publishers Weekly* reviewer commented, and Rochman noted that her conversations with the strangers she meets "yield glimpses of family and exile that can sometimes change us."

Speaking with Joy Castro in an interview for *MELUS,* Nye expounded on the importance of personal connections and personal honesty in the struggle for understanding in the world, a continuing theme in her work. "Most of us aren't politicians," Nye told Castro, "so personal connections are all we have. I guess I've always wished that people could speak up with their honest, true, insightful feelings and needs when they have them—but of course, it's not always so easy in real life: inhibitions confound us, expectations hinder us. We have all lost many opportunities to speak out about crucial issues. . . . In books, I hope that my characters are brave and strong. I want them to use their voices. I want young people to be reminded, always, that voices are the best tools we have."

Biographical and Critical Sources

BOOKS

Children's Literature Review, Volume 59, Gale (Detroit, MI), 2000.

Contemporary Poets, 6th edition, St. James Press (Detroit, MI), 1996.

Contemporary Southern Writers, St. James Press (Detroit, MI), 1999.

Dictionary of Literary Biography, Volume 120: *American Poets since World War II,* Gale (Detroit, MI), 1992.

Sale, Richard, editor, *Texas Poets in Concert: A Quartet,* introduction by Lisa Russ Spaar, University of North Texas Press (Denton, TX), 1990.

PERIODICALS

Booklist, October 15, 1992, Hazel Rochman, review of _This Same Sky: A Collection of Poems from around the World,_ p. 425; March 15, 1993, p. 1338; March 15, 1994, Hazel Rochman, review of _Sitti's Secrets,_ p. 1374; October 15, 1994, Patricia Monaghan, review of _Red Suitcase,_ p. 395; March 1, 1995, Patricia Monaghan, review of _Words under the Words: Selected Poems,_ p. 1175; May 1, 1995, Hazel Rochman, review of _Benito's Dream Bottle,_ p. 1580; September 15, 1995, Hazel Rochman, review of _The Tree Is Older than You Are: A Bilingual Gathering of Poems and Stories from Mexico with Paintings by Mexican Artists,_ p. 151; April 1, 1996, Hazel Rochman, review of _I Feel a Little Jumpy around You: A Book of Her Poems and His Poems Collected in Pairs,_ p. 1351; August, 1996, Hazel Rochman, review of _Never in a Hurry: Essays on People and Places,_ p. 1875; September 15, 1997, Hazel Rochman, review of _Habibi,_ p. 224; November 1, 1997, Stephanie Zvirin, review of _Lullaby Raft,_ p. 483; March 1, 1998, Hazel Rochman, review of _The Space between Our Footsteps: Poems and Paintings from the Middle East,_ p. 1131; November 1, 1998, review of _Words under the Words,_ p. 483; March 15, 1999, Hazel Rochman, review of _The Space between Our Footsteps,_ p. 1343; April 1, 1999, Hazel Rochman, review of _What Have You Lost?,_ p. 1397; March 15, 2000, Gillian Engberg, review of _Salting the Ocean: One Hundred Poems by Young Poets,_ p. 1378, and March 15, 2000, Gillian Engberg, review of _What Have You Lost?,_ p. 1380; June 1, 2000, Stephanie Zvirin, review of _This Same Sky,_ p. 1874; October 15, 2000, Shelle Rosenfeld, review of _Come with Me: Poems for a Journey,_ p. 442; April 1, 2002, Hazel Rochman, review of _Nineteen Varieties of Gazelle: Poems of the Middle East,_ p. 1315; September 15, 2003, Hazel Rochman, review of _Baby Radar,_ p. 239; January 1, 2005, Gillian Engberg, review of _A Maze Me: Poems for Girls,_ p. 852; April 1, 2005, Hazel Rochman, review of _Going Going,_ p. 1355; August, 2005, Donna Seaman, review of _You and Yours,_ p. 1962; August, 2007, Hazel Rochman, review of _I'll Ask You Three Times, Are You OK?: Tales of Driving and Being Driven,_ p. 64; August 1, 2008, Gillian Engberg, review of _Honeybee: Poems and Short Prose,_ p. 57.

Bulletin of the Center for Children's Books, March, 1994, Betsy Hearne, review of _Sitti's Secrets,_ p. 228; November, 1995, Deborah Stevenson, review of _The Tree Is Older than You Are,_ p. 101; April 1, 1996, review of _I Feel a Little Jumpy around You,_ p. 131; October, 1997, Deborah Stevenson, review of _Lullaby Raft,_ pp. 84-85; November, 1997, Elizabeth Bush, review of _Habibi,_ p. 94.

Cobblestone, May, 2002, Ruth Tenzer Felman, "Naomi Shihab Nye and the Power of Stories," pp. 126-129.

Horn Book, March-April, 1993, Mary M. Burns, review of _This Same Sky,_ p. 215; May-June, 1994, Maeve Visser Knoth, review of _Sitti's Secrets,_ p. 317; March-April, 1996, Nancy Vasilakis, review of _The Tree Is Older than You Are,_ p. 218; November-December, 1996, Nancy Vasilakis, review of _I Feel a Little Jumpy_

around You, p. 755; November-December, 1997, Jennifer M. Brabander, review of _Habibi,_ p. 683; March-April, 1998, review of _The Space between Our Footsteps,_ p. 229; March-April, 1999, Jennifer M. Brabander, review of _What Have You Lost?,_ p. 218; July-August, 2000, review of _Salting the Ocean,_ p. 472; September, 2000, review of _Come with Me,_ p. 592; September-October, 2002, Jennifer M. Brabander, review of _Nineteen Varieties of Gazelle,_ pp. 59-60; July-August, 2004, Susan P. Bloom, review of _Is This Forever, or What?: Poems and Paintings from Texas,_ p. 464; July-August, 2005, Lauren Adams, review of _Going Going,_ p. 476; May-June, 2008, Jennifer M. Brabander, review of _Honeybee,_ p. 336.

Journal of Adolescent and Adult Literacy, February, 2000, Mary Kay Rummel, review of _What Have You Lost?,_ p. 496.

Kirkus Reviews, April 1, 1996, review of _I Feel a Little Jumpy around You,_ p. 534; April 1, 1998, review of _The Space between Our Footsteps,_ p. 499; July 1, 1998, review of _Fuel,_ p. 930; April 15, 2002, review of _Nineteen Varieties of Gazelle,_ p. 575; August 1, 2003, review of _Baby Radar,_ p. 1021; April 15, 2004, review of _Is This Forever, or What?,_ p. 399.

Kliatt, May, 2005, Claire Rosser, review of _Going Going,_ p. 17.

Library Journal, August, 1982, David Kirby, review of _Hugging the Jukebox,_ p. 1466; December, 1986, Grace Bauer, review of _Yellow Glove,_ p. 116; February 1, 1995, Rochelle Ratner, review of _Words under the Words,_ p. 77.

MELUS, summer, 2002, Joy Castro, interview with Nye, pp. 225-237.

Middle East, November, 1997, McDonnel Twair, "Divided Loyalties," p. 41.

New York Times Book Review, November 16, 1997, Karen Leggett, "Where Rage Lives."

Ploughshares, winter, 1998, Victoria Clausi, review of _Fuel,_ p. 224.

Poetry, March, 1999, F.D. Reeve, review of _Fuel,_ p. 357.

Progressive, November, 2006, Robert Hirschfield, "A Poet Walks the Line," p. 30.

Publishers Weekly, April 24, 1995, review of _Benito's Dream Bottle,_ p. 71; May 13, 1996, review of _I Feel a Little Jumpy around You,_ p. 77; June 27, 1997, review of _Lullaby Raft,_ p. 90; September 8, 1997, review of _Habibi,_ p. 77; March 2, 1998, review of _The Space between Our Footsteps,_ p. 69; April 27, 1998, review of _Fuel,_ p. 62; March 13, 2000, review of _Salting the Ocean,_ p. 86; September 4, 2000, review of _Come with Me,_ p. 108; April 16, 2001, review of _Mint Snowball,_ p. 60; May 20, 2002, review of _Nineteen Varieties of Gazelle,_ pp. 69-70; September 29, 2003, review of _Baby Radar,_ p. 63; March 14, 2005, review of _A Maze Me,_ p. 69, and _Going Going,_ p. 69; July 25, 2005, review of _You and Yours,_ p. 49; September 24, 2007, review of _I'll Ask You Three Times, Are You OK?,_ p. 74.

School Library Journal, December, 1992, Lauralyn Persson, review of _This Same Sky,_ p. 139; June, 1994, Luann Toth, review of _Sitti's Secrets,_ p. 112; June, 1995, Judy Constantinides, review of _Benito's Dream Bottle,_

p. 94; May, 1996, Kathleen Whalen, review of *I Feel a Little Jumpy around You,* p. 143; November, 1996, Dottie Kraft, review of *Never in a Hurry,* p. 142; September, 1997, Alicia Eames, review of *Lullaby Raft,* p. 189, and Kate McClelland, review of *Habibi,* p. 223; May, 1998, Angela J. Reynolds, review of *The Space between Our Footsteps,* p. 159; April, 1999, Nina Lindsay, review of *What Have You Lost?,* p. 152; July, 2000, Linda Zoppa, review of *Salting the Ocean,* p. 120; September, 2000, Nina Lindsay, review of *Come with Me,* p. 221; May, 2002, Nina Lindsay, review of *Nineteen Varieties of Gazelle,* p. 175; September, 2003, Diane S. Marton, review of *Baby Radar,* p. 186; July, 2004, Nina Lindsay, review of *Is This Forever, or What?,* p. 127; March, 2005, Nina Lindsay, review of *A Maze Me,* p. 233; May, 2005, Leigh Ann Morlock, review of *Going Going,* p. 134; March, 2008, Jill Heritage Maza, review of *Honeybee,* p. 223; April, 2008, Rick Margolis, interview with Nye, p. 29.

Teacher Librarian, November, 1998, Teri Lesesne, "Honoring the Mystery of Experience," p. 59.

Voice of Youth Advocates, April, 1993, Jim Morgan, review of *This Same Sky,* p. 59; December, 1995, Delia A. Culbertson, review of *The Tree Is Older than You Are,* p. 333; August, 1996, review of *I Feel a Little Jumpy around You,* p. 178; August, 1998, Gloria Grover, review of *The Tree Is Older than You Are,* p. 228.

Washington Report on Middle East Affairs, August, 2006, Robert Hirschfield, "Naomi Shihab Nye: Portrait of a Palestinian-American Poet," p. 73.

Writing!, October, 2007, interview with Nye, p. 8.

ONLINE

Academy of American Poets Web site, http://www.poets.org/ (March 1, 2009), "Naomi Shihab Nye."

Book Wholesalers Web site, http://bwibooks.com/ (March 1, 2009), interview with Nye.

HarperChildren's Web site, http://www.harperchildrens.com/ (March 1, 2009), "Naomi Shihab Nye."

Pifmagazine.com, http://www.pifmagazine.com/ (October 1, 2003), Rachel Barenblatt, interview with Nye.

Public Broadcasting Service Web site, http://www.pbs.org/now/transcripts/ (October 11, 2002), Bill Moyers, interview with Nye.*

O-P

OLSON, David J. 1974-

Personal
Born 1974.

Addresses
Home and office—Corona del Mar, CA.

Career
Author and educator.

Writings

Lazy Daisy, illustrated by Jenny Campbell, Ideals (Nashville, TN), 2000.
The Thunderstruck Stork, Albert Whitman (Morton Grove, IL), 2007.

Sidelights
California-based author David J. Olson has written two books for young readers. Designed for young readers, *Lazy Daisy* introduces perhaps the laziest girl in the world. Daisy is so lazy that she never cleans her room, but when her closet finally erupts under the strain, Daisy's grandmother becomes lost in the mess and the girl has to save her. *The Thunderstruck Stork* is the story of Webster the stork, who flies into an airborne hot-air balloon and bumps his head. Confused by the injury, the stork delivers baby animals to the wrong parents. When Webster comes to his senses and realizes his mistakes, he finds that the mismatched parents have come to love their untraditional children.

"Preschoolers will giggle at the mismatched families," wrote Julie Cummins in her *Booklist* review of *The Thunderstruck Stork,* the critic adding that parents will likely appreciate Olson's message of unconditional love.

School Library Journal contributor Jayne Damron also appreciated the book's theme, but predicted that, even without it, "younger listeners who simply love a good animal tale will find much to appreciate" in *The Thunderstruck Stork.* A *Kirkus Reviews* contributor commented that "the reason this rhymed, topsy-turvy saga feels honest and natural is that Olson's verse is never forced."

Biographical and Critical Sources

PERIODICALS

Booklist, October 15, 2007, Julie Cummins, review of *The Thunderstruck Stork,* p. 54.
Kirkus Reviews, September 1, 2007, review of *The Thunderstruck Stork.*
School Library Journal, September, 2007, Jayne Damron, review of *The Thunderstruck Stork,* p. 173.*

*   *   *

ORGILL, Roxane

Personal
Born in Mount Vernon, NY. *Hobbies and other interests:* Playing the violin, singing in the choir.

Addresses
E-mail—roxane@roxaneorgill.com.

Career
Author. Worked as a music critic for over twenty years for newspapers, including *Champaign-Urbana News Gazette,* Bergen County *Record,* and *Wall Street Journal.*

Awards, Honors
Deems Taylor Award, American Society of Composers, Authors, and Publishers, 1985, for music critic writings.

Writings

Dream Lucky: When FDR Was in the White House, Count Basie Was on the Radio, and Everyone Wore a Hat (for adults), Smithsonian Books (New York, NY), 2008.

FOR CHILDREN

If I Only Had a Horn: Young Louis Armstrong, illustrated by Leonard Jenkins, Houghton Mifflin (Boston, MA), 1997.
Shout, Sister, Shout!: Ten Girl Singers Who Shaped a Century, Margaret K. McElderry (New York, NY), 2001.
Mahalia: A Life in Gospel Music, Candlewick Press (Cambridge, MA), 2002.
Go-go Baby!, illustrated by Steven Salerno, Marshall Cavendish (New York, NY), 2004.
Footwork: The Story of Fred and Adele Astaire, illustrated by Stéphane Jorisch, Candlewick Press (Cambridge, MA), 2007.

Sidelights

In 1997, Roxane Orgill expanded upon her career as a music critic by penning a picture book biography of Louis Armstrong titled *If I Only Had a Horn: Young Louis Armstrong.* In this story about the famous jazz musician, Orgill retells some of the more important events in Armstrong's early years in New Orleans, including his stay at a home for delinquent children. His time at the institution turned out to be a life-changing event, however, as he joined the home's band and started his path to musical fame. According to a *Publishers Weekly* contributor, the author shares the history of the young trumpeter "overcoming incredible odds to achieve his dream, without becoming too dark, maudlin or even overly hopeful."

Another noted New Orleans native is featured in Orgill's *Mahalia: A Life in Gospel Music.* Geared toward middle-grade readers, the biography covers the life of the noted singer Mahalia Jackson, from growing up in a poor family, to opening a beauty salon, to eventually taking part in the civil rights movement and singing at Carnegie Hall. Throughout her retelling of Jackson's life, the author includes historical information about race relations in the United States, giving readers extra insight into the struggles many African Americans faced during the early parts of the twentieth century. Several reviewers remarked favorably on Orgill's departure from traditional biographies in *Mahalia* by using a less formal narrative pattern. "More colloquial and impressionistic" than typical biographies, according to *Booklist,* Carolyn Phelan, the author's text "creates vivid scenes and sometimes stream-of-consciousness passages." Similarly, *School Library Journal* reviewer Ginny Gustin thought that Orgill's "rhythmic sentences . . . capture the beat of gospel music." Reviewing the book in *Black Issues Book Review,* Mondella S. Jones declared the biography of the gospel great to be "a fascinating read for all ages."

Orgill covered another form of entertainment in *Footwork: The Story of Fred and Adele Astaire,* a profile of the famous dancing siblings. Although most readers would likely pair Fred Astaire with his memorable dance partner, actress Ginger Rogers, the tap dancer actually began dancing in the shadow of his older sister, Adele. For nearly thirty years the two performed together, dancing in popular vaudeville acts in both the United States and England. While Adele stopped dancing professionally after her marriage to an English lord, Fred continued with his career, making the transition into motion pictures and earning his greatest fame. "The pleasantly written" narrative offers "a charming glimpse into the world of vaudeville," concluded *School Library Journal* critic Carol Schene.

Geared for an older audience, *Dream Lucky: When FDR Was in the White House, Count Basie Was on the Radio, and Everyone Wore a Hat* offers readers a "lively look at the late 1930s," observed Vanessa Bush in her *Booklist* review. Framed by two historic fights by boxer Joe Louis, Orgill recounts the development of the Big Band era at the end of the Great Depression, contextualizing her story by including other historical events, such as the rising power of Adolf Hitler in Germany, the social activism of Eleanor Roosevelt, and the achievements of aviatrix Amelia Earhart. A *Kirkus Reviews* contributor particularly enjoyed the author's efforts in recreating the pre-World War II mood of the nation. "Not content to help readers remember," the contributor wrote, Orgill's "evocation of those past days bids us to listen."

Biographical and Critical Sources

PERIODICALS

Black Issues Book Review, March-April, 2002, review of *Mahalia: A Life in Gospel Music,* p. 11.
Booklist, November 1, 1997, Bill Ott, review of *If I Only Had a Horn: Young Louis Armstrong,* p. 476; January 1, 2001, Carolyn Phelan, review of *Shout, Sister, Shout!: Ten Girl Singers Who Shaped a Century,* p. 952; February 15, 2002, Carolyn Phelan, review of *Mahalia,* p. 1024; November 1, 2007, Jennifer Mattson, review of *Footwork: The Story of Fred and Adele Astaire,* p. 60; May 1, 2008, Vanessa Bush, review of *Dream Lucky: When FDR Was in the White House, Count Basie Was on the Radio, and Everyone Wore a Hat,* p. 66.
Book Report, May-June, 2002, Terry Day, review of *Mahalia,* p. 63.
Kirkus Reviews, September 15, 2007, review of *Footwork;* March 1, 2008, review of *Dream Lucky.*
Library Journal, May 1, 2008, William G. Kenz, review of *Dream Lucky,* p. 81.
Publishers Weekly, July 14, 1997, review of *If I Only Had a Horn,* p. 82; March 15, 2004, review of *Go-go Baby!,* p. 73; October 7, 2007, review of *Footwork,* p. 53; February 25, 2008, review of *Dream Lucky,* p. 62.

School Library Journal, May, 2001, Carol Durusau, review of *Shout, Sister, Shout!,* p. 170; January, 2002, Ginny Gustin, review of *Mahalia,* p. 164; June, 2004, Linda Staskus, review of *Go-go Baby!,* p. 116; December, 2007, Carol Schene, review of *Footwork,* p. 114.

ONLINE

Roxane Orgill Home Page, http://www.roxaneorgill.com (February 6, 2009).*

* * *

PALMERO CACERES, Ana

Personal
Born in Venezuela.

Addresses
Home—Canary Islands.

Career
Graphic designer and illustrator. Ediciones Ekaré (publisher), Venezuela, book designer.

Awards, Honors
Américas magazine Commended Title selection, 2008, for *A Small Nativity.*

Illustrator
Carmen Sánchez and Aquiles Nazoa, *Viaje de poesía y color por la navidad,* Ministerio de Energía y Minas (Caracas, Venezuela), 2000, translated by Hugh Hazelton as *A Small Nativity,* Groundwood Books (Toronto, Ontario, Canada), 2007.

Biographical and Critical Sources

PERIODICALS

Booklist, October 15, 2007, Carolyn Phelan, review of *A Small Nativity,* p. 53.
Horn Book, November-December, 2007, Kitty Flynn, review of *A Small Nativity,* p. 634.
Resource Links, December, 2007, Linda Berzowski, review of *A Small Nativity,* p. 8.*

* * *

PINKNEY, Jerry 1939-

Personal
Born December 22, 1939, in Philadelphia, PA; son of James H. (a carpenter) and Williemae (a homemaker) Pinkney; married Gloria Maultsby, 1960; children: Troy

Jerry Pinkney (Photo by Myles C. Pinkney. Courtesy of Jerry Pinkney.)

Bernadette Pinkney-Ragsdale, Jerry Brian, Scott Cannon, Myles Carter. *Education:* Attended Philadelphia Museum College of Art (now University of the Arts), 1957-59. *Hobbies and other interests:* "I am a lover of music, with a large music collection. I enjoy all kinds of music: jazz, classical, rock, and pop."

Addresses
Home—Croton-on-Hudson, NY. *Office*—P.O. Box 667, Croton-on-Hudson, NY 10520.

Career
Illustrator and educator. Former designer/illustrator for Rustcraft Greeting Card Co., Dedham, MA, and Barker-Black Studio, Boston, MA; cofounder of Kaleidoscope Studio; founder of Jerry Pinkney Studio, Croton-on-Hudson, NY, 1971. Rhode Island School of Design, Providence, visiting critic, 1969-70, member of visiting committee, 1991; Pratt Institute, Brooklyn, NY, associate professor of illustration, 1986-87; University of Delaware, distinguished visiting professor, 1986-88, associate professor of art, 1988-92; University of Buffalo, Buffalo, NY, visiting artist, 1989; Syracuse University, Syracuse, NY, guest faculty, 1989; Fashion Institute of Technology, New York, NY, art mentor, 1989; State University of New York—Buffalo, visiting professor,

1991; guest lecturer at numerous schools and universities. National Council of the Arts, member, beginning 2002; member of judging committees for numerous art and illustration shows. Member of United States Postal Service (USPS) Stamp Advisory Committee, 1982-92, Quality Assurance Committee, 1986-92; member of National Aeronautics and Space Administration (NASA) Artist Team for space shuttle *Columbia;* Eric Carle Museum of Picture Book Art, member of board of trustees, 2001; appointed to National Council on the Arts, 2003; Katonah Museum of Art, Katonah, NY, member of board of trustees, 2003—. Designer of commemorative stamps for USPS "Black Heritage" series and "Honey Bee" commemorative envelope; designer of art for National Park Service's Freedman's Village exhibit. *Exhibitions:* Works included in numerous group and one-man shows throughout the United States and internationally, including at Brooklyn Museum, Brooklyn, NY; Art Institute of Chicago, Omaha Children's Museum, Omaha, NE; National Center of Afro-American Artists, Boston, MA; Air and Space Museum, Washington, DC; Boston Museum of Fine Arts; National Center for Children's Illustrated Literature, Abilene, TX; and Storyopolis, Studio City, CA.

Member

Society of Illustrators, Society of Children's Book Writers and Illustrators (member of board of trustees).

Awards, Honors

Numerous Society of Illustrators awards; New Jersey Institute of Technology award, 1969, for *Babushka and the Pig;* Council on Interracial Books for Children Award, 1973, and Children's Book Showcase selection, and Jane Addams Book Group Award, both 1976, all for *Song of the Trees,* written by Mildred D. Taylor; Newbery Medal, American Library Association (ALA), *Boston Globe/Horn Book* Honor Book designation, Jane Addams Book Group Award, and National Book Award finalist, all 1977, and Young Readers Choice Award, 1979, all for *Roll of Thunder, Hear My Cry,* written by Mildred D. Taylor; *Boston Globe/Horn Book* Award, and Carter G. Woodson Award, National Council for the Social Studies (NCSS), both 1980, both for *Childtimes,* written by Eloise Greenfield and Lessie Jones Little; *Childtimes* and *Tonweya and the Eagles, and Other Lakota Indian Tales* were American Institute of Graphic Arts Book Show selections, 1980; Outstanding Science Book Award, National Association of Science Teachers, 1980, Carter G. Woodson Award, and Coretta Scott King Award runner-up, all for *Count on Your Fingers African Style,* written by Claudia Zaslavsky; Christopher Award, and Coretta Scott King Award for Illustration, both 1986, both for *The Patchwork Quilt,* written by Valerie Flournoy; *Redbook* Award, 1987, for *Creatures of the Desert World and Strange Animals of the Sea,* written by Barbara Gibson; Coretta Scott King Award for Illustration, 1987, for *Half a Moon and One Whole Star* by Crescent Dragonwagon; Coretta Scott

King Award for Illustration, 1988, and Caldecott Honor Book designation, 1989, both for *Mirandy and Brother Wind* by Patricia McKissack; Caldecott Honor Book designation, 1989, for *The Talking Eggs* by Robert D. San Souci; Golden Kite Award, 1990, for *Home Place* by Dragonwagon; Drexel University citation for children's literature, 1992; Philadelphia College of Art and Design Alumni Award, 1992; David McCord Children's Literature citation, Framingham State College, 1992; *Boston Globe/Horn Book* Award for picture books, and Caldecott Honor Book designation, both 1995, and Nebraska Golden Sower Award, 1997, all for *John Henry* retold by Julius Lester; Golden Kite Honor Award, 1996, and Coretta Scott King Award for Illustration, and Christopher Award, both 1997, all for *Minty,* written by Alan Schroeder; Ten Best Illustrated Books of the Year designation, *New York Times,* 1997, for *The Hired Hand,* retold by San Souci; Virginia Hamilton Literary Award, 2000, for body of work; named Outstanding Pennsylvania Author, Pennsylvania School Librarians Association, 2000; Children's Book of Distinction designation, *Riverbank Review,* 2000, for *Journeys with Elijah,* retold by Barbara Diamond Goldin; Washington Irving Children's Choice Award, Westchester Library Association, 2000, for *Black Cowboy, Wild Horses* by Lester; Caldecott Honor Book designation, 2000, for *The Ugly Duckling;* Coretta Scott King Award for Illustration, 2002, and Bill Martin, Jr., Picture Book Award, Lab School of Washington, DC, 2004, both for *Goin' Someplace Special* by McKissack; Caldecott Honor Book designation, 2002, for *Noah's Ark;* Outstanding Learning Disabled Achievers Award, 2003; University of Southern Mississippi Medallion, 2004; Roberta Long Medal Award, University of Alabama at Birmingham, 2004; honorary doctorate of fine arts from Art Institute of Boston at Lesley University, Cambridge, MA, 2004; Coretta Scott King Award for Illustration, 2004, for *God Bless the Child* written by Arthur Herzog, Jr.

Writings

ADAPTOR AND ILLUSTRATOR

Rudyard Kipling, *Rikki-Tikki-Tavi,* Morrow (New York, NY), 1997.

Hans Christian Andersen, *The Little Match Girl,* Phyllis Fogelman Books (New York, NY), 1999.

Hans Christian Andersen, *The Ugly Duckling,* Morrow (New York, NY), 1999.

Aesop's Fables, SeaStar Books (New York, NY), 2000.

Hans Christian Andersen, *The Nightingale,* Phyllis Fogelman Books (New York, NY), 2002.

Noah's Ark, SeaStar Books (New York, NY), 2002.

The Little Red Hen, Dial Books (New York, NY), 2006.

Little Red Riding Hood, Little, Brown (New York, NY), 2007.

ILLUSTRATOR

Joyce Cooper Arkhurst, reteller, *The Adventures of Spider: West African Folk Tales,* Little, Brown (Boston, MA), 1964.

Adeline McCall, *This Is Music,* Allyn & Bacon (Boston, MA), 1965.

V. Mikhailovich Garshin, *The Traveling Frog,* McGraw (New York, NY), 1966.

Lila Green, compiler, *Folktales and Fairytales of Africa,* Silver Burdett (Morristown, NJ), 1967.

Ken Sobol, *The Clock Museum,* McGraw (New York, NY), 1967.

Harold J. Saleh, *Even Tiny Ants Must Sleep,* McGraw (New York, NY), 1967.

John W. Spellman, editor, *The Beautiful Blue Jay, and Other Tales of India,* Little, Brown (Boston, MA), 1967.

Ralph Dale, *Shoes, Pennies, and Rockets,* L.W. Singer (Syracuse, NY), 1968.

Traudl (pseudonym of Traudl Flaxman), *Kostas the Rooster,* Lothrop (New York, NY), 1968.

Cora Annett, *Homerhenry,* Addison-Wesley (Boston, MA), 1969.

Irv Phillips, *The Twin Witches of Fingle Fu,* L.W. Singer (Syracuse, NY), 1969.

Fern Powell, *The Porcupine and the Tiger,* Lothrop (New York, NY), 1969.

Ann Trofimuk, *Babushka and the Pig,* Houghton (Boston, MA), 1969.

Thelma Shaw, *Juano and the Wonderful Fresh Fish,* Addison-Wesley (Boston, MA), 1969.

Ken Sobol, *Sizes and Shapes,* McGraw (New York, NY), 1969.

Francine Jacobs, adapter, *The King's Ditch: A Hawaiian Tale,* Coward (New York, NY), 1971.

Joyce Cooper Arkhurst, *More Adventures of Spider,* Scholastic (New York, NY), 1972.

Adjai Robinson, *Femi and Old Grandaddie,* Coward (New York, NY), 1972.

Mari Evans, *JD,* Doubleday (Garden City, NY), 1973.

Adjai Robinson, *Kasho and the Twin Flutes,* Coward (New York, NY), 1973.

Berniece Freschet, *Prince Littlefoot,* Ginn (Lexington, MA), 1973.

Beth P. Wilson, *The Great Minu,* Follett (Chicago, IL), 1974.

Mildred D. Taylor, *Song of the Trees,* Dial (New York, NY), 1975, reprinted, Puffin Books (New York, NY), 2003.

Cruz Martel, *Yagua Days,* Dial (New York, NY), 1976.

Mildred D. Taylor, *Roll of Thunder, Hear My Cry,* Dial (New York, NY), 1976, twenty-fifth anniversary edition, Penguin (New York, NY), 2000.

Phyllis Green, *Mildred Murphy, How Does Your Garden Grow?,* Addison-Wesley (Boston, MA), 1977.

Eloise Greenfield, *Mary McLeod Bethune* (biography), Crowell (New York, NY), 1977.

Verna Aardema, *Ji-Nongo-Nongo Means Riddles,* Four Winds Press (New York, NY), 1978.

Lila Green, reteller, *Tales from Africa,* Silver Burdett (Morristown, NJ), 1979.

Rosebud Yellow Robe, reteller, *Tonweya and the Eagles, and Other Lakota Indian Tales,* Dial (New York, NY), 1979.

Eloise Greenfield and Lessie Jones Little, *Childtimes: A Three-Generation Memoir,* Crowell (New York, NY), 1979.

Virginia Hamilton, *Jahdu,* Greenwillow (New York, NY), 1980.

Claudia Zaslavsky, *Count on Your Fingers African Style,* Crowell (New York, NY), 1980.

William Wise, *Monster Myths of Ancient Greece,* Putnam (New York, NY), 1981.

Barbara Michels and Bettye White, editors, *Apples on a Stick: The Folklore of Black Children,* Coward (New York, NY), 1983.

Valerie Flournoy, *The Patchwork Quilt,* Dial (New York, NY), 1985.

Crescent Dragonwagon, *Half a Moon and One Whole Star,* Macmillan (New York, NY), 1986.

Barbara Gibson, *Creatures of the Desert World and Strange Animals of the Sea,* edited by Donald J. Crump, National Geographic Society (Washington, DC), 1987.

Nancy White Carlstrom, *Wild, Wild Sunflower Child Anna,* Macmillan (New York, NY), 1987.

Julius Lester, reteller, *The Tales of Uncle Remus* (also see below), Dial (New York, NY), 1987.

Julius Lester, reteller, *More Tales of Uncle Remus: Further Adventures of Brer Rabbit, His Friends, Enemies, and Others* (also see below), Dial (New York, NY), 1988.

Julia Fields, *The Green Lion of Zion Street,* Macmillan (New York, NY), 1988.

Pat McKissack, *Mirandy and Brother Wind,* Knopf (New York, NY), 1988.

Verna Aardema, *Rabbit Makes a Monkey of Lion,* Dial (New York, NY), 1989.

Robert D. San Souci, *The Talking Eggs,* Dial (New York, NY), 1989.

Marilyn Singer, *Turtle in July,* Macmillan (New York, NY), 1989.

Crescent Dragonwagon, *Home Place,* Macmillan (New York, NY), 1990.

Jean Marzollo, *Pretend You're a Cat,* Dial (New York, NY), 1990.

Julius Lester, reteller, *Further Tales of Uncle Remus: The Misadventures of Brer Rabbit, Brer Fox, Brer Wolf, the Doodang, and All the Other Creatures* (also see below), Dial (New York, NY), 1990.

Sonia Levitin, *The Man Who Kept His Heart in a Bucket,* Dial (New York, NY), 1991.

Arnold Adoff, *In for Winter, Out for Spring,* Harcourt (San Diego, CA), 1991.

Zora Neale Hurston, *Their Eyes Were Watching God,* University of Illinois Press (Urbana, IL), 1991.

Virginia Hamilton, *Drylongso,* Harcourt (San Diego, CA), 1992.

Gloria Jean Pinkney, *Back Home,* Penguin (New York, NY), 1992.

Colin Eisler, selector, *David's Songs: His Psalms and Their Story,* Dial (New York, NY), 1992.

Thylias Moss, *I Want to Be,* Dial (New York, NY), 1993.

Johanna Hurwitz, *New Shoes for Silvia,* Morrow (New York, NY), 1993.

Nancy Willard, *A Starlit Somersault Downhill,* Little, Brown (Boston, MA), 1993.

Julius Lester, reteller, *John Henry,* Dial (New York, NY), 1994.

Julius Lester, reteller, *The Last Tales of Uncle Remus* (also see below), Dial (New York, NY), 1994.

Gloria Jean Pinkney, *The Sunday Outing,* Dial (New York, NY), 1994.

Valerie Flournoy, *Tanya's Reunion,* Dial (New York, NY), 1995.

Rudyard Kipling, *The Jungle Book: The Mowgli Stories,* Morrow (New York, NY), 1995.

Alan Schroeder, *Minty: A Story of Young Harriet Tubman,* Dial (New York, NY), 1996.

Julius Lester, reteller, *Sam and the Tigers: A New Telling of Little Black Sambo,* Dial (New York, NY), 1996.

Robert D. San Souci, reteller, *The Hired Hand: An African-American Folktale,* Dial (New York, NY), 1997.

Gary Paulsen, *Sarny, a Life Remembered,* Delacorte (New York, NY), 1997.

Julius Lester, reteller, *Black Cowboy, Wild Horses: A True Story,* Dial (New York, NY), 1998.

Julius Lester, reteller, *Uncle Remus: The Complete Tales* (contains *The Tales of Uncle Remus, More Tales of Uncle Remus, Further Tales of Uncle Remus,* and *The Last Tales of Uncle Remus*), Phyllis Fogelman Books (New York, NY), 1999.

Barbara Diamond Goldin, reteller, *Journeys with Elijah: Eight Tales of the Prophet,* Harcourt (San Diego, CA), 1999.

Johanna Hurwitz, *New Shoes for Sylvia,* Morrow (New York, NY), 1999.

Patricia C. McKissack, *Goin' Someplace Special,* Atheneum (New York, NY), 2000.

Julius Lester, reteller, *Albidaro and the Mischievous Dream,* Phyllis Fogelman Books (New York, NY), 2000.

(With Brian Pinkney and Myles C. Pinkney) Gloria Jean Pinkney, *In the Forest of Your Remembrance: Thirty-three Goodly News Tellings for the Whole Family,* Penguin (New York, NY), 2001.

Arthur Herzog, Jr. and Billie Holiday, *God Bless the Child* (with CD), HarperCollins (New York, NY), 2003.

(With Brian Pinkney and Myles C. Pinkney) Gloria Jean Pinkney, compiler, *Music from Our Lord's Holy Heaven,* HarperCollins (New York, NY), 2005.

Julius Lester, *The Old African,* Dial Books (New York, NY), 2005.

Ann Grifalconi, *Ain't Nobody a Stranger to Me,* Jump at the Sun (New York, NY), 2007.

Patricia C. McKissack, *The All-I'll-Ever-Want Christmas Doll,* Schwartz & Wade (New York, NY), 2007.

Dianna Hutts Aston, *Moon over Star,* Dial Books (New York, NY), 2008.

Contributor of illustrations to textbooks and to anthologies, including *Why Did the Chicken Cross the Road?,* Dial (New York, NY), 2006. Contributor to magazines, including *Boys' Life, Contact, Essence, Post,* and *Seventeen.* Also illustrator of Helen Fletcher's *The Year around Book,* and of a series of limited-edition books for adults published by Franklin Library that includes *Wuthering Heights, The Winthrop Covenant, Early Autumn, Rabbit Run, Gulliver's Travels, Selected Plays,* *Tom Jones, The Flowering of New England, These Thirteen, The Covenant, Lolita, Rabbit Redux,* and *The Education of Henry Adams.*

Adaptations

The Patchwork Quilt, Half a Moon and One Whole Star, and *Yagua Days* were presented on *Reading Rainbow,* PBS-TV; *John Henry, Rikki Tikki Tavi, The Ugly Duckling,* and *Noah's Ark* were adapted for audio and video by Weston Woods (Norwalk, CT).

Sidelights

From the day he began copying drawings from comic books and photo magazines, illustrator Jerry Pinkney has aspired to be the best artist he can. Now nationally recognized for his work in children's books, Pinkney is recognized in particular for those that pay tribute to his African-American heritage. The winner of Coretta Scott King awards for illustration, Caldecott Honor Book designations, and many other honors, Pinkney has also combined his art with his own texts, producing original versions of time-honored tales such as *Little Red Riding Hood* and *Noah's Ark* as well as updates of childhood classics by Hans Christian Andersen and Rudyard Kipling. The patriarch of a creative family, Pinkney has also collaborates with author wife Gloria Jean Pinkney, children Myles C. Pinkney, Brian Pinkney, and Troy Pinkney-Ragsdale, and daughter-in-law Andrea Davis Pinkney to expand the children's literature cannon.

Pinkney was born into a large family living on an all-black block in the Germantown section of Philadelphia, Pennsylvania. His neighborhood and extended family provided the young Pinkney with an active childhood, and his artistic urges were rewarded in school, where his teachers and fellow students admired and encouraged his work. Although Pinkney was an excellent student and received consistently high marks in his classes, he continued to doubt his abilities and worried about fulfilling the expectations of both himself and others.

Supported by his parents in his study of art, Pinkney attended Dobbins Vocational High School, which had an excellent program in commercial art. There he received encouragement and guidance from his teachers and peers. After graduation, he earned a four-year scholarship to the Philadelphia Museum College of Art, becoming the first in his family to go to college. There he met and married his wife, Gloria, and established the network of contacts that have helped support him throughout his artistic career. Those contacts also landed Pinkney his first job, with a greeting card company near Boston.

Pinkney's commitment to expanding his artistic range eventually inspired him to co-found Kaleidoscope Studio, where he worked for two years before moving on to a studio of his own. In addition to advertising clients, Pinkney was soon creating illustrations for a wide variety of projects, including African-American historical calendars, a number of limited-edition books for Franklin Library and, in 1983, a set of stamps for the U.S. Postal Service's "Black Heritage" series that featured Harriet Tubman, Martin Luther King, Jr., Scott Joplin, and Jackie Robinson.

Pinkney's book illustration projects brought him the greatest satisfaction, and also earned him critical attention. His work for *The Patchwork Quilt,* with a text by Valerie Flournoy, tells of a wonderful relationship between a grandmother and a granddaughter and celebrates the strength of the black family. Pinkney found people to model the relationships described in the book, and he created his drawings from these modeling sessions. The book won a number of awards, including two that were very important to the illustrator: the Christopher Award and the Coretta Scott King Award for Illustration.

Pinkney's collaboration with author Julius Lester allowed him to further develop his live-model concept. Describing the collaborators' work on *The Tales of Uncle Remus,* June Jordan commented in the *New York Times Book Review* that "every single illustration . . . is fastidious, inspired and a marvel of delightful imagination." Another joint project, *John Henry,* was, as Pinkney later noted in his acceptance speech for the *Boston Globe/Horn Book* Award, an attempt "to create an African-American hero that would inspire all." Based on published versions of the traditional folk song as well as on additional verses remembered by Lester, the picture book depicts the mythic life of John Henry from birth through his fatal contest with a steam drill. Praising Pinkney's "challenging visual imagery" in her review for the *Bulletin of the Center for Children's Books,* Elizabeth Bush added that his "earthy, craggy watercolors capture the sober, thoughtful side of Henry's story."

Pinkney's thoughtful approach to his art is reflected in his work on *John Henry.* "As far back as I can recall, I have sustained the memory of the legend of John Henry," he once explained. "I am not sure why it took me so long to entertain the notion to unlock John Henry from its place in my memories. After all, he had been a part of my most cherished remembrance of African-American perseverance, along with Harriet Tubman, Fredrick Douglass, and Sojourner Truth. And John Henry and High John de Conquer were the only tall-tale black heroes to come from that period in American history. I became intrigued with the realization that black heroes did not exist in African-American folklore until after the U.S. Civil War. Before emancipation, African-American story characters, like the enslaved, had only two weapons that they were able to use: good old-fashioned common sense, and that of trickster. . . . Only after freedom could African Americans afford to create black heroes in our folklore."

"How fortunate I was when Julius Lester embraced the idea to create the text; who better to take on the task than Julius, a civil rights advocate, folk-singer and

author. . . . Our collaboration is a John Henry that represents and symbolizes the men and boys who made up the crews, whose muscles built the roads and railroads in this country in the late 1800s. One can only imagine the stamina and endurance of the men and boys, black and white, employed for such dangerous work. I tried to give reverence to the men, by instilling in each person I portrayed a sense of his own history. . . . With this book we strived to create an African-American hero that would inspire all."

Other Pinkney-Lester projects include three more collections of "Uncle Remus" tales as well as a new version of a somewhat controversial picture book titled *Sam and the Tigers: A New Telling of Little Black Sambo.* In yet another work, *Black Cowboy, Wild Horses: A True Story,* author and illustrator combine to tell the story of Texan Bob Lemmons, a former slave who became a legend due to his skill in coralling wild mustangs. *The Old African,* also a Lester-Pinkney collaboration, is based on a slave legend that finds those who succumbed during the horrific middle passage given supernatural rebirth to help living slaves endure and transcend their fate. Calling *The Old African* "an eloquent visual expression of the heroism" of those who were forcibly transported to the New World, *Horn Book* contributor Joanna Rudge described Pinkney's illustrations as a "superb" mix of "muted tones of worn fabric; impressionistic shadows . . . ; resolute dramatic focus; . . . steadfast courage; [and] quiet jubilation." "The stirring illustrations . . . beautifully depict the dramatic escape fantasy" of enslaved Africans, "but they never deny the horror," Rochman noted, while in *School Library Journal* Nina Lindsay dubbed Pinkney's work for *The Old African* as "stunning, showing power in landscape and emotional energy in posture."

Using the few facts known about the childhood of former slave and abolitionist Harriet Tubman, author Alan Schroeder teamed up with Pinkney to produce another picture book focusing on African-American history. *Minty: A Story of the Young Harriet Tubman* tells the story of how Minty—taken from Tubman's cradle name, Araminta—acquires the skills she needs to escape and survive alone in the wilderness and how she ultimately uses those same skills to lead hundreds of fellow slaves to freedom. In a *School Library Journal* review, Louise L. Sherman wrote of the book that "Pinkney's illustrations are outstanding . . . and his depictions of Minty are particularly powerful and expressive."

Another picture book in which Pinkney explores African-American history is *Goin' Someplace Special,* one of several collaborations between Pinkney and author Patricia C. McKissack. In the story a little girl named 'Tricia Ann is allowed to go Someplace Special, alone, for the very first time. Her journey takes place in the Jim Crow South, and it is made more challenging because 'Tricia Ann has to sit at the back of the bus and the park benches she passes on her way are labeled for "whites only." The racism the girl faces almost makes her give up, but with her grandmother's encouragement she perseveres. Finally, she arrives at Someplace Special: the Nashville Public Library. In Pinkney's illustration, the library building is "bathed in a hopeful lemon sunshine" that illuminates the sign over the door: "Public Library: All Are Welcome," as Robin Smith observed in her *Horn Book* review of *Goin' Someplace Special*. Other reviewers commented upon the bright turquoise-and-yellow dress worn by the young heroine, a *Kirkus Reviews* critic observing that it "jumps out of every picture."

Pinkney's adaptations and retelling of classic stories include Rudyard Kipling's *Rikki-Tikki-Tavi;* Hans Christian Andersen's *The Little Match Girl, The Ugly Duckling,* and *The Nightingale; Aesop's Fables,* and storybook classics such as *Little Red Riding Hood.* His version of *The Ugly Duckling* garnered him his fourth Caldecott Honor Book designation, and *Booklist* contributor Carolyn Phelan called Pinkney's *The Little Match Girl* a "beautifully illustrated version of a classic tale." A *Horn Book* critic dubbed the newly illustrated *Aesop's Fables* the "quintessential Aesop, lovingly retold in a contemporary yet timeless style embellished with a profusion of glorious illustrations." For his adaptation of *The Nightingale,* Pinkney transports Andersen's tale from China to Morocco, resulting in an interpretation that is "fresh, but true to the spirit of the original," according to Phelan. The book's "gouache and watercolor illustrations have the stained radiance of sunlight through glass; even his figures appear lit from within," commented a *Kirkus Reviews* contributor.

Described by Rochman as a "delightful, old-fashioned version of a familiar tale," Pinkney's *Little Red Riding Hood* features high-contrast art due to its somewhat unconventional setting: a snowy woodland setting. Noting that the character of the wolf provides a comical touch despite its unhappy fate at the hands of the burly woodcutter, a *Publishers Weekly* concluded that Pinkney's "spry and satisfying" retelling will appeal to those "looking for traditional tales that feature a multiracial cast." *The Little Red Hen* is also characteristic of Pinkney's high standards: the author/illustrator's "meticulously crafted watercolors depicting a cast of unique characters," according to Cooper, and a *Publishers Weekly* critic praised the book for its "resplendent artwork." Calling the story of the hen who has trouble getting help with dinner a "lush, light-filled rendition of a folktale staple," *School Library Journal* critic Kathy Krasniewicz explained that "important lessons of work ethics, initiative, and . . . consequence[s] are delivered in the latest addition to . . . the 'Pinkney classic bookshelf.'"

Pinkney turns to the ancient world in both *Noah's Ark* and *Aesop's Fables,* both of which figured strongly in his own childhood. A *Publishers Weekly* reviewer described *Noah's Ark* as containing "some of the finest illustrations of [Pinkney's] . . . career." Here the author/illustrator adheres closely to the events as told in the Bible, and he "seems utterly comfortable with the majesty of the tale," as Stephanie Zvirin commented in *Booklist.* According to a *Kirkus Reviews,* the book's "sweeping spreads of dappled paintings . . . capture brilliantly the hugeness of the Ark," and Zvirin observed that Pinkney's "strong, straightforward" language evokes "the deep rumble of a distant voice." Calling Pinkney "one of America's most honored illustrators," Rosemary Wells noted in her *New York Times Book Review* appraisal of *Aesop's Fables* that the work is a "visible treat. . . . combining pencil, colored pencil and watercolor with a light-as-air touch." In addition, Wells added, "Pinkney's . . . text is better than most traditional tellings."

Biographical and Critical Sources

BOOKS

African American Almanac, edited by Jessie Carnie Smithland and Joseph Palmisano, 8th edition, Gale (Detroit, MI), 2000.
Cederholm, Theresa Dickason, compiler and editor, *Afro-American Artists: A Bibliographical Directory,* Boston Public Library (Boston, MA), 1973.
Children's Literature Review, Volume 43, Gale (Detroit, MI), 1997.
Contemporary Black Biography, Volume 15, Gale (Detroit, MI), 1997.
Kingman, Lee, and others, compilers, *Illustrators of Children's Books: 1957-1966,* Horn Book (Boston, MA), 1968.
Marcus, Leonard S., *Ways of Telling,* Dutton (New York, NY), 2001.
Marcus, Leonard S., *Side by Side,* Walker (New York, NY), 2002.
McKissack, Patricia, *Goin' Someplace Special,* illustrated by Jerry Pinkney, Atheneum (New York, NY), 2000.
Twelve Black Artists from Boston, Brandeis University (Waltham, MA), 1969.

PERIODICALS

Black Issues Book Review, March-April, 2002, Mondella S. Jones, "Awards Spotlight," p. 9.
Booklist, October 15, 1999, Carolyn Phelan, review of *The Little Match Girl,* p. 443; January 1, 2000, review of *The Ugly Duckling,* p. 825; July, 2001, Stephanie Zvirin, review of *Aesop's Fables,* p. 2011; September 1, 2002, Carolyn Phelan, review of *The Nightingale,* p. 121; October 1, 2002, Stephanie Zvirin, review of *Noah's Ark,* p. 342; February 15, 2004, Ilene Cooper, review of *God Bless the Child;* July, 2005, Hazel Rochman, review of *The Old African,* p. 1923; October 1, 2005, Ilene Cooper, review of *Music from Our Lord's Holy Heaven,* p. 70; March 1, 2006, Ilene Cooper, review of *The Little Red Hen,* p. 96; September 1, 2007, Hazel Rochman, review of *Little Red Riding Hood,* p. 121.

Bulletin of the Center for Children's Books, October, 1994, Elizabeth Bush, review of *John Henry,* p. 54; January, 2003, review of *Noah's Ark,* p. 188; February, 2004, review of *God Bless the Child,* p. 233

Horn Book, January-February, 1996, Jerry Pinkney, "John Henry," pp. 32-34; January, 2001, review of *Aesop's Fables,* p. 100; November-December, 2001, Robin Smith, review of *Goin' Someplace Special,* pp. 736-737; November-December, 2002, Mary M. Burns, review of *The Nightingale,* p. 733; May-June, 2003, Barbara Bader, "Multiculturalism in the Mainstream," pp. 265-292; September-October, 2005, Joanna Rudge-Long, review of *The Old African,* p. 593.

Kirkus Reviews, April 1, 1996, review of *Minty: A Story of Young Harriet Tubman,* p. 537; September 15, 2001, review of *Goin' Someplace Special,* p. 1362; August 1, 2002, review of *The Nightingale,* p. 1120; October 1, 2002, review of *Noah's Ark,* p. 1478; January 15, 2004, review of *God Bless the Child,* p. 83; August 1, 2005, review of *The Old African,* p. 852; April 1, 2006, review of *The Little Red Hen,* p. 354; September 1, 2007, review of *Little Red Riding Hood.*

New York Times, August 21, 2001, Doreen Carvajal, "Illustrating Familiar Tales for a New Generation," p. E1.

New York Times Book Review, May 17, 1987, June Jordan, "A Truly Bad Rabbit," p. 32; November 13, 1995, Jack Zipes, "Power Rangers of Yore," p. 30; November 19, 2000, Rosemary Wells, review of *Aesop's Fables,* p. 50; February 20, 3003, review of *Goin' Someplace Special,* p. 20; December 2, 2007, review of *The All-I'll-Ever-Want Christmas Doll,* p. 58.

Publishers Weekly, February 25, 2002, review of *In the Forest of Your Remembrance: Thirty-three Goodly News Tellings for the Whole Family,* p. 63; July 8, 2002, review of *The Nightingale,* p. 49; September

30, 2002, review of *Noah's Ark,* p. 69; July 25, 2005, review of *Music from Our Lord's Holy Heaven,* p. 80; October 24, 2005, review of *The Old African,* p. 58; June 5, 2006, review of *The Little Red Hen,* p. 63; October 1, 2007, review of *Little Red Riding Hood,* p. 55; October 22, 2007, review of *The All-I'll-Ever-Want Christmas Doll,* p. 56.

School Library Journal, May, 1996, Louise L. Sherman, review of *Minty,* p. 108; November, 2000, Julie Cummins, review of *Albidaro and the Mischievous Dream,* p. 126; September, 2001, Mary Elam, review of *Goin' Someplace Special,* p. 199, Kathryn Kosiorek, review of *In the Forest of Your Remembrance,* p. 252; November, 2002, Kathy Piehl, review of *Noah's Ark,* pp. 146-147; February, 2004, review of *God Bless the Child,* p. 132; September, 2005, Nina Lindsay, review of *The Old African,* p. 206; December, 2005, Linda L. Walkins, review of *Music from Our Lord's Holy Heaven,* p. 132; May, 2006, Kathy Krasniewicz, review of *The Little Red Hen,* p. 116; May, 2007, Wendy Lukehart, review of *Ain't Nobody a Stranger to Me,* p. 97.

Watercolor, fall, 2003, Daniel Grant, "Jerry Pinkney Joins the National Council on the Arts," pp. 18-23.

Wilson Library Bulletin, April, 1989, Donnarae MacCann and Olga Richard, "Picture Books for Children," and Frederick Woodard, review of *Mirandy and Brother Wind,* both p. 92; January, 1993, Frances Bradburn, review of *Nightjohn,* p. 88.

ONLINE

Children's Book Council Web site, http://www.cbcbooks. org/cbcmagazine/ (June 15, 2008), "Jerry Pinkney."

National Endowment for the Arts Web site, http://www. nea.gov/ (June 15, 2008), "Jerry Pinkney."

Autobiography Feature

Jerry Pinkney

Pinkney contributed the following autobiographical essay to *SATA:*

I was born in 1939 to a family of six children; there were three boys and three girls. I was a middle child—two older brothers, one older sister, and two younger sisters. We were all three years apart. Edward, who was the oldest, was just incredible to me in terms of the perfect big brother. He was nine years older than myself. Eddie had the magical tendency of always being around when you needed some kind of help or guidance.

Billy was an interesting child. He was a kid who most of us considered very, very straight. Unlike Eddie, who was always a leader with lots of followers. Billy was quite different; he was a loner and always had a strong sense of . . . I guess morality might be the word. He was the practical one of my two older brothers.

Joan was certainly the one who got the most attention, being the firstborn girl. In some way that was her place in the family and my father certainly adored her; I should say my father and mother both adored her, their first girl. Joan has always had an interest in art that she and I have been able to share since art school. Claudia was a rebel and a very high-spirited child. And my youngest sister, Helen, was, as you might suspect, the baby of the family. I was very close to Claudia and Helen as a teenager and often went to parties and concerts with them. Over the years my family has maintained a close and loving relationship.

We lived on an all-black block in a section called Germantown in Philadelphia, Pennsylvania, on Earlham Street—an all-black block in a neighborhood that was mostly Italians and Jews.

As a kid, I don't remember growing up thinking much about the fact that my neighbors were all African Americans. I think it had to do with the fact that we saw ourselves on that small block as all family so that there was no great need to go outside of it for a social life. If you were to do something that was not quite right, then you might get scolded by a friend's mother or some other elder. I don't remember feeling that we were isolated because there were many kids and always a lot of activity. For example, I remember we always had a variety of projects. We had a stand where we would sell lemonade. Much later on we used to barbe-cue chickens and sell them right out there on the sidewalk. So you can see there was a lot of socializing among the people who lived on Earlham Street.

As peers, I remember we always traveled together. I had a shoeshine kit and we had somewhat of a business—a number of us, four or five, would go out to earn extra money by shining shoes. We always traveled as a group. My father, at that time, was employed in produce; he worked for a co-op chain of fruit stores in Philadelphia. Mother stayed home most of the time and took care of the children. I do remember periods when, for extra money, she would go out and do domestic work. I don't quite recall the extent of how much of that she did. Something in the back of my mind remembers that she did that kind of work to supplement the

Mother, Williemae Pinkney (Courtesy of Jerry Pinkney.)

Father, James H. Pinkney (Courtesy of Jerry Pinkney.)

family income. My mother had a grace and a style about her and her appearance was very important to her. My feeling is that she also worked to buy things for herself. I remember that fondly because she was a person with a tremendous amount of self-respect, and I can say that of my father also. He was a very proud man. When I think back or look at some of the old pictures of my mother and father as young adults, it amazing to see the quality and the style and the dignity they both had.

We were the family on the block that had the most in terms of money and material things. I remember as a child that we were one of the first families to get a car. It was a wonderful car—a Ford Woodie. I remember always polishing that car; it was a handsome vehicle. So very early on in life I experienced people looking up to me or to the family, because we seemed to have more than most families on Earlham Street. That's not to say that there was an abundance of money, because really there wasn't. My mother and father had a certain kind of savvy that enabled us to feel like we had enough.

I took an interest in drawing very early in my life. It had a lot to do with both brothers drawing, not only from comic books, which were popular then, but from photo magazines—which at that time were large, for-matted magazines. One that I certainly remember very

clearly was *Life* magazine. So they would draw things that were current issues. Unfortunately, there was potential for war at that time, so tanks and airplanes became a big thing. I actually started out drawing, mimicking my brothers, because I thought that if they could sit down to draw and make pictures that looked terrific, then I could sit down and do the same. So drawing started very early for me. At some point I realized that I actually enjoyed it and that very often I'd rather sit and draw than go out and play with the other children. I think this caused a great deal of conflict for me, because I remember very early that I was always caught in the middle between the thing that I wanted to do, which would be to sit and draw, and the other side of me that really wanted to be more social; and yet, being social was more work for me. I was well liked, however.

My first recollection of feeling that art would play an important part in my life was early in elementary school. I found that by using a drawing for a project, my teachers soon realized this was something other children weren't doing, and that there was potential talent in my work. Two things happened: I was able to solve certain class projects in a unique way, and I enjoyed the response that I got and the encouragement from teachers and fellow students. So I knew then that expressing myself with marks on a paper was going to be a part of my life.

Elementary school was an interesting time for me because I think some of the security and insecurity that I feel now stemmed from being in a school where the teachers and certainly my parents emphasized my success and achievement. Somehow I hooked into that competitive mode so that it became very important that I succeed and, in some ways, that was not always constructive for me. I found, in terms of sports, that I always had difficulty—not in actually playing the sport or having the skill or talent, but in always thinking that I had to win. If I did not win, I felt that I wasn't living up to what people expected or, in reality, I wasn't living up to what I thought I should be doing, or I wasn't playing as well as I should have been playing. I never really understood how to enjoy playing sports of any kind, because I was there to succeed and win and if I didn't win then I didn't think very much of myself. It's interesting to draw parallels to things like that because you wonder if, as a "drawer," I expected the attention being paid to me in terms of my drawing to be the same kind of attention that should be paid to me in sports and everything else. I don't know whether or not I was comparing these attentions. Anyway, as a result, it made it very difficult for me to feel comfortable playing any kind of sports.

I was not a terrific speller or a fast reader so throughout elementary school I always felt that, again, I was not achieving the way that I wanted to. I always got fairly good grades, and if I had a problem in a subject I could always study very hard and bring those marks up. I remember in spelling, for instance, that on Fridays we would have a spelling test on a group of words we had had to study all week. I would study on Thursday, pass the test on Friday, and forget the words by Monday. That was the kind of baggage that I dragged through elementary school and to me it implied that I was not very bright.

Anyway, come graduation day at Hill Elementary School, I graduated with the top male honors in the class. So very early I started receiving awards, but I was still unable to make a connection between what I thought about myself and how others felt about my achievements. Gosh, I wish I had that medal now because I would look at it in a different way.

After graduation, I went to Roosevelt Junior High School. There I did not participate in art activities. I shouldn't say I did not participate because there really were no art classes as such and I don't remember having any opportunity to actually apply my artistic talent. I joined the orchestra and played an E-flat alto horn, which is a little deeper in tone than the trumpet I wanted to play but couldn't because they were all taken. If there's a parallel between some of the things that have happened to me with peers in junior high school and in elementary school, then it might be making the decision to play that particular horn and the fact that I started

Age six (Courtesy of Jerry Pinkney.)

taking classes other than those offered in school. I found a private teacher. I remember on Saturday mornings I would get up very early and take these lessons. But I was always the only kid around who was doing that kind of thing, so I always felt a kind of separation. Remember I talked earlier about the conflict between wanting to draw and wanting to be social. I found in junior high school, while taking these Saturday classes, that I was beginning to separate myself from the direction of most of my peers.

*

My family was very social, especially my father, so a strong and full social life was very much prevalent in growing up. I spent a great deal of time with aunts and uncles and cousins. I was very close to my cousins. I remember part of the family doing fairly well—aunts and uncles—and we would spend weekends or a Saturday or Sunday with them. We had relatives who lived in suburban Philadelphia, and we would go and spend time there. I remember an aunt and uncle who owned a pony and having the experience of being able to ride on his back or in a cart. So there was a kind of balance to the life I was living in the city. I think that was an important experience. The other things that happened, in terms of family, were holidays and barbecues. We met often for these huge barbecues. We would purchase a live pig and chickens and slaughter and cook them. This took on a kind of family ritual. We would find wood and actually dig a pit and burn the wood till we got charcoal. Of course, this meant getting up very early in the morning and starting this whole process, a process where everybody had some chore to do. In the evening we would eat and dance and just enjoy being with each other.

The other thing that I vividly remember was building a house for my aunt Helen and uncle Ausbie. They had bought some land in New Jersey and decided to build on that land. They had a number of acres, and it was the first time I knew about African-American people owning that much land. They actually had acres of land where they were going to farm and raise chickens. All the families got together and the menfolk lent their expertise, whether it was in laying brick, carpentry, plumbing, or electricity. Every weekend and for weeks during the summer we went to the site. After the foundation was laid we actually spent the night either outside or inside in sleeping blankets. It was a rich experience of sharing with cousins and uncles and aunts. I think that was important in many ways and I have tried to express those times in my work by concentrating much of it on the African American and in celebration of our heritage and culture.

At some point, my father left the co-op in produce and decided that he was going to go out on his own. Where his experience came from, I don't know, but he had some intuitive sense of how to do things. He liked working with his hands, like painting and wallpapering, much of it certainly self-taught and probably much of it coming from working on our own house. But he did go out on his own and, in the summers, I would spend time helping him. I think back on that and in some ways am not quite sure how we actually related to each other: I certainly worked with him and we did share in whatever project we were focused on at the time. I don't remember sharing much more than that. Now we go back to my old insecurity. My father's love of baseball was very important to him—and my older brother Eddie was a sports enthusiast—so it always seemed to me that my father had a favorite son, and that was Eddie. And certainly with my lack of interest and my lack of involvement in sports, we didn't have that common platform to relate on. I think, in terms of fathers and sons, that's one way of communicating. Certainly there was a big age difference also. The age difference of thirty-four years. The other thing was that I felt my father was larger than life and, in some ways, I think that intimidated me and might also have played a role in our relationship.

He was very supportive in an interesting way in my pursuit of art. He did not discourage me but he did not *encourage* me. That part gets tricky because he was responsible for many of the Saturday and afternoon classes. But my pursuit of art had mostly to do with my mother. My mother was my true supporter. She was not one to talk very much so it certainly didn't come out in conversation, But she certainly understood and made it very clear to everyone, and especially to my dad, that if art was what I wanted to pursue then that's what she wanted to have happen. In thinking back, I realize that my father did not know about the potential of one making a living from art, so he was somewhat skeptical. But my mother was always in my corner, saying that I had something and that it was special and I should be left to pursue it. Whether that affected my relationship with my father I really don't know; it's always a possibility. When I was about thirty-five, we became very close, and we remained that way until he died in 1990.

As for my mother, I remember that with her there was always room to grow and, pursue art, and also room to be different from the other kids. That's a very important thing as you grow up one of six children. There were six children and one child was very different; it could've gone the other way but it didn't in this case. My mother felt that there was something different about me that I needed to be left alone and also encouraged. As I have already noted, my mother had a tremendous amount of elegance and grace, and I remember that over everything else. Her sixth sense about me has always been a source of strength and determination. I was very fortunate in many ways that I became successful as an artist very early, and she got the chance to see the beginnings of that success before she died in 1965.

As a youngster, I went to an all-black school and I grew up feeling that it was natural to attend an all-black

High school graduation, 1957 (Courtesy of Jerry Pinkney.)

school and live in an all-black neighborhood. I didn't feel that I was less than equal to anyone else. A large part of this feeling also had to do with going to Roosevelt Junior High School, which was a mixed school, and having very strong relationships with some of the white students there. Another side of it was the fact that my father worked for himself as a jack-of-all-trades. His clients or customers were most often white, and because I was young when I used to work with him I could only do so much to help with his projects. I often ended up playing with the children of his customers, so there were also very strong bonds there when we became friends. Later on I would baby-sit for some of the younger children. As a result, even though I had that dichotomy between a black neighborhood and a black school and my relationships with whites and a mixed junior high school, in that whole time I don't remember any incidents where I was told that I was less than equal to anyone else.

I met John Liney while in junior high school. John was a cartoonist of the "Little Henry" comic strip. I had a newsstand and I would take a drawing pad with me to work. I would sketch people passing by as well as the display windows of a department store adjacent to my newsstand. John noticed me sketching one day and invited me to visit his studio. There he shared with me the work he was doing and gave me materials to work with. I still remember that experience fondly. In many ways he was the first person to plant a seed of the possibilities of making a living as an artist.

*

In junior high school I had to make a decision as to what high school I would attend. There were two options: Germantown High School, which was basically liberal-arts orientated, and Dobbins Vocational School. I chose Dobbins and the commercial art course. To get into Dobbins you had to pass a test. Whether you had to show a portfolio or let them know some other way that you had the talent to go into the art program, I don't remember. But I did pass the test and I took the commercial art course. How and why I made that decision, I'm not quite sure. It might have had something to do with the feeling that the liberal-arts school really wasn't where I wanted to be. And it probably had to do with my insecurity of how well I would be able to achieve in that kind of situation. John Liney and his friendship must have been in there somewhere, too. So I attended Dobbins and that changed my life on many different levels. For one, I now was going to a school that was outside the neighborhood. Dobbins was forty-five minutes away from home by bus and trolley, which meant that I would meet new friends. That in itself would be a new experience. Another change was common to all teenagers going to high school: you are trying to discover who you are.

For the second time I started to get some idea of how to make a living by making marks on paper. My first instructor, Samuel Brown, was an African American. He was the second real artist that I had ever met and, interestingly enough, he was black. So that was positive. He was a teacher and a sign-painter, so he was in my eyes a success.

Dobbins was a very good school for me. It was the first time I had to deal with a very structured program orientated toward a goal, and that goal was to apply what you learned to make a living in art. It had a good three-year program. Most of the time was spent on sharpening skills and techniques; we had calligraphy, perspective drawing, product rendering, and experimented with different media. We weren't allowed to have live models in our drawing class. So we all enrolled in, as part of the classroom experience, a class at night to draw from a model and get a grade. It was in south Philadelphia and we would travel to these drawing classes in the evening. That was also a very new experience: a high-school student drawing from a live model.

I met and had a very close relationship with another student, Warren Neal, an African American. He didn't live very far from me in Germantown so we traveled back and forth by public transportation and, since we were in the same class, we worked on many problems together; we were able to help each other and spur each

other on. We had extremely talented students in our class and I did well, but not as well as I thought I should be doing. Not only could you get an A in this class, you could get an "A with wings." By the end of the senior year, I think I got more "A's with wings" than anyone else in the class. So you can see that I was always getting some kind of encouragement that I was talented.

The first time that I encountered any kind of discrimination was when the class was in its senior year and we were applying for scholarships to art schools. I remember our counselor coming to class and taking the most talented of the white students down to his office to help them fill out applications. He completely ignored the African-American students. I've always felt good about myself in that I was aggressive enough to go down to the counselor's office and actually get applications, not only for myself but for the other African-American students, making them aware of what was going on. I filled out the applications and I, along with Warren Neal, got a scholarship to the Philadelphia Museum College of Art, a four-year scholarship paying all the tuition. That was exciting! It also validated my efforts.

Jerry and Gloria Pinkney, 1960s (Courtesy of Jerry Pinkney.)

In my senior year at Dobbins I met my future wife, Gloria. Our relationship started on the night of a Valentine's Day dance and we dated all through high school and into college.

Going off to college, the Philadelphia Museum College of Art, I was extremely excited and could not help patting myself on the back for getting a scholarship. I was also the first in my family to go off to college. So there was a whole lot of new experiences to be excited and anxious about.

My freshman orientation year at PCA was a difficult year for me. I had mentioned that the focus or the orientation of Dobbins was basically in terms of craft and a representational interpretation of subject matter and product rendering. PCA was the opposite. It was orientated more towards abstract painting and self-expression, and these things were very new for me. At the same time, I felt that I had a lot going for me because I had been so successful in high school. So the first year was a mixture of excelling in some areas and not so much in others, yet I felt the school had much to offer. Certainly that was backed up with what was happening to me in the area of fine arts at the time, and this was all new. I was going into galleries for the first time. I had never been in an art gallery until then, nor had I been in

a museum until art school. You can imagine the excitement and also the questioning that went on in my head about what I was going to be and what I had learned at Dobbins and just exactly how talented I was. I took all this very seriously because I knew that I really wanted to become an artist. I was excited about the whole concept of expressing oneself in a much freer way. I began to change my thinking in terms of moving from representational interpretation to more expressionistic works.

I also met a whole mix of people who came from out of state and from different parts of the city. There was the GI Bill. As a result, you had students who were ex-soldiers coming back to school. You had cultural differences and age differences. All very exciting. One of the things I did find to be a problem was the fact that I didn't live on campus. I went home every evening, back to the same neighborhood, and that was awkward for me.

After my freshman year, my concentration was in the area of graphic design. I was very fortunate in that I had to fulfill other credits and they were in the areas of drawing, painting, and printmaking. I chose the area of graphic design because I knew there were possible jobs and, I think as a result of coming from Dobbins, I knew what I wanted to be in terms of the kind of position or kind of money I could make. There was, at that time, little awareness about the possibility of careers in illustration. I was an extremely dedicated student and my grades were good. So I did do well in the schools with drawing, painting, and printmaking being the areas that I enjoyed, the most.

Something very interesting happened when I was in PCA's design department. The way artists looked at the applied arts was changing. Illustrators were designing and designers were illustrating, which did have an impact on some of the philosophy in the school. When I entered the school, the advertising design philosophy was that you dealt with editorial, graphic design, and typography—symbols and magazine layout.

The illustration department's school of thought was from the N.C. Wyeth and Howard Pyle type interpretation and narrative illustration, for instance, the Brandywine School of illustration. That all changed while I was there and the design class began to solve some problems with illustrations.

During that time my relationship with Gloria got stronger and richer and we made the decision that we were going to be in each other's lives. We got married in the beginning of my third year of school. Gloria had graduated from Dobbins and was working, and the intent was that I would go to school and do some freelance work and she would take a nine-to-five job.

We were expecting our first child, and shortly after Troy Bernardette was born I left school. But knowing that art and to be an artist was what I wanted in my

Daughter, Troy Bernardette (Courtesy of Jerry Pinkney.)

Sons Scott Cannon and Myles Carter (Courtesy of Jerry Pinkney.)

life, I immediately started looking for work as a freelancer. I did some calligraphy for a department store, but work was spotty. Eventually I started driving a delivery truck for a florist. Later I moved up to arranging flowers inside the shop. I took the job extremely seriously and started studying floral design by looking at what the Japanese had done traditionally. We were a very prestigious flower shop; we entered different floral contests and won a number of awards. It gave me a feeling that I was still connected to something that was artistic.

I had met one of the adjunct professors at PCA and evidently he took a liking to me; Sam Maitin was his name. He was a designer and sometimes students would apprentice with him. He was very concerned with what happened to students after they left PCA.

Whether I had gone to him or he had found out that I had left school and was looking for work, I don't remember. But he called to tell me about a position that was open at Rustcraft Greeting Card Company in Massachusetts and said that if I could put a portfolio together there was a possibility that I could get an interview. I put a portfolio together and went up to see the people in Dedham, Massachusetts. They offered me the position as a designer in their studio-card department. So I left for Boston and, shortly after that Gloria and our three-month-old daughter joined me. I had been in Boston by myself, trying to raise the money to bring Gloria and Troy out and to find a place to live. So there we were, the three of us in Boston, not knowing anyone and being the first of our families to really leave home and go live in another city (excluding those

in the armed services). We were excited about being in Boston, a town of universities and colleges and completely different from Philadelphia.

*

Meeting new people included individuals who had come from other greeting-card companies. Hallmark Cards had had a great impact on all the other greeting-card firms. A number of people working at Rustcraft were from Hallmark and they brought a certain sense of professionalism and craft to their trade. Jan Coffman was from Hallmark. She was the art director of the department. I met Joe Brancato, who was from New York and had come up to work at Rustcraft. He had done quite a bit of editorial and advertising cartooning in New York City. Meeting new people formed new possibilities for what I would do with my life and work.

I worked in the studio-card department, but I was curious about how things were being done and what other options there were for me to move into new areas. Rustcraft printed their cards right on the premises—I was often in with the printing press and the printers, trying to understand how things were produced. I also visited the design department, and eventually ended up designing and illustrating some posters for the studio-card department. So it was a valuable time for me and, again, a widening of my experiences as an artist.

I went to a small graphic-printing workshop run by George Lockwood, who was giving classes in lithography. I remember taking some of his classes one or two nights a week and at the same time starting again to paint in oils. I was now dealing with the fact of having a child, and providing for a family. It was important for me to work out a way so that I could do that—provide for the family—yet at the same time I realized that the work I was doing with studio cards was not what I wanted to do for the rest of my life. I was always trying to make inroads into other areas.

Eventually we had four children and we had them very quickly, at a time when I was still trying to develop as an artist and person. In some respects, that had a lot to do with the way I organized my life so that I did the things that had to be taken care of, tried to spend some time with my family and, at the same time, develop my art; I wasn't developing my art at Rustcraft, I was doing what had to be done.

Boston was also rich in its community of artists. It was the first time I connected with artists who were working in different areas—painting, drawing, and printmaking. They were teachers as well as illustrators and I think that was very healthy for me. I met other African-American artists working in creative areas and there was dialogue—this time on a level of professionals and cultural sharing, professionals who wanted to expand on what they were doing.

It was the sixties and the time of the civil rights movement. Music was changing and expanding at the time also, and Boston was a city that embraced musicians and many kinds of music. So all of this was filtering in and I think in many ways shaping who I am now in a very positive way, through being exposed to different kinds of music and artists working in a variety of areas as teachers, painters, illustrators, and musicians. As a result, I worked toward being a well-rounded artist and I chose not to focus on one style or put all my energies into one visual discipline.

I left Rustcraft Greeting Cards to take a position in an illustration house in Boston, Barker-Black Studio. I worked there for two years doing illustration and design work and developing a reputation as an illustrator. I think that was a very good time because it helped me get financially set; it paid better than Rustcraft. While working at Barker-Black, they hired another young, talented artist, Joe Vino. He and I got along very well and it wasn't long before we had begun thinking about the possibilities of freelancing—starting our own studio. Now I should mention here, because it's important, that while at Barker-Black I illustrated my first children's book, *The Adventures of Spider,* by Joyce Arkhurst. It was published in 1964, so it was in about 1969 that I went to Barker-Black and started working on that project.

I also worked on a number of textbooks that got me started in that area and made it easier for me eventually to leave Barker-Black because I already had clients. The first textbook was a series called "You Can Spell" which was illustrated in a much more stylized and decorative way than my work is today.

After working at Barker-Black for two years I realized that I wanted to do it on my own. I needed to go out and be more in control of my work. I was not fully in control at Barker. So I left and, along with Joe Vino and Rob Howard, another illustrator, formed a studio—Kaleidoscope Studio. This created a mixture of excitement, anxiety, joy, frustration, you name it. We were all focused on the same thing—we were trying to make a living as freelancers and at the same time trying to make our mark as creative artists. There was this balancing act, especially for me, to meet the needs of the industry, provide for my family, and at the same time express myself freely. Working with two other artists who had the same kind of goals in mind, we were able to encourage each other quite a bit. At a later point, George Price, an illustrator and designer, joined the studio.

I've been very lucky in that respect, when I think back on my life in terms of becoming an artist. Even at age eleven or twelve when I had the newsstand and met John Liney. Then there were the teachers at Dobbins-Sam Brown and William Wilcox—who were extremely encouraging. Sam Maitin, who got me the interview at Rustcraft Greeting Cards. Ben Black, who brought me

Son Jerry Brian (Courtesy of Jerry Pinkney.)

into the Barker-Black Studio to work. All very, very supportive. Being in a studio with the kind of energy and excitement generated by working with young illustrators sharing the same aspirations was also very helpful. We urged each other on and kept ourselves strong and focused.

Around the same time, I became involved some what in the civil rights movement through the Boston Action Group (BAG). Even though I didn't do much in the way of demonstrating, I did take part in some voter-registration programs. Most of my time with that group was spent handing out leaflets and pamphlets and going door-to-door to try to get people to register to vote. It was an extremely stimulating time for me because I had the opportunity to sit in meetings where people who had just come back from the South—clergymen and fellow artists—were talking and telling stories of their experiences. It certainly helped effect and shape my attitudes because I felt that I was, to a limited degree, involved.

I became aware of Elma Lewis's National Center of Afro-American Artists in Boston and decided to volunteer my help as a graphic designer. The only time there was an exchange of money was when I had people working for me and with me on projects, and with the printer. But I did a number of things for them and, during that time, Gloria and the children got involved with the school and took classes in ballet, African dance, music, and theater. All of our children took an interest in the arts.

Prior to that we had bought a house in Sharon, Massachusetts, which is in the suburbs of Boston, thinking that that would be the best place for our children to grow up and go to school. Sharon was a predominantly white, middle-class suburban neighborhood, and eventually we opted for the city again. Even though the children were getting a fairly decent education, culturally the suburbs were a void. We felt that it would be important, too, for the children to grow up in the city where there were more things going on culturally and where they could take an even greater role in their classes at the Elma Lewis Center of Afro-American Artists. And they would be going to schools and to the center with a much larger percentage of African-American children. That was very important to us at that time.

Kaleidoscope lasted a little over two years and in many respects it was a successful experience. However, there was difficulty in a studio like that being able to exist in Boston with the limited amount of work available. So I left Kaleidoscope and started my own studio—Jerry Pinkney Studio—and have been freelancing ever since. I moved into a different space where I worked for a number of years. And as a freelancer, I worked all the time. I became more and more conscious of the fact that I was not spending the kind of time with my family that I would have liked, so while we were still in Sharon I started working out of the studio in the house one, maybe two, times a week. When we moved back into the city, we had an old townhouse in Boston and eventually made studio space on the fifth floor. This way, I could spend more time with my family, even though I still worked the same number of hours, ten to twelve a day.

*

Most of my work at this point was in, advertising and textbook illustration. Boston was an important publishing city because it had houses there like Houghton Mifflin, Allyn and Bacon, D.C. Heath, Ginn, and Little, Brown. So there was plenty of work to keep me busy. I'd done one trade book and a number of textbooks where I was the sole illustrator for the whole book, which was kind of unusual. I did several reading anthologies, also the "You Can Spell" and "This Is Music" series. A part of me liked the idea of working with books because of the infusion of typography and art. With my background as a designer, this was an area that intrigued and interested me.

As much as possible, I did get down to New York to see publishers and magazines and at one point got a job from *Seventeen* magazine. That work was discovered by Cullen Rapp, an agent in New York, who called me up and asked if I wanted to be represented. He did represent me for about a year; nothing much happened, but I had the opportunity of working with an agent. Eventually I got a call from Eric Simonson, who was handling publishing work. I took on a couple of projects with him and he ended up representing me.

I started doing projects out of New York and began to think about the possibilities of moving there. Other factors also made me start thinking about New York—part of my personality wanted to be the best at something and in order to be the best in illustration, or be able to get some of the better assignments in illustration, you had to be in New York City. At that time, New York was the proving ground and I felt that it was important that I eventually go there. The other thing was our children. Culturally, Boston was an enriching city to grow up in, but the schools were not. We lived in an area with a progressive school and experimental teaching methods which were constructive in one way but on another level not so. Our children didn't get structured classes in reading or writing and the basics, and we thought that was important. With these things in mind, along with getting together again with Cullen Rapp, it seemed like a good idea to seriously think about leaving. And we did. In 1970 I decided that I was going to leave Boston. We put our house on the market, rented a van, and packed ourselves up (I moved most of the things myself) to Croton-on-Hudson, New York.

So, another move. I think within ten years we moved seven or eight times, owning two houses. On my part, I felt a surging of many things. I was trying to establish myself as an illustrator and also provide a living and life-style for my family. Why and from where this drive came, I don't know. I was always taking a risk by moving—from Philadelphia to Boston to New York. Even though I had an agent, I really didn't know exactly what the climate in freelance work would be in New York. I didn't know whether I was going to be able to keep my Boston clients. But I did know what I wanted to be and I knew when things weren't as fulfilling as they should be. I've always thought there was more to see and more to learn, and I was curious about whether I could make it in New York doing the kinds of projects that I wanted to do. That was my intent in leaving Boston. I knew there was a larger editorial and book publishing market and I was coming to New York to get involved in it.

I had done a number of books while in Boston for Lothrop, Lee & Shepard. I had also worked for McGraw-Hill and Golden Books in New York, and I felt very strongly that there was no reason why this work couldn't continue. And there was no reason why I shouldn't be able to get even more clients. The thing I didn't count on in New York was the difference in the cost of living, the impact of my children growing up, and what all that would mean. I turned my sights to advertising because that was where the money was. Again, though I structured my schedule so that I spent time doing more advertising projects, I still managed to do one or two books a year, because I loved it. The marriage of typography and illustration was always very important to me and the picture-book area provided me with the opportunity to illustrate and design. I controlled all the production, mechanicals and everything, and I especially enjoyed doing that. It was for the love—totally for the love—of seeing the book printed. I still think one of the most exciting things is to get a copy of a book's first edition in the mail. You open it and you hear it crack—everything about that experience is very rewarding.

The late sixties and early seventies brought an awareness of black writers. Publishers sought out black artists to illustrate black subject matter and the work of black writers. And there I was—it was almost like a setup. I had worked in publishing in Boston and in the sixties had been a small part of the black civil rights movement in this country. Now here was the opportunity to work on projects that related directly to that time and directly to my culture.

                                    *

Books became more and more important to me and took up a greater share of my time. Gloria started representing me in the area of publishing, so I was getting exposure from my reviews and Gloria's meetings with other clients. I started working for a number of publishers, which I still work for today, that were very supportive. Dial Press was one of them. Atha Tehon, Dial's art director, and I go back to the seventies—she has been a person who's been important in terms of encouragement and projects in publishing.

The move to New York City turned out to be a good one. New York City had the markets—the editorial, the publishing, and certainly the advertising market. I did fairly well in advertising work, but that also was a problem. It provided me the income to live in the New York area, but I was not happy doing it. The book was still the vehicle for me to express myself. I think New York was good in other ways too. The connection with the Society of Illustrators and peers through the society and through the juried shows, gave me the national recognition I was looking for and dialogue with fellow artists, unlike Boston where most of the artists were into the fine arts. I was now relating to fellow illustrators. Alan E. Cober became very important to me at that time. He knew many people in the business; he enjoyed what I was doing, and we shared a great deal. That was a very good experience and helped shape me in my approach to what I was striving for in my work. Also, Alan was showing work in galleries in New York City, and he was balancing his fine arts and his commissioned work. I began to relate that with things that had happened to me in Boston and my friendships with the fine artists there, and began to think about not necessarily fine art, but how to incorporate some of their ideas and concepts into the work I was doing at the time.

I also began to think a great deal about some of the African-American artists whose books I had collected: Charles White, Romare Bearden, and Jacob Lawrence. I started looking at their work and discovering in all these cases that they were doing some narrative art. And that's exactly what I wanted to do through the picture book. All these ideas started to come together supported by the projects I was getting. I did get very special projects while I was in New York, one being the African-American historical calendars for Seagrams. I did a number of paintings for them over the course of four years: four calendars. it was a very exciting time because I could begin to think about my work in terms of paint quality and express my connection, concerns, and knowledge about African-American history. It was a terrific project for me. Gloria did the research and legends on these. They became quite successful in an interesting way, and are now collector's items.

Another project that was a turning point was my work on a group of limited-edition books for Franklin Library. I illustrated William Faulkner's *These Thirteen,* Swift's *Gulliver's Travels,* Tennessee Williams's *Cat on a Hot Tin Roof,* and a number of limited-illustration books. My eyes were open now to numerous possibilities of what one can do within the format of the illustrated book.

In New York City I spent even more time in galleries and museums. There was a time when it was incredibly important that I spend a day every other week in the city going to the galleries and museums so that all I saw had an impact on the kind of things I was doing. Part of me was storing all these ideas away, looking forward and planning to reach a point, through commissioned work, where making aesthetic decisions would become foremost.

In 1983 I was commissioned to do a postage stamp of Harriet Tubman for the Black Heritage series that was being issued by the U.S. Postal Service. That was terrific for me. It had to do with some of the things I had thought about as being African American. I wanted to do works that expressed my attitude about living in this country, and I had to deal with the dichotomy, always around me, of African Americans who were doing well versus those who were not, for many different reasons. Certainly, discrimination was and is one reason, but I believe there are many opportunities in this country. I addressed this belief by working for government agencies, and I spent some time in Washington, DC, showing my portfolio to clients. I ended up doing a poster of the Carver National Monument for the U.S. Parks Department; I did a portrait of Jesse Jackson for the U.S. Information Agency. This kind of assignment was exciting because U.S.I.A. prints brochures in about sixteen or eighteen different languages and they re sent all over the world to represent what's happening in this country.

Family (from left): Troy, Brian, Jerry, Gloria, Myles, and Scott, 1970s (Courtesy of Jerry Pinkney.)

I illustrated an article on the Underground Railroad written by Charlie Blockson for *National Geographic* magazine. I was trying to use these projects as vehicles to address the issues of being an African American and the importance of African-American contributions to society.

I did nine Black Heritage stamps as well as the United Way and the Help End Hunger stamps. In 1983 I was invited by the U.S. Postal Service to serve on the Citizens' Stamp Advisory Committee. The committee reviews recommendations for stamp issues. We also review sketches and finished art for stamp projects. At the time I was not thinking consciously about this whole thing of becoming a role model, but when I think back on it, it was probably there. I wanted to show that an African-American artist could certainly make it in this country on a national level in the visual graphic arts. And I wanted to show my children the possibilities that lay ahead for them. That was very important. I wanted to be a strong role model for my family and for other African Americans.

While all this was going on, recognition and quality jobs were coming in. I began to deal with the fact that I had been wrestling with insecurity about the quality of

my work. I had been in therapy for a while trying to work out this feeling along with finding out more about myself. In starting a project, from the beginning of the process, my attitude was always, "It's never going to work," or "This will never work." Because it was commissioned work and there were deadlines, I always carried the project to completion. And my efforts worked! What I was doing was quality work and was being recognized. It was time for me to deal with my self-doubts and begin to enjoy the process, my work process, more. I was always satisfied when the work was completed. I also understood that in doing creative work there was a lot of pain, but I felt for me that I was experiencing more than I was comfortable with. So I began dealing with it, trying to look at what I had done in the past and relating that work to what I was doing at the time. I realized that there was continuity within the whole body of work. Continuity when translated, to me, represents my own style.

*

With all these things going on in my head, I was fortunate enough to get a manuscript that summed up some of the feelings I had about embracing and celebrating black culture—*The Patchwork Quilt* by Valerie Flournoy. I had been doing folk tales of Native Americans and from all different countries—Mexico, Puerto Rico, India, Europe, and Africa—but *The Patchwork Quilt* provided me with the chance to do something that was contemporary and dealt directly with the black family at a time when the black family was in crisis. This was an incredible opportunity to address the fact that there are many successful African-American families. *The Patchwork Quilt* is also a wonderful story about the relationship between a grand mother and granddaughter. And it is a celebration of the strength of the black family. So the timing couldn't have been better for me. The book became very successful and received a number of awards, two that were very special: the Christopher Award and the Coretta Scott King Award.

The Patchwork Quilt also changed the way I was using models. I had been using myself and my family as models for a number of my assignments, with Gloria photographing me or me photographing Gloria or the children. But they were always just that: models, mannequins. I posed them and took Polaroids and I would do drawings from the Polaroids. *The Patchwork Quilt* dealt with family-caring relationships, and I needed models who responded to the text, and at the same time knew and cared for each other. We were very lucky to find models to fit the bill. I began to realize that this was an interesting way of approaching text—getting the models actually involved with the story.

To carry this concept further in *The Tales of Uncle Remus,* retold by Julius Lester, I wanted the animals to be more anthropomorphic and struggled with achieving the results I was after. After a number of preliminary drawings, I realized that the answer was for me to model and pose as the animals. And that's what I did. I got dressed up in vests and baggy pants and I took on the posture and attitude of whatever that animal might be. I think it worked out very successfully from that point of view.

For *The Green Lion of Zion Street* I used the children from the Star of Bethlehem Baptist Church in Ossining to act out the story while I photographed them. There again, the models were relating and expressing—actually responding to—the text. The necessity for using models is to get the anatomy and action and then to invent the staging and manipulate the figures. So you achieve a drawing that on one level appears real and at the same time takes the viewer into a place he or she could not get to without that illustration.

The use of models and the roles they play and my interest and love of drawing animals were, and are, two important elements of my work. I always tried to pay equal attention to doing figurative work and doing projects dealing with animals and nature. Many projects came along where I combined the two. Good examples

Jerry Pinkney and his father (Courtesy of Jerry Pinkney.)

would be *The Tales of Uncle Remus* and *Pretend You're a Cat,* by Jean Marzollo. In *Turtle in July,* by Marilyn Singer, the animals are in more of a natural environment, although the intent was to make those animals recite the poems. When drawing animals, I work from a number of reference sources to create my own animal that does what I want it to do. I always try to reach a balance between fantasy, realism, and naturalism.

I think if one wants to get a better idea of what I'm trying to do, an easy way might be by looking at works like *Tales of Uncle Remus, Turtle in July,* and *Rabbit Makes a Monkey out of Lion*—all dealing with animals, but all with a different intent in stylization. I think it's a good way of seeing and comparing the varied kind of styling that I'm interested in doing. I want the text to be the springboard for stylizing my characters.

Mirandy and Brother Wind marked a turning point in the amount of time that I spend on a project. I work fairly fast and I tend to do my book dummies like a sketchbook. I then move to very rough pencils and those pencils are transferred onto drawing paper using a light box. *Mirandy and Brother Wind*, I thought, was a text that required a little more detail. The fact that there were a lot of figures certainly made it a project on which I had to spend a great deal more of time. But *Mirandy and Brother Wind* was also the book where I finally made the commitment to spend a greater portion of my time on books. The book won a Caldecott Honor Book award and I felt my career was now very solid in the area of picture books.

In spring 1986, I took a position teaching illustration at Pratt Institute, a senior portfolio project, another factor that helped me devote more energy and time to children's books. At that time, the University of Delaware, in Newark, was also talking about the possibility of my teaching there in the fall. I did take that post as a distinguished visiting professor for two years, and then was asked to join the faculty. I was now in the position to be able to turn down work that I didn't want to do and focus more time and energy on children's books. Presently, I am on leave from the University of Delaware and am teaching in the department of art at the University of Buffalo as a visiting professor.

Teaching is very rewarding for me on many levels. Certainly one reward is in hearing myself speak on illustration, having to organize my thoughts about illustration and my own work. I think that's been very important in my own artistic growth. I'm now involved in doing my own personal projects. Another reward is in working with fellow faculty. The faculty show is important to me and something that I look forward to.

Still another is having the feeling that I can function very well in many different arenas—teaching, the Citizens' Stamp Advisory Committee, my freelance work, and dealing with clients.

The awards keep coming and my concept of my artistic possibilities no longer has any boundaries. Gloria and I have been married thirty years now—happily married—and the children are growing, risking, failing, succeeding, and dealing with all the curves that life throws at them. Troy is a director of Child Life at the Children's Friedman Rehabilitation Center in Ossining, New York, and has a beautiful daughter, Gloria Nicole. Brian just finished a graduate program at the School of Visual Arts and is off to a brilliant career in children's book illustration; he is engaged to Andrea Davis, a writer and editor at Scholastic, Inc. Scott, who is married to Kimm, is a senior art director and group head at Ogilvy & Mather Direct. At this time, he's in England working with Ogilvy & Mather. Kimm works in the accounting department at Ogilvy. Myles is married to Sandra and has two beautiful children, Leon and Charnelle, which make three grandchildren for us to date. Myles has taken a position with a photography studio and is a freelance photographer and student at Dutchess Community College. Sandra is assistant to the director of the Liberty Partnership Program at Marist College.

Gloria, my wife, has sold her second manuscript to Dial Books and is currently working on her third manuscript. So she's off to a career in writing.

I've been thinking a great deal about the continuity in my personal and professional life lately, and certainly while putting this autobiography together. In my personal life, continuity started with my mother and father and the support I had there, as well as the support from my brothers and sisters and friends along the way. When I remember and think back on my early career days, there has always been support and encouragement, most of all from Gloria, who has certainly been by my side from the very beginning when there was no clear vision about the possibilities or potential of making it in this business. My children have also been extremely supportive.

In terms of my professional life, if we include schooling, certainly my teachers, along with mentors and peers, were extremely supportive. The encouragement I have received has been the common thread that's run through all of these different elements. Over the many years I've been in this business, the awards have also been recognition for the kind of work I've been doing.

As far as my future goals, one would be to have my work continually grow and to have something artistic to put back into the pot. That's one of the things that is always been important to me. Another goal is to continue acting as a role model, sharing my time with young artists and children. As for the work itself, my interest is in doing more multicultural projects. I started with *Pretend You're a Cat,* which is a multicultural book. This interest has stemmed from my talks—visiting schools and seeing the changing color of the fabric of this country. *Home Place,* by Crescent Dragonwagon, is another example of the kind of books that I'd like to do in the future, where there's a very natural integration between African Americans and whites. Other future projects which I've signed up for will deal with Hispanic Americans. These are the kind of projects I'm looking for. These books are needed and are my contribution in terms of my concern for this country and the issue of racism.

I would like to think of myself as one who responds to signals life sends out. I hope always to play an important role in whatever projects I take on, and my other wish would be that I will be able to continue this commitment for many years to come.

Jerry Pinkney contributed the following update to *SATA* in 2008:

It's early November 2007. I am at the Houston Airport in Texas waiting for a flight to Austin. I arrived from Washington, DC, where I attended a meeting of the National Endowment for the Arts. I have served as a member of the National Council on the Arts for the last six years. I was appointed by President George W. Bush and it required a congressional approval. I was sworn in by Justice Sandra Day O'Connor in one of the Supreme Court Chambers and can easily say it was one of my most memorable moments. What I can call back in my mind's eye is walking up the stairs to the Supreme Court building. It was a beautiful day with few clouds and a bright sun. The sun reflecting off of the white marble stairs was almost blinding and made the body feel warm. Gloria Jean was able to join me and share in such a notable event.

My relationship with the White House goes back to early September, 2001. I was working in my studio, when the phone rang. The person on the other end of the phone explained that the call was from the White House and she was calling on behalf of the First Lady, Laura Bush. Mrs. Bush had requested that the call be made to see if I was willing and interested in illustrating the 2001 Christmas program. We decided a visit to the White House and to meet with the staff would be in order. I left for Washington, DC, on Thursday the 6th. As you can imagine, the day was filled with the excitement of being in the White House for the first time. Meetings were held and the project was explained to me in detail. More material needed for me to start the program was to be sent the following week. I agreed to rework my schedule to be able to fit the project in. The excitement and energy I felt leaving the White House was at an all-time high. The honor and privilege of designing and illustrating the program was all I could think of. On the plane home, I immediately started thinking and sketching possible solutions. Sketching on whatever I could find.

Once I was home and back in my studio, I called my publisher and explained the project and they were all too eager to accommodate my new opportunity. The following Monday, I started the week anticipating the delivery of the material from Washington. That Tuesday, the 11th of September, Gloria and I went for our morning walk. When we returned, the phone rang. The call was from our daughter Troy informing us that a plane had just crashed into World Trade Center. Immediately turning on the TV, we watched as another plane struck the second tower. Most of that day, Gloria and I watched the TV news coverage, as many of us did on that tragic day. The next morning, I decided to continue working on the project as a way of dealing with my fear and my sense of loss. That Friday, I would ship to Washington a mock of my thoughts on the White House program. It would arrive that Monday, and by Wednesday I received a response on the material I had sent to Mrs. Bush. The project would finally be completed in early November with many obstacles and challenges due to the tragedy of 9/11. In December, Gloria Jean and I were invited to a reception at the White House for those who had contributed to the Christmas program and we met with Mrs. Bush privately (if you don't count the press). I truly feel this experience played a substantial role in allowing me to become a member of the National Council on the Arts and I have visited the White House several times since.

In many ways, this honor and privilege speaks to the way my life has broadened through the many life-changing experiences that have inspired and motivated my work. I am also a trustee on the boards of the Katonah, New York, Museum of Art, the Eric Carle Museum of Picture Book Art in Amherst, Massachusetts, and the Society of Children's Book Writers and Illustrators. As a trustee I have learned to wear many different hats, hats quite different than that of a solitary

Gloria Jean Pinkney and Jerry Pinkney in Kingston, Jamaica, 1997 (Courtesy of Jerry Pinkney.)

artist. Working with fellow board members as well as the institution directors and their staff, my charge is to advise and help to forward the museum and organizations mission. I am also there to support artists and their exhibitions. This position has—in many ways—deepened my appreciation and understanding for the work of other artists and has opened up new ways for me to approach my own work and the process in which I do it.

Travel has consumed much more of my time than it used to. At times, I stop and ask myself 'how did this all come about?' The answer, I feel, has a lot to do with my passion and need for creating images and narrative illustrations for over forty years and counting. There is something to say for following through with a dream that rings true for oneself. Visual storytelling—drawing and painting—is one of the times when I am the most centered. This is especially so when I am working on the stories that reflect my interest and in many ways my growth as a person and as an artist. Work which has provided me the means to visit far-off places and meet people of different cultures as well as see sights I've never dreamed of seeing. Much like the path my books and art have traveled.

In 1984, I illustrated a project titled "The Wild Children" for Reader's Digest Condensed Books. The story takes place in Moscow and one of the images occurs outside of Red Square. In October of 2007, I stood in the exact spot I had imagined in my picture over twenty years before. This opportunity came when I was invited to represent the United States at Bibliobraz in Moscow (which was actually my second time there since my first trip in 2005). There I toured the Kremlin and experienced places I never thought possible to visit. In 1996, I had the opportunity to travel to the Bologna Book Fair in Italy, which was celebrating its thirtieth anniversary. The reason for my visit was to take part in the celebration of the book fair and also participate in an exhibition of thirty artists chosen from countries around the world to create an image with the theme being "a secret garden." The original art was exhibited and all the work was reproduced into a publication. There I was able to not only see the whole breath of children's literature around the world but also meet many of the other artists contributed to the thirty-work portfolio. Artists I had known only through their books. The opportunity to meet those artists—not always speaking the same language but all speaking the same visual language—was truly an amazing moment.

It's fascinating for me at this point to see how many of my books have been translated and published in other countries. To date, my books have been published in over fourteen languages in eleven other countries, with China and South Korea having the most publications. Traveling exhibitions of my work have crisscrossed the country. I have had over thirty one-man retrospectives. I've exhibited in over 100 group shows in the United States, Japan, Russia, Italy, Taiwan, Jamaica, and the United Kingdom.

Over the last ten years, I have started adapting the classics and retelling many of the stories that excited me as a young person. Collaborating with some of the best authors, like Julius Lester and Robert D. San Souci, we have recreated those classic tales for the modern day. I learned a great deal from them, especially the collaborations with my friend Julius Lester. We partnered on nine books: *The Tales of Uncle Remus* (four volumes), *Sam and the Tigers, Black Cowboy, Wild Horses, John Henry, Albidaro and the Mischievous Dream,* and *The Old African.* Julius is a master writer and storyteller and it was through these collaborations that I became to understand how to reshape a well-known story and make it my own.

This was no simple task. There were two hurtles I had to clear. The first was being intimidated by Julius's gift with language, and the power of his storytelling. And second were my learning challenges. I was concerned with my dyslexia getting in the way of creative writing. It took me some time to understand that the main thing was to write it without concern for spelling, grammar, or punctuation. *Rikki-Tikki-Tavi* by Rudyard Kipling was my first adaptation, although it was more of an abridgement of a story than an adaptation of the text. This allowed me to fully illustrate it in a way that had not been done before. *The Ugly Duckling* was my first truly recreated project, with a more accessible language. It was said to be one of Hans Christian Andersen's favorite fairy tales he wrote. It certainly was one of my favorites. I think we all, in some way or at some time, identify with the lonely duckling. My sister has told me of my mother reading that story to us as children. I don't personally recall her reading it, but hearing my sister's remembrance of my mother sharing *The Ugly Duckling* with us brought a certain energy and importance to my adaptation. This was my first experience with the responsibility of being both writer and illustrator and allowing me the ability to work back and forth from text to art. This would become a sea change in my work. At times there was difficulty finding the right language to speak to a passage. I learned that the solution was to actually do a sketch and have my language trail those elements in the illustration. What was most important here was to reach that point that it actually became liberating.

Reviews of *The Ugly Duckling* were positive, which gave me the confidence to consider other classics. *Aesop's Fables* conjured up for me an astounding range of unforgettable stories. From my earliest years, my parents used the powerful themes from these tales to teach my siblings and me about the folly and virtue of human beings. There was, and still is, a strong magnetic pull drawing me ever so close to the engaging characters (both human and animal). How interesting and magical it is for me to work and even play at making pictures where animals stand in for humans.

Jerry Pinkney in his studio, Croton-on-Hudson, NY, 2006 (Courtesy of Jerry Pinkney.)

In my illustrations, it is easy to see the influence of both Arthur Rackham and A.B. Frost, two masters of personification. Other artists have always played a large role in my understanding of visual arts and its many interpretations of subject. My art publications in my personal library number over five hundred. These publications have influenced, enlarged, and informed the works that I have created. It's hard for me to tell just how I use their works as inspiration. Oftentimes, I will pick an artist who works in the same manner that I am working in. There are other times where the artist's work is different than what I'm working on, and it is important for me to step away from what I am creating and immerse myself in another visual world. For example, about ten years ago I became very interested in the Ashcan School of Painting. What I responded to in their work was the way they approached their urban subject matter. Streets would be crammed with people shopping, children playing, cramped buildings, and scenes that seemed to be in chaos. Up until this time, most of my works did not include large crowds. Yet in some way, I was fascinated to do so.

To give an example of how it came into play with my own work is with *The Little Match Girl.* There you will

see a definite influence by the Ashcan artist William Glackens. This November, I was in Ft. Lauderdale to give a presentation at the African-American Research Center. It happened to pass the Ft. Lauderdale Museum of Art and decided to see what was on exhibition there. The museum has a large holding of William Glackens' work and I had never seen his original work before. All the work I was familiar with was in publications. I can't tell you how it felt to stand in front of those drawings and paintings that I had so admired and coveted. In my adaptation of *The Little Match Girl,* you will find images of crowds of people shopping, talking, and laughing as they prepare for their New Years Eve celebration. After *The Little Match Girl,* I went on to adapt *The Nightingale.*

Up until this point, my contribution to these classic tales was making the language more accessible, staging the story in the twentieth century, and of course bringing my style to the story. *The Little Red Hen* was a story I adapted with a twist. We're all familiar with the red hen seeking advice from barnyard animals. In my version, the animals include a short brown dog, a thin gray rat, a tall black goat, and a round pink pig. What I believe makes my version different is that the animals the red hen asks for help from can all help with the task. For example, she asks from the short brown dog if he will help plant the seeds. When she requests that the dog help plant the seeds, she says, "surely you will . . . you are so fond of digging." Of course the dog responds with, "Not I." There lies the twist. This was a new take for me and I followed *The Little Red Hen* with *Little Red Riding Hood.* Once again, I searched for a way to retell this story from a new perspective. I imagined it through a different lens. The staging would be the answer. I decided to place Little Red Riding Hood in a winter setting with a snow-covered forest. This staging created challenges but at the same time opened a window to bring new aspects to the story.

We all know that in the original, Little Red takes treats to her grandmother and picks flowers along the way. There are no flowers in winter. When you run into a challenge like this, it forces you to be more creative. I happened to be working on this project during the winter and after a fresh snowfall, I had noticed that it had brought down several small branches around my yard. That would be the answer. Red Riding Hood would take kindling to her grandmother so she could start a fire. It has always been interesting to me to see that when an artist runs into these challenges, and once they find solutions to these challenges, they often produce their most creative work.

In thinking about other stories that left lasting impressions on me, the revisiting of my past has turned out to be more interesting than I ever imagined. I thought not only about stories but also about my friends—the way we spent our playtime, the movies we went to see—and the teachers and mentors who became my helping hands. I then thought about how these past experiences were the springboards for future projects to come.

As a young boy growing up in Philadelphia, I dreamed of exploring the Wild West. On Saturdays, after household chores were finished, I would meet up with my best buddies. Off we would run, not walk, to the movies, where we could catch a double feature for ten cents. I was most excited when there were westerns playing. When we returned, we imitated cowboys like Tom Mix, Roy Rogers, and Gene Autry and explorers like Daniel Boone. I even had my very own coonskin hat. With much enthusiasm and intensity, we inhabited the characters portrayed on the black-and-white screen. If one were to have asked me at that time, "Was this due to an early interest in history?," my answer would have been, "Not me!" However, looking back, I now realize that answer was not entirely true. Yes, we did have fun, and yes, our flights into the past seemed to be more about action than about learning history, but that role-playing seeded my interest in discovery, and learning, as an adult, that one out of three cowboys was black or Mexican was moving and profound. It's no surprise that *Black Cowboy, Wild Horses* by Julius Lester was an important book for me, given the impact the western theme had on my childhood and the historical significance of Lester's story.

In 1984, I was commissioned by *National Geographic* to illustrate a project on the Underground Railroad. This led me to do an in-depth study on that time period with the help of consultants from *National Geographic.* The project consisted of five illustrations, one of which was to speak to the importance of the Underground Railroad. I chose to use Harriet Tubman as the subject matter, showing her crossing over a bridge into freedom: Canada. I can't tell you how much of an impact and a learning process it was for me to understand that time period and the heroic figures who occupied it. The section in Philadelphia I grew up in, Germantown, had a strong Quaker influence and the Quakers were known for being very active in the abolishment of the slave trade. What I remember as a child going to school was passing these limestone buildings with bronze plaques. I never stopped to read those plaques, but what I do remember was the uniqueness of the architecture. Little did I know these buildings had such historical significance. It so happened that many slaves escaping north traveled through Germantown, and in the course of researching the *National Geographic* project I was not too far from the place that I was born, raised, and educated.

Jerry and Gloria Jean Pinkney, in Moscow, Russia, 2005 (Courtesy of Jerry Pinkney.)

The Pinkney clan: (left to right) Myles, Gloria Jean, Jerry, Brian, and Andrea (Photo by Myles C. Pinkney. Courtesy of Jerry Pinkney.)

Some time after that project was finished, I was asked to do *Minty: A Story of Young Harriet Tubman.* I was able use some of the reference I had acquired during the research with *National Geographic.* I had also just finished a project for the National Parks Service for the Booker T. Washington National Monument in West Virginia. They also had consultants to support my research. In working on *Minty,* I was able to use those consultants in my research process. It is amazing to see that by the choices of many of the projects I have made through the years I was brought full circle, back to where I grew up.

One of the most striking differences in how I have changed my thinking in the way I approach a project is to not be overly concerned with the book's pagination. I choose not to try and force a concept to fit into thirty-two or forty pages but let the story tell me what it needs. I start with thumbnail sketches of as many visual ideas as come to mind. I then edit out those that do not move the story along. Considering the text length and the look and feel of the book, I then decide how many

pages are necessary to serve my vision. This way of working sets up new and challenging hurdles to clear concerning deadlines.

A good example would be Lester's illustrated novel *The Old African,* which is the legend of Ibo Landing. I don't recall when I first heard of the story or its source, but it has been coursing through my veins for what seems to be like my entire adult life. The novel was based on a legend that was said to have taken place on a landing on St. Simons Island, Georgia. As the story goes, a group of enslaved Ibo walk away from the plantation they have worked and journey back to Ibo land in Nigeria on foot, by way of the ocean floor. The book was scheduled to be completed in a year but it ended up taking two and a half years to complete the eighty-page novel.

I am presently working on a project with poet Marilyn Nelson that will also be about eighty pages. And yes, we have already pushed back the publication date. Recently, I finished a project for the National Parks Service, illustrating works for a brochure on the Arlington House: The Robert E. Lee Memorial in Virginia. Currently, I am working with the Parks Department on a project for the African-American Burial Ground Museum in lower Manhattan. I marvel at the different steps and places my career has taken me over these past years, and it truly has been one magnificent journey.

Journey is a good metaphor for my personal life as well. Gloria Jean and I have been married for forty-eight years. We still live in Croton-on-Hudson, New York, the one place that keeps us centered. Our home is the hub for our children, our grandchildren, and our great grandchild. Gloria Jean has authored a collection of short narratives that tell of her spiritual journey titled *In the Forest of Your Remembrance,* a collaboration with Brian, Myles, and me. *Music from Our Lord's Holy Heaven* was another family collaboration with Gloria Jean, Brian, Myles, our daughter Troy, and me. For this project, Gloria compiled twenty-two hymns and spirituals from her childhood. These songs were illustrated with Brian's scratchboard technique, Myles' photographs, my watercolors, and a foreword by Troy. The book also includes a CD of the songs, sung by Gloria Jean.

Troy is now the director of Child Life at Bank Street College here in New York. Her daughter now has a baby girl. Brian continues to produce exciting new projects, often collaborating with his wife, Andrea, who now holds the position as editor-at-large with Scholastic Books. Brian and Andrea have two children. Our middle son, Scott, is a creative director in Toronto with his wife Kimm. They have three children. More recently, Scott has also become a painter being represented by a gallery in Cape Cod. Myles divides his photography between children's books written by his wife, Sandra, and portraits and weddings. They have three children as well. There are three grandchildren in college, two in art school, and the others are all showing the interest and the gift for creative expression.

Today is January 6, 2008, and I just returned back from a visit to the Brandywine River Museum in Pennsylvania. I was there to discuss plans for an exhibition of my work, "Jerry Pinkney: Aesop's Fables and Other Tails." The purpose of the exhibit is to focus on my works that portray animals. As a professor of art at the University of Delaware, I would take my students to the museum to view the current exhibitions. It was important because of the collection of narrative figure painters. There I would introduce my students to the inspirational power and wonder of painting and drawing. The museum is located in Chadds Ford, a town most notable for the presence of the Wyeth family (N.C. and Andrew Wyeth). Other prominent artists who lived and worked in that area include Howard Pyle and Harvey Dunne, members of what would become the Ashcan School of Painting who got their start illustrating for the *Philadelphia Inquirer,* not a stones throw away from Chadds Ford. All these artists contributed in a big way to the world of visual storytelling.

It has been over forty years since my first book was published. I often end my school visits by asking the students, "Do you think I am just as excited today about my work and what I do as I was years ago?" The answer is always a resounding "Yes," and they are right.

*　　　*　　　*

PRIESTLEY, Chris 1958-

Personal

Born 1958, in England; children: one son.

Addresses

Home—Cambridge, England. *Agent*—Philippa Milnes-Smith, Lucas Alexander Whitley, Ltd., 14 Vernon St., London W14 0RJ, England.

Career

Author, illustrator, artist, and cartoonist.

Writings

SELF-ILLUSTRATED

Dog Magic!, Young Corgi (London, England), 2000.
Jail-Breaker Jack, Hodder (London, England), 2001.

"TOM MARLOWE ADVENTURE" SERIES

Death and the Arrow, Knopf (New York, NY), 2003.
The White Rider, Doubleday (London, England), 2004.
Redwulf's Curse, Doubleday (London, England), 2005.

ILLUSTRATOR

Russell Stannard, *World of 1,001 Mysteries,* Faber & Faber (London, England), 1993.
Terrance Dicks, *Escape from Everytown,* Longman (Harlow, England), 1995.
Martin Waddell, *Poor Tom and the Smugglers of Mourne,* Longman (Harlow, England), 1998.
Mary Gribbin and John Gribbin, *Chaos and Uncertainty,* Hodder (London, England), 1999.
Gillian Cross, *The Monster from Underground,* Mammoth (London, England), 2000.
Lynne Markham, *Barney's Headcase,* Mammoth (London, England), 2001.
Mark Barratt, *Joe Rat,* Red Fox (London, England), 2008.

OTHER

(With Sandra Woodcock and Karen Wildgust) *Routeing around the Heart of England,* NEWMAT/National Institute of Adult Education, 1988.

Battle of Britain: Harry Woods, England, 1939-1941, Scholastic (London, England), 2002, published as *Battle of Britain: A Second World War Spitfire Pilot, 1939-1941,* 2008.

Witch Hunt, Hodder (London, England), 2003.

The Battle of Hastings, Scholastic (London, England), 2003.

Billy Wizard, Young Corgi (London, England), 2005.

Uncle Montague's Tales of Terror, illustrated by David Roberts, Bloomsbury (New York, NY), 2007.

New World, Corgi (London, England), 2007.

Tales of Terror from the Black Ship, illustrated by David Roberts, Bloomsbury (New York, NY), 2008.

Creator of weekly comic strip "Payne's Grey" for *New Statesman.*

Sidelights

Although published in the author's native England for over a decade, children's books by author and illustrator Chris Priestley did not reach U.S. readers until the 2003 publication of his novel *Death and the Arrow.* The first installment in Priestley's "Tom Marlowe Adventure" series, *Death and the Arrow* introduces readers to a fifteen year old named Thomas, who lives in early-eighteenth-century London. An apprentice printer, Thomas begins investigating a series of mysterious deaths after his friend, an orphan named Will, turns up strangled with a sinister-looking picture of Death attached to his corpse. Through the help of his acquaintance Dr. Harker, Tom soon realizes that Will's was part of a larger mystery involving the murders of several Londoners at the hand of a Mohawk from North America who is bent on avenging the massacre of his fellow villagers. According to *School Library Journal* reviewer Lynn Evarts, *Death and the Arrow* possesses "enough excitement and intrigue to keep even reluctant readers turning the pages." Writing in *Kirkus Reviews,* a contributor suggested that fans of Philip Pullman's Victorian novels would likely enjoy Priestley's "Tom Marlowe" books due to their "similar level of violence and almost tangibly miasmic setting."

Priestley's "Tom Marlowe Adventures" series continues with *The White Rider* and *Redwulf's Curse.* Set during the violent conflict between those citizens loyal to England's King George and the Jacobites, *The White Rider* focuses on a horseback rider who terrorizes travelers by robbing and murdering all those who cross his path. While attempting to determine the identity of this criminal—who is said to have a skull for a head—Thomas faces additional challenges as he worries about the safety of Dr. Harker, a supposed Jacobean sympathizer, and witnesses the sudden appearance of a man from the American colonies who claims to be Thomas's long-absent father. "The action never lets up" in *The White Rider,* wrote *Booklist* reviewer Hazel Rochman, the critic adding that there are "surprising discoveries and reversals in every chapter." In a *Kliatt* review of the novel, Ernie Cox also commended *The White Rider,*

calling Priestley's novel "a valuable contribution to historical fiction collections for the middle grades."

Now nearing age eighteen in *Redwulf's Curse,* Thomas and Dr. Harker stumble upon a mystery of a different sort in the tidal bogs of Norfolk: while visiting an acquaintance, the doctor unearths the tomb of a seventh-century ruler. Meanwhile, two recent and unexplained deaths in the area have led locals to believe that the grave is cursed, and this leads Thomas to explore the circumstances surrounding these two murders. *Redwulf's Curse* "will intrigue reluctant readers, mystery seekers, and history buffs alike," predicted *Booklist* reviewer Frances Bradburn, while *School Library Journal* contributor Elizabeth Bird praised the fast pace of the novel, as well as Priestley's ability to blend "the essence of a good old-fashioned murder mystery with ghostly undertones."

In *Uncle Montague's Tales of Terror* Priestley introduces a boy named Edgar and chronicles Edgar's visits to his sinister relative. While meeting with his uncle ev-

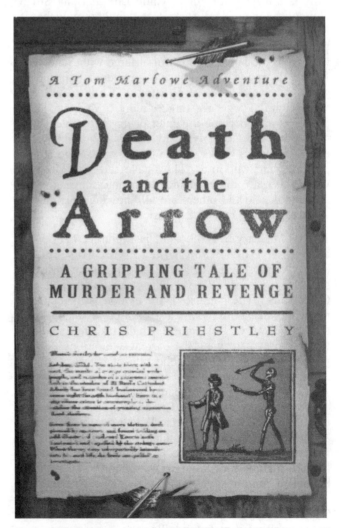

Cover of Chris Priestley's murder mystery Death and the Arrow, *part of his "Tom Marlowe" series set in London during the 1700s.* (Illustration copyright © 2003 by Chris Priestley. All rights reserved. Reproduced by permission of Random House Group, Ltd.)

ery day, Edgar enjoys hearing the horrible consequences befalling individuals doing things they should not. Soon, however, the young narrator begins to wonder how his uncle came by all these stories: are they more than just the product of an overactive imagination? Comparing *Uncle Montague's Tales of Terror* favorably to "the best of Edward Gorey in wickedness and humour," London *Observer* critic Katie Toms thought the collection of ten stories would make for a great read aloud for families who enjoy being scared. Reviewing *Uncle Montague's Tales of Terror* in *School Library Journal*, Terrie Dorio wrote that Priestley's compilation contains "enough creepy atmosphere (and some gruesome action) to hold readers' attention." Combined with illustrations by David Roberts, the tales comprise "a wonderfully old-fashioned anthology of ghost stories that is genuinely chilling without losing its sense of fun," determined *New Statesman* book reviewer Elinor Cook.

Biographical and Critical Sources

PERIODICALS

Booklist, October 15, 2005, Hazel Rochman, review of *The White Rider,* p. 50; November 1, 2005, Frances Bradburn, review of *Redwulf's Curse,* p. 38.

Guardian (London, England), May 10, 2003, Julia Eccleshare, review of *Death and the Arrow,* p. 33.

Kirkus Reviews, May 1, 2003, review of *Death and the Arrow,* p. 682; October 15, 2005, review of *Redwulf's Curse,* p. 1145; September 1, 2007, review of *Uncle Montague's Tales of Terror.*

Kliatt, November, 2005, Ernie Cox, review of *The White Rider,* p. 17; November, 2007, Olivia Durant, review of *Death and the Arrow* and *The White Rider,* p. 21.

New Statesman, November 5, 2007, Elinor Cook, "Creepy Relatives," review of *Uncle Montague's Tales of Terror,* p. 59.

Observer (London, England), October 21, 2007, Katie Toms, review of *Uncle Montague's Tales of Terror,* p. 25.

Publishers Weekly, May 19, 2003, review of *Death and the Arrow,* p. 73.

School Library Journal, July, 2003, Lynn Evarts, review of *Death and the Arrow,* p. 134; December, 2005, Elizabeth Bird, review of *Redwulf's Curse,* p. 152; February, 2008, Terrie Dorio, review of *Uncle Montague's Tales of Terror,* p. 126.

ONLINE

Chris Priestley Web Log, http://chrispriestley.blogspot.com/ (March 7, 2009).

Uncle Montague's Tales of Terror Web site, http://www.talesofterror.co.uk/ (March 8, 2009).*

PROSE, Francine 1947-

Personal

Born April 1, 1947, in Brooklyn, NY; daughter of Philip (a physician) and Jessie (a physician) Prose; married Howard Michels (a sculptor), September 24, 1976; children: Bruno, Leon. *Education:* Radcliffe College, B.A., 1968; Harvard University, M.A., 1969. *Religion:* Jewish.

Addresses

Home—New York, NY.

Career

Writer and book reviewer. Harvard University, Cambridge, MA, teacher of creative writing, 1971-72; University of Arizona, Tucson, visiting lecturer in fiction, 1982-84; Warren Wilson College, Swannanoa, NC, member of faculty in M.F.A. program, beginning 1984. Instructor at Breadloaf Writers Conference, summer, 1984, Iowa Writers' Workshop, Sewanee Writers' Conference, Johns Hopkins University, Harvard University, Sarah Lawrence University, and University of Utah.

Member

PEN (former president), Associated Writing Programs.

Awards, Honors

Jewish Book Council Award, 1973, for *Judah the Pious; Mademoiselle* magazine award, 1975; Edgar Lewis Wallant Memorial Award, Hartford (CT) Jewish Community Center, 1984, for *Hungry Hearts;* Fulbright fellowship, 1989; named director's fellow, New York Public Library's Center for Scholars and Writers, 1999; National Book Award finalist, 2000, for *Blue Angel;* Dayton Literary Peace Prize in fiction, 2006, for *A Changed Man;* New York Institute for the Humanities fellow; two National Endowment for the Arts grants; PEN Translation Prize.

Writings

JUVENILE FICTION

Stories from Our Living Past (Jewish tales; includes teacher's guide), illustrated by Erika Weihs, Behrman (New York, NY), 1974.

Dybbuk: A Story Made in Heaven, illustrated by Mark Podwal, Greenwillow (New York, NY), 1996.

(Reteller) *The Angel's Mistake: Stories of Chelm* (folklore), illustrated by Mark Podwal, Greenwillow (New York, NY), 1997.

You Never Know: A Legend of the Lamed-Vavniks (folklore), illustrated by Mark Podwal, Greenwillow (New York, NY), 1998.

Francine Prose (Reproduced by permission of Barry Goldstein.)

The Demon's Mistake: A Story from Chelm (folklore), illustrated by Mark Podwal, Greenwillow (New York, NY), 2000.

After (young-adult novel), HarperCollins (New York, NY), 2003.

Leopold, the Liar of Leipzig, illustrated by Einav Aviram, Joanna Cotler Books (New York, NY), 2004.

Bullyville (young-adult novel), HarperCollins (New York, NY), 2007.

Rhino, Rhino, Sweet Potato, illustrated by Matthew S. Armstrong, HarperCollins (New York, NY), 2009.

ADULT FICTION

Judah the Pious (novel), Atheneum (New York, NY), 1973.

The Glorious Ones (novel), Atheneum (New York, NY), 1974.

Marie Laveau (novel), Berkley Publishing (New York, NY), 1977.

Animal Magnetism (novel), Putnam (New York, NY), 1978.

Household Saints (novel), St. Martin's (New York, NY), 1981.

Hungry Hearts (novel), Pantheon (New York, NY), 1983.

Bigfoot Dreams (novel), Pantheon (New York, NY), 1986.

Women and Children First (short stories), Pantheon (New York, NY), 1988.

Primitive People (novel), Farrar, Straus & Giroux (New York, NY), 1992.

The Peaceable Kingdom (short stories), Farrar, Straus & Giroux (New York, NY), 1993.

Hunters and Gatherers (novel), Farrar, Straus & Giroux (New York, NY), 1995.

Guided Tours of Hell (novellas), Holt (New York, NY), 1997.

Blue Angel (novel), HarperCollins (New York, NY), 2000.

Household Saints (novel), HarperCollins (New York, NY), 2003.

A Changed Man (novel), HarperCollins (New York, NY), 2005.

Goldengrove (novel), HarperCollins (New York, NY), 2008.

ADULT NONFICTION

(With others) *On Writing Short Stories,* edited by Tom Bailey, Oxford University Press (New York, NY), 2000.

The Lives of the Muses: Nine Women and the Artists They Inspired, HarperCollins (New York, NY), 2002.

Sicilian Odyssey, National Geographic Society (Washington, DC), 2003.

Gluttony: The Seven Deadly Sins, New York Public Library (New York, NY), 2003.

(Editor) *The Mrs. Dalloway Reader,* Harcourt (Orlando, FL), 2003.

Caravaggio: Painter of Miracles, HarperCollins (New York, NY), 2005.

(Author of text) *Loretta Lux,* Aperture (New York, NY), 2005.

Reading like a Writer: A Guide for People Who Love Books and for Those Who Want to Write Them, HarperCollins (New York, NY), 2006.

TRANSLATOR

(With Madeline Levine) Ida Fink, *A Scrap of Time; and Other Stories,* Pantheon (New York, NY), 1987.

(With Joanna Weschler) Ida Fink, *The Journey,* Farrar, Straus & Giroux (New York, NY), 1992.

Carter Wilson, *A Green Tree and a Dry Tree* (fiction), University of New Mexico Press (Albuquerque, NM), 1995.

(With Philip Boehm) Ida Fink, *Traces: Short Stories,* Metropolitan Books (New York, NY), 1997.

OTHER

Contributor of fiction and articles to periodicals, including *Mademoiselle, Redbook, Harper's Bazaar, Glamour, New York Times Magazine, Atlantic Monthly, Village Voice, Elle, O, Redbook, Real Simple, Victoria,* and *Commentary.*

Adaptations

Household Saints was adapted for film, Fine Line Features, 1993. *The Glorious Ones* was adapted as a one-act musical, book and lyrics by Lynn Ahrens and music by Stephen Flaherty, produced in New York, NY, 2007.

Sidelights

Francine Prose has enjoyed a long and accomplished career penning novels and short stories for adults as well as books for children. Her fiction blends elements of the real with the fantastic. The president of the PEN American Center, Prose has received numerous honors for her writings, including the Dayton Literary Peace Prize in fiction and two National Endowment for the Arts grants. According to *New Republic* contributor Evgenia Peretz, "Prose is remarkably perceptive about the pretensions and the anomalies of modern people," and Rosellen Brown, writing in the *New Leader,* emphasized "Prose's unique skill at embodying our eccentricities and uncertainties" in her works.

Prose completed her first novel, *Judah the Pious,* when she was in her twenties, and many critics praised it as a work beyond its author's years. The story is about an eighteenth-century rabbi who teaches the king of Poland that there are some things in the world that defy ordinary reason. In this book, Prose first demonstrates the techniques, themes, and writing styles that have become characteristic of her work. She adds elements of the fanciful, allegorical, or magical to nearly every book she has written, whether it is the voodoo conjured by the title character of *Marie Laveau,* a work set in nineteenth-century New Orleans, the strange belief in a "universal fluid" that connects all creatures and can do

Cover of Prose's young-adult novel **After,** *featuring cover art by Barry* **Goldstein.** (Jacket art © 2003 by Jonathan Barkat. Reproduced by permission.)

almost anything in *Animal Magnetism,* or the confusion between appearances and reality and elements of spirituality in *Hungry Hearts.*

Although Prose's adult works touch on various subjects, in her books for children she grounds her stories in Jewish folklore. In the picture book *Dybbuk: A Story Made in Heaven* she combines a Jewish legend about how heavenly angels match lovers before they are born with the supernatural folk-tale character the dybbuk. In the book, Leah and Chonon are two youngsters from nearby shtetls who fall in love. However, Leah's parents want her to marry Benya, an old, mean man who is rich. Just as she is about to wed Benya, Leah begins to talk and sneeze the same way Chonon does. The rabbi declares that she is possessed by Chonon's dybbuk, and nothing can be done to help her until the two lovers are allowed to wed. Reviewers such as *Booklist* critic Hazel Rochman found *Dybbuk* to be "wonderfully theatrical; there's no way to read this without acting the parts and laughing out loud." *Bulletin of the Center for Children's Books* commentator Betsy Hearne wrote that Prose's story is "fun and it's funny—one of those picture books which, by staying true to an ethnic tradition, reaches beyond it as well."

In the role of reteller in *The Angel's Mistake: Stories of Chelm,* Prose presents the Jewish legend of a town inhabited entirely by foolish people. The founders of Chelm, the legend goes, arrived on Earth when two angels accidentally dropped a bag of foolish souls and they all ended up in one spot instead of being scattered through the world as God intended. The townspeople of Chelm do such ridiculous things as wear their hats upside down to keep them dry and carry a huge rock up a mountain to let it roll down because that is supposedly easier than carrying it to its original destination. The villagers burn the town down after lighting a fire that goes out of control when the firemen try to smother it with wooden logs, and the fools finally scatter across the countryside as the angels had first planned. Hannah B. Zeiger, writing in *Horn Book,* called Prose's retelling "a pleasant addition to the many stories of Chelm." The author's matter-of-fact tone, which is characteristic of her adult fiction, makes the Chelmites' exploits all the more funny. As one *Kirkus Reviews* critic noted, Prose has created an "understated, humorous narrative. Families will find this a savory treat for sharing."

Her deceptively simple style and fanciful subject matter have paired well in Prose's children's stories. *You Never Know: A Legend of the Lamed-Vavniks* tells the story of poor, stupid Schmuel, a cobbler. Because of his habit of fixing shoes for free, Schmuel is thought by the town to be a fool. However, when his successful prayers end both a drought and a flood, his fellow townspeople realize that the cobbler is actually a Lamed-Vavnik, one of the thirty-six righteous men born in every generation. *You Never Know* was praised as "fresh and memorable" by a *Publishers Weekly* critic and as "an excellent read-aloud" by *School Library Journal* contributor Susan Scheps.

Prose examines the value of storytelling in *Leopold, the Liar of Leipzig,* another work for young readers. Every Sunday at the Leipzig Zoo, Leopold spins marvelous tales about Carthaginian caterpillars and the Gelato galaxy, to the delight of the assembled crowds. His incredible yarns, however, infuriate Doctor Doctor Professor Morgenfresser, a scientist who brands Leopold a liar and has the man arrested. At his trial, Leopold uses his flair for the dramatic to sway the jury. Writing in *Booklist,* Hazel Rochman stated that *Leopold, the Liar of Leipzig* affirms "the exciting truth of imaginative play."

Prose branched out into the YA genre with *After,* a story about the lingering effects of a school shooting. Following a tragic shooting at Pleasant Valley High, nearby Central High is taken over by purported grief counselor Dr. Willner, but instead of providing counseling, Willner transforms Central into a virtual prison. Protagonist Tom's friends are caught up in Willner's web of control, and some are sent away and never heard from again. Eventually, Tom learns that the repression at his school is only a small part of a wider plan: students all across the country are being sent away to gulag-style camps as part of something called "Operation Turnaround." As Tom gains more knowledge of these events, he and his friend Becca fight against Willner's evil administration as well as their own brainwashed parents, risking their lives in the process. "Because the narrative is kept faithfully inside [Tom's] mind, readers are skillfully left just as unsettled, frightened, and confused as he is himself," commented a *Kirkus Reviews* critic.

After "raises all-too-relevant questions about the fine line between safety as a means of protection versus encroachment on individual rights and free will," noted a *Publishers Weekly* contributor. This was the point, as Prose explained in an interview for *Publishers Weekly:* "I'd been doing a lot of thinking about the new security measures . . . taken in schools since the Columbine shootings. I'd even heard that a hotline had been formed for students to report any kids acting 'weird' at their school. I mean really, don't all kids act weird in adolescence? The issue of security and the loss of civil liberties are suddenly so much in our culture, but no one's asking kids how they feel about it."

Prose was inspired to write her next work for teens, *Bullyville,* while touring schools to discuss *After.* "I love talking to kids—asking them what their lives are like, what it's like to be their age, what they enjoy, what they're worried about," she noted on her home page. "Shockingly, the fear of bullies came up in almost every single conversation." In *Bullyville,* Prose introduces Bart Rangely, a fourteen year old who is offered a scholarship to a prestigious academy after his father is killed during the terrorist attacks of September 11, 2001. Known for their intense hazing rituals, the students at Bailywell immediately target Bart, and he retaliates by damaging the car of ringleader Tyro Bergen. As punishment, Bart must perform community service at a local

Cover of Prose's teen novel Bullyville, *featuring cover art by Jonathan Barkat.* (Cover art © 2007 by Jonathan Barkat. Used by permission of HarperCollins Children's Books, a division of HarperCollins Publishers.)

hospital where he forms a close bond with Nola, a patient who is also Tyro's sister. "Bart is a sympathetic character that readers will pull for," Heath Booth noted in *Booklist,* and Connie Tyrrell Burns remarked in *School Library Journal* that the author's "skewering of elite prep-school society while probing the serious issues of the aftermath of 9/11 and of bullying is riveting." "Connecting grief, rage and violence, Prose's insights are piercing and powerful," a *Publishers Weekly* reviewer observed.

A thirteen year old deals with the painful aftermath of her sister's tragic death in *Goldengrove,* "a very wise novel about the family dynamics of grief and loss," wrote *BookPage* online contributor Alden Mudge. The novel centers on Nico, a sensitive, intelligent young woman whose distracted parents offer little support after their older daughter, Margaret, drowns while swimming. In her grief, Nico enters a confusing relationship with Aaron, Margaret's boyfriend. According to Heller McAlpin, writing in the *Los Angeles Times,* "*Goldengrove,* is a simple tale of a haunted summer of profound, multi-pronged loss" that Prose "transforms . . . into a moving meditation on how, out of the painful passing of innocence and youth, sexuality and identity can miraculously emerge."

A creative imagination continues to drive Prose. As a child, she recalled to *W* contributor Vanessa Lawrence, "I was always reading, and I wanted to be in the world of the book. Once I realized I could create that world, it was a revelation."

Biographical and Critical Sources

BOOKS

Contemporary Literary Criticism, Volume 45, Gale (Detroit, MI), 1987.

Dictionary of Literary Biography, Volume 234: *American Short-Story Writers since World War II,* Gale (Detroit, MI), 2001.

PERIODICALS

Booklist, April 15, 1996, Hazel Rochman, review of *Dybbuk: A Story Made in Heaven,* p. 1444; June 1, 1998, Hazel Rochman, review of *You Never Know: A Legend of the Lamed-Vavniks,* p. 1774; August, 2000, Hazel Rochman, review of *The Demons' Mistake: A Story from Chelm,* p. 2144; June 1, 2003, Bill Ott, review of *After,* p. 1762; December 1, 2004, Joanne Wilkinson, review of *A Changed Man,* p. 619; September 1, 2005, Hazel Rochman, review of *Leopold, the Liar of Leipzig,* p. 146; September 1, 2007, Heather Booth, review of *Bullyville,* p. 103; May 1, 2008, Donna Seaman, review of *Goldengrove,* p. 6.

Bulletin of the Center for Children's Books, April, 1996, Betsy Hearne, review of *Dybbuk,* p. 276.

Horn Book, July-August, 1997, Hanna B. Zeiger, review of *The Angel's Mistake: Stories of Chelm,* p. 468; July-August, 1998, Hanna B. Zeiger, review of *You Never Know,* p. 504; May-June, 2003, Roger Sutton, review of *After,* p. 357.

Interview, October, 2005, Patrick Giles, "Francine Prose: It Could Be Said That without Caravaggio's Innovations Film Noir Would Not Have Come to Exist," p. 76.

Kirkus Reviews, April 15, 1997, review of *The Angel's Mistake,* p. 648; March 15, 2003, review of *After,* p. 476; September 1, 2005, review of *Leopold, the Liar of Leipzig,* p. 981.

Kliatt, September, 2007, Paula Rohrlick, review of *Bullyville,* p. 17.

Los Angeles Times, October 14, 2002, Susan Salter Reynolds, interview with Prose, p. E11; September 13, 2008, Heller McAlpin, review of *Goldengrove.*

Nation, June 16, 2003, review of *After,* p. 41.

New Leader, December 16-30, 1996, review of *Hunters and Gatherers,* p. 24.

New Republic, November 13, 1995, Evgenia Peretz, review of *Guided Tours of Hell,* p. 47.

New York Times Book Review, October 18, 1998, Robin Tzannes, review of *You Never Know,* p. 31.

Publishers Weekly, February 12, 1996, review of *Dybbuk,* p. 71; April 28, 1997, review of *The Angel's Mistake,* p. 76; May 18, 1998, review of *You Never Know,* p. 79; August 28, 2000, review of *The Demons' Mistake,* p. 83; February 24, 2003, interview with Prose, p. 72, and review of *After,* p. 73; December 20, 2004, Anne Sanow, interview with Prose, p. 35; October 3, 2005, review of *Leopold, the Liar of Leipzig,* p. 68; August 6, 2007, review of *Bullyville,* p. 190; May 12, 2008, review of *Goldengrove,* p. 31.

School Library Journal, April, 1996, Marcia W. Posner, review of *Dybbuk,* pp. 127-128; August, 1998, Susan Scheps, review of *You Never Know,* p. 154; October, 2000, Teri Markson, review of *The Demons' Mistake,* p. 152; May, 2003, Vicki Reutter, review of *After,* p. 160; September, 2005, Amy Lilien-Harper, review of *Leopold, the Liar of Leipzig,* p. 185; August, 2007, Connie Tyrrell Burns, review of *Bullyville,* p. 124.

W, Vanessa Lawrence, "Elegant Prose: In Her Latest Novel, Master Satirist Francine Prose Reveals Her Softer Side" (interview), p. 388.

ONLINE

Atlantic Unbound, http://www.theatlantic.com/ (March 11, 1998), Katie Bolick, "As the World Thrums: A Conversation with Prose."

Barnes & Noble.com, http://www.barnesandnoble.com/ (March 1, 2009), Jamie Brenner, interview with Prose.

BookPage.com, http://www.bookpage.com/ (March 1, 2009), Alden Mudge, review of *Goldengrove.*

Bookreporter.com, http://www.bookreporter.com/ (July 28, 2000), interview with Prose.

HarperCollins Web site, http://www.harpercollins.com/ (March 1, 2009), Francine Prose, essay on *Bullyville.*

* * *

PULLMAN, Philip 1946-

Personal

Born October 19, 1946, in Norwich, England; son of Alfred Outram (an airman) and Audrey (a homemaker) Pullman; married Judith Speller (a teacher), August 15, 1970; children: James, Thomas. *Education:* Oxford University, B.A., 1968; Weymouth College of Education, earned teaching degree. *Politics:* "Liberal." *Hobbies and other interests:* Drawing, playing the piano.

Addresses

Home—Oxford, England.

Career

Author, playwright, scriptwriter, and educator. Teacher at Ivanhoe, Bishop Kirk, and Marston middle schools, Oxford, England, 1970-86; writer, 1986—. Lecturer at Westminster College, North Hinksey, Oxford, 1988-95.

Member

Society of Authors (chairman, 2001-03).

Philip Pullman (Reproduced by permission of Philip Pullman.)

Awards, Honors

Lancashire County Libraries/National and Provincial Children's Book Award and Best Books for Young Adults listing, *School Library Journal,* both 1987, Children's Book Award, International Reading Association, Preis der Leseratten, ZDF Television (Germany), and Best Books for Young Adults listing, American Library Association (ALA), all 1988, all for *The Ruby in the Smoke;* Best Books for Young Adults listing, ALA, 1988, and Edgar Allan Poe Award nomination, Mystery Writers of America, 1989, both for *Shadow in the North;* Carnegie Medal, British Library Association, and London *Guardian* Children's Fiction Award, both 1996, both for *Northern Lights,* Top of the List designation, *Booklist,* 1996, for *The Golden Compass;* Smarties Award, Rowntree Mackintosh Co., 1996, for *The Firework-Maker's Daughter;* Whitbread Book of the Year Award and Children's Book Award, both 2001, and Best Books for Young Adults listing, ALA, 2002, all for *The Amber Spyglass;* Securicor Omega Express Author of the Year, 2002, Whitaker/BA Author of the Year, 2002; Eleanor Farjeon Award, 2002; named commander, Order of the British Empire, 2003; Astrid

Lindgren Memorial Award, 2005; International Humanist Award, 2008; honorary degree from University of East Anglia.

Writings

FOR CHILDREN; FICTION

Count Karlstein; or the Ride of the Demon Huntsman, Chatto & Windus (London, England), 1982, illustrated by Patrice Aggs, Doubleday (London, England), 1991, illustrated by Diane Bryan, Knopf (New York, NY), 1998, illustrated by Peter Bailey, Corgi (London, England), 2007.

Spring-Heeled Jack: A Story of Bravery and Evil (graphic novel), illustrated by David Mostyn, Doubleday (London, England), 1989, Knopf (New York, NY), 1991.

The Wonderful Story of Aladdin and the Enchanted Lamp (retelling), illustrated by David Wyatt, Picture Hippo (London, England), 1995.

The Firework-Maker's Daughter illustrated by Peter Bailey, Corgi (London, England), 1995, illustrated by S. Saelig Gallagher, Arthur A. Levine Books (New York, NY), 1999.

Clockwork; or, All Wound Up, illustrated by Peter Bailey, Doubleday (London, England), 1996, illustrated by Leonid Gore, Scholastic/Arthur A. Levine Books (New York, NY), 1998.

I Was a Rat!, illustrated by Kevin Hawkes, Knopf (New York, NY), 2000.

Puss in Boots: The Adventures of That Most Enterprising Feline, illustrated by Ian Beck, Knopf (New York, NY), 2000.

The Scarecrow and His Servant, illustrated by Peter Bailey, Doubleday (London, England), 2004, Knopf (New York, NY), 2005.

Aladdin and the Enchanted Lamp, illustrated by Sophy Williams, Scholastic (London, England), 2004, Arthur A. Levine Books (New York, NY), 2005.

"THE NEW CUT GANG" SERIES; NOVELS

Thunderbolt's Waxworks, illustrated by Mark Thomas, Viking (New York, NY), 1994.

The Gas-Fitter's Ball, illustrated by Mark Thomas, Viking (New York, NY), 1995.

YOUNG-ADULT FICTION

How to Be Cool (humorous fiction), Heinemann (London, England), 1987.

The Broken Bridge, Macmillan (London, England), 1990, Knopf (New York, NY), 1992, revised edition, Picador (London, England), 2004.

The White Mercedes (realistic fiction), Macmillan (London, England), 1992, Knopf (New York, NY), 1993.

(Editor) *Detective Stories,* illustrated by Nick Hardcastle, Kingfisher (New York, NY), 1998, published as *Whodunit?: Detective Stories,* Kingfisher (Boston, MA), 2007.

"SALLY LOCKHART" QUARTET; YOUNG-ADULT HISTORICAL FICTION

The Ruby in the Smoke, Knopf (New York, NY), 1985.

The Shadow in the Plate, Oxford University Press (Oxford, England), 1987, published as *Shadow in the North,* Knopf (New York, NY), 1988, reprinted, 2008.

The Tiger in the Well, Knopf (New York, NY), 1990.

The Tin Princess, Knopf (New York, NY), 1994.

"HIS DARK MATERIALS" SERIES; YOUNG-ADULT FANTASY NOVELS

Northern Lights, Scholastic (London, England), 1995, tenth anniversary edition, 2005, published as *The Golden Compass,* Knopf (New York, NY), 1996, tenth anniversary edition, 2006.

The Subtle Knife, Knopf (New York, NY), 1997.

The Amber Spyglass, Knopf (New York, NY), 2000.

Lyra's Oxford, illustrated by John Lawrence, Knopf (New York, NY), 2003.

Once upon a Time in the North, illustrated by John Lawrence, Scholastic (London, England), 2004, Knopf (New York, NY), 2008.

PLAYS

Sherlock Holmes and the Adventure of the Sumatran Devil (produced in Wimbledon, England, 1984), published as *Sherlock Holmes and the Adventure of the Limehouse Horror,* Thomas Nelson (London, England), 1993.

The Three Musketeers (for children; adapted from Alexandré Dumas's novel), produced in Wimbledon, England, 1985.

Frankenstein (adapted from Mary Shelley's novel), produced in Wimbledon, England, 1987), Oxford University Press (Oxford, England), 1990.

Puss in Boots, produced in Wimbledon, England, 1997.

Author of scripts for television.

OTHER

Ancient Civilizations (nonfiction), illustrated by G. Long, Wheaton (Exeter, England), 1978.

Galatea (adult fantasy), Gollancz (London, England), 1978, Dutton (New York, NY), 1979.

(Author of introduction) Kate Agnew, editor, *Life and Death: A Collection of Classic Poetry and Prose,* Wizard, 2004.

(Author of introduction) John Milton, *Paradise Lost,* Oxford University Press (New York, NY), 2005.

(Author of introduction) Lewis Carroll (pseudonym of Charles L. Dodgson) *Through the Looking-Glass: And What Alice Found There,* Macmillan (London, England), 2006.

Adaptations

How to Be Cool was televised by Granada-TV in the United Kingdom, 1988; *The Golden Compass* and *The Amber Spyglass* were made into sound recordings; two plays based on "His Dark Materials," adapted by Nicholas Wright, were produced in London, England, 2003-04; *The Golden Compass* was adapted as a major motion picture and released by New Line Cinema, 2007.

Sidelights

"Philip Pullman has been described as a storytelling mariner, a [J.R.R.] Tolkien of our time," wrote Wendy Parsons and Catriona Nicholson in the *Lion and the Unicorn.* Considered a writer of great range, depth, and imagination, Pullman is recognized as one of the most talented creators of children's literature of his generation. Best known for the "Sally Lockhart" and "His Dark Materials" books, Pullman packs his complex stories with humor and high drama. "I am first and foremost a storyteller," he once told *SATA.* "In whatever form I write—whether it's the novel, or the screenplay, or the stage play, or even if I tell stories (as I sometimes do)—I am always the servant of the story that has chosen me to tell it and I have to discover the best way of doing that. I believe there's a pure line that goes through every story and the more closely the telling ap-

Cover of Pullman's acclaimed fantasy novel The Golden Compass, *featuring artwork by Eric Rohmann.* (Cover art copyright © 1996 by Eric Rohmann. Used by permission of Laurel-Leaf, an imprint of Random House Children's Books, a division of Random House, Inc.)

proaches that pure line, the better the story will be. . . ." The story must tell me."

In 2001 Pullman won the Whitbread Book of the Year Award for *The Amber Spyglass,* an unprecedented accolade for someone who is seen primarily as a writer for younger readers. Most critics agree that the award recognizes Pullman's unique and imaginative "His Dark Materials" trilogy, a bestselling epic set in an Arctic-like region. The series revolves around the concept of daemons, animal familiars containing the souls of their human counterparts, and the quest of Lyra Belacqua, a feisty, shrewd teen, to find the origin of Dust, a mysterious substance that is integral to the composition of the universe. Drawing its energy from myth, science fiction, classical literature, the Bible, and speculative philosophy, Pullman's trilogy succeeds for children as a ripping good-versus-evil adventure, and for teens and adults as a thoughtful venture into alternative realities.

Produced beginning in the late 1980s, Pullman's "Sally Lockhart" quartet, including *The Ruby in the Smoke, The Shadow in the Plate, The Tiger in the Well,* and *The Tin Princess,* chronicles the adventures of a young woman named Sally who finds herself caught up in mysteries set against the backdrop of the nineteenth-century London underworld. In addition to the "His Dark Materials" and "Sally Lockhart" books, Pullman has also written several other works of young-adult fiction, as well as an adult novel and several plays, essays, and picture books.

Although Pullman was born in Norwich, England, much of his early childhood was spent traveling the world because both his father and stepfather served in the Royal Air Force and were assigned to a series of international postings. While living briefly in Australia, Pullman discovered the joys of comics, reveling particularly in the exploits of Batman and Superman. When he was eleven, the family returned to Great Britain, settling in North Wales. Pullman eventually studied English literature at Oxford University's Exeter College, earning his bachelor's degree in 1968. In the first four years after leaving Oxford, Pullman worked at a variety of odd jobs around England. In 1972, Pullman returned to the town of Oxford and took a position as a middle school teacher with the Oxfordshire Education Authority. In his spare time, he began to write.

In 1978, Pullman published his first novel, *Galatea,* a book for adults that outlines how flautist Martin Browning, searching for his missing wife, embarks on a series of surreal adventures. After completing *Galatea,* Pullman began writing and producing plays for his students; he wrote in the *Something about the Author Autobiography Series (SAAS,).* "I enjoyed doing school plays so much that I've written for children ever since." Pullman's first book for young people is *Ancient Civilizations,* a nonfiction title about the cultures of several Mediterranean, Eastern, Middle Eastern, and South American countries that *Junior Bookshelf* critic R. Baines called "a lively and informative work."

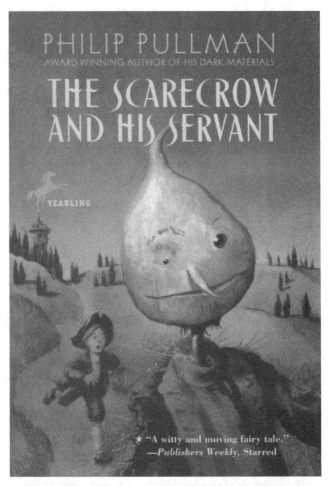

Cover of Pullman's **The Scarecrow and His Servant,** *featuring artwork by Kevin Hawkes.* (Cover art © 2005 by Kevin Hawkes. Used by permission of Yearling, an imprint of Random House Children's Books, a division of Random House, Inc.)

Pullman's next book, *Count Karlstein,* is an adaptation of a story that the author had originally written as a play. The book was also published as a graphic novel. Taking his inspiration from Victorian pulp fiction and from such tales of derring-do as Anthony Hope's *The Prisoner of Zenda,* Pullman weaves together a gothic farce set in a Swiss castle that describes how a fourteen-year-old servant girl and her English tutor foil a plot by the evil Count Karlstein to sacrifice his two young nieces to Zamiel, the Demon Huntsman, in exchange for riches. Writing in *New Statesman,* Charles Fox noted, "To compare this book with T.H. White's *Mistress Masham's Repose* is to risk hyperbole, yet it shares a similar concern with making the improbable seem remarkably precise."

In 1986, Pullman published *The Ruby in the Smoke,* a historical novel for young adults that became the first of his series of books about Sally Lockhart. A thriller set in Victorian London that was inspired by the English melodramas of the period, *The Ruby in the Smoke* concerns the whereabouts of a priceless stone that mysteriously disappeared during the Indian mutiny. Sixteen-year-old Sally, a recently orphaned girl who is savvy about such subjects as business management, military strategy, and firearms, becomes involved in the opium trade when she receives a cryptic note written in a strange hand soon after hearing word of her father's drowning off the coast of Singapore. Like its successors, *The Ruby in the Smoke* includes abundant—often violent—action, murky atmosphere, and an examination of Victorian values from a modern perspective. Writing in *British Book News Children's Books,* Peter Hollindale called it "a splendid book" and "a first-rate adventure story." As David Churchill commented in the *School Librarian:* "There are not many books that offer such promise of satisfaction to so many children, of both sexes, of secondary age."

The next volume in the series, *The Shadow in the Plate,* was released to U.S. readers as *Shadow in the North.* In this novel, Sally, now a financial consultant, and Frederick Garland, a photographer turned detective, solve a mystery with connections to the aristocracy, the Spiritualism movement, and a conspiracy that involves the production of an ultimate weapon. Pullman introduces readers to such issues as the moral implications of the Industrial Revolution while profiling Sally's growing love for Frederick. Writing in *School Librarian,* Dennis Hamley called *The Shadow in the Plate* a "super read and a story to mull over afterwards for a significance which belies its outward form," while Michael Cart in *School Library Journal* noted that Pullman "once again demonstrates his mastery of atmosphere and style."

In *The Tiger in the Well* Sally is a successful tycoon as well as a single mother with a two-year-old daughter, Harriet. When she receives a court summons informing her that she is being sued for divorce by a man she does not know, the heroine is faced with the prospect of losing her daughter and her property. After her court date, Sally—who has lost custody of Harriet as well as her home and her job—disappears into the Jewish ghetto of London's East End in order to find out who is behind the ruse. Pullman outlines Sally's developing social conscience through her experiences, which expose her to an anti-Semitic campaign while also drawing parallels between her treatment and that of other ghetto residents. Writing in *Voice of Youth Advocates,* Joanne Johnson noted that, as in his previous books in the series, Pullman "has recreated 19th century London in good detail. His portrayal of the chauvinism rampant in British law during that time is a lesson to all." Marcus Crouch commented in *Junior Bookshelf:* "Not for the first time in the sequence, but with greater relevance, the name of Dickens comes to mind." The critic concluded that, like its predecessors, *The Tiger in the Well* "is compulsively readable. Unlike them the strong action runs parallel with sound social observations."

The final volume of the "Sally Lockhart" quartet, *The Tin Princess,* takes place in Central Europe rather than in Victorian London. A swashbuckling adventure set in the tiny kingdom of Razkavia, which lies between Germany and Austria, the novel introduces two new protagonists, Cockney Adelaide, a former prostitute featured in *The Ruby in the Smoke* who is now queen of Razkavia, and Adelaide's friend and translator, Becky Winter. During the course of the story, Adelaide and Becky become caught up in political intrigue and romance, and Sally Lockhart makes a cameo appearance. Writing in *Booklist,* Ilene Cooper noted that the author's passion for details "gets in the way" and that "too many names and places and plot twists" confuse readers; however, the critic concluded, fans of Pullman's writing "should find much to enjoy here." Roger Sutton in *Bulletin of the Center for Children's Books* commented in a similar vein, noting that the plot "is far too complicated for its own good" but concluded that while Pullman "appreciates the excesses of Victorian melodrama he is never seduced by them."

With the popular and critical reaction to "His Dark Materials," a series named for a phrase from John Milton's *Paradise Lost,* Pullman became an international phenomenon. It is one of those rare publishing successes that finds as many readers among adults as it does among children and is particularly popular with college students—and their professors, who sometimes use it in classes on how to write children's literature. "The books can obviously be read at more than one level," observed John Rowe Townsend in *Horn Book.* "To younger readers they offer narratives of nonstop excitement with attractive young central characters. Adolescents and adults, putting more experience into their reading, should be able to draw more out. There are features of 'His Dark Materials' that will give older readers a great deal to think about." The chief elements that Pullman asks his older readers to ponder are no less than the nature of God, Satan, and the power that organized religion exerts on the independent mind. Townsend concluded: "This [work] has weight and richness, much that is absorbing and perceptive, and ample food for serious thought. It has flaws; but a large, ambitious work with flaws can be more rewarding than a cabined and confined perfection and 'saying something truthful and realistic about human nature' is surely what all fiction, including fantasy, should be trying to do."

In the first volume of "His Dark Materials," which was published in the United Kingdom as *Northern Lights* and in the United States in 1996 as *The Golden Compass,* Pullman describes an alternate world—parallel to our own but featuring technology from a hundred years ago as well as inventions from the future and the recent past—in which humans and daemons in animal form are tied with emotional bonds that if broken cause considerable damage, even death. Lyra, a young orphan girl with the skills of a natural leader, lives with her daemon Pantalaimon at Oxford. After children around the country begin disappearing and her uncle Lord Asriel is imprisoned during an expedition to the Arctic, Lyra embarks on a journey North with an alethiometer, a soothsaying instrument that looks like a golden compass. There she discovers that the youngsters are being held in a scientific experimental station where they are subjected to operations to separate them from their daemons. As the story progresses, Pullman discloses that Lyra, the key figure in an ancient prophecy, is destined to save her world and to move into another universe. Writing in the *Times Educational Supplement* about *Northern Lights,* Jan Mark noted: "Never did anything so boldly flout the usual protective mimicry of the teen read. This novel really does discuss the uniqueness of humanity—the fact of the soul." Julia Eccleshare commented in *Books for Keeps:* "The weaving together of story and morality is what makes *Northern Lights* such an exceptional book. Never for a moment does the story lose ground in the message it carries." Writing in *Horn Book,* Ann A. Flowers called *The Golden Compass* an "extraordinary, compelling fantasy" that is "touching, exciting, and mysterious by turns."

In the next novel in the "His Dark Materials" series, *The Subtle Knife,* Lyra meets Will Parry, a boy from Oxford who escapes into an alternative city after killing a man. Like Lyra, Will is destined to help save the universe from destruction; in addition, he possesses a counterpart to her golden compass, a knife that can cut through anything—even the borders between worlds. While Lyra and Will search for Dust and for Will's explorer father, it becomes evident that Lord Asriel, Lyra's guardian from the first book, is preparing to re-stage the revolt of the angels against God and that Lyra has been chosen to be the new Eve. In *Horn Book* Flowers commented that while Pullman "offered an exceptional romantic fantasy in *The Golden Compass,* . . . *The Subtle Knife* adds a mythic dimension that inevitably demands even greater things from the finale." Writing in *Voice of Youth Advocates* about both *The Subtle Knife* and its predecessor, Jennifer Fakolt commented that these volumes "are, simply, magnificent. Pullman has the power of a master fantasist. He imbues an age-old classical struggle with a new mythic vision, the depth and realization of which are staggering." Fakolt concluded that the "two titles stand in equal company with the works of J.R.R. Tolkien and C.S. Lewis."

The Amber Spyglass is perhaps the most successful of the first three "His Dark Materials" novels. The saga culminates with Will and Lyra descending into the realm of death and returning to life again, reversing the loss of Dust from the universe, and—by expressing their love for one another—putting an end to the iron autocracy led by Metatron and the demented deity. "The witches and wizards in the Harry Potter books will seem like cartoon characters compared with those in Pullman's religious pantheon," declared Cooper in *Booklist.* "The first two books in the series exposed the Church as corrupt, bigoted, and evil. Now Pullman takes on Heaven itself. . . . His Dark Materials has taken readers on a wild, magnificent ride that, in its totality, represents an astounding achievement." Eva Mitnick in *School Library Journal* found the message in *The Amber Spyglass* "clear and exhilarating," adding that the book offers "a subtle and complex treatment of the eternal battle between good and evil."

Originally envisioned as a trilogy, "His Dark Materials" expanded to several volumes and was adapted as a major motion picture. Pullman also penned a novella set in the Dark Materials universe, titling it *Lyra's Oxford.* The story was published as a specially packaged gift book including a pullout map of Oxford, a travel brochure, and a postcard from Mary Malone, the inventor of the amber spyglass. Set a few years after the end of the trilogy, *Lyra's Oxford* describes an encounter between Lyra, her daemon, Pantalaimon, and a witch's daemon named Ragi that is searching for the home of alchemist Sebastian Makepeace. Sutton offered praise for a tale "that even in its brevity manages to capture some of the majesty—and mystery—of the parent work."

Once upon a Time in the North, a prequel to the "His Dark Materials" trilogy, features three of the most popular characters from the series: gunslinging aeronaut Lee Scoresby, Lee's jackrabbit daemon, Hester, and the armored bear Iorek Byrnison. When a young Scoresby crash-lands on the island of Novy Odense, he finds himself at odds with a corrupt politician who wants to rid the area of the bears that labor in the region's mines. "Readers will appreciate this story's larger-than-life tenor," commented a *Publishers Weekly* critic, and Claire E. Gross stated in *Horn Book* that the short novel "exudes all the breezy charm of an old-fashioned Western, mostly thanks to its fast-talking, straight-shooting, rashly honorable hero."

Pullman returned to nineteenth-century London for the setting of his "New Cut Gang" series, comic mysteries for middle graders that feature a gang of urchins in the 1890s. In a review of the first book in the series, *Thunderbolt's Waxworks,* D.A. Young in *Junior Bookshelf* commented that Pullman "creates a convincing picture of his chosen time and place with the lightest of touches," while Jan Mark, reviewing the same title in *Carousel,* noted that the narrative introduces "an extraordinary vocabulary of scientific terms and 19th century slang. You get very educated without noticing it." Pullman has also written works that reflect his fascination with folktale and myth. In his award-winning *The Firework-Maker's Daughter,* the author describes how Lila, the daughter of a fireworks maker who is in the final stages of apprenticeship, goes on a quest with Hamlet, a talking white elephant that belongs to the king of her country, and Chulak, the elephant's keeper. Their journey takes them to the lair of the Fire-fiend, a figure who holds the key to firework making. In the process, Lila discovers herself. As a critic in *Reading Time* concluded: "This is the stuff of myths. . . . It is an exciting story, not only for its own sake but for the other layer of meaning which lurks beneath the surface."

In addition to his series fiction, Pullman has also had success with stand-alone books for readers of various ages. For example, *How to Be Cool,* a humorous satire in which a group of teens expose a government agency that decides which fashions will be hip, was called "a perfect gift for iconoclastic teenagers" by Peter Hollindale in the *British Book News Children's Supplement.* Considered a departure for Pullman, *The Broken Bridge* features Ginny Howard, a sixteen-year-old Haitian/English girl living with her single father in a small Welsh town. Anxious to begin her career as a painter, Ginny learns that she is illegitimate, that she has a half-brother, and that her mother, whom she assumed was dead, is actually alive. When she meets this woman, she learns more about her parents and begins to evaluate her own heritage, character, and direction. Writing in the *New York Times Book Review,* Michael Dorris wrote of *The Broken Bridge* that "it's a credit to the storytelling skill of Philip Pullman that this contemporary novel succeeds as well as it does. As the plot tumbles forward, . . . the writing remains fresh, the settings original and the central characters compelling."

Clockwork; or, All Wound Up, a short novel with echoes of *Faust* and the ballet *Coppelia,* weaves an examination of the process of storytelling with a spine-tingling tale. In the book Pullman describes how Fritz, a talented tale-spinner, and Karl, a clockmaker's apprentice who has failed to complete his latest assignment, a clockwork child, are joined with the subject of one of Fritz's stories, Dr. Kalmerius, a clockmaker thought to have connections with the Devil. In *Books for Keeps* George Hunt dubbed the book a "fascinating meditation on the intricate machinations of narrative" as well as "a funny, frightening, and moving story." Writing in *Carousel,* Adèle Geras concluded of *Clockwork:* "This story could not be more modern, yet it has the weight and poetry of the best folktales."

In *I Was a Rat!,* a scruffy little boy tries to convince people that he actually is a rat. By some trick of magic he was turned into a boy in order to accompany a woman to a ball—and then, at the stroke of midnight, he was playing when he should have been transformed back into a rat. Now he seeks help wherever he can find it—from the tabloid press, from his adoptive parents, and from the new princess herself, who he remembers as his old friend Mary Jane. The story turns the Cinderella fairy tale on its head in a humorous way but also manages to make points about modern society and the way people respond to unconventional requests. In *School Library Journal* Connie Tyrrell Burns noted that, while Pullman is having fun in *I Was a Rat!,* he still "leaves readers with some thought-provoking ideas."

Pullman blends elements of both Cervantes' novel *Don Quixote* and L. Frank Baum's *The Wizard of Oz* in *The Scarecrow and His Servant,* a "picaresque story of a gallant farmyard mannequin who comes to life and the orphaned boy who signs on as his Sancho Panza," according to Laura Miller in the *New Yorker.* After an eccentric scarecrow sets off in search of adventure, he joins forces with Jack, a sensible youngster whose energies are devoted to keeping his master safe as they search for treasure, enlist in the army, and battle the despicable Buffaloni family. Cooper lauded Pullman's ability to create "unique characters to charm young readers." Reviewing the work in *Horn Book,* Deirdre F. Baker stated that the author's "language has a comic flamboyance and precision that make this one outstanding."

Pullman has also put his unique spin on a pair of childhood favorites: *Puss in Boots: The Adventures of That Most Enterprising Feline* and *Aladdin and the Enchanted Lamp,* the former based on Pullman's 1997 play for children. "I had great fun with the story," the author noted on his home page. In his version of the Aladdin story, Pullman updates the original tale with exotic language and a dollop of humor. According to Jennifer Mattson in *Booklist,* the "big, lavish volume is undeniably enticing," and a *Publishers Weekly* critic observed of *Aladdin and the Enchanted Lamp* that "there's plenty of humor and wordplay for adults as well as children."

Asked by Kit Alderdice in *Publishers Weekly* what he finds most satisfying about his career, Pullman responded: "The fundamental thing that I do find important and gratifying is that I simply have the time—never as much time as I would like—but I simply have the time to sit here and enjoy the company of my stories and my characters. That's an enormous pleasure, and a great privilege." The author added in *SAAS,* "Sometimes I can hardly believe my luck."

Biographical and Critical Sources

BOOKS

Children's Literature Review, Volume 20, Gale (Detroit, MI), 1990.

Colbert, David, *The Magical Worlds of Philip Pullman: Inside His Dark Materials,* Puffin (London, England), 2006.

Gallo, Donald, editor, *Speaking for Ourselves, Too,* National Council of Teachers of English, 1993.

Gribbon, Mary, and John Gribbin, *The Science of Philip Pullman's His Dark Materials,* Hodder (London, England), 2003.

Marcus, Leonard S., editor, *The Wand in the Word: Conversations with Writers of Fantasy,* Candlewick Press (Cambridge, MA), 2006.

Parker, Vic, *Philip Pullman,* Heinemann (Oxford, England), 2006.

Silvey, Anita, editor, *Children's Books and Their Creators,* Houghton Mifflin (Boston, MA), 1995.

Simpson, Paul, *The Rough Guide to Philip Pullman's His Dark Materials,* Rough Guides (London, England), 2007.

Something about the Author Autobiography Series, Volume 17, Gale (Detroit, MI), 1993.

Squires, Claire, *Philip Pullman's "His Dark Materials" Trilogy: A Reader's Guide,* Continuum (New York, NY), 2003.

Squires, Claire, *Philip Pullman, Master Storyteller: A Guide to the Worlds of His Dark Materials,* Continuum (Oxford, England), 2006.

Twentieth-Century Young-Adult Writers, St. James Press (Detroit, MI), 1994.

PERIODICALS

Book, September, 2000, Jennifer D'Anastasio and Kathleen Odean, "Built to Last," p. 88; November-December, 2002, Anna Weinberg, "Are You There, God? It's Me, Philip Pullman," p. 11.

Booklist, February 15, 1994, Ilene Cooper, review of *The Tin Princess,* p. 1075; July, 1997, Sally Estes, review of *The Subtle Knife,* p. 1818; October 1, 2000, Ilene Cooper, review of *The Amber Spyglass,* p. 354; February 1, 2004, Ilene Cooper, review of *Lyra's Oxford,* p. 977; May 1, 2005, Jennifer Mattson, review of *Aladdin and the Enchanted Lamp,* p. 1582; September 1, 2005, Ilene Cooper, review of *The Scarecrow and His Servant,* p. 125; May 15, 2008, Ilene Cooper, review of *Once upon a Time in the North,* p. 57.

Bookseller, June 29, 2001, Caroline Sylge, "Performing Books," p. 8.

Books for Keeps, May, 1992, Geoff Fox, "Philip Pullman," p. 25; September, 1996, Julia Eccleshare, "Northern Lights and Christmas Miracles," p. 15; March, 1997, George Hunt, review of *Clockwork; or, All Wound Up,* p. 25.

British Book News Children's Books, March, 1986, Peter Hollindale, review of *The Ruby in the Smoke,* pp. 33-34; December, 1986, Peter Hollindale, review of *The Shadow in the Plate,* pp. 30-31; March, 1988, Peter Hollindale, review of *How to Be Cool,* p. 30.

Bulletin of the Center for Children's Books, February, 1994, Roger Sutton, review of *The Tin Princess,* pp. 199-200.

Carousel, spring, 1997, Adèle Geras, review of *Clockwork,* p. 19; spring, 1997, Jan Mark, review of *Thunderbolt's Waxwork,* p. 19.

Commonweal, November 17, 2000, Daria Donnelly, "Big Questions for Small Readers," p. 23.

Horn Book, March-April, 1992, Nancy Vasilakis, review of *The Broken Bridge,* p. 211; July-August, 1996, Ann A. Flowers, review of *The Golden Compass,* pp. 464-465; September-October, 1997, Ann A. Flowers, review of *The Subtle Knife,* pp. 578-579; January, 2000, review of *I Was a Rat!,* p. 82; July-August, 2002, John Rowe Townsend, "Paradise Reshaped," p. 415; January-February, Roger Sutton, review of *Lyra's Oxford,* p. 90; September-October, 2005, Deirdre F. Baker, review of *The Scarecrow and His Servant,* p. 586; May-June, 2008, Claire E. Gross, review of *Once upon a Time in the North,* p. 326.

Junior Bookshelf, April, 1982, R. Baines, review of *Ancient Civilizations,* p. 75; December, 1986, Marcus Crouch, review of *The Shadow in the Plate,* pp. 229-230; June, 1991, Marcus Crouch, review of *The Tiger in the Well,* p. 127; December, 1994, D.A. Young, review of *Thunderbolt's Waxwork,* pp. 231-232; November, 2000, Gregory Maguire, review of *The Amber Spyglass,* p. 735.

Library Journal, February 15, 1996, Julie C. Boehning, "Philip Pullman's Paradise," p. 175.

Lion and the Unicorn, January, 1999, Wendy Parsons and Catriona Nicholson, interview with Pullman, pp. 116-134.

Magpies, May, 1997, Rayma Turton, review of *The Firework-Maker's Daughter,* p. 35.

National Review, March 25, 2002, Andrew Stuttaford, "Sunday School for Atheists," p. 56.

New Statesman, December 3, 1982, Charles Fox, "Once and Future Image," pp. 21-22; October 30, 2000, Amanda Craig, "Burning Dazzle," p. 53.

Newsweek, October 30, 2000, "Pullman's Progress," p. 80.

New Yorker, December 26, 2005, Laura Miller, "Far from Narnia: Philip Pullman's Secular Fantasy for Children."

New York Times Book Review, May 17, 1992, Michael Dorris, "Galloping Adolescence," p. 24; May 19, 1996, Jane Langton, "What Is Dust?," p. 34.

Publishers Weekly, January 1, 1992, review of *The Broken Bridge,* p. 56; May 30, 1994, Kit Alderdice, interview with Pullman, pp. 24-25; September 25, 2000, review of *The Amber Spyglass,* p. 119; September 25, 2000, Kit Alderdice, interview with Pullman, p. 119; December 18, 2000, Shannon Maughan, "Whose Dark Materials?," p. 25; October 13, 2003, review of *Lyra's Oxford,* p. 80; April 4, 2005, review of *Aladdin and the Enchanted Lamp,* p. 60; February 18, 2008, review of *Once upon a Time in the North,* p. 155.

Reading Time, May, 1997, review of *The Firework-Maker's Daughter,* p. 30.

School Librarian, June, 1986, David Churchill, review of *The Ruby in the Smoke,* p. 174; December, 1986, Dennis Hamley, review of *The Shadow in the Plate,* p. 368; November, 1990, Derek Paget, review of *Frankenstein,* p. 157; May, 1997, Chris Routh, review of *Clockwork,* p. 90.

School Library Journal, May, 1988, Michael Cart, review of *Shadow in the North,* p. 112; March, 2000, Connie Tyrrell Burns, review of *I Was a Rat!,* p. 241; October, 2000, Eva Mitnick, review of *The Amber Spyglass,* p. 170; January, 2004, Tim Wadham, review of *Lyra's Oxford,* p. 134.

Spectator, March 22, 2008, A.S.H. Smyth, "Pullman Gives God a Break for Easter," p. 16.

Time, April 14, 2008, Lev Grossman, review of *Once upon a Time in the North,* p. 16.

Times Educational Supplement, July 21, 1995, Jan Mark, review of *Northern Lights,* p. 23.

Voice of Youth Advocates, October, 1987, Brooke L. Dillon, review of *The Ruby in the Smoke,* p. 206; December, 1990, Joanne Johnson, review of *The Tiger in the Well,* p. 288; June, 1998, Jennifer Fakolt, reviews of *The Golden Compass* and *The Subtle Knife,* p. 133.

ONLINE

Philip Pullman Home Page, http://www.philip-pullman.com (March 1, 2009).

Random House Web site, http://www.randomhouse.com/ (March 1, 2009), "Philip Pullman."*

R

RAMÍREZ, José 1967-

Personal
Born 1967.

Addresses
Home—Los Angeles, CA. *E-mail*—joseram@aol.com.

Career
Artist and educator. Teacher of art in Los Angeles, CA.

Writings

SELF-ILLUSTRATED

Memories of Mexico, privately published, 2005.

ILLUSTRATOR

Max Benavidez and Katherine del Monte, *A New Sun = Un nuevo sol,* Latino Literacy Press (Los Angeles, CA), 2002.

Elena Poniatowski, *Zapata para los niños,* Telemundo, 2004.

Ina Cumpiano, *Quinito's Neighborhood = El vecindario de Quinito,* Children's Book Press (San Francisco, CA), 2005.

Victor Villaseñor, *The Frog and His Friends Save Humanity = La rana y sus amigos salvan a la humanidad,* Piñata Books (Houston, TX), 2005.

Victor Villaseñor, *Goodnight, Papito Dios = Buenas noches, Papito Dios,* Piñata Books (Houston, TX), 2007.

Ina Cumpiano, *Quinito, Day and Night = Quinito, dia y noche,* Children's Book Press (San Francisco, CA), 2008.

Sidelights

José Ramírez is an artist and illustrator who uses heavy lines and saturated color to document the Latino culture of contemporary Los Angeles, where he makes his home. Ranging in his focus from warm family relations to frustrations over politics and racial issues, Ramírez works primarily in oil paints, creating his primitive-style images on both canvas and wood. In addition to the paintings he exhibits in local galleries and shows, the artist has also contributed artwork to bilingual picture books by Victor Villaseñor, Ina Cumpiano, and Max Benavidez and Katherine del Monte.

Collaborations between Ramírez and Cumpiano include *Quinito's Neighborhood = El vecindario de Quinito* and *Quinito, Day and Night = Quinito, dia y noche.* In these picture books about an enthusiastic young boy, the artist contributes what *School Library Journal* contributor Ann Welton described as "vibrant acrylic-on-canvas paintings" that "fairly burst . . . from the book's pages." In the first-mentioned title, the artist's "colors and textures, the absence of white space, and the folk-art representation of the neighbors make every page seem like a mural," according to *Booklist* critic Julie Kline. Opposites are the focus of *Quinito, Day and Night,* and the contrasts of Cumpiano's text are captured in what *Booklist* critic Hazel Rochman dubbed "exuberant" images.

Several stories by Hispanic writer Victor Villaseñor are introduced and paired with Ramírez's art in the picture books *Goodnight Papito Dios = Buenas noches, Papito Dios* and *The Frog and His Friends Save Humanity = La rana y sus amigos salvan a la humanidad,* A gentle bed-time story, *Goodnight, Papito Dios* features a lullaby from the author's childhood while *The Frog and His Friends Save Humanity* retells a creation story from Mexico. In the latter book, Ramírez's "vibrant, stylized illustrations . . . echo pre-Columbian motifs and Mexican folk-art forms," according to Kline, while in *School Library Journal* Maria Otero-Boisvert wrote that the illustrator's "dark, swirling illustrations, done in a symbolic, indigenous [pre-Columbian] style, are fascinating."

In an interview with Roberto Flores for *In Motion* online, Ramírez discussed the changes in his art over time.

At first, the artist explained, "I would try to paint something that looked like something in a photograph. Now I have gotten away from that and I go straight into working with that flat piece and make that colorful. It's more relaxing for me to focus on that. My work is more stylized." He also shared his thoughts on artist in general, noting: "We are complex people. We are not just one-minded. We can think a lot of different thoughts. Just as musicians can do different things with music, artists can do different kinds of paintings."

Biographical and Critical Sources

PERIODICALS

Booklist, August, 2005, Julie Kline, review of *The Frog and His Friends Save Humanity = La rana y sus amigos salvan a la humanidad,* p. 2037; December 1, 2005, Julie Kline, review of *Quinito's Neighborhood = El vecindario de Quinito,* p. 52; July 1, 2008, Hazel Rochman, review of *Quinito, Day and Night = Quinito, dia y noche,* p. 73.

Kirkus Reviews, May 1, 2005, review of *The Frog and His Friends Save Humanity,* p. 548; August 1, 2005, review of review of *Quinito's Neighborhood,* p. 846.

School Library Journal, October, 2005, Ann Welton, review of *Quinito's Neighborhood,* p. 148; June, 2006, Maria Otero-Boisvert, review of *The Frog and His Friends Save Humanity,* p. 145; March, 2008, Tim Wadham, review of *Goodnight, Papito dios = Buenas noches, Papito Dios,* p. 178.

ONLINE

José Ramírez Home Page, http://www.ramirezart.com (February 2, 2009).

In Motion Online, http://www.inmotionmagazine.com/ (August 25, 2001), Roberto Flores, interview with Ramírez.*

*   *   *

RÁTZ de TAGYOS, Paul 1958-

Personal

Born January 30, 1958, in New Rochelle, NY; son of Paul (a fine artist) and Helen Rátz de Tagyos. *Education:* Attended Parsons School of Design. *Politics:* "Hopeful pessimist." *Hobbies and other interests:* Music, walking, bicycling, Indian food ("eating, not cooking").

Addresses

Home and office—30 Eastchester Rd., Apt. 6A, New Rochelle, NY 10801. *E-mail*—PaulRátz@paulRátz.com.

Career

Illustrator and author of children's books

Awards, Honors

Certificate of Merit, Society of Illustrators; Certificate of Design Excellence, *Print* magazine.

Writings

SELF-ILLUSTRATED

(Self-illustrated) *A Coney Tale,* Clarion (New York, NY), 1992.

Showdown at Lonesome Pellet, Clarion (New York, NY), 1994.

ILLUSTRATOR

Karen Rostoker-Gruber, *Rooster Can't Cock-a-Doodle-Doo,* Dial Books for Young Readers (New York, NY), 2004.

Jacquelyn Mitchard, *Ready, Set, School!,* HarperCollins (New York, NY), 2007.

Katie Speck, *Maybelle in the Soup,* Henry Holt (New York, NY), 2007.

Katie Speck, *Maybelle Goes to Tea,* Henry Holt (New York, NY), 2008.

Sidelights

Paul Rátz de Tagyos is an author and illustrator who has created the original picture books *A Coney Tale* and *Showdown at Lonesome Pellet* as well as contributing artwork to books by other writers. Appraising his work in bringing to life Karen Rostoker-Gruber's *Rooster Can't Cock-a-Doodle-doo,* *Horn Book* critic Kitty Flynn wrote that the "comical pencil, ink, and marker" illustrations in the book "give the cartoon-like animals personality plus." His images also "add tremendously to the humor" of Jacquelyn Mitchard's *Ready, Set, School!,* noted a *Kirkus Reviews* writer, the critic adding that the "numerous examples of visual humor" in Mitchard's book "should amuse readers."

Both original picture books by Rátz de Tagyos focus on a society of rabbits living in seventeenth-century Flanders. After it is discovered that a huge tree is actually an enormous carrot in *A Coney Tale,* the rabbits find a way to unearth and harvest the vegetable, ultimately creating a delightful work of art. The setting shifts forward to the 1870s in *Showdown at Lonesome Pellet,* and Rátz de Tagyos's rabbits are now living in the American West, where life in their peaceful town is disrupted by the wild and roughhousing Pointy Brothers. "Skewed perspectives create an amiably offbeat effect in the clean, crisp artwork," proclaimed one *Publishers Weekly* critic in reviewing *A Coney Tale,* while another reviewer described the author's picture-book sequel as a humorous story with "droll illustrations" featuring "hard to resist" flop-eared characters.

As an illustrator, Rátz de Tagyos's work has appeared in several picture books by Katie Speck that follow the adventures of a coquettish cockroach and her common-sense friend Henry the Flea: *Maybelle in the Soup* and *Maybelle Goes to Tea.* Reviewing *Maybelle in the Soup, School Library Journal* critic Cheryl Ashton wrote that Rátz de Tagyos's "wonderfully energetic illustrations bring . . . [Speck's story] to life," and *Horn Book* critic Betty Carter noted that the artist's use of shifting viewpoints "reinforce[s] the humor and reveal[s] the action" in the story.

Rátz de Tagyos comes from a family of painters. As he once explained to *SATA*, while he was "neither encouraged nor discouraged to pursue" art, he decided to train as a commercial artist at Parsons School of Design. After studying illustration, he worked a series of odd jobs, then began to pursue "comp work": creating "quick, mostly disposable, marker drawings of proposed ads used by ad agencies to show to their clients." The "usage of marker and pencil became an available technique" and "a key factor in attempting to create a children's picture book," Rátz de Tagyos later noted.

The rabbit characters in Rátz de Tagyos's self-illustrated picture books are the "result of a longtime involvement I have with someone named Constance; I called her Coney. And it was she, in fact, who told me what a coney is. It's a bunny-rabbit, or dupe." *A Coney Tale* "is a direct adaptation from a bedtime story," he continued. "The prototype text [of the story] was verbose and endless (that's where editors come in, and I'm lucky with mine). I came to this project more as an illustrator with a story rather than an author with pictures. I feel much more comfortable with being the illustrator, it comes naturally."

Biographical and Critical Sources

PERIODICALS

Booklist, August, 2007, Gillian Engberg, review of *Ready, Set, School!*, p. 83; November 15, 2007, Suzanne Harold, review of *Maybelle in the Soup,* p. 49.

Horn Book, November-December, 2007, Betty Carter, review of *Maybelle in the Soup,* p. 687; July-August, 2008, Kitty Flynn, review of *Rooster Can't Cock-a-Doodle-Doo,* p. 441.

Kirkus Reviews, March 1, 1992, review of *A Coney Tale;* May 1, 2004, review of *Roosters Can't Cock-a-Doodle-Doo,* p. 447; June 15, 2007, review of *Ready, Set, School!*

Publishers Weekly, March 30, 1992, review of *A Coney Tale;* November 14, 1994, review of *Showdown at Lonesome Pellet,* p. 67; June 18, 2007, review of *Ready, Set, School!*, p. 52.

School Library Journal, September, 2007, Rachel G. Payne, review of *Ready, Set, School!*, p. 172; December, 2007, Cheryl Ashton, review of *Maybelle in the Soup,* p. 100.

ONLINE

Paul Rátz de Taygos Home Page, http://www.prdt.net (February 2, 2009).

REMPT, Fiona 1973-

Personal

Born 1973, in The Hague, Netherlands; married; husband's name Harold; children: Elza.

Addresses

Home—Amsterdam, Netherlands. *E-mail*—fiona@fionarempt.nl.

Career

Editor and writer. Formerly worked as an editor of a Dutch publishing company; currently manager of a photography gallery, Amsterdam, Netherlands.

Writings

FOR CHILDREN

Kidsgids Utrecht: voor gezinnen met kinderen van 0 tot 12 jaar, illustrated by Jet Violier, Kidsgids (Amsterdam, Netherlands), 2001.

Kidsgids Nederland: uitjes voor kinderen en ouders, illustrated by Jet Violier, Kidsgids (Amsterdam, Netherlands), 2002.

(Translator) Roger Priddy, *Mijn grote treinboek* (translation of *My Big Train Book*), Piccolo (Amsterdam, Netherlands), 2004.

(Translator) *Ik hou van alle dieren* (translation of *I Love Animals*), Piccolo (Amsterdam, Netherlands), 2004.

Feestjes voor beestjes: spelletjes en verwentips voor huisdieren, illustrated by Guida Joseph, Gottmer (Haarlem, Netherlands), 2006.

Geknipt voor de keuken: knutselkookboek, illustrated by Mirèn van Alphen, Pimento (Amsterdam, Netherlands), 2006.

Supervrienden, illustrated by Noëlle Smit, Gottmer (Haarlem, Netherlands), 2006, translated as *Snail's Birthday Wish,* Boxer Books (London, England), 2007.

Kampioenen, illustrated by Noëlle Smit, Gottmer (Haarlem, Netherlands), 2006.

Dieren ABC, Gottmer (Haarlem, Netherlands), 2008.

Wat hoort bij wie? Bij de dieren, Gottmer (Haarlem, Netherlands), 2008.

Biographical and Critical Sources

PERIODICALS

Kirkus Reviews, September 15, 2007, review of *Snail's Birthday Wish.*

School Library Journal, November, 2007, Blair Christolon, review of *Snail's Birthday Wish,* p. 99.

ONLINE

Fiona Rempt Home Page, http://www.fionarempt.nl (February 2, 2009).*

ROWE, John A. 1949-

Personal

Born 1949, in Kingston-upon-Thames, Surrey, England; son of Alfred and Joan Elaine Rowe; married Lisbeth Zwerger (an illustrator; divorced, 1990); married Michelle Kuipers (a manager), March 8, 1992. *Education:* Attended Richmond School of Art, 1968, Twickenham College of Technology, 1970, and Hochschule für Angewandte Kunst, 1974; Epsom School of Art & Design, fine arts diploma, c. 1974. *Hobbies and other interests:* Mountain biking, walking, reading, music, history, playing flute and recorder.

Addresses

Home—Australia; England. *Home and office*—The Cottage, Higher Putham, Cutcombe, Minehead, Somerset TA24 7AS, England.

Career

Writer and illustrator. Worked variously as a grave digger, bicycle mechanic, plumber, cinema cleaner, and television set maker. *Exhibitions:* Work included in exhibitions at Royal Academy, London, England, 1973, 1974, 1977, 1979, 1982; Galerie Wittman, Vienna, Austria, 1975; Surrey Artists Exhibition, Surrey, England, 1976; United Nations, Vienna, Austria, 1978, 1980; Künstlerhaus, Vienna, 1981; Galerie im Kelterhaus, Hochheim, Germany, 1998; and Every Picture Tells a Story, Los Angeles, CA, 2000.

Awards, Honors

Golden Apple award, Biennial of Illustrations Bratislava, 1991; UNICEF honorary diploma, Bologna Book Fair, 1992; Rattenfänger Literaturepreis, 1992; Österreichischer Kinder-und Jugendbuchpreis, 1993, 1995; UNICEF Recognition award, 1995; *Storytelling World* Award, 1995; Biennial of Illustrations Bratislava Grand Prix, 1995; Fällt aus dem Rahmen award, 1996; Federhasenpreis for design (Austria), 1997; Austrian Honors listee, 2000; Deutscher Jugendliteratur Preis nomination, 2000; UNICEF Books of Tolerance nomination, 2002.

Writings

SELF-ILLUSTRATED

Rabbit Moon, Picture Book Studios (Saxonville, MA), 1992.

How Many Monkeys?: A Counting Book in English, French, German, Hutchinson (London, England), 1993.

Jack the Dog, Picture Book Studios (Saxonville, MA), 1993.

John A. Rowe (Reproduced by permission.)

Baby Crow (also see below; originally published in Switzerland as *Raben-Baby*), North-South Books (New York, NY), 1994.

Can You Spot the Spotty Dog?, Red Fox (London, England), 1996, published as *Can You Spot the Spotted Dog?,* Doubleday Books for Young Readers (New York, NY), 1996.

Peter Piglet (also see below; originally published in Switzerland as *Ferkel Ferdinand*), North-South Books (New York, NY), 1996.

Smudge (also see below; originally published in Switzerland as *Schmutzfink*), North-South Books (New York, NY), 1997.

Monkey Trouble (originally published in Switzerland as *Affenzoff*), North-South Books (New York, NY), 1999.

Favorite Stories by John A. Rowe: Three Complete Tales (contains *Baby Crow, Peter Piglet,* and *Smudge*), Smithmark (New York, NY), 1999.

Jasper the Terror (originally published in Switzerland as *Theodor Terror*), North-South Books (New York, NY), 2001.

Tommy DoLittle (originally published in Switzerland under the same title), North-South Books (New York, NY), 2002.

Amazing Animal Hide and Seek, Barron's (Hauppauge, NY), 2003.

Hamlet: Life Is a Feast, 2004.

Hansenmond, Minedition, 2004.

Moondog, Minedition (New York, NY), 2005.

Objectif: La lune, NordSud, 2005.

J.A. Teddy, Minedition (New York, NY), 2006.

I Want a Hug (originally published in Switzerland as *Bitte nimm mich in die Arme!*) Minedition (New York, NY), 2007.

Smile (originally published in Switzerland as *Nur nicht Lächeln!*), Minedition (New York, NY), 2008.

The Secret, 2009.

ILLUSTRATOR

Rudyard Kipling, *The Sing-Song of Old Man Kangaroo,* Picture Book Studios (Saxonville, MA), 1990.

The Gingerbread Man: An Old English Folktale, Picture Book Studios (London, England), 1993, North-South Books (New York, NY), 1996.

Rudyard Kipling, *The Beginning of the Armadillos,* North-South Books (New York, NY), 1995.

Rudyard Kipling, *The Elephant's Child,* North-South Books (New York, NY), 1995.

Brigitte Weninger, reteller, *Zwergen Mütze,* translated by J. Alison James as *The Elf's Hat,* North-South Books (New York, NY), 2000.

Karl Rühmann, *Aber Ich Will . . . ,* translated by J. Alison James as *But I Want To!,* North-South Books (New York, NY), 2002.

Hans Christian Anderson, *The Emperor's New Clothes,* Minedition (New York, NY), 2005.

Sidelights

British-born author and illustrator John A. Rowe has garnered consistent high praise for his illustrated picture books. Compared to the works of Dutch painter Hieronymus Bosch, Rowe's detailed illustrations feature offbeat animal and human characters. Reviewing Rowe's illustrated version of Hans Christian Andersen's *The Emperor's New Clothes, School Library Journal* critic Robin L. Gibson dubbed the artwork "highly unusual" and "delightfully expressive," while his watercolor art for his self-illustrated *Moondog* "offer a satiric punch," according to Linda Ludke in the same periodical. Taken on a trip to Grumpy Land in the author/illustrator's *Smile,* readers are treated to art that a *Kirkus Reviews* writer characterized as "colorful and charming and [full of] . . . quirky details."

In *Jack the Dog,* one of Rowe's early works, the author/illustrator takes readers on a trip to the unfamiliar places in a canine's dreams as a dog named Jack wanders onto a ship and sails to Japan, where he has to overcome cultural barriers and follow unusual procedures to get a cup of tea. Before he can sample the beverage, however, the pup wakes up in his own home, safe and sound and close to his own food bowl. A *Publishers Weekly* reviewer called *Jack the Dog* a "sophisticated flight of fancy" in which Rowe's "illustrations might be more at home on a gallery wall."

Like many of Rowe's books for children, *Baby Crow* was originally published in Switzerland. In this story, a little bird discovers that he cannot caw or call or sing like the other crows in his well-mannered family. Instead, Baby Crow is only able to make a beeping noise. Fortunately, Grandpa Crow, a former opera singer, is a wise old bird and gladly helps the young bird find his true voice. Rowe's "haunting pictures are rich in color and tone and have a dream-like reality," wrote Raymond Briggs in a *Times Educational Supplement* review of *Baby Crow,* while a *Books for Keeps* reviewer commented that Rowe's picture book is "unusual and visually striking."

In *Peter Piglet* Peter the pig finds a pair of beautiful golden shoes. The shoes quickly become the pig's prized possession, and he learns to walk, dance, swim, and do other amazing things while wearing them. The next morning, however, the shoes are gone, and Peter sets out to find the scoundrel he believes has taken his precious shoes. What he finds is something quite unexpected: One shoe is being used by an old tortoise who lost his home in a storm, and the other serves as a nest for a growing blackbird family. Rowe's "touching message is delivered in a gentle manner" with the aid of the author/illustrator's "accomplished artwork," observed Julie Corsaro in a *Booklist* review of *Peter Piglet.* Calling the book's text "image-rich," Lee Bock added in *School Library Journal* that *Peter Piglet* "is an exquisitely designed book that children will love."

Smudge, the lead character of Rowe's book of the same name, is an old rat, a grandfatherly storyteller with a vivid imagination and a clear recollection of the adventures he experienced during his youth. In *Smudge*—first published as *Schmutzfink*—the rodent relates how, as a child, he was abducted by a bird. Smudge tries to fit in with the bird family, but eventually the birds fly off and leave him behind. Through a series of surrogate families—dogs, rabbits, fish, squirrels, and more—the rat tries again and again to fit in but to no avail: He cannot hop like rabbits, swim like fish, or run like dogs. One day, however, Smudge encounters a brown rat with a familiar smile: his mother has found him and brings him back into the rat family where he belongs.

Anji Keating, writing in *Bloomsbury Review,* commented that *Smudge* "is not only humorous but enchanting," while *School Librarian* critic Hazel Townson deemed Rowe's book "clever and amusing." A *Kirkus Reviews* contributor called Smudge a "delightfully eccentric character" and declared the author's own illustrations to be "dauntingly emotional." In a *Booklist* review, Michael Cart commented favorably on "Rowe's striking pictures" and deemed *Smudge* "an eccentric but engaging book."

Little Monkey finds himself in difficult situations in *Monkey Trouble,* as the wind takes the startled primate on an instructive journey. Far from home, Little Monkey is mistaken for an elephant couple's new baby and is clad in a pink dress, even though he objects that he is not a little girl. When he finally arrives back at home, the monkey is given a special present to discourage him from repeating his adventure. In *Monkey Trouble* Rowe's "whimsical artistic interpretation adds a sense of character to each animal and humor to each situation," according to *School Library Journal* Tina Hudak. A *Publishers Weekly* reviewer noted that "the artwork is the real draw" of the book.

Jasper the Terror introduces an earnest but accident-prone young dragon whose allergy-induced sneezing causes fires. Problems come when Jasper sets his friends' pants ablaze, and is consequently banished, purely for the sake of everyone else's safety. Eventually, Professor Owl discovers that Jasper has tickleyitis from the tall grass that constantly tickles the dragon's nose, and the wise bird offers a solution that pleases everyone. Rowe's "bold cartoon illustrations" for *Jasper the Terror* "are strong crowd pleasers," claimed Eunice Weech in a *School Library Journal* review, while Stephanie Merrit remarked in the London *Observer* upon the story's "ingenious solution."

A young porcupine named Little Elvis is the star of *I Want a Hug*, a large-format picture book that is "sure to spark lots of hugs and kisses," according to *Booklist* contributor Hazel Rochman. In the story, the prickly, diaper-clad youngster yearns for some physical contact, but his prickles put off everyone he meets. Finally Little Elvis meets a lonely crocodile with a similar dilemma, and in helping Colin the croc he helps himself as well. According to a *Kirkus Reviews* writer, *I Want a Hug* features "a cozy tale" in which Rowe's message—"that differences should be embraced—literally"—takes center stage.

"I was born in Kingston-upon-Thames, Surrey, England, in 1949," Rowe once told *SATA*. 'My parents separated when I was three to four years old, so, along with my three sisters and one brother, I was raised by my mother. I started drawing more and more around this time.

"After the usual soul-destroying school years, I worked, amongst other things, as a bicycle mechanic, grave digger, cinema cleaner, plumber, and TV set maker, before attending life drawing classes at Richmond School of Art in 1968. This led to a Foundation Year at Twickenham College of Technology, and then a three-year fine art (painting) course at Epsom School of Art & Design.

"In 1974, I moved to Vienna, Austria, after a two-week holiday there, during which time I fell in love with [illustrator] Lisbeth Zwerger. I studied two semesters at the Hochschule für Angewandte Kunst. I also worked in a design studio, did some set painting at a theatre, but mainly painted and exhibited. Lisbeth and I married, and I stayed in Vienna for sixteen years, until our divorce.

"After a trip to Australia, I started a series of small paintings based on Kipling's *Just-So Stories*. These pictures were not intended to be illustrations, but they were seen by the Austrian publisher Michael Neugebauer, and I was offered the chance to turn them into a book. This was a major turning point for me and the point where my life as an illustrator, and author, of children's books began."

Biographical and Critical Sources

PERIODICALS

Bloomsbury Review, November-December, 1997, Anji Keating, review of *Smudge,* p. 33; September-October, 1999, review of *Monkey Trouble,* p. 22.

Bookbird, summer, 1995, review of *Baby Crow,* p. 56.
Booklist, November 1, 1996, Ellen Mandel, review of *Can You Spot the Spotted Dog?,* p. 510; December 1, 1996, Julie Corsaro, review of *Peter Piglet,* p. 669; December 1, 1997, Michael Cart, review of *Smudge,* pp. 643-644; September 15, 2007, Hazel Rochman, review of *I Want a Hug,* p. 72.
Books for Keeps, July, 1996, review of *Raben-Baby,* p. 7; November, 1996, review of *Jack the Dog,* p. 7.
Kirkus Reviews, April 15, 1996, review of *The Gingerbread Man: An Old English Folktale,* p. 606; September 1, 1996, review of *Peter Piglet,* p. 1327; October 1, 1997, review of *Smudge,* p. 1536; August 15, 2007, review of *I Want a Hug;* August 1, 2008, review of *Smile.*
Observer (London, England), October 28, 2001, Stephanie Merrit, review of *Jasper the Terror,* p. 16.
Publishers Weekly, November 23, 1992, review of *Rabbit Moon,* p. 61; April 26, 1993, review of *Jack the Dog,* p. 77; April 15, 1996, review of *Baby Crow,* p. 70; December 2, 1996, review of *Jack the Dog,* p. 62; May 12, 1997, review of *Rabbit Moon,* p. 77; September 17, 2001, review of *Monkey Trouble,* p. 82.
School Librarian, spring, 1998, Hazel Townson, review of *Smudge,* p. 22.
School Library Journal, June, 1993, Anna Biagioni Hart, review of *Rabbit Moon,* p. 88; August, 1993, Steven Engelfried, review of *Jack the Dog,* p. 151; November, 1994, Christine A. Moesch, review of *Baby Crow,* p. 90; January, 1996, Patricia Lothrop Green, review of *The Beginning of the Armadillos,* p. 86; August, 1996, Pam Gousner, review of *The Gingerbread Man,* p. 136; November, 1996, Lee Bock, review of *Peter Piglet,* pp. 91-92; December, 1996, Martha Topol, review of *Can You Spot the Spotted Dog?,* p. 104; February, 1998, Alicia Eames, review of *Smudge,* p. 90; October, 1999, Tina Hudak, review of *Monkey Trouble,* p. 125; March, 2002, Eunice Weech, review of *Jasper the Terror,* p. 200; July, 2002, Bina Williams, review of *But I Want To!,* pp. 97-98; November, 2003, Rachel G. Payne, review of *Amazing Animal Hide and Seek,* p. 114; January, 2005, Robin L. Gibson, review of *The Emperor's New Clothes,* p. 85; January, 2006, Linda Ludke, review of *Moondog,* p. 113.
Times Educational Supplement, December 2, 1994, Raymond Briggs, review of *Baby Crow,* p. 14; May 19, 2000, Ted Dewan, review of *The Elf's Hat,* p. 23.

ONLINE

John A. Rowe Home Page, http://www.johnarowe.com (February 2, 2009).*

* * *

RUSCH, Elizabeth 1966-

Personal

Born October 14, 1966, in New York, NY; married; children: two. *Education:* Duke University, bachelor's degree; University of California at Berkeley, master's degree.

Elizabeth Rusch (Photograph by David Friedman.)

Addresses

Home—Portland, OR. *E-mail*—author@elizabethrusch. com.

Career

Children's book author, freelance magazine writer, and editor. Former managing editor, *Teacher* magazine; editor-in-chief, *PointsBeyond.com.* Member of faculty, Attic Writers' Workshop.

Awards, Honors

Education Writers Associaton honorable mention, 1991; Benjamin Fine Award honorable mention, 1992; International Reading Association Children's Book Award finalist, and Notable Children's Book selection, *Smithsonian* magazine, both 2002, both for *Generation Fix;* Maggie Award for Best How-to magazine article, 2003; Kate Snow Literary Award for Juvenile Literature, 2004, for *The Big Brothers' Guide;* Oregon literary fellowship, 2006; *Natural History* magazine Best Books designation, 2007, for *Will It Blow?;* Outstanding Science Picturebook designation, 2007, for *Will It Blow?,* 2008, for *The Planet Hunter;* Eloise Jarvis McGraw Award

for Children's Literature, 2008, and Monarch Children's Choice Award finalist, 2009, both for *A Day with No Crayons.*

Writings

Generation Fix: Young Ideas for a Better World, Beyond Words (Hillsboro, OR), 2002.
The Planet Hunter: The Story behind What Happened to Pluto, illustrated by Guy Francis, Rising Moon (Flagstaff, AZ), 2007.
A Day with No Crayons, illustrated by Chad Cameron, Rising Moon (Flagstaff, AZ), 2007.
Will It Blow? Become a Volcano Detective at Mount St. Helens, illustrated by K.E. Lewis, Sasquatch (Seattle, WA), 2007.
Girls' Tennis: Conquering the Court, Capstone Press (Mankato, MN), 2007.

Contributor to books, including *Classroom Crusaders: Twelve Teachers Who Are Trying to Change the System,* Jossey-Bass, 1994; *Thoughtful Teachers, Thoughtful Schools,* Allyn & Bacon, 1996; *More Backcountry Cooking: Moveable Feasts by the Experts and Backpacker Magazine,* Mountaineers, 2003; and *The Power of Kindness for Teens,* Ideals, 2005. Contributor to periodicals, including *Smithsonian, Portland Monthly, Muse, Read, American Girl, Harper's, Mother Jones, Backpacker, Oregonian,* and *Parenting.* Contributing editor to *Child* and *Fit Pregnancy.*

Sidelights

Elizabeth Rusch is an award-winning magazine writer and children's book author. She writes both fiction and nonfiction for children and adults in the areas of science, art, humor, child development, health, the environment, sports, outdoors, travel, and social issues: anything that catches her fancy. In addition to writing, Rusch enjoys teaching, inspiring and mentoring students and adults about writing and about the topics she has grown to love, such as volcanoes, space exploration, art exploration, and youth activism. Her books include *The Planet Hunter: The Story behind What Happened to Pluto* and *Will It Blow? Become a Volcano Detective at Mount St. Helens.*

In *The Planet Hunter* Rusch tells the true story of Michael E. Brown, an astronomer at the California Institute of Technology. Taking readers through Brown's life, from backyard experiments as a child to research at leading universities in the United States, Rusch assembles a biography of a scientist determined to prove the existence of solar system planets beyond the set of nine that was traditionally taught in school. *Sky and Telescope* contributor Stuart J. Goldman called *The Planet Hunter* "fun and informative,"while *School Library Journal* critic John Peters suggested that the work "makes an inspiring, energizing addition to any collection."

Rusch introduces young readers to the world of geology in *Will It Blow?,* encouraging children to gather clues to determine what clues might predict a volcanic eruption. Page by page, the author explains the process leading to a volcano exploding, not only defining scientific terminology but also providing simple experiments children can perform at home to reinforce the geological principals covered in the book. Writing in *Children's Bookwatch,* a reviewer described *Will It Blow?* as an "ideal" starting point for young readers exploring volcanic activity, claiming that the title is as "engaging and entertaining as it is informed and informative." *School Library Journal* contributor Patricia Manning favorably commented on the book's "breezy" narrative, finding it filled with "light humor masking the fact that it is packed with information."

A Day with No Crayons is a picture book in which little Liza's world suddenly goes gray when her mother takes her crayons away. How does the budding artist respond? She squirts her toothpaste angrily and stomps through mud puddles. Through these acts, Liza inadvertently creates art, and eventually discovers color in the world around her. *Generation Fix: Young Ideas for a Better World,* another book for young readers, tells the inspiring true stories of more than fifteen young activists who overcame daunting obstacles to work for a more-perfect

Rusch's nonfiction picture book The Planet Hunter ***features artwork by Guy Francis.*** (Illustration © 2007 by Guy Francis. All rights reserved. Reproduced by permission.)

world. The children's many accomplishments include collecting more than 5,000 boxes of cereal for food pantries, recycling 30,000 gallons of oil, and raising a quarter of a million dollars to buy school supplies for needy students. Jennifer Hubert wrote in the *Voice of Youth Advocates* that *Generation Fix* serves as "an inspirational and practical guide for youth interested in serving their communities."

Biographical and Critical Sources

PERIODICALS

Children's Bookwatch, October, 2007, review of *Will It Blow? Become a Volcano Detective at Mount St. Helens.*

School Library Journal, July, 2008, Patricia Manning, review of *Will It Blow?,* p. 120; January, 2008, John Peters, review of *The Planet Hunter: The Story behind What Happened to Pluto,* p. 110; April, 2008, Rachael Vilmar, review of *A Day with No Crayons,* p. 121.

Sky and Telescope, March, 2008, Stuart J. Goldman, review of *The Planet Hunter,* p. 82.

Voice of Youth Advocates, December, 2002, Jennifer Herbert, review of *Generation Fix: Young Ideas for a Better World,* p. 410.

ONLINE

Elizabeth Rusch Home Page, http://www.elizabethrusch.com (February 6, 2009).

Embracing the Child Web site, http://www.embracingthechild.org/ (February 5, 2009), interview with Rusch.

S

SAKAMOTO, Miki

Personal

Married; husband's name Kevin. *Education:* California State University, Long Beach, B.A. (fine arts and illustration).

Addresses

Home—Orange County, CA. *Agent*—Shannon Associates, LLC, 630 9th Ave., Ste. 707, New York, NY 10036.

Career

Illustrator.

Illustrator

Steve Metzger, *We're Going on a Leaf Hunt,* Scholastic, Inc. (New York, NY), 2005.

Allia Zobel Nolan, *What I Like about Me,* Reader's Digest Children's Publishing (New York, NY), 2005.

Fran Shaw, *Sharing: How Kindness Grows,* Reader's Digest Children's Publishing (New York, NY), 2006.

Allia Zobel Nolan, *What I Do Best!,* Reader's Digest Children's Publishing (New York, NY), 2006.

Todd Dunn, *We Go Together!,* Sterling Publishing (New York, NY), 2007.

Wendy Lewison, *My First Garden,* Simon & Schuster (New York, NY), 2009.

Biographical and Critical Sources

PERIODICALS

Booklist, December 1, 2007, Shelle Rosenfeld, review of *We Go Together!,* p. 50.

Kirkus Reviews, October 15, 2007, review of *We Go Together!*

School Library Journal, December, 2007, Carolyn Janssen, review of *We Go Together!,* p. 88.*

* * *

SCHINDLER, S.D. 1952-
(Steven D. Schindler)

Personal

Born September 27, 1952, in Kenosha, WI; son of Edwin C. and Bettie L. Schindler; married. *Education:* University of Pennsylvania, degree (biology). *Politics:* "Green." *Religion:* Christian. *Hobbies and other interests:* Playing piano, recorder, and harpsichord; tennis, squash, gardening, wildflower propagation, creating ponds to attract amphibians like frogs and toads.

Addresses

Home—Philadelphia, PA. *Agent*—Publishers' Graphics Inc., 251 Greenwood Ave., Bethel, CT 06801.

Career

Illustrator.

Awards, Honors

Parents' Choice Award for Illustration, Parents' Choice Foundation, 1982, for *The First Tulips in Holland;* Best Book selection, *School Library Journal,* 1985, for *Every Living Thing,* and 1995, for *If You Should Hear a Honey Guide; Smithsonian* magazine award for outstanding natural history title, 1995, for *If You Should Hear a Honey Guide;* California Young Reader Medal, 1996-97, for *Don't Fidget a Feather!;* Best Children's Book of the Year, Age Five to Eight category, Bank Street College, 1998, for *Creepy Riddles;* Notable Children's Book designation, American Library Association, 1999, for *How Santa Got His Job;* Notable Wisconsin Children's Author designation, Wisconsin Library Association, 2005; Newbery Honor Book designation, 2006, for *Whittington* by Alan Armstrong.

Writings

SELF-ILLUSTRATED

My First Bird Book, Random House (New York, NY), 1989.

ILLUSTRATOR

G.C. Skipper, *The Ghost in the Church,* Children's Press, 1976.

Susan Saunders, *Fish Fry,* Viking (New York, NY), 1982.

Phyllis Krasilovsky, *The First Tulips in Holland,* Doubleday (New York, NY), 1982.

Morrell Gipson, reteller, *Favorite Nursery Tales,* Doubleday (New York, NY), 1983.

Leon Garfield, *Fair's Fair,* Doubleday (New York, NY), 1983.

Deborah Perlberg, *Wembley Fraggle Gets the Story,* Holt (New York, NY), 1984.

Cynthia Rylant, *Every Living Thing,* Bradbury Press (New York, NY), 1985.

Elizabeth Bolton, *The Tree House Detective Club,* Troll Associates (Metuchen, NJ), 1985.

Laurence Santrey, *Moon,* Troll Associates (Metuchen, NJ), 1985.

Virginia Haviland, reteller, *Favorite Fairy Tales Told around the World,* Little, Brown (Boston, MA), 1985.

Eric Suben, editor, *The Golden Goose and Other Tales of Good Fortune,* Golden Books, 1986.

Cynthia Rylant, *Children of Christmas: Stories for the Season,* Orchard (New York, NY), 1987.

Ursula K. Le Guin, *Catwings,* Orchard (New York, NY), 1988.

Margery Williams, *The Velveteen Rabbit,* adapted by David Eastman, Troll Associates (Metuchen, NJ), 1988.

Ursula K. Le Guin, *Catwings Return,* Orchard (New York, NY), 1988.

Steven Kroll, *Oh, What a Thanksgiving!,* Scholastic (New York, NY), 1988.

Bobbi Katz, *The Creepy, Crawly Book,* Random House, 1989.

Deborah Hautzig, *The Pied Piper of Hamelin,* Random House (New York, NY), 1989.

Melvin Berger, *As Old as the Hills,* F. Watts (New York, NY), 1989.

Morgan Matthews, *The Big Race,* Troll Associates (Metuchen, NJ), 1989.

William H. Hooks, *The Three Little Pigs and the Fox,* Macmillan (New York, NY), 1989.

Mary Blount Christian, *Penrod's Party,* Macmillan (New York, NY), 1990.

Mark Twain, *The Prince and the Pauper,* retold by Raymond James, Troll Associates (Metuchen, NJ), 1990.

Carollyn James, *Digging up the Past: The Story of an Archaeological Adventure,* F. Watts (New York, NY), 1990.

Joanne Oppenheim, *Could It Be?,* Bantam (New York, NY), 1990.

Jonathan Swift, *Gulliver's Travels,* retold by Raymond James, Troll Associates (Metuchen, NJ), 1990.

Megan McDonald, *Is This a House for Hermit Crab?,* Orchard (New York, NY), 1990.

Janet Craig, *Wonders of the Rain Forest,* Troll Associates (Metuchen, NJ), 1990.

Betsy Rossen Elliot and J. Stephen Lang, *The Illustrated Book of Bible Trivia,* Tyndale, 1991.

Evan Levine, *Not the Piano, Mrs. Medley!,* Orchard (New York, NY), 1991.

Joanne Oppenheim, *Eency Weency Spider,* Bantam (New York, NY), 1991.

Mary Blount Christian, *Penrod's Picture,* Macmillan (New York, NY), 1991.

The Twelve Days of Christmas, music copying and calligraphy by Christina Davidson, HarperCollins (New York, NY), 1991.

Megan McDonald, *Whoo-oo Is It?,* Orchard (New York, NY), 1992.

Erica Silverman, *Big Pumpkin,* Macmillan (New York, NY), 1992.

Susanne Santoro Whayne, *Night Creatures,* Simon & Schuster (New York, NY), 1992.

Elizabeth Jaykus, editor, *For Dad,* Peter Pauper, 1992.

Christina Anello, editor, *For Grandma,* Peter Pauper, 1992.

Jennifer Habel, editor, *For Mom,* Peter Pauper, 1992.

Rita Freedman, editor, *For My Daughter,* Peter Pauper, 1992.

Walter Retan, compiler, *Piggies, Piggies, Piggies,* Simon & Schuster (New York, NY), 1992.

Dawn Langley Simmons, *The Great White Owl of Sissinghurst,* Margaret K. McElderry Books (New York, NY), 1993.

Noah Lukas, *The Stinky Book,* Random House (New York, NY), 1993.

Constance C. Greene, *Odds on Oliver,* Viking (New York, NY), 1993.

Noah Lukas, *Tiny Trolls' 1, 2, 3,* Random House (New York, NY), 1993.

Noah Lukas, *Tiny Trolls' A, B, C,* Random House (New York, NY), 1993.

Leah Komaido, *Great Aunt Ida and Her Great Dane, Doc,* Doubleday (New York, NY), 1994.

Joanne Oppenheim, *Floratorium,* Bantam (New York, NY), 1994.

William Kennedy, *Charlie Marlarkie and the Singing Moose,* Viking (New York, NY), 1994.

Erica Silverman, *Don't Fidget a Feather!,* Macmillan (New York, NY), 1994.

Tres Seymour, *I Love My Buzzard,* Orchard (New York, NY), 1994.

Rose Wyler, *Spooky Tricks,* HarperCollins (New York, NY), 1994.

Patricia Brennan Demuth, *Those Amazing Ants,* Macmillan (New York, NY), 1994.

Ursula K. Le Guin, *Wonderful Alexander and the Catwings,* Orchard (New York, NY), 1994.

Jeff Sheppard, *Full Moon Birthday,* Atheneum (New York, NY), 1995.

April Pulley Sayre, *If You Should Hear a Honey Guide,* Houghton Mifflin (Boston, MA), 1995.

Mary DeBall Kwitz, *Little Vampire and the Midnight Bear,* Dial (New York, NY), 1995.

Tres Seymour, *The Smash-Up Crash-Up Derby,* Orchard (New York, NY), 1995.

Tony Johnston, *The Ghost of Nicholas Greebe,* Dial (New York, NY), 1996.

Lucille Recht Penna, *Landing at Plymouth,* David McKay, 1996.

Candace Fleming, *Madame LaGrande and Her So High, to the Sky, Uproarious Pompadour,* Knopf (New York, NY), 1996.

Lucille Recht Penner, *The Pilgrims at Plymouth,* Random House (New York, NY), 1996.

Crescent Dragonwagon, *Bat in the Dining Room,* Marshall Cavendish (New York, NY), 1997.

Stuart J. Murphy, *Betcha!,* HarperCollins (New York, NY), 1997.

Arthur Dorros, *A Tree Is Growing,* Scholastic (New York, NY), 1997.

Megan McDonald, *Tundra Mouse: A Storyknife Tale,* Orchard (New York, NY), 1997.

Carolyn White, *Whuppity Stoorie: A Scottish Folktale,* Putnam (New York, NY), 1997.

Janet Craig, *Wonders of the Rain Forest,* Troll Associates (Metuchen, NJ), 1997.

Cynthia DeFelice, *Clever Crow,* Atheneum (New York, NY), 1998.

Katy Hall and Lisa Eisenberg, *Creepy Riddles,* Dial (New York, NY), 1998.

Caron Lee Cohen, *How Many Fish?,* HarperCollins (New York, NY), 1998.

Stephen Krensky, *How Santa Got His Job,* Simon & Schuster (New York, NY), 1998.

Virginia Walters, *Are We There Yet, Daddy?,* Viking (New York, NY), 1999.

Candace Fleming, *A Big Cheese for the White House: The True Tale of a Tremendous Cheddar,* Dorling Kindersley (New York, NY), 1999.

Harriet Ziefert, *First Night,* Putnam (New York, NY), 1999.

Verla Kay, *Gold Fever,* Putnam (New York, NY), 1999.

Ursula K. Le Guin, *Jane on Her Own: A Catwings Tale,* Orchard (New York, NY), 1999.

Marilyn Singer, *Josie to the Rescue,* Scholastic (New York, NY), 1999.

David Greenberg, *Whatever Happened to Humpty Dumpty?, and Other Surprising Sequels to Mother Goose Rhymes,* Little, Brown (Boston, MA), 2000.

Verla Kay, *Covered Wagons, Bumpy Trails,* Putnam (New York, NY), 2000.

M.C. Helldorfer, *Hog Music,* Viking (New York, NY), 2000.

Nancy Antle, *Sam's Wild West Christmas,* Dial (New York, NY), 2000.

Kenneth Oppel, *Sunwing,* Simon & Schuster (New York, NY), 2000.

Irma Joyce, *Never Talk to Strangers,* Golden Books (New York, NY), 2000.

Rosemary Benét and Stephen Vincent Benét, *Johnny Appleseed,* Margaret K. McElderry Books (New York, NY), 2001.

Patricia Rae Wolff, *Cackle Cook's Monster Stew,* Golden Books (New York, NY), 2001.

Mark Kurlansky, *The Cod's Tale,* Putnam's (New York, NY), 2001.

Stephen Krensky, *How Santa Lost His Job,* Simon & Schuster (New York, NY), 2001.

Kenneth C. Davis, *Don't Know Much about the Pilgrims,* HarperCollins (New York, NY), 2002.

Kenneth C. Davis, *Don't Know Much about the Kings and Queens of England,* HarperCollins (New York, NY), 2002.

Margery Cuyler, *Skeleton Hiccups,* Margaret K. McElderry Books (New York, NY), 2002.

Eileen Spinelli, *Three Pebbles and a Song,* Dial (New York, NY), 2003.

Kevin Lewis, *The Runaway Pumpkin,* Orchard Books (New York, NY), 2003.

Laura Leuck, *One Witch,* Walker (New York, NY), 2003.

Melvin Berger, *Spinning Spiders,* HarperCollins (New York, NY), 2003.

Douglas Rees, *Grandy Thaxter's Helper,* Atheneum (New York, NY), 2004.

Jon Koons, *A Confused Hanukkah: An Original Story of Chelm,* Dutton Children's (New York, NY), 2004.

Anne Rockwell, *Honey in a Hive,* HarperCollins (New York, NY), 2005.

Kathleen V. Kudlinski, *Boy, Were We Wrong about Dinosaurs!,* Dutton Children's (New York, NY), 2005.

Kenneth C. Davis, *Don't Know Much about Mummies,* HarperCollins (New York, NY), 2005.

Alan Armstrong, *Whittington,* Random House (New York, NY), 2005.

Deborah O'Neal and Angela Westengard, *The Trouble with Henry: A Tale of Walden Pond,* Candlewick Press (Cambridge, MA), 2006.

Carol Otis Hurst, *Terrible Storm,* Greenwillow (New York, NY), 2006.

Jane O'Connor, *The Snow Globe Family,* Putnam (New York, NY), 2006.

Mark Kurlansky, *The Story of Salt,* Putnam (New York, NY), 2006.

Louise Borden, *Off to First Grade,* Margaret K. McElderry Books (New York, NY), 2007.

Julian Fellowes, *The Curious Adventures of the Abandoned Toys,* Henry Holt (New York, NY), 2007.

Gennifer Choldenko, *Louder, Lili,* Putnam (New York, NY), 2007.

Margery Cuyler, *Monster Mess!,* Margaret K. McElderry Books (New York, NY), 2008.

Deborah Hopkinson, *Home on the Range: John A. Lomax and His Cowboy Songs,* Putnam (New York, NY), 2009.

Jacqueline Davies, *Tricking the Tallyman,* Knopf (New York, NY), 2009.

Linda Ashman, *Come to the Castle: A Visit to a Castle in Thirteenth-Century England,* Flash Point, 2009.

ILLUSTRATOR; "EINSTEIN ANDERSON, SCIENCE DETECTIVE" SERIES

Seymour Simon, *Einstein Anderson Science Sleuth,* Viking Penguin (New York, NY), 1980, published as *The Howling Dog and Other Cases,* Morrow (New York, NY), 1997.

Seymour Simon, *Einstein Anderson Shocks His Friends,* Viking Penguin (New York, NY), 1980, published as *The Halloween Horror and Other Cases,* Morrow (New York, NY), 1997.

Seymour Simon, *Einstein Anderson Tells a Comet's Tale,* Viking Penguin (New York, NY), 1981, published as *The Time Machine and Other Cases,* Morrow (New York, NY), 1997.

Seymour Simon, *Einstein Anderson Makes up for Lost Time,* Viking Penguin (New York, NY), 1981, published as *The Gigantic Ants and Other Cases,* Morrow (New York, NY), 1997.

Seymour Simon, *Einstein Anderson Lights up the Sky,* Viking Penguin (New York, NY), 1982, published as *The Mysterious Lights and Other Cases,* Morrow (New York, NY), 1998.

Seymour Simon, *Einstein Anderson Goes to Bat,* Viking Penguin (New York, NY), 1982, published as *Wings of Darkness and Other Cases,* Morrow (New York, NY), 1998.

Seymour Simon, *Einstein Anderson Sees through the Invisible Man,* Viking Penguin (New York, NY), 1982, published as *The Invisible Man and Other Cases,* Morrow (New York, NY), 1998.

Seymour Simon, *The On-Line Spaceman and Other Cases,* Morrow, 1997.

ILLUSTRATOR; "LOTTERY LUCK" SERIES

Judy Delton, *Winning Ticket,* Hyperion (New York, NY), 1995.

Judy Delton, *Prize-winning Private Eyes,* Hyperion (New York, NY), 1995.

Judy Delton, *Ten's a Crowd,* Hyperion (New York, NY), 1995.

Judy Delton, *Moving Up,* Hyperion (New York, NY), 1995.

Judy Delton, *Ship Ahoy!,* Hyperion (New York, NY), 1995.

Judy Delton, *Next Stop, the White House!,* Hyperion (New York, NY), 1995.

Judy Delton, *Royal Escapade,* Hyperion (New York, NY), 1995.

Judy Delton, *Cabin Surprise,* Hyperion (New York, NY), 1995.

Sidelights

Accomplished in many media and diverse styles, S.D. Schindler has illustrated over one hundred books since beginning his career in 1976. His whimsical pen-and-ink drawings, which have drawn comparison to the work of noted illustrator Edward Gorey, often appear decked out with gouache and watercolor tones, while other projects feature colored pencil drawings or acrylic paintings. Praising Schindler's work for Stephen Krensky's picture book *How Santa Lost His Job,* a *Kirkus Reviews* writer hailed his images as "masterworks of detail," while in *School Library Journal* a critic dubbed the book's ink and gouache illustrations "wonderfully energetic and detailed." The writers whose texts have been brought to life through Schindler's creative talent reads like a who's who of award-winning modern chil-

dren's authors: Melvin Berger, Judy Delton, Arthur Dorros, Cynthia Rylant, Margery Cuyler, Kenneth Oppel, Cynthia DeFelice, Ursula K. LeGuin, and Virginia Haviland, among others.

As Schindler once recalled to *SATA:* "I began drawing and coloring at an early age. My first award was when I was four; I won a red wagon at a coloring contest at a summer playground program. My favorite kinds of pictures were of animals. I had a total fascination with animals and their habitats. I loved going out looking for animals to bring home as pets as much as I loved drawing. I would bring home rabbits, snakes, polliwogs, rats, mice, and even a bat once. I have an older brother and we would do coloring or drawing together. He was more advanced and was certainly a stimulus. We continued to draw together until he was in junior high school, then he stopped drawing."

Schindler is self-taught and never took art courses; like other children, he liked to copy cartoons and characters, especially from *Mad* magazine and Disney films. In school he was known as the class artist, and his teachers put him in charge of class bulletin boards and posters in grade school. His parents acknowledged his talent, but ultimately encouraged Schindler to pursue a technical degree because of the difficulty of making a living in the art field. During junior high school, he began giving his drawings as presents; then in high school, he decided to set up at a local outdoor art exhibit to sell his botanical drawings. The teen was so successful that he continued to set up booths at art exhibits as a way to earn money for college. Although he entered the University of Pennsylvania as a pre-med major, he later admitted to *SATA:* "The first two years I goofed off and did a lot of drawing. I didn't really care too much for the biology courses, which was a surprise." During his junior year in college he realized that he wanted to make art his life, and although he majored in biology, after graduation he went to New York City in search of a job in the art field. When no jobs developed, he returned to selling his artwork at outdoor exhibits. An agent visiting an exhibit noticed some pieces of Schindler's work that related to children and got him involved in textbook illustration. Eventually he was approached by someone about illustrating a children's story, thus launching his career as a children's book illustrator.

Schindler has built a reputation as an accomplished illustrator who works in a variety of styles and media. He typically works on five to six projects at a time, jumping from one style to the next without carrying over the previous style of work. As Schindler once explained to *SATA,* the style of art called for in any book "depends on the feel of the story," which, he noted, he determines by reading "the text over and over until I'm sure of its tone, then the pictures appear." Schindler often finds that after he draws a story's characters, he encounters them in real life. He related, for example, that while working on *Not the Piano, Mrs. Medley!,* he went

A versatile artist, S.D. Schindler ranges in his style from detailed drawings to the cartoon art he contributes to Stuart J. Murphy's **Betcha!** (Jacket art ©
1997 by S.D. Schindler. Used by permission of HarperCollins Children's Books, a division of HarperCollins Publishers.)

to the New Jersey shore to take photographs for his research on the book and, while there, found a woman that matched the image of the character, Mrs. Medley.

Schindler's work is also known for its whimsy and humor. As the artist explained: "Visual humor is so easy; I never have to think of ways to achieve it." The amount of detail in his drawings is inspired by "the appeal of diversity. I've always enjoyed observing the details and what they mean. And in drawing or painting them I enjoy combining them to achieve a whole." When asked how long it takes to complete a particular book, Schindler explained that it depends on how detailed the characters and background are and the type of medium he uses. On the average, he requires four weeks of work, working eight to ten hours per day, to complete a picture book.

One of Schindler's early projects, illustrating *The First Tulips in Holland* by Phyllis Krasilovsky, received the Parents' Choice Award for Illustration from the Parents'

Choice Foundation. *The First Tulips in Holland* retells the story of how tulips, originally a Middle-Eastern flower, were introduced in Holland during the seventeenth century and started a horticultural craze that created several fortunes. Krasilovsky imagines a Dutch merchant who, after visiting Persia, returns with some flower bulbs for his daughter, Katrina. Katrina plants the flower bulbs in a pot in her window. When the tulips bloom, they receive much public attention and the merchant is offered huge sums of money for the tulips. He refuses the offers, instead giving the flower bulbs to Katrina as a dowry when she marries a young florist. The florist eventually builds them into a Holland trademark for everyone to enjoy. "Brilliantly colored illustrations that echo Dutch paintings spill out to the edges of nearly every page," hailed Joyce Maynard in a *New York Times Book Review* of *The First Tulips in Holland.* Citing Schindler's illustrations for the book as "reminiscent of the Dutch masters," *School Library Journal* reviewer Eva Elisabeth Von Ancken also praised the artist's eye for telling details. A contributor to *Booklist* described Schindler's work as a "visual feast," while a *Publishers Weekly* critic called the artist's renderings "marvelous paintings." Commenting on the accurate detail given to elements of architecture, costume, and botany in the book, a *Bulletin of the Center for Children's Books* contributor claimed that *The First Tulips in Holland* "is lovely to look at."

Another early project was illustrating Cynthia Rylant's *Every Living Thing.* This collection of short stories by one of Schindler's favorite writers expresses the positive influence animals have on people. One story shows how getting a hermit crab as a pet helps a young orphaned child relate to the elderly aunt who has become his new caretaker. Another story demonstrates how a turtle assists a learning-impaired child develop a friendship. Schindler's artwork is represented as "decorations" because small pen-and-ink renderings of the featured animal of each story are the book's only illustrations. His skill is nonetheless evident, a *Publishers Weekly* contributor noted, writing that the drawings "adorn as well as illustrate" the tales in Rylant's book. Praising the "finely detailed" drawings, *School Library Journal* critic Ruth S. Vose, added that the images at the beginning of each short story "express its tone" as well.

Schindler has illustrated several children's books by noted science-fiction novelist Ursula K. Le Guin. *Catwings* follows four winged kittens who are encouraged by their mother to flee the dangerous city for the safety of the countryside. Writing in the *New York Times Book Review,* Crescent Dragonwagon pointed out that Le Guin's story and Schindler's "marvelous ink and watercolor illustrations, especially the kitten closeups: personable, enchanting, believable," captivate the reader. "Fine illustrations show the delightfully furry and winged cats to perfection," asserted Ann A. Flowers in her *Horn Book* review, the critic adding that "every cat lover will wish for one of his or her own." Schindler has also illustrated several sequels to Le-Guin's book, among them *Catwings Return, Wonderful Alexander and the Catwings,* and *Jane on Her Own: A Catwings Tale.*

I Love My Buzzard ranks as one of Schindler's favorite picture-book project, as he told *SATA.* In the book author Tres Seymour tells a rhyming story of a young boy who brings home unusual pets, including a buzzard, warthog, squid, and even slugs. When his mother cannot take the surprises anymore and leaves, the boy realizes that he must find new homes for his pets. "Schindler adds considerably to the merriment with artfully detailed depictions of the irrepressible collector, his righteously indignant mom, and the realistic yet delightfully expressive creatures he's harboring," noted a contributor to *Kirkus Reviews.* His contribution to another nature-themed story, April Pulley Sayre's *If You Should Hear a Honey Guide,* also earned praise from critics,

Booklist reviewer Julie Corsaro writing that "the realistically detailed mixed-media paintings are executed in earth tones that suggest the almost colorless terrain of the region."

Schindler has also been complimented for his work on a wide variety of other books for children, such as Candace Fleming's *Madame LaGrande and Her So High, to the Sky, Uproarious Pompadour* and *Whittington,* a first-novel by Alan Armstrong that earned the illustrator a Newbery Honor Book designation. In *Booklist* Kay Weisman noted of *Madame LaGrande and Her So High, to the Sky, Uproarious Pompadour* that the artist's "fanciful illustrations match the delightful silliness of the text." Praising Schindler's work for Eileen Spinelli's *Three Pebbles and a Song* as containing "some of his most striking work to date," a *Publishers Weekly* critic also cited the "wonderful story" about a family of mice preparing for winter. In *School Library Journal* Robyn Walker wrote of Spinelli's story that "Schindler's painterly artwork captures perfectly the chill of the coming winter and the warmth of a happy home." Schindler's "warm, energetic illustrations highlight the elements of humor" that Gennifer Choldenko weaves into her story

Cover of Kenneth Oppel's novel Silverwing, *featuring Schindler's detailed artwork.* (Aladdin Paperbacks, 1999. Reproduced by permission.)

Schindler teams up with noted author Ursula K. LeGuin for a series of books that includes **Wonderful Alexander and the Catwings.** (Illustration copyright © 1994 by S.D. Schindler. Reproduced by permission of Orchard Books, an imprint of Scholastic, Inc.)

for *Louder, Lili,* according to *School Library Journal* critic Barbara Katz, and in *Kirkus Reviews* a critic deemed the artist's "bright, cartoon-style illustrations . . . just right" and full of "eye-catching details."

Although many critics maintain that some of Schindler's best work brings to life animal-centered stories, the versatile artist also demonstrates his knack for grotesquely amusing monsters in several picture books. Reviewing his pictures for Katy Hall and Lisa Eisenberg's *Creepy Riddles,* a *Horn Book* contributor wrote that Schindler's "detailed color illustrations . . . are spooky enough to produce a shiver, yet amusing enough to scare up a smile." *Skeleton Hiccups* and *Monster Mess,* two picture books by Margery Cuyler, also benefit from the illustrator's eye for the amusingly horrific, and his bold, inky pictures for the former "make the most out of every situation, instilling humor in every scene," according to Piper L. Nyman in *School Library Journal.* In Cuyler's rhyming story, Skeleton spends an entire day trying to rid himself of the jarring need to issue a rattling "hic-hic-hiccup" until Ghost implements a time-tested solution. *Monster Mess,* which finds a scary monster tidying up the room of a sleeping child before

curling up in its nighttime haunt, also earned praise for its illustrator; in *School Library Journal* Linda M. Kenton wrote that Cuyler's "rhyming, repetitive text and [Schindler's] whimsical images whirl on the pages, making [*Monster Mess*] . . . a fun read-aloud."

Described by a *Kirkus Reviews* writer as a "witch's brew of ABC's," *Cackle Cook's Monster Stew* by Patricia Rae Wolff also brings out Schindler's playful side; in following a witch's efforts to put together the most disgusting stew ever, the illustrator colors his drawings "with just the right bilious colors, and his population of witches and ogres are comfortably spooky," the *Kirkus Reviews* writer added. *School Library Journal* critic Gay Lynn Van Vleck agreed, writing that in the artist's watercolor-and-gouache rendering of Igor the ogre's trip to his local witch-friendly grocery story, "bits of 'furry odds and ends' and iguana toes are not for the squeamish."

In a similar fashion, Schindler's work on *How Santa Got His Job* brings out the whimsical, understated quality of Krensky's story. "Schindler knows exactly how to make his artwork play off the humor," wrote Ilene Cooper in *Booklist.* Also notable are his illustrations for *A Big Cheese for the White House: The True Tale of a Tremendous Cheddar,* a story by Candace Fleming that is based on an incident that occurred during Thomas Jefferson's U.S. presidency. Calling the book "as pleasing to look at as it is delightful to read," a *Horn Book* critic paid compliment to Schindler's "droll, elegantly limned pen, ink and watercolor illustrations." In "endearing pen-and-ink spot illustrations," as well as full-page color paintings, Schindler imbues Julian Fellowes' *The Curious Adventures of the Abandoned Toys* with a nostalgic quality that "will appeal to those with a fondness for old-fashioned storybooks," concluded Jayne Damron in a review of yet another Schindler work in *School Library Journal.*

Schindler proves his expertise in bringing historical themes to life in *Gold Fever,* a tale of California's mining country that was penned by Verla Kay. He also mines historical research in creating art for the volumes in Kenneth C. Davis's "Don't Know Much About . . ." nonfiction series for elementary graders. A *Horn Book* contributor noted that in *Gold Fever* "Schindler's colored-pencil drawings on rough textured paper aptly convey" the landscape and the arduous and dirty work of searching for gold, while in *Don't Know Much about the Pilgrims* the illustrator's "precise and lively ink drawings . . . put a very human (and often amusing) face on the past," according to *Booklist* reviewer Carolyn Phelan.

For all his successes, Schindler acknowledges that illustrating is not an easy career to establish. He points out that, although his style has not changed since his graduation from college, when he first went to New York City, no one was interested in his work until he found an agent to represent him. "Art directors do not have to look for illustrators for children's books," he once explained to *SATA*. "It is easier to get work once you have been published." Based on his own experiences, he advises aspiring illustrators to "be sure of yourself" and "draw, draw, draw."

Biographical and Critical Sources

PERIODICALS

Booklist, May 15, 1982, review of *The First Tulips in Holland,* p. 1258; November 15, 1994, Linda Ward-Callaghan, review of *Don't Fidget a Feather!;* September 1, 1995, Julie Corsaro, review of *If You Should Hear a Honey Guide;* July 19, 1996, Kay Weisman, review of *Madame LaGrande and Her So High, to the Sky, Uproarious Pompadour;* January 1, 1998, Susan Dove Lempke, review of *Tundra Mouse: A Storyknife Tale;* September 1, 1998, Ilene Cooper, review of *How Santa Got His Job;* June 1, 2001, Denise Wilms, review of *Johnny Appleseed,* p. 1885; August, 2002, Carolyn Phelan, review of *Don't Know Much about the Pilgrims,* p. 1952; September 15, 2002, John Peters, review of *Skeleton Hiccups,* p. 245; October 15, 2005, Carolyn Phelan, review of *The Trouble with Henry: A Tale of Walden Pond,* p. 58; December 1, 2005, Carolyn Phelan, review of *Boy, Were We Wrong about Dinosaurs!,* p. 61; July 1, 2006, Hazel Rochman, review of *The Story of Salt,* p. 53; October 1, 2006, Gillian Engberg, review of *The Snow Globe Family,* p. 60; November 15, 2006, Ilene Cooper, review of *Terrible Storm,* p. 44; August, 2007, Gillian Engberg, review of *Louder, Lili,* p. 84; October 1, 2007, Shelle Rosenfeld, review of *The Curious Adventures of the Abandoned Toys,* p. 56; June 1, 2008, Hazel Rochman, review of *Monster Mess!,* p. 91.

Bulletin of the Center for Children's Books, June, 1982, review of *The First Tulips in Holland,* pp. 190-191.

Horn Book, November-December, 1988, Ann A. Flowers, review of *Catwings,* p. 781; September, 1999, Mary M. Burns, review of *A Big Cheese for the White House,* p. 594; January, 2001, Mary A. Burns, review of *Covered Wagons, Bumpy Trails,* p. 84; November-December, 2001, Betty Carter, review of *The Cod's Tale,* p. 773; September-October, 2002, Joanna Rudge Long, review of *Skeleton Hiccups,* p. 549; July-August, 2005, Joanna Rudge Long, review of *Whittington,* p. 463; November-December, 2005, Danielle J. Ford, review of *Boy, Were We Wrong about Dinosaurs!,* p. 739; September-October, 2006, Betty Carter, review of *The Story of Salt,* p. 607; November-December, 2006, Martha V. Parravano, review of *The Snow Globe Family,* p. 702.

Kirkus Reviews, March 15, 1994, review of *I Love My Buzzard;* August 1, 1997, review of *Tundra Mouse;* August 15, 2001, review of *Cackle Cook's Monster Stew,* p. 1224; September 15, 2001, review of *How Santa Lost His Job,* p. 1360; August 1, 2002, review of *Skeleton Hiccups,* p. 1125; April 15, 2003, review of *Spinning Spiders,* p. 604; July 1, 2003, review of

Three Pebbles and a Song, p. 916; September 15, 2004, review of *Grandy Thaxter's Helper,* p. 919; November 1, 2004, review of *A Confused Hanukkah: An Original Story of Chelm,* p. 1051; July 1, 2005, review of *Whittington,* p. 729; August 1, 2005, review of *The Trouble with Henry,* p. 855; August 1, 2006, review of *The Story of Salt,* p. 790; September 1, 2006, review of *The Snow Globe Family,* p. 910; August 15, 2007, review of *The Curious Adventures of the Abandoned Toys;* September 1, 2007, review of *Louder, Lili;* July 1, 2008, review of *Monster Mess!*

New York Times Book Review, April 25, 1982, Joyce Maynard, review of *The First Tulips in Holland,* p. 38; November 13, 1988, Crescent Dragonwagon, review of *Catwings;* October 19, 2003, Susan Marie Swanson, review of *The Runaway Pumpkin,* p. 26; March 13, 2005, Beth Gutcheon, review of *Grandy Thaxter's Helper,* p. 20.

Publishers Weekly, April 23, 1982, review of *The First Tulips in Holland;* September 20, 1985, review of *Every Living Thing,* p. 108; October 9, 2000, review of *Covered Wagons, Bumpy Trails,* p. 87; June 25, 2001, review of *Johnny Appleseed,* p. 72; September 3, 2001, review of *The Cod's Tale,* p. 88; August 25, 2003, review of *Three Pebbles and a Song,* p. 63; September 20, 2004, review of *Grandy Thaxter's Helper,* p. 61; September 27, 2004, review of *A Confused Hanukkah,* p. 60; October 23, 2006, review of *The Snow Globe Family,* p. 50; January 15, 2007, review of *Terrible Storm,* p. 51; October 29, 2007, review of *The Curious Adventures of the Abandoned Toys,* p. 55.

School Library Journal, March, 1982, Eva Elisabeth Von Ancken, review of *The First Tulips in Holland,* p. 136; December, 1985, Ruth S. Vose, review of *Every Living Thing,* p. 106; May, 2000, Lee Bock, review of *Hog Music,* p. 142; November, 2000, Catherine T. Quattlebaum, review of *Covered Wagons, Bumpy Trails,* p. 125; August, 2001, Wendy Lukehart, review of *Johnny Appleseed,* p. 166; October, 2001, review of *How Santa Lost His Job,* p. 67; November, 2001, Gay Lynn Van Vleck, review of *Cackle Cook's Monster Stew,* p. 139; July, 2002, Barbara Buckley, review of *Don't Know Much about the Kings and Queens of England,* p. 133; October, 2002, Piper L. Nyman, review of *Skeleton Hiccups,* p. 100; August, 2003, James K. Irwin, review of *One Witch,* p. 136; September, 2003, Robyn Walker, review of *Three Pebbles and a Song,* p. 192; November, 2004, Marge Loch-Wouters, review of *Grandy Thaxter's Helper,* p. 116; August, 2005, Beth Wright, review of *Whittington,* p. 121; September, 2005, Karey Wehner, review of *Honey in a Hive,* p. 195; October, 2005, Shawn Brommer, review of *The Trouble with Henry,* p. 124; December, 2005, Patricia Manning, review of *Boy, Were We Wrong about Dinosaurs!,* p. 131; October, 2006, Carol S. Surges, review of *The Story of Salt,* p. 138; January, 2007, Catherine Threadgill, review of *Terrible Storm,* p. 98; September, 2007, Barbara Katz, review of *Louder, Lili,* p. 161; January, 2008, Jayne Damron, review of *The Curious Adventures of the Abandoned Toys,* p. 86; July, 2008, Linda M. Kenton, review of *Monster Mess!,* p. 70.*

SCHINDLER, Steven D.
See SCHINDLER, S.D.

*   *   *

SCOTT, Elaine 1940-

Personal

Born June 20, 1940, in Philadelphia, PA; daughter of George Jobling, Jr. (a banker) and Ethel (a homemaker) Watts; married Parker Scott (a geophysical engineer), May 16, 1959; children: Cynthia Ellen, Susan Elizabeth. *Education:* Attended Southern Methodist University, 1957-59, 1979-81, and University of Houston, 1979-81. *Religion:* Methodist. *Hobbies and other interests:* Reading, traveling, sailing, teaching.

Addresses

Home—Houston, TX. *E-mail*—Elaine@elainescott.com.

Career

Writer, 1975—. Teacher of workshops for Texas Conference of the United Methodist Church, 1978; teacher of writing workshops at Southwest Writer's Conference, Houston, TX, 1979, and at Trinity University, San Antonio, TX, 1980. Volunteer teacher of leadership workshops at United Methodist Church, Houston, 1959-77; volunteer publicity director for Camp Fire Girls of America, 1973-74. Board member and chair of committee on international adoptions, Homes of St. Mark (private non-profit adoption agency), Houston, 1980-89.

Member

Authors Guild, Authors League of America, Society of Children's Book Writers and Illustrators, Writer's League of Texas.

Awards, Honors

Reading Magic Award, *Parenting* magazine, and American Library Association Notable Book citation, 1988, both for *Ramona: Behind the Scenes of a Television Show;* Best Books designation, *School Library Journal,* and *Voice of Youth Advocates* nonfiction honor list includee, both 1995, and Children's Literature Choice, and Beehive Award nomination, both 1996, all for *Adventure in Space;* Outstanding Trade Book for Children designation, National Science Teachers Association, and Science Writing Award, American Institute of Physics, both 1999, both for *Close Encounters;* Notable Social Studies Trade Books for Young People designation, Children's Book Council/National Center for the Social Studies, and Cooperative Children's Book Center Choice, both 2005, both for *Poles Apart;* Golden Spur Award for Children's Literature, Texas State Reading Association, and Teacher's Choice selection, International Reading Association, both 2008, both for *When Is a Planet Not a Planet?*

Elaine Scott (Reproduced by permission of Elaine Scott.)

Writings

NONFICTION

Adoption, Franklin Watts (New York, NY), 1980.

The Banking Book, illustrated by Kathie Abrams, Warne, 1981.

Doodlebugging for Oil: The Treasure Hunt for Oil, Warne, 1982.

Oil! Getting It, Finding It, Selling It, Warne, 1984.

Stocks and Bonds, Profits and Losses, Franklin Watts (New York, NY), 1985.

Ramona: Behind the Scenes of a Television Show, photographs by Margaret Miller, Morrow (New York, NY), 1987.

Could You Be Kidnapped?, Franklin Watts (New York, NY), 1988.

Safe in the Spotlight: The Dawn Animal Agency and the Sanctuary for Animals, photographs by Margaret Miller, Morrow Junior Books (New York, NY), 1991.

Look Alive: Behind the Scenes of an Animated Film, photographs by Richard Hewett, Morrow Junior Books (New York, NY), 1992.

Funny Papers: Behind the Scenes of the Comics, photographs by Margaret Miller, Morrow Junior Books (New York, NY), 1993.

From Microchips to Movie Stars: The Making of Super Mario Brothers, Hyperion (New York, NY), 1995.

Movie Magic: Behind the Scenes with Special Effects, Morrow Junior Books (New York, NY), 1995.

Adventure in Space: The Flight to Fix the Hubble, photographs by Margaret Miller, Hyperion (New York, NY), 1995.

Twins!, photographs by Margaret Miller, Atheneum (New York, NY), 1998.

Close Encounters: Exploring the Universe with the Hubble Space Telescope, Hyperion (New York, NY), 1998.

Friends!, photographs by Margaret Miller, Atheneum (New York, NY), 2000.

Poles Apart: Why Penguins and Polar Bears Will Never Be Neighbors, Viking (New York, NY), 2004.

When Is a Planet Not a Planet?: The Story of Pluto, Clarion (New York, NY), 2007.

All about Sleep from A to Zzzz, Viking (New York, NY), 2008.

Mars and the Search for Life, Clarion (New York, NY), 2008.

YOUNG ADULT FICTION

Choices, Morrow (New York, NY), 1988.

Secrets of the Cirque Medrano, Charlesbridge (Watertown, MA), 2008.

Adaptations

Several of Scott's books have been adapted as audiobooks by Recorded Books, including *Movie Magic, Friends!, Adventure in Space,* and *Funny Papers.*

Sidelights

Texas-based writer Elaine Scott creates children's books that reveal the behind-the-scenes story about how things work. Among Scott's titles are *Oil! Getting It, Finding It, Selling It, Poles Apart: Why Penguins and Polar Bears Will Never Be Neighbors,* and *When Is a Planet Not a Planet?: The Story of Pluto.* "The kinds of nonfiction photo essays I write are rewarding, but difficult books to research and write," the author stated in an online interview with Cynthia Leitich Smith. "For one thing, I insist on first-hand research, and it isn't always easy to get access to the folks I want to interview. Fortunately, I'm persistent—and I try to be polite."

In *Ramona: Behind the Scenes of a Television Show,* Scott follows the progress of a television series based on Beverly Cleary's book series featuring popular preteen Ramona Quimby. Illustrated with black and white photographs, *Ramona* covers all aspects of the production cycle, from deciding on a plot and auditioning actors to designing costumes and sets and filming each episode. Commending Scott's ability to clearly explain the technical aspects of television production, a critic for *Kirkus Reviews* called the book "attractive and engagingly written." Elizabeth S. Watson, writing in *Horn Book,* remarked on the effective pairing of text and pictures, and added that *Ramona* is "rich in information" about what goes on behind the scenes in a television show. In the *Bulletin of the Center for Children's Books,* Zena Sutherland called Scott's text "direct, clear, sequential, and informative."

Safe in the Spotlight: The Dawn Animal Agency and the Sanctuary for Animals focuses on a farm owned by Leonard and Bunny Brook, a couple who rescue abandoned, abused, and neglected animals. After their farm had taken in over seven hundred animals—including camels, elephants, and even lions—private funds could no longer support the sanctuary. To sustain their beneficial venture, the Brookses founded the Dawn Animal Agency, a company that provides animals for use in television commercials and films. Following established guidelines that ensure that animals are treated properly, professionals can film a variety of exotic animals, with the proceeds going to support the farm. In *Horn Book,* Ellen Fader dubbed the photographs "engaging" and wrote that "Scott's lively reporting is packed with details." Calling *Safe in the Spotlight* "enticingly formatted," Betsy Hearne wrote in the *Bulletin of the Center for Children's Books* that in her text Scott clearly emphasizes the importance "of human respect and responsibility for animal life."

Animals of a different sort are the focus of *Poles Apart,* as Scott explains how the relatively recent understanding of plate tectonics helps our growing understanding of Earth's two coldest points: the north and south poles. In addition to discussing the movement of Antarctica to its current location, Scott also outlines the history of settlement and exploration in these frigid regions, including the arduous expeditions led by British Captain James Cook along the northern coasts, Norwegian Roald Amundsen to the geographical South Pole, and Robert Peary to the North Pole. In addition to explaining that creatures such as polar bears would not survive the brutal climate in Antarctica, Scott discusses ongoing research at the poles and includes a useful list of books and Web sites for interested readers. Noting that "Scott writes well, never talking down" to readers, *Booklist* contributor Carolyn Phelan praised *Poles Apart* as a "handsome, informative book," while in *Horn Book* Bush cited the "clearly written text" featured in "this attractive geographic history."

Funny Papers: Behind the Scenes of the Comics explores a subject dear to most young readers' hearts: cartoons and comic books. Beginning with a brief history of comic strips and comic books, Scott explains how cartoons are syndicated, printed, and published. She also provides information and commentary on some of the most popular names in the cartoon field, such as Charles Schultz and Hank Ketcham. Kathryn Jennings, writing in the *Bulletin of the Center for Children's Books,* claimed that Scott's text reads at times like a "well-written but under-researched college research paper," but added that the author describes the printing and distributing process extremely well. "Very readable and lively" was the way *School Library Journal* reviewer Carol Schene described *Funny Papers,* the critic adding that Scott's book provides "an entertaining and well-organized introduction" to its subject.

Several of Scott's books focus on behind-the-scenes stories that also take place above the clouds. The details of the space shuttle mission to repair the Hubble telescope are the focus of her award-winning *Adventure in*

Cover of Scott's nonfiction picture book Funny Papers, *featuring artwork by Margaret Miller.* (Photograph copyright © 1993 by Margaret Miller. Used by permission of HarperCollins Children's Books, a division of HarperCollins Publishers.)

Space: The Flight to Fix the Hubble. Here Scott discusses the problems space scientists discovered in the orbiting space telescope, and then describes the steps taken to solve them. Seven astronauts were sent into space aboard the space shuttle to correct a defective lens on the Hubble, and Scott provides interesting insight into the personal lives of these men and women, including interviews with the astronauts' families. According to a reviewer for the *Voice of Youth Advocates,* this additional background "enhance[s] a vivid, fact-filled portrayal of an important space mission." Appreciating the "lively text which holds the interest of the reader," a critic in *Reading Time* applauded Scott's ability to capture the excitement of the mission and recommended *Adventure in Space* for children interested in space.

The results of the mission profiled in *Adventure in Space* are covered in *Close Encounters: Exploring the Universe with the Hubble Space Telescope,* which contains pictures sent back from the orbiting craft and explains the information scientists have learned about our solar system as a result. Noting the "striking photographs"

included in Scott's book, *Horn Book* contributor Margaret A. Bush added that the volume "extend[s] a marvelous invitation to readers" who are fascinated by the life cycle of stars, black holes, and the discovery of new planets.

In Scott's award-winning *When Is a Planet Not a Planet?* she offers a history of astronomical discoveries, concentrating on the decision to redefine Pluto as a "dwarf" planet. As Scott noted, this book actually began as a study of Eris, a celestial body that was almost considered the tenth planet in our solar system; her focus shifted after the International Astronomical Union reclassified Pluto in 2006. "It's a challenge to write science in real time," the author told Smith, "but it's also exhilarating." Critiquing *When Is a Planet Not a Planet?,* Phelan complimented the author for explaining "how scientists come to conclusions—and occasionally change their minds." Betty Carter, writing in *Horn Book,* remarked that the volume "reiterates the powerful assertion that we don't know what we will know in the future."

Discussing her work writing nonfiction, Scott once told *SATA:* "When I write a book it is important to me to tell all the facts about the subject, but it is equally important to tell these facts in a way that is not boring. After all, a book that bores people usually isn't finished, and every writer wants his books to be read. So I try and include anecdotes about real people and real events in my work. Often boys and girls will ask me if everything in my books is true, and I delight in being able to answer, 'Yes. Everything happened just as I said.'

"I write about subjects I know and care about. I believe that without caring about the subject, the writer is in real danger of becoming nothing but a flesh and blood word processor—spitting out facts and nothing more. I think a writer should share himself, as well as his information, with his reader. It should be his voice that says to the reader, 'Come with me and together we'll explore sensitive issues like adoption, or complicated subjects like banking. Together you and I will visit the remote corners of the world, searching for oil with the doodlebuggers.' For me that is the essence of writing—it's really a dialogue between me and my reader. I'm grateful for the reader, and out of that gratitude comes a willingness to share myself and my experience of life with him."

In addition to her nonfiction, Scott authored the young-adult novel *Choices*. The work focuses on Beth, a popular senior at Millington High School. Just before an important school football game, students discover that their team mascot has been stolen. Suspecting that students from rival Woodrow Wilson High are to blame, Beth and several friends decide to settle the score by vandalizing the building of their longtime opponent. Although she is only a minor participant in the destruction, Beth is caught by the police and made a scapegoat by the school administration. Placed in a juvenile detention center for six weeks, she suffers the consequences of an unfair punishment. Aldor L. Matta, reviewing *Choices* in *Voice of Youth Advocates,* highly recommended the novel and stated that Scott "has packed many messages" into her relatively brief text.

Set in 1904, Scott's *Secrets of the Cirque Medrano* is a work of historical fiction for young adults. The novel concerns Brigitte Dubrinsky, a fourteen-year-old orphan who leaves Warsaw, Poland, to live with her aunt and uncle in Paris, France. Although Brigitte busies herself in helping to run her family's café, which is frequented by a young Pablo Picasso, her imagination is captured by the Cirque Medrano, located in Montmartre. When one of the circus performers disappears, the curious girl investigates and finds herself drawn into a world of political intrigue involving the Russian secret police. *School Library Journal* reviewer Caitlin Augusta wrote that *Secrets of the Cirque Medrano* "evokes the riotous, layered culture of Montmartre in the early 20th century," and Kathleen Isaacs described Scott's novel in *Booklist* as "an agreeable introduction to an unusual political, artistic, and social world."

Discussing the transition from nonfiction writer to novelist, Scott remarked in her online interview with Smith that "making things up didn't come easily to me, so creating an entire world out of whole cloth was a different kind of writing experience. But I loved giving my imagination free reign, getting inside my characters' heads, wondering what animated them, pondering their hopes and dreams—it was a heady experience."

Biographical and Critical Sources

PERIODICALS

Booklist, November 15, 1996, Jeanette Larson, review of *Adventure in Space: The Flight to Fix the Hubble,* p. 604; May 15, 1998, Carolyn Phelan, review of *Twins!,* p. 16; May 15, 2000, Shelley Townsend-Hudson, review of *Friends!,* p. 1746; December 1, 2004, Carolyn Phelan, review of *Poles Apart,* p. 670; September 1, 2007, Carolyn Phelan, review of *When Is a Planet Not a Planet? The Story of Pluto,* p. 113; January 1, 2008, Kathleen Isaacs, review of *Secrets of the Cirque Medrano,* p. 82.

Cover of Scott's middle-grade novel Secrets of the Cirque Medrano, *featuring artwork by Jamie Hogan.* (Illustration copyright © 2008 by Jamie Hogan. Used with permission of Charlesbridge Publishing, Inc. All rights reserved.)

Bulletin of the Center for Children's Books, October, 1988, Zena Sutherland, review of *Ramona: Behind the Scenes of a Television Show,* pp. 52-53; July-August, 1991, Betsy Hearne, review of *Safe in the Spotlight: The Dawn Animal Agency and the Sanctuary for Animals,* pp. 274-275; January, 1994, Kathryn Jennings, review of *Funny Papers: Behind the Scenes of the Comics,* p. 167.

Horn Book, January-February, 1989, Elizabeth S. Watson, review of *Ramona,* pp. 92-93; June, 1989, Aldor L. Matta, review of *Choices,* p. 107; September-October, 1991, Ellen Fader, review of *Safe in the Spotlight,* p. 615; July-August, 1998, Margaret A. Bush, review of *Close Encounters,* p. 516; January-February, 2005, Margaret A. Bush, review of *Poles Apart,* p. 114; November-December, 2007, Betty Carter, review of *When Is a Planet Not a Planet?,* p. 701.

Kirkus Reviews, July, 15, 1988, review of *Ramona,* p. 1065; September 15, 2004, review of *Poles Apart,* p. 920; August 15, 2007, review of *When Is a Planet Not a Planet?;* December 15, 2007, review of *Secrets of the Cirque Medrano;* September 1, 2008, review of *All about Sleep from A to Zzzz.*

Publishers Weekly, May 25, 1998, review of *Twins!,* p. 91; August 3, 1998, review of *Adventure in Space,* p. 87; May 22, 2000, review of *Friends!,* p. 92.

Reading Time, May, 1996, review of *Adventure in Space,* pp. 43-44.

School Library Journal, November, 1993, Carol Schene, review of *Funny Papers,* pp. 119-120; July, 1998, review of *Adventure in Space,* p. 35, and Joy Fleishhacker, review of *Twins!,* p. 91; May, 1998, John Peters, review of *Close Encounters,* p. 160; May, 2000, Susan Hepler, review of *Friends!,* p. 164; December, 2004, Patricia Manning, review of *Poles Apart,* p. 169; March, 2008, Caitlin Augusta, review of *Secrets of the Cirque Medrano,* p. 210.

Voice of Youth Advocates, June, 1989, Aldor L. Matta, review of *Choices,* p. 107; August, 1996, review of *Adventure in Space,* p. 151.

ONLINE

Balkin Buddies Web site, http://www.balkinbuddies.com/ (March 1, 2009), "Elaine Scott."

Cynsations Web log, http://cynthialeitichsmith.blogspot.com/ (November-December, 2001), Cynthia Leitich Smith, interview with Scott; (May 1, 2008) Smith, interview with Scott.

Elaine Scott Home Page, http://www.elainescott.com (March 1, 2009).*

*   *   *

SMATH, Jerry 1933-

Personal

Born 1933.

Addresses

Home—Croton-on-Hudson, NY.

Career

Author and illustrator.

Awards, Honors

Children's Choice and Parent's Choice awards.

Writings

SELF-ILLUSTRATED

But No Elephants, Parents Magazine Press (New York, NY), 1979.

The Housekeeper's Dog, Parents Magazine Press (New York, NY), 1980.

Elephant Goes to School, Parents Magazine Press (New York, NY), 1984.

Up Goes Mr. Downs, Parents Magazine Press (New York, NY), 1984.

Leon's Prize, Parents Magazine Press (New York, NY), 1987.

(With Valerie Smath) *Mr. Digby's Bad Day,* Simon & Schuster (New York, NY), 1989.

Peek-a-Bug, Random House (New York, NY), 1990.

Wheels on the Bus, Grosset & Dunlap (New York, NY), 1991.

Jumbo Jet, Grosset & Dunlap (New York, NY), 1992.

Space Shuttle, Grosset & Dunlap (New York, NY), 1992.

Helicopters, Grosset & Dunlap (New York, NY), 1992.

Elephant Goes to School, Parents Magazine Press (New York, NY), 1993.

A Hat So Simple, Bridgewater Books (Mahwah, NJ), 1993.

Up Goes Mr. Downs, Parents Magazine Press (New York, NY), 1993.

Investigator in New Ghouls on the Block, WhistleStop (Mahwah, NJ), 1994.

Mystery at Camp Crump, WhistleStop (Mahwah, NJ), 1994.

The Nutcracker, Grosset & Dunlap (New York, NY), 1994.

Thumbelina, Grosset & Dunlap (New York, NY), 1995.

One, Two, Buckle My Shoe, Western Publishing (Racine, WI), 1995.

Agnes Mouse, Troll Associates (Mahwah, NJ), 1995.

Baker Bunny, Troll Associates (Mahwah, NJ), 1995.

Eloise Elephant, Troll Associates (Mahwah, NJ), 1995.

Leopold Frog, Troll Associates (Mahwah, NJ), 1995.

The Frog Prince, Grosset & Dunlap (New York, NY), 1995.

Investigator in Classroom Capers, WhistleStop (Mahwah, NJ), 1995.

Mrs. Claus, WhistleStop (Mahwah, NJ), 1995.

Santa Claus, WhistleStop (Mahwah, NJ), 1995.

The Three Little Kittens, Western Publishing (Racine, WI), 1995.

Night-night Sleep Tight, Grosset & Dunlap (New York, NY), 1998.

Yum, Yum, All Done, Grosset & Dunlap (New York, NY), 1998.

The Magic Carousel Pony, Grosset & Dunlap (New York, NY), 1999.

Yes, Yes, Get Dressed!, Grosset & Dunlap (New York, NY), 1999.

The Animals' Christmas Carol: Adapted from Charles Dickens's A Christmas Carol, Bridgewater Books (Mahwah, NJ), 2000.

Long Ago in Bethlehem, Cook Communications Ministries (Colorado Springs, CO), 2002.

Wee Witches' Halloween, Scholastic (New York, NY), 2002.

The Best Easter Eggs Ever!, Scholastic (New York, NY), 2003.

I Like Pumpkins, Scholastic (New York, NY), 2003.

Kitty Goes to School, Scholastic (New York, NY), 2003.

Spiders, Bats, and Pumpkin Eaters: Halloween Fun with Mother Goose, Scholastic (New York, NY), 2004.

Sammy Salami, Abrams Books for Young Readers (New York, NY), 2007.

ILLUSTRATOR

Essie E. Lee and Elaine Israel, *Alcohol and You,* Messner (New York, NY), 1975.

Joanna Cole, *The Clown-Arounds,* Parents Magazine Press (New York, NY), 1981.

Joanna Cole, *The Clown-Arounds Have a Party,* Parents Magazine Press (New York, NY), 1982.

Joanna Cole, *Get Well, Clown-Arounds!,* Parents Magazine Press (New York, NY), 1982.

Joanna Cole, *The Clown-Arounds Go on Vacation,* Parents Magazine Press (New York, NY), 1983.

Joanna Cole, *Sweet Dreams, Clown-Arounds!,* Parents Magazine Press (New York, NY), 1985.

Bonnie Pryor, *Perfect Percy,* Simon & Schuster (New York, NY), 1988.

Jane Caraway, *One Windy Day,* Raintree Publishers (Milwaukee, WI), 1990.

Annie Ingle, *The Smallest Elf,* Random House (New York, NY), 1990.

Clement C. Moore, *The Night before Christmas,* Western Publishing (Racine, WI), 1991.

Mike Thaler, *Seven Little Hippos,* Simon & Schuster (New York, NY), 1991.

Dorothy Baustian Chapman, *Little Tune and the Misplaced Sounds,* American Guidance Service (Circle Pines, MN), 1992.

Lynn Offerman, *Hide-and-Seek around the House,* Starlight (New York, NY), 1992.

Lynn Offerman, *Let's Go to the Farm!,* Starlight (New York, NY), 1992.

Lynn Offerman, *Playground Peek-a-Boo!,* Starlight (New York, NY), 1992.

Lynn Offerman, *Who's Who at the Zoo?,* Starlight (New York, NY), 1992.

Eric Suben, reteller, *The Elves and the Shoemaker,* Golden Books (New York, NY), 1992.

Linda Williams Aber, *The Big Golden Book of Riddles, Jokes, Giggles, and Rhymes,* Golden Books (New York, NY), 1993.

Tom Chapin and John Forster, *Sing a Whale Song,* Random House (New York, NY), 1993.

Joanna Cole, *Get Well, Clown-Arounds!,* 1993.

Joanna Cole, *Sweet Dreams, Clown-Arounds!,* Parents Magazine Press (New York, NY), 1993.

Lee Hansen, *My Christmas Counting Book,* Golden Books (New York, NY), 1993.

Gail Herman, *Double-header,* Grosset & Dunlap (New York, NY), 1993.

Dayle Ann Dodds, *Someone Is Hiding: A Lift-the-Flap Counting Game,* Simon & Schuster (New York, NY), 1994.

Maxine P. Fisher, *The Country Mouse and the City Mouse,* Random House (New York, NY), 1994.

Mike Thaler, *Never Mail an Elephant,* Troll Associates (Mahwah, NJ), 1994.

Mike Thaler, *Uses for Mooses and Other Popular Pets,* Troll Associates (Mahwah, NJ), 1994.

Jennifer Dussling, *The Princess Lost Her Locket,* Grosset & Dunlap (New York, NY), 1996.

Wendy Cheyette Lewison, *Don't Wake the Baby!,* Grosset & Dunlap (New York, NY), 1996.

Mike Thaler, *Never Give a Fish an Umbrella and Other Silly Presents,* 1996.

Dina Anastasio, *Fly Trap,* Grosset & Dunlap (New York, NY), 1997.

Schuyler M. Bull, adaptor, *The Nutcracker,* Grosset & Dunlap (New York, NY), 1998.

Jennifer Dussling, *The Magic Carpet Ride,* Grosset & Dunlap (New York, NY), 1998.

Johanna Maron, *The Secret Valentine,* Grosset & Dunlap (New York, NY), 1999.

Catherine Daly, *Bugs, Bugs, Bugs,* Grosset & Dunlap (New York, NY), 2000.

Sonali Fry, adaptor, *Cinderella,* Grosset & Dunlap (New York, NY), 2000.

Nat Gabriel, *A Day with May,* Reader's Digest Children's Books (Pleasantville, NY), 2000.

Lucille Recht Penner, *Lights Out!,* Kane Press (New York, NY), 2000.

Jerry Smath's cartoon art brings to life Daphne Skinner's picture-book text for **All Aboard!** (Kane Press, Inc., 2007. Illustration copyright © 2007 by Jerry Smath. All rights reserved. Reproduced by permission.)

Jane Werner Watson, *The Story of Jesus,* Golden Books (New York, NY), 2000.

Linda Williams Aber, *The Big Golden Book of Laughs: A Treasury of Poems, Jokes, Riddles, and Rhymes,* Golden Books (New York, NY), 2001.

Gail Herman, *Keep Your Distance!,* Kane Press (New York, NY), 2001.

Sue Kassirer, *Math Fair Blues,* Kane Press (New York, NY), 2001.

Wendy Cheyette Lewison, *Princess Buttercup: A Flower Princess Story,* Grosset & Dunlap (New York, NY), 2001.

Monique Z. Stephens, *Halloween Parade,* Grosset & Dunlap (New York, NY), 2001.

Tui Sutherland, *Glittering Galaxies: A Trip through the Stars!,* Grosset & Dunlap (New York, NY), 2001.

William Boniface, *Five Little Ghosts,* Price, Stern, Sloan (New York, NY), 2002.

William Boniface, *Five Little Pumpkins,* Price, Stern, Sloan (New York, NY), 2002.

Lucille Recht Penner, *X Marks the Spot!,* Kane Press (New York, NY), 2002.

Gail Herman, *Buried in the Backyard,* Kane Press (New York, NY), 2003.

Daphne Skinner, *Almost Invisible Irene,* Kane Press (New York, NY), 2003.

Sue Kassirer, *What Daddy Loves,* Reader's Digest Children's Books (Pleasantville, NY), 2003.

Laura Driscoll, *My Brother, the Knight,* Kane Press (New York, NY), 2004.

Lori Haskins, *Butterfly Fever,* Kane Press (New York, NY), 2004.

Daisy Alberto, *No Rules for Rex!,* Kane Press (New York, NY), 2005.

Iris Hudson, *Mac and the Messmaker,* Kane Press (New York, NY), 2005.

Anna Jane Hays, *The Secret of the Circle-K Cave,* Kane Press (New York, NY), 2006.

Daphne Skinner, *Palapalooza,* Kane Press (New York, NY), 2006.

Daphne Skinner, *All Aboard!,* Kane Press (New York, NY), 2007.

Kirsten Larsen, *The Ghost Town Mystery,* Kane Press (New York, NY), 2008.

Monica Kulling and Nan Walker, *The Messiest Room on the Planet,* Kane Press (New York, NY), 2009.

Sidelights

Author and illustrator Jerry Smath has contributed to more than one hundred children's books. In his self-illustrated picture book *A Hat So Simple,* Edna Alligator purchases a new hat that draws the attention of her friends, who attempt to spruce it up by adding such decorative measures as a flower pot and a bunch of grapes. When a flock of hungry birds spies Edna walking outdoors, it swoops down, driving her into a rushing stream. *Booklist* critic Julie Corsaro praised the work, stating that young readers will enjoy "pratfalls captured in the rhyming text and sunny, watercolor cartoons."

Smath's use of bright colors and engaging characters enhance his illustrations for Butterfly Fever *by Lori Haskins.* (Illustration copyright © 2004 by Jerry Smath. All rights reserved. Reproduced by permission.)

The generous owner of a diner adopts a meat-loving cat in *Sammy Salami,* another self-illustrated work. After Pete finds a scrawny feline scrounging through his garbage, he brings the cat home, names it Sammy, and fattens it on the cat's favorite food, salami. When Pete heads to the mountains for a weekend, Sammy tries to follow him aboard the train. The confused cat is rescued by kind-hearted Lolly, who just happens to be preparing for a vacation herself. "Busily detailed and cartoonish illustrations play up the humor and silliness" in *Sammy Salami,* observed a contributor in *Kirkus Reviews.* In *Booklist,* Randall Enos also complimented Smath's illustrations, writing that "panoramic scenes and close-ups . . . provide plenty for the eyes to feast upon."

In addition to creating original picture books, Smath has also provided the artwork for dozens of titles by other authors. *X Marks the Spot!,* a tale by Lucille Recht Penner, centers on two brothers who discover a number of treasure maps after they move into their grandfather's house, prompting them to explore their new neighborhood. "Smath's detailed, light-dappled illustrations amplify the fun," Carolyn Phelan remarked in *Booklist.* In Anna Jane Hays's *The Secret of the Circle-K Cave,* another adventure tale, a youngster finds clues to a century-old bank robbery while spelunking with his cousins. According to *Booklist* contributor Gillian Engberg, young readers "will look to [Smath's] . . . appealing pencil-and-watercolor pictures for textual clues."

Smath has also contributed illustrations to several titles that teach science and math concepts to beginning readers. In *Math Fair Blues* by Sue Kassirer, Seth and his bandmates are invited to play at the big school event. Unfortunately, they spend so much time preparing music and decorating their shirts with geometric figures that they forget to complete a project. "Smath's colorful cartoons are lively and appealing," Barbara Auerbach commented in *School Library Journal.* In Recht's *Lights Out!,* a young girl stays up late one night, counting the darkened windows in the neighboring apartment building as each occupant prepares for bed. According to Lucinda Snyder Whitehurst, reviewing the tale in *School Library Journal,* "Smath's exuberant cartoon drawings add a great deal of humor to the story."

A grandmother and her two grandchildren face a tight schedule as they journey by train to a family wedding in *All Aboard!,* a book by Daphne Skinner. "Colorful cartoon art adds a touch of humor" to this story, noted Anne L. Tormohlen in *School Library Journal.* A shy girl attempts to camouflage herself by dressing to match her surroundings in *Almost Invisible Irene,* another work by Skinner. Here Smath's "soft, lighthearted paintings show how she manages to blend in with a variety of backgrounds," Erlene Bishop Killeen observed in her *School Library Journal* review of the book

Biographical and Critical Sources

PERIODICALS

Booklist, January 1, 1994, Julie Corsaro, review of *A Hat So Simple,* p. 833; April 15, 2002, Carolyn Phelan, review of *X Marks the Spot!,* p. 1408; February 15, 2004, Carolyn Phelan, review of *Butterfly Fever,* p. 1062; August 1, 2006, Gillian Engberg, review of *The Secret of the Circle-K Cave,* p. 86; January 1, 2007, Randall Enos, review of *Sammy Salami,* p. 95.

Kirkus Reviews, October 1, 2007, review of *Sammy Salami.*

Publishers Weekly, April 19, 1993, review of *Sing a Whale Song,* p. 28.

School Library Journal, June, 2000, Lucinda Snyder Whitehurst, review of *Lights Out!,* p. 111; October, 2000, review of *The Animals' Christmas Carol: Adapted from Charles Dickens's A Christmas Carol,* p. 63; June, 2001, Barbara Auerbach, review of *Math Fair Blues,* p. 100; August, 2001, Maura Bresnahan, review of *Princess Buttercup: A Flower Princess Story,* p. 156; December, 2001, Thomas Pitchford, review of *Keep Your Distance!,* p. 90; October, 2003, Karen Land, review of *Buried in the Backyard,* p. 125; January, 2004, Erlene Bishop Killeen, review of *Almost Invisible Irene,* p. 100; June, 2004, Erlene Bishop Killeen, review of *Butterfly Fever,* p. 110; June, 2007, Anne L. Tormohlen, review of *All Aboard!,* p. 124; July, 2008, Laura Scott, review of *The Ghost Town Mystery,* p. 76.*

*   *   *

SPALENKA, Greg 1958-

Personal

Born March 13, 1958, in Arcadia, CA. *Education:* Art Center College of Design, B.F.A., 1982. *Hobbies and other interests:* Playing the drums.

Addresses

Home—CA. *Office*—P.O. Box 884, Woodland Hills, CA 91365. *Agent*—Allen Spiegel Fine Arts, 221 Lobos Ave., Pacific Grove, CA 93950. *E-mail*—service@spalenka. com.

Career

Illustrator and educator. Instructor at art colleges, including School of Visual Arts, New York, NY, 1989-90; Art Center College of Design, Pasadena, CA, 1991-97; Laguna College of Art and Design, Laguna Beach, CA, 1992-2004; California State University at Northridge, 1997; and Otis College of Art and Design, Los Angeles, CA, 2000-03. Lecturer and speaker at workshops. Contributor to films, including *The Ant Bully, The Golden Compass,* and *Escape from Planet Earth. Exhibitions:* Works included in exhibits at Art Institute of Southern California, Laguna Beach, 1991; Storyopolis, Los Angeles, CA, 1996; and University of the Arts, 2007.

Awards, Honors

Gold and silver medals from Society of Illustrators.

Greg Spalenka created the evocative artwork for Elizabeth E. Wein's fantasy novel **A Coalition of Lions.** (Reproduced by permission of Viking Children's Books, a division of Penguin Putnam Books for Young Readers. All rights reserved.)

Illustrator

Teresa Bateman, *The Eyes of the Unicorn,* Holiday House (New York, NY), 2007.

Contributor of illustrations to periodicals, including *Rolling Stone, Atlantic Monthly, Business Week, Time, Newsweek, New York Times Magazine,* and *Sports Illustrated.*

Sidelights

Throughout his artistic career, Greg Spalenka has worked in a variety of different areas, creating illustrations for national magazines, teaching at art colleges, and even working in art departments for the film industry. In 2007, he again expanded his reach, creating the artwork for *The Eyes of the Unicorn,* a fairy tale written by Teresa Bateman. Set in a fantasy world, *The Eyes of the Unicorn* tells the story of a young girl named Tanisa and her special relationship with a white unicorn and the duke's son Chris. Unfortunately, hunters in the kingdom consider unicorns an exceptionally desirable prize. As one of these sportsmen, Chris takes aim at a unicorn while on a hunting outing, but instead hits Tanisa, his best friend from childhood. Using his magical powers, the unicorn saves the beautiful girl's

Spalenka's artwork is a highlight of Teresa Bateman's fantasy story in **The Eyes of the Unicorn.** (Illustration copyright © 2007 by Greg Spalenka. All rights reserved. Reproduced by permission of Holiday House, Inc.)

life, an act so touching that Chris vows never to hunt the creatures again. To preserve both his friend Tanisa and the unicorn, Chris sends the pair into hiding until the day comes when he can govern his father's land with kindness and wisdom.

Although a *Publishers Weekly* critic wrote that Spalenka's "digitally manipulated illustrations" for *The Eyes of the Unicorn* "compete for readers' attention," a *Kirkus Reviews* contributor described the artwork as "simply magical." "Spalenka's images often look like Renaissance portraits or still lifes," the critic added, particularly commending the illustrator's ability to bring the unicorn to life. Writing in *School Library Journal,* Margaret Bush cited Spalenka's "vigorous, cinematic views," claiming that the artist's pictures "lend a dramatic, surreal tone" to the novel.

Biographical and Critical Sources

PERIODICALS

Kirkus Reviews, September 1, 2007, review of *The Eyes of the Unicorn.*
Publishers Weekly, September 10, 2007, review of *The Eyes of the Unicorn,* p. 60.
School Library Journal, September, 2007, Margaret Bush, review of *The Eyes of the Unicorn,* p. 157.

ONLINE

Greg Spalenka Home Page, http://www.spalenka.com (January 31, 2009).*

*   *   *

STIER, Catherine

Personal

Born in MI; married; children: one son, one daughter.

Addresses

Home—Southwest TX. *E-mail*—info@catherinestier. com.

Career

Teacher, journalist, and writer. Central Business District Association, Detroit, MI, communications assistant; Twinbrook YMCA, Schaumburg, IL, preschool instructor for five years; Pioneer Press, Arlington Heights, IL, former columnist for *Schaumberg Review* newspaper. William Rainey Harper College, Palatine, IL, former instructor in continuing education program.

Member

Society of Children's Book Writers and Illustrators.

Catherine Stier (Photograph courtesy of Catherine Stier.)

Awards, Honors

Society of School Librarians International Honor Book designation, and International Reading Association Best Book designation, both for *If I Were President.*

Writings

If I Were President, illustrated by DyAnne DiSalvo-Ryan, Albert Whitman (Morton Grove, IL), 1999.
If I Ran for President, illustrated by Lynne Avril, Albert Whitman (Morton Grove, IL), 2007.
Bugs in My Hair?!, illustrated by Tammie Lyon, Albert Whitman (Morton Grove, IL), 2008.

Contributor to periodicals, including *Woman's Day, Woman's World, Chicago Parent, Child Life, Chicago Sun-Times, Schumburg Review, Elk Grove Times,* and *Highlights for Children.* Work anthologized in books, including *Reading and Writing Excellence, Playtime Props for Toddlers, The Family Travel Guide,* and *Children's Writer's and Illustrator's Market: 2008.*

Sidelights

Teacher and former newspaper columnist Catherine Stier features a multicultural cast of characters in her beginner's look at civics, *If I Were President.* Selected as part of the Chicago Public Schools Literacy Program in 2005, *If I Were President* introduces young children

to life in the White House, with its grand rooms, resident chef, and private bowling alley. The duties and responsibilities of the White House's most important resident are also covered, from working with Cabinet members to dealing with congress to serving as commander in chief of the U.S. military. Describing the book as presenting "a rosy picture of a very stressful job," *Booklist* critic Lauren Peterson added that *If I Were President* contains "good general information" that is conveyed in "short, simple sentences and mostly broad, nonspecific terms."

In a companion volume, *If I Ran for President,* Stier follows the path of a presidential candidate in vying for White House residency, from stumping for votes on the campaign trail to determining a political platform, choosing a running mate, and articulating answers to questions from the press as well as from political opponents. Reviewing *If I Ran for President* in *Booklist,* John Peters wrote that Stier's book will help elementary-grade students to have "a better understanding of the complex election process and, just maybe, an enduring respect for it." In *School Library Journal* Barbara Katz described Stier's volume as "a step above the usual election books," adding that Lynne Avril's "lively cartoons cheefully clarify the action and reinforce the concepts." "Honesty is a virtue" in Stier's "bright-eyed" election guidebook, as a *Kirkus Reviews* critic wryly remarked. The author presents "a campaign to yearn for, all issues and not a spin doctor in sight."

Turning to fiction, Stier creates an utterly perfect heroine in *Bugs in My Hair?!* At least, Ellie LaFleur THOUGHT she was perfect until the school nurse discovered that the girl has a case of head lice. At first shocked, Ellie eventually comes to terms with her situation, and she ultimately role-models a positive way to deal with this personal setback. Tammie Lyon's cartoon images "capture Ellie's emotions as she goes from feeling grossed out to upset, sullen, and, finally, elated to be free of the bugs," observed *School Library Journal* contributor Lisa Gangemi Kropp. In *Booklist,* Hazel Rochman concluded that in *Bugs in My Hair?!* "Stier packs in lots of useful information."

Stier has enjoyed writing since childhood. Although she found the time to contribute articles and stories to a variety of magazines and newspapers while working as a teacher, in more recent years she has been able to devote increasing time to the writer's craft, and her published books are the result. Now, "I write all the time!," she exclaimed on her home page. "In the last ten years, I have worked as a newspaper columnist and feature writer. I've taught writing classes for kids and grown-ups at a college. I even helped run a Teen Writing Club! Best of all, I still have opportunities to visit schools to talk about being an author. I am VERY happy that writing is such a BIG part of my life."

Biographical and Critical Sources

PERIODICALS

Booklist, October 1, 1999, Lauren Peterson, review of *If I Were President,* p. 360; November 1, 2007, John Peters, review of *If I Ran for President,* p. 43; July 1, 2008, Hazel Rochman, review of *Bugs in My Hair?!,* p. 74.

Daily Herald (Arlington Heights, IL), September 25, 1999, Pam Baert, "Author Has First Book Published," p. 1.

Kirkus Reviews, September 15, 2007, review of *If I Ran for President.*

School Library Journal, September, 2007, Barbara Katz, review of *If I Ran for President,* p. 187; May, 2008, Lisa Gangemi Kropp, review of *Bugs in My Hair?!,* p. 110.

ONLINE

Catherine Stier Home Page, http://catherinestier.com (February 1, 2009).

T

TAN, Shaun 1974-

Personal
Born 1974, in Western Australia, Australia. *Education:* University of Western Australia, B.A. (with honours), 1995.

Addresses
Home—Australia.

Career
Writer and illustrator. Concept artist on films, including *Horton Hears a Who* and *WALL-E*; director of a short film with Passion Pictures Australia.

Awards, Honors
L. Ron Hubbard Illustrators of the Future Contest winner, 1992; Ditmar Award for best professional artwork, 1995; Ditmar Award for best cover artwork, 1996, and 2000, for *The Coode St. Review of Science Fiction*; Crichton Award, 1998, and Spectrum Gold Award for Book Illustration, 2000, both for *The Viewer* by Gary Crew; Aurealis Coverners' Award for excellence, Children's Book Council of Australia (CBCA) Picture Book of the Year designation, and Spectrum Gold Award for Book Illustration, all 1999, all for *The Rabbits* by John Marsden; CBCA Honor Book designation, and APA Design Award, both 2000, both for *Memorial* by Crew; Best Artist Award, World Fantasy Convention, 2001; Ditmar Awards for best artwork and best professional achievement, and CBCA Picture Book of the Year designation, all 2001, all for *The Lost Thing*; Patricia Wrightson Prize, New South Wales Premier's Literary Awards, and CBCA Honour Book designation, both 2002, both for *The Red Tree*; Book of the Year designation, New South Wales Premier's Literary Awards, and World Fantasy Award for Best Artist, both 2007, and Angoulême International Comics Festival Prize for Best Comic Book, and Hugo awards for Best Professional Artist nomination and Best Related Book nomination, all 2008, all for *The Arrival*.

Writings

SELF-ILLUSTRATED

The Playground, Lothian (Port Melbourne, Victoria, Australia), 1998.

The Lost Thing, Lothian (Port Melbourne, Victoria, Australia), 2000.

The Red Tree, Lothian (South Melbourne, Victoria, Australia), 2001.

The Arrival (graphic novel), Lothian (South Melbourne, Victoria, Australia), 2006, Arthur A. Levine (New York, NY), 2007.

Picture Books: Who Are They For?, Primary English Teaching Association (Marrickville, New South Wales, Australia), 2006.

The Haunted Playground, Stone Arch (Minneapolis, MN), 2008.

Tales from Outer Suburbia, Arthur A. Levine (New York, NY), 2008.

ILLUSTRATOR

Terry Dowling, *The Man Who Lost Red,* MirrorDanse (Parramatta, New South Wales, Australia), 1994.

Greg Egan, *Our Lady of Chernobyl,* MirrorDanse (Parramatta, New South Wales, Australia), 1995.

Steven Paulsen, *The Stray Cat,* Lothian (Port Melbourne, Victoria, Australia), 1996.

James Moloney, *The Pipe,* Lothian (Port Melbourne, Victoria, Australia), 1996, published as *Trapped,* Stone Arch (Minneapolis, MN), 2008.

Garry Disher, *The Half Dead,* Lothian (Port Melbourne, Victoria, Australia), 1997.

Janine Burke, *The Doll,* Lothian (Port Melbourne, Victoria, Australia), 1997, published as *The Deadly Doll,* Stone Arch (Minneapolis, MN), 2008.

Gary Crew, *Crew's Thirteen: Classic Tales of the Macabre and Fantastic,* Australian Broadcasting Corporation (Sydney, New South Wales, Australia), 1997.

Gary Crew, *The Viewer,* Lothian (Port Melbourne, Victoria, Australia), 1997.

John Marsden, *The Rabbits,* Lothian (Port Melbourne, Victoria, Australia), 1998.

Gary Crew, *Forces of Evil,* Reed (Port Melbourne, Victoria, Australia), 1998.

Gary Crew, *Memorial,* Lothian (Port Melbourne, Victoria, Australia), 1999.

Nette Hilton, *The Hicksville Horror,* Lothian (Port Melbourne, Victoria, Australia), 1999.

Ian Bone, *The Puppet,* Lothian (Port Melbourne, Victoria, Australia), 1999, published as *The Puppet's Eye,* Stone Arch (Minneapolis, MN), 2009.

(With others) Susan V. Bosak, *Dream: A Tale of Wonder, Wisdom, and Wishes,* 2004.

Kelly Link, *Pretty Monsters: Stories,* Viking (New York, NY), 2008.

Contributor of illustrations to periodicals.

Sidelights

Award-winning Australian illustrator Shaun Tan's talents were recognized early in his career. As a teen, Tan began illustrating for science-fiction periodicals, and he was recognized by the L. Ron Hubbard Illustrators of the Future contest when he was eighteen years old. As he noted on his home page, Tan earned the title of "good drawer" early on, which he notes made up a little bit for always being the shortest student in his class.

Tan first began illustrating texts by other authors, among them John Marsden, author of *The Rabbits,* and Gary Crews, with whom he has collaborated on several books. *The Rabbits* was a breakthrough book for Tan; as he explained in *Asia Africa Intelligence Wire* this "book is significant for me because it's the first time I had full creative licence." *The Rabbits* comments on the impact European immigrants had on Australia, likening immigrants to the invasive and plague-like rabbits that overwhelmed many of the continent's native species. Karen Jameyson cited "Tan's elaborate, intricate paintings and provocative design" in her review of *The Rabbits* for *Horn Book,* and Nancy Palmer wrote in *School Library Journal* that the illustrator's "stunning ink, oil, and wash artwork . . . adds complexity and the visual experience of a culture and landscape being overrun."

In illustrating Crew's *The Viewer,* Tan depicts a different type of apocalyptic landscape, one that can be seen through the lens of a strange Viewmaster that is found by a young boy. "Tan loads his marvelous, shadowy images with post-apocalyptic clutter," wrote a contributor to *Publishers Weekly* in reviewing the book.

Tan's original self-illustrated titles include *The Playground,* and *The Lost Thing,* the latter which explores the idea of not fitting in. Nicolette Jones, writing in the London *Sunday Times,* described *The Lost Thing* as "illustrated with a bizarre and extremely skilled collage," and stated that although the narrator, who finds an odd charm on the beach and is told to discard it, might not know the moral of the tale, readers certainly will. Concluding her review of the book in *School Library Journal,* Teresa Pfeifer called Tan "a singular talent."

Tan's *The Red Tree* also delves into ideas of loneliness and not fitting in, this time depicting a young girl who suffers from childhood depression. One day, a red tree begins to sprout in the girl's room, and as it grows the girl is able to leave some of her depression behind. A *Kirkus Reviews* contributor called *The Red Tree* "an imaginative, sad, and ultimately uplifting tale of very few words and extraordinary images," while in *Resource Links* Antonia Gisler noted: "Rather than using a multitude of words to express the feelings of a little girl, Tan relies on illustrations to get the point across."

With *The Arrival,* Tan gained international attention, receiving nominations and awards from such notable organizations at the Hugo Awards and the Angoulême International Comics Festival Prize for Best Comic Book of France. The 128-page, wordless graphic novel follows the voyage of an immigrant to a strange new world. Like others, he is fleeing a bad situation at home and he hopes to find freedom and opportunity in this land full of odd creatures that adopt each newcomer as he or she becomes a resident. The main character of *The rrival* writes home, looking forward to the day when his family can join him. "By flawlessly developing nuances of human feeling and establishing the enigmatic setting, [Tan] compassionately describes an immigrant's dilemma," wrote a contributor to *Publishers Weekly.* Jennifer Sweeney, in *Kliatt,* considered the book an "exquisite tale of imaginatively mastered fantasy," and a *Kirkus Reviews* contributor called it "an unashamed paean to the immigrant's spirit, tenacity and guts, perfectly crafted for maximum effect." Jesse Karp, writing in *Booklist,* concluded that "*The Arrival* proves a beautiful, compelling piece of art, in both content and form."

Another self-illustrated book by Tan, *The Haunted Playground* features a higher proportion of text to illustration. Designed for reluctant readers, *The Haunted Playground* tells the story of Gavin, who joins in a game only to find that his strange playmates want to keep him trapped in the playground. Noting the prose, which she described as simple enough for reluctant readers without seeming "babyish," Stephanie Zvirin wrote in *Booklist* that "Tan's black-and-white sketches give the story much of its dark lure." As Bethany A. Lafferty wrote of *The Haunted Playground* in *School Library Journal,* the "suspense . . . lasts until the very end."

Tan discussed his creative process with Rick Margolis in an interview for *School Library Journal.* "When I start a book, I'm attracted to very specific imagery, and I'm usually not aware of what the story is about until I'm well into it," he explained. To develop the surreal details and creatures in books like *The Arrival,* Tan creates preliminary sketches that are "very small and very scribbly. There's something about being scribbly that creates an accidental form. . . . From that silliness and chaos, I often get really good ideas."

Biographical and Critical Sources

PERIODICALS

Asia Africa Intelligence Wire, January 3, 2004, "He Aims to Inspire Children."

Australasian Business Intelligence, May 28, 2002, "WA Writers Score in NSW Awards."

Booklist, May 1, 2003, Gillian Engberg, review of *The Red Tree,* p. 1589; September 1, 2007, Jesse Karp, review of *The Arrival,* p. 115; November 1, 2007, Stephanie Zvirin, review of *The Haunted Playground,* p. 46; December 15, 2007, Carolyn Phelan, review of *Trapped,* p. 48.

Guardian (London, England), February 2, 2008, Julia Eccleshare, review of *The Arrival,* p. 20.

Horn Book, May, 1999, Karen Jameyson, "Brush Strokes with History," p. 364; November-December, 2007, Roger Sutton, review of *The Arrival,* p. 669.

Kirkus Reviews, January 15, 2003, review of *The Red Tree,* p. 148; January 1, 2005, review of *The Lost Thing,* p. 58; September 1, 2007, review of *The Arrival.*

Kliatt, September, 2007, Jennifer Sweeney, review of *The Arrival,* p. 30.

New York Times Book Review, November 11, 2007, Gene Lang Yuen, "Stranger in a Strange Land," p. 21.

Publishers Weekly, January 27, 2003, review of *The Red Tree,* p. 259; January 5, 2004, review of *The Rabbits,* p. 61; May 3, 2004, review of *The Viewer,* p. 192; November 15, 2004, review of *Dream: A Tale of Wonder, Wisdom, and Wishes,* p. 60; July 16, 2007, review of *The Arrival,* p. 166; September 8, 2008, review of *Pretty Monsters,* p. 51.

Resource Links, April, 2003, Antonia Gisler, review of *The Red Tree,* p. 7; December, 2003, Adriane Pettit, review of *The Rabbits,* p. 5; April, 2004, Antonia Gisler, review of *The Viewer,* p. 3; October, 2004, Joanne de Groot, review of *Memorial,* p. 3; January 31, 2005, review of *The Lost Thing,* p. 68; June, 2005, Anne Hatcher, review of *The Lost Thing,* p. 9.

School Library Journal, April, 2003, Liza Graybill, review of *The Red Tree,* p. 140; March, 2004, Dona Ratterree, review of *The Viewer,* p. 204; April, 2004, Nancy Palmer, review of *The Rabbits,* p. 119; December, 2004, Ellen Fader, review of *Memorial,* p. 144; May, 2005, Teresa Pfeifer, review of *The Lost Thing,* p. 140; September, 2007, Rick Margolis, "Stranger in a Strange Land: Shaun Tan's 'The Arrival' May Be the Most Brilliant Book of the Year," p. 34, Alana Abbott, review of *The Arrival,* p. 225; February, 2008, Bethany A. Lafferty, reviews of *Trapped* and *The Haunted Playground,* p. 113.

Sunday Times (London, England), December 30, 2007, Nicolette Jones, review of *The Arrival,* p. 48.

ONLINE

Shaun Tan Home Page, http://www.shauntan.net (March 9, 2009).*

TAVARES, Matt 1975-

Personal

Born 1975, in Boston, MA; married, 2002; wife's name Sarah; children: two daughters. *Education:* Bates College, B.A., 1997.

Addresses

Home—Ogunquit, ME. *E-mail*—matt@matttavares.com.

Career

Author and illustrator. Worked part-time for Tavares Design Associates, 1997-2000.

Awards, Honors

Oppenheim Toy Portfolio Gold Seal Award, and Massachusetts Book Award Honor, both 2000, both for *Zachary's Ball;* Parents' Choice Gold awards, for *Mudball, Jack and the Beanstalk,* and *Lady Liberty;* Parents' Choice Silver Honor, for *Oliver's Game;* Arkansas Diamond Honor Book designation, for *Mudball.*

Writings

SELF-ILLUSTRATED

Zachary's Ball, Candlewick Press (Cambridge, MA), 2000.
Oliver's Game, Candlewick Press (Cambridge, MA), 2004.
Mudball, Candlewick Press (Cambridge, MA), 2005.
Henry Aaron's Dream, Candlewick Press (Cambridge, MA), 2010.

ILLUSTRATOR

Clement Clarke Moore, *'Twas the Night before Christmas; or, Account of a Visit from St. Nicholas,* Candlewick Press (Cambridge, MA), 2002.
E. Nesbit, reteller, *Jack and the Beanstalk,* Candlewick Press (Cambridge, MA), 2006.
Stephen Mitchell, reteller, *Iron Hans: A Grimm's Fairy Tale,* Candlewick Press (Cambridge, MA), 2007.
Doreen Rappaport, *Lady Liberty: A Biography,* Candlewick Press (Cambridge, MA), 2008.
Kristin Kladstrup, *The Gingerbread Pirates,* Candlewick Press (Cambridge, MA), 2009.
E. Nesbit, reteller, *Sleeping Beauty in the Wood,* Candlewick Press (Cambridge, MA), 2010.

Contributor of illustrations to books, including *This Place I Know: Poems of Comfort* by Georgia Heard, Candlewick Press (Cambridge, MA), 2002.

Sidelights

When Matt Tavares was studying art at Bates College, he had no intention of becoming a children's book writer and illustrator. Then, during his junior year, a friend showed him several books by author/illustrator Chris Van Allsburg and Tavares was hooked. "I was so amazed, I started spending time in bookstores and libraries, looking at all kinds of children's books," he recalled on the *Candlewick Press Web site*. "And I decided to make my own." Tavares began his new career right away, with his college thesis, and created a story that embodies every young baseball fan's wildest dream. Originally titled *Sebastian's Ball,* the book was published two years after its original creation as *Zachary's Ball.*

In Tavares's tale, a boy and his father are at a game at Boston's historic Fenway Park. When the father catches a baseball, he gives it to his son. The ball is magical; it transports the boy to the pitcher's mound where he throws a strike against the batter, winning the game for the Red Sox. His father explains that all baseballs are magical, and the boy keeps the ball with him, continuing to dream of baseball heroics. As he grows older, the ball is lost, however. An adult, he catches an over-the-wall fly ball and, remembering the magic of his own lost baseball, he gives this new ball to a little girl walking by the ball park.

Setting *Zachary's Ball* at Fenway Park was only natural for Tavares, who had been raised a Boston Red Sox fan and whose admitted fantasy is "catching a foul ball at a Red Sox game." "I've never been anywhere that feels more magical than Fenway Park," the author/illustrator added.

Many reviewers wrote that Tavares captures the magic of America's favorite pastime in his book; according to Tim Arnold, writing in *Booklist, Zachary's Ball* "is at once a tribute to the spell of baseball and to parks like Fenway and Wrigley Field." A *Publishers Weekly* critic wrote that "the timeless quality of Tavares's black-and-white pencil illustrations is in perfect pitch with the story's setting and theme."

Tavares has used the game of baseball as a theme for his other self-illustrated titles as well. *Oliver's Game* is set near Wrigley Field in Chicago. Oliver enjoys working at his grandfather's baseball memorabilia store, located right across the street from the historic ball park. Exploring the store's dusty corners one day, the boy discovers an old Cubs uniform; when he questions his grandfather about it, he learns that the older man, also named Oliver, once had a chance to play for the Chi-

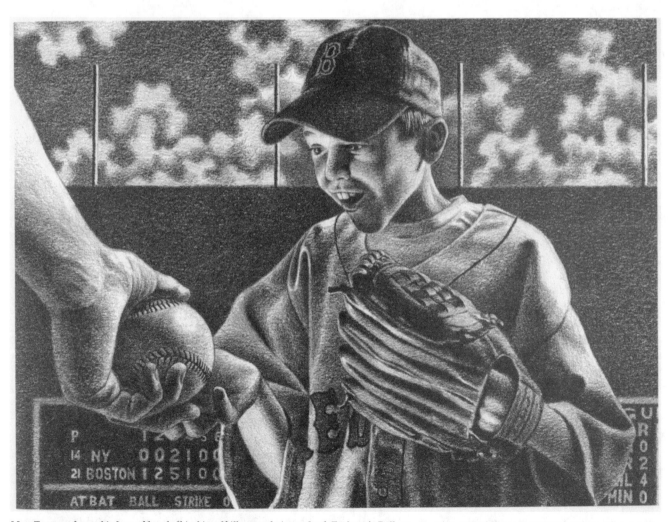

Matt Tavares shares his love of baseball in his self-illustrated picture book **Zachary's Ball.** (Candlewick Press, 2000. Copyright © 2000 Matt Tavares. Reproduced by permission of the publisher Candlewick Press, Inc., Somerville, MA.)

cago major league team. The elder Oliver tells the story of how, when he was eighteen years old, the manager of the Cubs saw him hit a home run while playing stickball with some friends on the streets outside of Wrigley Field. Impressed with the young man' skills, the manager invited him to practice with the Cubs, and later asked him to try out for the team. However, the United States entered World War II at that point, and instead of trying out for the Cubs the older Oliver joined the U.S. Marines.

A *Kirkus Reviews* critic called *Oliver's Game* "an intimate, poignant episode for fans who revel in the game's less tangible aspects," while in *Publishers Weekly* a contributor wrote that "Tavares suffuses his text, his art, and both of his characters with a tangible love of baseball." Marilyn Taniguchi, reviewing *Oliver's Game* for *School Library Journal,* noted that "the text masterfully weaves together tradition, perseverance, loyalty, and family lore, and the result will enchant baseball fans young and old."

Mudball is based on a baseball legend about the shortest grand-slam homerun in the history of the game. In 1903, Little Andy Oyler was the shortest player on his team, the Minneapolis Millers, and probably in the whole league. In Tavares's story, Andy has been going through a dry spell, wrestling with a problem hitting the ball. When it is his turn at bat, with bases loaded and the Millers three runs behind with only one strike left, the pressure is on and the situation seems pretty hopeless. Then it starts to rain, making things go from bad to worse. However, Andy manages to make a hit. In the heavy downpour the opposing team cannot figure out where the ball went, allowing Andy and his surprised teammates the chance to run the bases and win the game.

A critic for *Publishers Weekly* proclaimed *Mudball* "another triumphant trip to the baseball field," while in *Kirkus Reviews* a writer praised the "humorous details and delightfully expressive faces" Tavares includes in his illustrations. Martha V. Parravano, writing for *Horn Book,* predicted that *Mudball* "should make a big splash with underdogs and baseball fans alike."

In his work as an illustrator, Tavares has brought to life several fairy tales and tall tales. Turning to the work of British children's author E. Nesbit, he revisioned Nesbit's 1908 version of *Jack and the Beanstalk,* producing a "witty, elegant retelling" that is enhanced by "realistic pencil-and-watercolor paintings" that have "a vintage look suitable to the old tale," according to *School Library Journal* critic Marie Orlando. Collaborating with author Stephen Mitchell, Tavares also reintroduces children to the Grimm Brothers' story *Iron Hans: A Grimm's Fairy Tale,* about a giant who helps a young prince learn about life and gain his fortune. Using pencil and water color in shades of gold and brown, Tavares creates "especially arresting" images that have an "enchanted" quality, according to *Booklist* contributor Jennifer Mattson. A *Kirkus Revews* writer also praised the

Tavares turns his artistic eye to the holiday season in his illustrated version of Clement C. Moore's classic 'Twas the Night before Christmas. (Candlewick Press, 2002. Illustrations copyright © 2002 Matt Tavares. Reproduced by permission of the publisher Candlewick Press, Inc., Somerville, MA.)

work, asserting that the illustrator's "tidy, literal, clean-lined" images imbue Mitchell's text with a "welcome grounding in reality."

Turning to the marvels of the more-recent past, Tavares' work for Doreen Rappaport's *Lady Liberty: A Biography* "convey[s] a vivid sense of the ingenuity, politics, and hardships involved in making the statue" that now stands in New York Harbor," according to *Horn Book* critic Michael Santangelo. Initially envisioned by Edouard de Laboulaye and designed by French sculptor Auguste Bartholdi, the Statue of Liberty was funded by newspaper giant Joseph Pulitzer and inspired artists, writers, and everyday Americans alike. In 1886 it was unveiled in New York, where it has served as a symbol of freedom to generations of immigrants ever since. "Large in scale and monumental in effect," Tavares's line and watercolor pictures "offer often beautiful views of [Lady Liberty's] . . . many-faceted story," noted *Booklist* critic Carolyn Phelan. In *Publishers Weekly* a reviewer cited the book's "realistic" images, which capture the "sweeping, angled perspective of the [monument's] construction." A *New York Times Book Review* contributor wrote that "Tavares creates images with a pageantlike grandeur" and imbues the images of the Lady's construction with a "muralistic monumentality," while *School Library Journal* critic Barbara Auerbach dubbed *Lady Liberty* "a beautiful, attractive volume."

Tavares has also illustrated Clement C. Moore's perennially popular holiday poem *'Twas the Night before*

***Tavares brings a monument to life in his work for Doreen Rappaport's picture book* Statue of Liberty.** (Candlewick Press. Text copyright © Doreen Rappaport. Illustrations copyright © 2008 by Matt Tavares. All rights reserved. Reproduced by permission of the publisher Candlewick Press, Inc., Somerville, MA.)

Christmas; or, Account of a Visit from St. Nicholas, using Moore's original 1823 text. In this version of the now-familiar poem, two of the reindeer were named Dunder and Blixem, instead of Donder and Blitzen. In his introduction, Tavares explains that because he uses the original text of the poem, he also uses details from that era in his illustrations; to prepare for this, he spent time studying the architecture of old houses in Boston's historical district and the nineteenth-century room interiors reproduced at Boston's Museum of Fine Arts. Susan Dove Lempke complimented Tavares's "low-key, very traditional treatment" of the poem in her review for *Booklist,* while a critic for *Kirkus Reviews* wrote that "the moody illustrations suggest the drama and excitement of the magical night in an unusual way."

Biographical and Critical Sources

PERIODICALS

Booklist, April 15, 2000, Tim Arnold, review of *Zachary's Ball,* p. 1546; September 1, 2004, Susan Dove

Lempke, review of *'Twas the Night before Christmas; or, Account of a Visit from St. Nicholas,* p. 141; June 1, 2004, GraceAnne A. DeCandido, review of *Oliver's Game,* p. 1729; September 15, 2006, Hazel Rochman, review of *Jack and the Beanstalk,* p. 64; December 15, 2007, Jennifer Mattson, review of *Iron Hans: A Grimm's Fairy Tale,* p. 48; April 15, 2008, Carolyn Phelan, review of *Lady Liberty: A Biography,* p. 46.

Horn Book, March-April, 2005, Martha V. Parravano, review of *Mudball,* p. 195; July-August, 2008, Michael Santangelo, review of *Lady Liberty,* p. 471.

Kirkus Reviews, November 1, 2002, review of *'Twas the Night before Christmas,* p. 1614; February 15, 2004, review of *Oliver's Game,* p. 186; March 15, 2005, review of *Mudball,* p. 359; October 1, 2006, review of *Jack and the Beanstalk,* p. 1021; August 1, 2007, review of *Iron Hans.*

New York Times Book Review, September 14, 2008, review of *Lady Liberty,* p. 16.

Publishers Weekly, March 27, 2000, review of *Zachary's Ball,* p. 80; February 23, 2004, review of *Oliver's Game,* p. 76; February 7, 2005, review of *Mudball,* p. 60; September 17, 2007, review of *Iron Hans,* p. 54; May 5, 2008, review of *Lady Liberty,* p. 62.

School Library Journal, August, 2000, Anne Parker, review of *Zachary's Ball,* p. 165; July, 2004, Marilyn Taniguchi, review of *Oliver's Game,* p. 89; November, 2006, Marie Orlando, review of *Jack and the Beanstalk,* p. 122; November, 2007, Barbara Scotto, review of *Iron Hans,* p. 110; May, 2008, Barbara Auerbach, review of *Lady Liberty,* p. 148.

ONLINE

Candlewick Press Web site, http://www.candlewick.com/ (February 2, 2009), "Matt Tavares."
Matt Tavares Home Page, http://www.matt-tavares.com (February 2, 2009).
Walker Books Web site, http://www.walkerbooks.co.uk/ (April 22, 2005), "Matt Tavares."

*   *   *

TERRILL, Beth
(Elizabeth Terrill)

Personal
Female.

Addresses
Home—Brooklyn, NY.

Career
Author and editor of children's books. Random House, New York, NY, children's book editor.

Writings

Fly away to Dragon Land, illustrated by Robbin Cuddy, Random House (New York, NY), 2000.
What Does Ernie Hear?, illustrated by David Prebenna, Random House/Children's Television Workshop (New York, NY), 2000.
(Under name Elizabeth Terrill) *Simba's Jungle Hunt* (lift-the-flap book), Disney/Random House (New York, NY), 2001.
(Under name Elizabeth Terrill) *Get Those Puppies* (lift-the-flap book), illustrated by Mike Peterlein, Random House (New York, NY), 2002.
The Counting Carnival, illustrated by Joe Ewers, Random House (New York, NY), 2003.
(Coauthor under name Elizabeth Terrill) Rev. W. Awdry, *Thomas & Friends: Go, Train, Go!,* illustrated by Tommy Stubbs, Random House (New York, NY), 2005.
The Barnyard Night before Christmas, illustrated by Greg Newbold, Random House (New York, NY), 2007.

Biographical and Critical Sources

PERIODICALS

Publishers Weekly, October 22, 2007, review of *The Barnyard Night before Christmas,* p. 52.

TERRILL, Elizabeth
See TERRILL, Beth

*   *   *

THOMPSON, Colin 1942-
(Amy Lissiat)

Personal
Born October 18, 1942, in London, England; married twice (divorced twice); married 1999; third wife's name Anne (a librarian); children: (first marriage) Charlotte; (second marriage) Hannah, Alice. *Education:* Attended art school (London, England).

Addresses
Home—Bellingen, New South Wales, Australia. *E-mail*—colin@colinthompson.com.

Career
Author and illustrator of children's books, 1990—. Worked as a silkscreen printer, graphic designer, stage manager, documentary filmmaker for British Broadcasting Corporation, ceramicist, and creator of Gelaskins for iPod.

Awards, Honors
Primary English Best Picture Book Award, 1994, for *Ruby;* Picture Book of the Year Award, English Association, for *Falling Angels;* Honor Book citation, Australian Children's Book Council, 2004, for *The Violin Man;* Aurealis Award, 2004, for *How to Live Forever;* Astrid Lindgren Memorial Award nomination (Sweden), 2005; Hampshire Picture Book of the Year Award, 2005, for *Castles;* Picture Book of the Year designation, Children's Book Council of Australia, 2006, for *The Short and Incredibly Happy Life of Riley,* 2008, for *Dust.*

Writings

SELF-ILLUSTRATED PICTURE BOOKS

Ethel the Chicken, Hodder & Stoughton (London, England), 1990.
A Giant Called Norman Mary, Hodder & Stoughton (London, England), 1991.
The Paperbag Prince, Julia MacRae (London, England), 1992, published as *The Paper Bag Prince,* Knopf (New York, NY), 1992.
Pictures of Home, Julia MacRae (London, England), 1992, Green Tiger Press (New York, NY), 1993.
Looking for Atlantis, Julia MacRae (London, England), 1993, Knopf (New York, NY), 1994.
Sid the Mosquito and Other Wild Stories, Knight (London, England), 1993.

Colin Thompson (Photograph by Roger Beresford-Jones. Reproduced by permission of Colin Thompson.)

Ruby, Knopf (New York, NY), 1994.

Attila the Bluebottle and More Wild Stories, Hodder & Stoughton (London, England), 1995.

How to Live Forever (also see below), Julia MacRae (London, England), 1995, Knopf (New York, NY), 1996.

Venus the Caterpillar and Further Wild Stories, Hodder & Stoughton (London, England), 1996.

The Haunted Suitcase and Other Stories, Hodder & Stoughton (London, England), 1996.

The Tower to the Sun, Julia MacRae (London, England), 1996, Knopf (New York, NY), 1997.

Castle Twilight and Other Stories, Hodder & Stoughton (London, England), 1997.

The Paradise Garden, Knopf (New York, NY), 1998.

The Last Alchemist, Hutchinson (London, England), 1999.

Falling Angels, Hutchinson (London, England), 2001.

The Violin Man, Hodder Headline (Sydney, New South Wales, Australia), 2003.

Castles, Hutchinson (London, England), 2006.

The Big Little Book of Happy Sadness, Kane/Miller (La Jolla, CA), 2008.

Sometimes Love Is under Your Foot, Scholastic Australia (Lisarow, New South Wales, Australia), 2008.

Free to a Good Home, Random House Australia (Sydney, New South Wales, Australia), 2009.

PICTURE BOOKS; AND ILLUSTRATOR, UNDER PSEUDONYM AMY LISSIAT

The Short and Incredibly Happy Life of Riley, Lothian Books (South Melbourne, Victoria, Australia), 2005, Kane/Miller (La Jolla, CA), 2007.

Norman and Brenda, Lothian Books (South Melbourne, Victoria, Australia), 2006.

PICTURE BOOKS

Sailing Home, illustrated by Matt Ottley, Hodder Headline (London, England), 1996.

The Last Circus, illustrated by Kim Gamble, Hodder Headline (London, England), 1997.

The Staircase Cat, illustrated by Anna Pignataro, Hodder Headline (Sydney, New South Wales, Australia), 1998.

The Puzzle Duck, illustrated by Emma Quay, Random House (Milsons Point, New South Wales, Australia), 1999.

Unknown, illustrated by Anna Pignataro, Walker (New York, NY), 2000.

The Last Clown, illustrated by Penelope Gamble, Hodder Headline (Sydney, New South Wales, Australia), 2001.

No Place like Home, illustrated by Anna Pignataro, Hodder Headline (Sydney, New South Wales, Australia), 2001.

One Big Happy Family, illustrated by Karen Carter, Hodder Headline (Sydney, New South Wales, Australia), 2002.

Round and Round and Round and Round, illustrated by Penelope Gamble, Hodder Headline (Sydney, New South Wales, Australia), 2002.

Gilbert, illustrated by Chris Mould, Lothian Books (South Melbourne, Victoria, Australia), 2003.

The Great Montefiasco, illustrated by Ben Redlich, Lothian Books (South Melbourne, Victoria, Australia), 2004, Star Bright Books (New York, NY), 2005.

Gilbert Goes Outside, illustrated by Chris Mould, Lothian Books (South Melbourne, Victoria, Australia), 2005.

Dust, illustrated by various artists, ABC Books (Sydney, New South Wales, Australia), 2007.

POETRY; FOR CHILDREN

The Dog's Been Sick in the Honda, illustrated by Peter Viska, Hodder Headline (Sydney, New South Wales, Australia), 1999, revised as *Fish Are So Stupid,* illustrated by Chris Mould, Hodder & Stoughton (London, England), 2000.

My Brother Drinks out of the Toilet, illustrated by Peter Viska, Hodder Headline (Sydney, New South Wales, Australia), 2000.

There's Something Really Nasty on the Bottom of My Shoe, illustrated by Peter Viska, Hodder Headline (Sydney, New South Wales, Australia), 2003.

NOVELS; FOR CHILDREN AND YOUNG ADULTS

Future Eden, Walker (London, England), 1999, published as *Future Eden: A Brief History of Next Time,* Simon & Schuster Books for Young Readers (New York, NY), 2000.

Pepper Dreams, Hodder Headline (Sydney, New South Wales, Australia), 2003.

How to Live Forever (novel; based on Thompson's picture book of the same title), Random House (Milsons Point, New South Wales, Australia), 2004.

Space the Final Effrontery (sequel to *Future Eden*), Lothian (South Melbourne, Victoria, Australia), 2005.

"FLOODS" SERIES; SELF-ILLUSTRATED

Neighbours, Random House (Milsons Point, New South Wales, Australia), 2005, published as *Good Neighbors,* HarperCollins (New York, NY), 2008.

Playschool, Random House (Milsons Point, New South Wales, Australia), 2006, published with illustrations by Crab Scrambly as *School Plot,* HarperCollins (New York, NY), 2008.

Home and Away, Random House (Milsons Point, New South Wales, Australia), 2006, published with illustrations by Crab Scrambly as *Witch Friend,* HarperCollins (New York, NY), 2008.

Survivor Random House (Milsons Point, New South Wales, Australia), 2007.

Prime Suspect Random House (Milsons Point, New South Wales, Australia), 2007.

The Floods Family Files, Random House (Milsons Point, New South Wales, Australia), 2007.

The Great Outdoors,, Random House (Milsons Point, New South Wales, Australia), 2008.

Top Gear, Random House (Milsons Point, New South Wales, Australia), 2008.

Better Homes and Gardens, Random House (Milsons Point, New South Wales, Australia), 2009.

OTHER

Laughing for Beginners (adult novel), Sceptre (Sydney, New South Wales, Australia), 2002.

Sidelights

Regarded as a gifted author and illustrator, Colin Thompson is lauded as a particularly imaginative artist as well as a committed supporter of the environment. He is recognized for providing young readers with demanding, yet satisfying, books that are considered both thought-provoking and entertaining. As an illustrator, Thompson creates colorful, intricate pictures filled with both realistic and surrealistic images as well as visual jokes and intertextual references; his work has been compared to such artists as Graeme Base and M.C. Escher. "People sometimes ask me what age group I write for and I have to say, I don't really think about it," Thompson noted on his home page. "I think I write and illustrate for a certain type of person not a certain age."

Thompson did not begin publishing his detailed and inventive picture books and fantasies until he was nearly fifty years old. Born in London, England in 1942, his early schooling in both Yorkshire and West London led to two years of art instruction in his hometown of Ealing and in Hammersmith. Employed for a period of time as a silkscreen painter and graphic designer, Thompson later studied film and worked for the British

Broadcasting Corporation (BBC) creating television documentaries. In the late 1960s he moved to Scotland's Outer Hebrides islands and in 1975 to Cumbria. During this time, he began crafting ceramics while living in a remote farmhouse; he also spent a good deal of free time planting trees due to his concern for the environment, as well as raising his family and caring for his numerous adopted pets. "As my kids got older and left home, I thought I'd like to get into drawing again," Thompson remarked to *Scan* interviewer Ian McLean. "I was always drawing; I have memories of doing really fine detailed drawings, even as a little child. I came to writing quite late (1990), but I now consider myself to be a writer/illustrator, rather than an illustrator."

Thompson's first children's book, the easy-reader *Ethel the Chicken,* appeared in 1990. Heroine Ethel, who lives in a box labeled First Class Oranges, has been all but forgotten since the death of the old woman who used to feed her. A rat named Neville happens upon Ethel's home in the vacant house and the two become friends until Neville and his family move away. Briefly overcome with loneliness, Thompson's talking chicken finds happiness and companionship once again when a human family moves into the old woman's house. Written with care and childlike simplicity, *Ethel the Chicken* is designed to teach young children how to read, to appeal to their sense of humor, and to address their particular anxieties about friendship, love, and loneliness. *Growing Point* reviewer Margery Fisher lauded the work, noting that "When words and illustrations consort

Colin Thompson's elementary-grade novel **The Great Montefiasco** *features Ben Redlich's whimsical art.* (Illustration copyright © 2004 by Ben Redlich. All rights reserved. Reproduced by permission of Thomas C. Lothian Pty., Ltd. In the U.S. by Star Bright Books.)

perfectly together, expressing both the warmth of humor and the tinge of wit, the result is a masterpiece and I think *Ethel the Chicken* is a masterpiece."

Thompson's second picture book, *The Paper Bag Prince,* is set in a town dump and expresses a pro-environmental message. The book's protagonist, an old man whose name has long since been forgotten, is known as the "Paper Bag Prince." He lives on the site, inhabiting a derelict railroad car and surviving off the town's refuse and junk. The arrival of Sarah from the city council and her announcement that the dump is to be shut down proves a welcome harbinger to the Paper Bag Prince: once the land on which the dump is located was his, and with the landfill closed nature can now begin to reclaim the soil so long abused by humans. A reviewer for *Kirkus Reviews* enthused, "In Thompson's lovely, intricate art . . . signs of life and renewal creep in everywhere. . . . More than just another ecological fantasy, this dump is a compelling symbol of the earth itself; it's to be hoped that, like the old man, humanity will be here to welcome nature back if the pollution ever abates." Writing in *School Library Journal,* Lori A. Janick commented that *The Paper Bag Prince* "effectively portrays the tenacity of nature as well as the resilience of the human spirit," while *Books for Keeps* critic Trevor Dickinson called the book one "which deserves to be widely popular through and beyond the school years."

Pictures of Home represents something of a departure for Thompson. The work consists of numerous detailed illustrations of houses along with several short, poetic texts composed by British schoolchildren. The texts describe each child's individual interpretation of home; for example, "Home is my parents./ You should have love in all homes./ Love is my parents." Although critics generally approved of Thompson's almost surreal paintings, many found *Pictures of Home* lacking a clear-cut connection between text and illustration. A *Kirkus Reviews* contributor found more to like, describing *Pictures of Home* as a "fascinating book, to pore over and share."

In *Looking for Atlantis* a man recalls his childhood and the return of his grandfather from an ocean voyage. Upon his arrival, the old man tells his grandson about a sea chest that contains the secret of a path to Atlantis. The rest of the story is a celebration of the joys of observation, accompanied by Thompson's detailed and engrossing drawings. Reviewing *Looking for Atlantis* in *School Library Journal,* Barbara Peklo Abrahams wrote that Thompson's "watercolor masterpieces . . . contain myriad images that are striking, mysterious, dreamlike, witty, and eternal, and the simple, spare prose holds transcendental truth." *Booklist* critic Mary Harris Veeder concluded that fans of *Where's Waldo?* will enjoy the book's illustrations due to their "combination of fine, realistic detailing and fantastical images"

In his award-winning picture-book mystery *Ruby* Thompson spins two interconnected tales involving an

automobile: a red 1934 Austin Seven called Ruby. One tale evokes Ruby's travels around the world to exotic locations such as China's Great Wall and England's Stonehenge, while the other presents a tiny family lured from the safety of their tree-home by the arrival of the shiny red car. The miniature family members find themselves trapped in the vehicle, while their son Kevin is doubly so, having locked himself inside a briefcase. As Kevin's family attempts to find the combination to the case in order to free the boy, Thompson invites his readers to do the same, informing them that Ruby's license plate number and the combination are one and the same. Only by actively exploring the book's illustrations can the mystery be solved. A *Publishers Weekly* critic commented that, "Once again Thompson breaks barriers of narrative space and time with an ornately crafted, multilevel picture book," while a *Kirkus Reviews* contributor called *Ruby* "two wonderful picture books in one."

Thompson once again displays his cleverness and artistic virtuosity in *How to Live Forever.* The story's hero, Peter, finds himself in a vast library of a thousand rooms that is purported to contain every book ever written. Peter learns that one book, alluringly titled *How to Live Forever,* is missing. Eventually he happens upon the Ancient Child, a creature suspended in time, apparently because he has read the elusive book, and Peter wisely decides to give up his search. A *Junior Bookshelf* commentator praised the control exhibited in "Thompson's brief sentences and still more precise and exquisite drawings." While a *Publishers Weekly* critic warned that "many of the visual puns are too sophisticated for younger readers but will delight adults," the reviewer added that *How to Live Forever* "excites [reader] interest on several levels."

Set in the not-too-distant future, *The Tower of the Sun* presents a planet cloaked in a yellow fog of pollutants which permanently obscure the sun. Thompson's novel opens as the world's wealthiest man promises his grandson that he will one day show the boy a blue sky and a shining sun. The man institutes an ambitious plan to construct a magnificent tower to achieve his goal, incorporating into his edifice such famous structures as the Guggenheim museum, the Taj Mahal, the Chrysler Building, and the Leaning Tower of Pisa. A *Publishers Weekly* critic mused that, "with its rich visual tapestry, a subtle message about what constitutes real wealth and an upbeat ending," Thompson's novel is "a crowd-pleaser," while a *Reading Time* contributor called *Tower of the Sun* an "extraordinary fantasy" that "challenges readers' moral insights and at the same time leaves those readers aesthetically satisfied."

In 1995 Thompson traveled from England to Sydney, Australia, to do a school visit, "and fell so much in love with the place that two weeks later I came back to live here," he wrote on his home page. Four years later, the divorced writer/illustrator married the librarian who first invited him to come to the school. Since moving to

Australia he has collaborated with Australian artists on works such as *Sailing Home,* a story illustrated by Matt Otley about a family who awakes one day and realizes that their house is no longer on firm land but instead is floating along in the middle of the sea.

Unknown, Thompson's collaboration with Aussie illustrator Anna Pignataro, teaches children an important lesson about pet ownership. The book takes its title from a shy little dog that has been abandoned at a local pound. All the animals in the shelter are named for the reasons why they wound up there: "Grown-Too-Large," "Owner-Died," "Unwanted-Christmas-Gift," and little "Unknown." None of the families who come to the pound looking for a pet take notice of the shy Unknown, hiding in the back of his cage, but the little dog proves his bravery when a fire threatens the shelter and its inhabitants. *Unknown* was deemed "a sure bet for any prospective young dog owner to stimulate discussion about owning a pet for life" by Holly Belli in her review for *School Library Journal.*

Thompson's other collaborative picture books include *The Staircase Cat,* about a cat who waits patiently in his long-time home after his caretaker disappears during a war; *The Puzzle Duck,* about an imaginative duck who makes up crazy stories and gives ill-thought-out advice; *Gilbert,* about a very skittish cat; and *The Great Montefiasco,* about the most incompetent magician on earth.

Thompson has continued to produce self-illustrated books since his move to Australia, including *The Paradise Garden,* in which, according to a *Publishers Weekly* reviewer, "his intricate, fantastical illustrations lure readers to a parallel universe where nothing is quite as it seems." In the book, the parallel universe is located in a small garden in the middle of a large, dirty, noisy city that is home to a boy named Peter. Peter runs away from his chaotic home to live in the garden and enjoy the fresh air and peace and quiet for a summer. Although he must eventually return home, he takes with him a newfound sense of peace along with a few seeds from the garden plants. Thompson's illustrations of Peter's refuge show glimpses of tiny fairy houses in the shrubbery and bamboo, along with many more of his trademark page-filling details.

The Last Alchemist is another solo effort by Thompson. A king who is determined to find an alchemist who can create gold is now on his nineteenth alchemist, Spiniflex. Spiniflex is highly motivated by the king's promises of treasure if he succeeds (and by a considerably worse fate if he fails), but he still cannot seem to find the correct formula. In the end the alchemist succeeds in turning the kingdom to gold, but not quite in the manner the king had hoped. Critics particularly praised Thompson's illustrations for *The Last Alchemist,* wherein "each page is a treasure chest bursting with color, minute detail, wit, and surprise," according to Shelle Rosenfeld in *Booklist.* A *Publishers Weekly*

contributor also pointed out "a running sight gag in Thompson's [more recent] oeuvre—the ubiquitous "Café Max," with its red-checked curtains, tucked in like a cheeky footnote."

Ethel the chicken, the warm-hearted subject of Thompson's first book, returns in a very different story in *Future Eden: A Brief History of Next Time.* This "wickedly barbed low fantasy," as *School Library Journal* contributor John Peters termed it, began life as a serial that ran on Thompson's home page. The story is set in 2287, when human beings are nearly extinct. One of the few remaining humans, Jay, has been camping out in a penthouse with the thickly feathered Ethel, but he gets bored and decides to go out and explore the world. Ethel is more than she seems, however: she is in fact a higher life form, originally from the planet Megatron. Since she created humans—and every other living thing on Earth—she feels responsible for all the pain, war, and suffering Earth's creatures have felt throughout history. Ethel the alien's quest to discover why Earth's humans were all happy for one brief hour in October of 2042 provides the plot of the story. Her companions on this quest include Jay, whom she declares the Chosen One; the Delphic Oracle reincarnated as a goldfish; and the wizard Merlin from the King Arthur legends.

In Thompson's fantasy tale *Falling Angels,* a young girl who possesses the gift of flight travels around the globe to retrieve such treasures as an African orchid and a Patagonian shell for her ailing grandmother. "The metaphor of imagination is tethered to Thompson's intricately detailed, dreamy illustrations," observed a contributor in *Kirkus Reviews.* A lonely boy adopts a needy animal in *The Big Little Book of Happy Sadness,* another self-illustrated tale. After the death of his parents, George goes to live with his kindly grandmother. On one of his weekly visits to the shelter, the youngster spots a three-legged dog that captures his heart. With his grandmother's help, George constructs an artificial leg for his new pet, named Jeremy, and provides him with a bright future. A critic in *Kirkus Reviews* again praised Thompson's artwork, stating that "the combination of facial expressions and interesting perspectives perfectly captures the mood."

For his award-winning self-illustrated title, *The Short and Incredibly Happy Life of Riley,* Thompson created a fictitious helper: artist Amy Lissiat (the name is an anagram for "it's my alias"). Lissiat claims to be a model, muse, and international imagination consultant who was born in France in 1920 and journeyed to Australia in a hot air balloon during the 1950s. Thompson's story focuses on a contented rat named Riley who finds most humans to be dissatisfied with their wasteful, materialistic lives. Lissiat's "witty art" was cited by a *Kirkus Reviews* contributor, who also remarked that Thompson's message-laden narrative "just might stir some readers to check their priorities."

Thompson also serves as author and illustrator of a creepily humorous series of books about the Floods, a

In **Good Neighbors** *Thompson's quirky story is paired with equally quirky art by Crab Scrambly.* (Illustration copyright © 2008 by Crab Scrambly. All rights reserved. Used by permission of HarperCollins Children's Books, a division of HarperCollins Publishers.)

family of wizards and witches. The books, including *School Plot* and *Prime Suspect,* describe the misadventures of Nerlin and Mordonna Flood and their seven children, some of whom were created through the use of magical spells, saucepans, and a chemistry set. In the series debut, *Neighbours* (published in the United States as *Good Neighbors*), the Floods must deal with the despicable Dents, an obnoxious family of hooligans that lives next door. One by one, the Dents meet their demise at the hands of the Floods, in the most imaginative of ways. "Middle-graders will enjoy the over-the-top humor, gore, and magic," Suzanne Harold observed in *Booklist.*

A prolific author, Thompson continues to produce his own picture books and to develop collaborative stories. In each of his works, however, his overall philosophy remains constant. "I have always believed in the magic of childhood and think that if you get your life right that magic should never end," he stated on his home page. "I feel that if a children's book cannot be enjoyed properly by adults there is something wrong with either

the book or the adult reading it. This of course, is just a smart way of saying I don't want to grow up."

Biographical and Critical Sources

BOOKS

Thompson, Colin, *Unknown,* illustrated by Anna Pignataro, Walker (New York, NY), 2000.

PERIODICALS

Booklist, December 1, 1992, Hazel Rochman, review of *The Paper Bag Prince,* p. 678; April 1, 1994, Mary Harris Veeder, review of *Looking for Atlantis,* p. 1441; July, 1999, Shelle Rosenfeld, review of *The Last Alchemist,* p. 1974; May 1, 2000, John Peters, review of *Unknown,* p. 1680; May 15, 2008, Suzanne Harold, review of *Good Neighbors,* p. 58.
Books for Keeps, May, 1992, Trevor Dickinson, review of *The Paperbag Prince,* p. 28.
Growing Point, July, 1991, Margery Fisher, review of *Ethel the Chicken,* pp. 5537-5538.
Junior Bookshelf, April, 1996, review of *How to Live Forever,* p. 63.
Kirkus Reviews, July 15, 1992, review of *The Paper Bag Prince,* p. 926; April 1, 1993, review of *Pictures of Home,* p. 465; November 11, 1994, review of *Ruby,* p. 1544; September 1, 2001, review of *Falling Angels,* p. 1302; December 15, 2004, review of *The Great Montefiasco,* p. 1209; August 1, 2007, review of *The Short and Incredibly Happy Life of Riley;* December 15, 2007, review of *Good Neighbors;* August 15, 2008, review of *The Big Little Book of Happy Sadness.*
New York Times Book Review, October 23, 1994, review of *Looking for Atlantis,* p. 30.
Publishers Weekly, August 31, 1992, review of *The Paper Bag Prince,* p. 79; April 19, 1993, review of *Pictures of Home,* p. 59; April 4, 1994, review of *Looking for Atlantis,* p. 77; October 24, 1994, review of *Ruby,* p. 60; May 13, 1996, review of *How to Live Forever,* p. 74; March 10, 1997, review of *The Tower to the Sun,* p. 65; March 16, 1998, review of *The Paradise Garden,* p. 64; June 14, 1999, review of *The Last Alchemist,* p. 70; December 17, 2001, review of *Falling Angels,* p. 94; January 14, 2008, review of *Good Neighbors,* p. 57.
Reading Time, February, 1997, review of *The Tower to the Sun,* p. 15.
Scan, May, 1999, Ian McLean, interview with Thompson, pp. 6-8.
School Librarian, February, 1997, reviews of *The Haunted Suitcase* and *The Tower to the Sun,* p. 34.
School Library Journal, February, 1993, Lori A. Janick, review of *The Paper Bag Prince,* p. 80; July, 1993, JoAnn Rees, review of *Pictures of Home,* p. 82; May, 1994, Barbara Peklo Abrahams, review of *Looking for Atlantis,* p. 118; December, 1994, Steven Engelfried, review of *Ruby,* p. 87; July, 1996, Heide Piehler, review of *How to Live Forever,* p. 74; May, 1998, Heide

Piehler, review of *The Paradise Garden,* p. 127; July, 2000, Holly Belli, review of *Unknown,* p. 88; November, 2000, John Peters, review of *Future Eden: A Brief History of Next Time,* p. 162.
Wilson Library Bulletin, November, 1992, Frances Bradburn, review of *The Paper Bag Prince,* p. 75.

ONLINE

Colin Thompson Home Page, http://www.colinthompson.com (March 1, 2009).
Random House Web site, http://www.randomhouse.com.au/ (March 1, 2009), "Colin Thompson."

* * *

TOLEDO, Francisco 1940-

Personal

Born July 17, 1940, in San Vicente, Oaxaca, Mexico; partner of Eliza Ramirez Castaneda (a poet and sociologist); partner of Ana Ekatherina (a textile artist); children: (with Ramirez Castaneda) Natalia, Jeronimo (Dr Lakra), Laureana; (with Ekatherina) Sara, Benjamin. *Education:* Attended Escuela de Bella Artes (Mexico City, Mexico), 1957, and Taller de Grafica Popular; attended Escuela de Diseno y Artesanias, beginning 1958.

Addresses

Home—Oaxaca, Mexico. *Office*—IAGO, Macedonia Alcala 507, Centro Oaxaca, Oaxaca City, Oaxaca 68000, Mexico. *E-mail*—froggallery@franciscotoledo.net.

Career

Painter, graphic artist, sculptor, and philanthropist. Graphic Arts Institute, Oaxaca, Mexico, cofounder; Casa de Cultura de Juchitaan, founder; Museo de Arte Contemporaneo de Oaxaca, cofounder, 1992; Editiones Toledo (publisher), cofounder, c. 1980s. *El Alcaravan* (art review), editor. Social activist and preservation advocate. *Exhibitions:* Work exhibited internationally, including in Galería Juan Martin, Mexico City, Mexico, 1967; Galería Arvil, Mexico City, 1970; (retrospective) Museo de Arte Moderno, Mexico City; (retrospective) Mexican Fine Arts Center, Chicago, IL, 1988; and Associated American Artists, New York, NY, 1998; Whitechapel Art Gallery, London, England, 2001; Centro de Arte Reina Sofia, Madrid, Spain; and Galería Quetzalli, Oaxaca City, Mexico.

Awards, Honors

Right Livelihood Award, 2005; numerous other awards for artwork.

Writings

FOR CHILDREN

Natalia Toledo, *Light Foot = Pies ligeros,* translated from Zapotec by Elisa Amado, Groundwood Books (Toronto, Ontario, Canada), 2007.

OTHER

Eliza Ramirez Castaneda, *Palabras,* 1971.
Wallace Stevens, *Trece maneras de mirar un mirlo,* 1981.
Veróonica Volkow, *El inicio,* 1983.
Manual de zoología a fantástica: Homenaje a Jorge Luis Borges, Secretaría de Educación Pública (Mexico City, Mexico), 1984, abridged versions, Prisma Editorial (Mexico City, Mexico), 1999, artwork published as *Zoología a fantástica: Tintas y acuarelas = Fantastic Zoology: Ink and Watercolor,* 2005.
Lo que el viento a Juárez, Ediciones Era (Mexico City, Mexico), 1986.
Alberto Blanco, *Canto a la sombra de los animales,* Galería a López Quiroga (Mexico), 1988.
José Emilio Pacheo, *Album de zoología = An Ark for the Next Millennium* (poetry), University of Texas Press (Austin, TX), 1993.
Obra Gráfica para Arvil, 1974-2001, text by Luis Carolos Emerich, Prisma Editorial (Mexico City, Mexico), 2001.

Contributor to periodicals, including *XX Siécle.*

Sidelights

Hailed as one of Mexico's most accomplished contemporary artists, Francisco Toledo creates gouache paintings that revision his Zapotec heritage through a surrealistic prism. In addition to his work as a painter, textile artist, and sculptor, Toledo is also a community activist; he dedicates much of his time and money to preserving and promoting the arts and crafts of the indigenous Zapotec people in his native Oaxaca. In addition, Toledo has supported the arts by working to establish a photography center, an art museum, and a library for the blind in Oaxaca, and he has received several Mexican and international honors and awards for his preservation efforts.

While growing up, Toledo was entertained by the Zapotec and Huave folktales told to him by family members. In his late teens he channeled his talent for art into a profession as a print maker, and then expanded to other mediums despite the lack of a formal education. According to *Americas* writer Caleb Bach, "creatures wild and domestic predominate" in Toledo's oeuvre. The artist "dares to rival the Divine Creator himself by reinventing animals or at least redefining our sense of what they can be and do. In Toledo's wild kingdom, disparate species consort in unimaginable ways, call all the shots, and even mock humankind for its self-centeredness, inhibitions, and ignorance of irrevocable rules of nature. . . . He is not a storyteller who narrates in a literal fashion regional myths and legends but rather a maker of Promethean proportions."

Toledo has published several collections of his artwork, pairing his graphic images with poetry or other text by noted Spanish-language writers. In 2004 he also joined oldest daughter Natalia Toledo in creating the picture book *Light Foot = Pies ligeros.* Originally written in

Francisco Toledo is well known in his native Mexico for his folk-art-inspired sculpture. ("Mask 3/4 View," by Francisco Toledo. Photograph by Art Resource. NY.)

Toledo teams with his daughter, Natalia Toledo to create the picture book **Light Foot = Pies ligeros.** (Groundwood Books/Libros Tigrillo/House of Anansi Press, 2006. Illustration copyright © 2007 by Francisco Toledo. All rights reserved. Reproduced by permission.)

the Toledos' native Zapotec, *Light Foot = Pies ligeros* captures many themes characteristic of Mexico in its story about how Death attempts to control all the creatures of the world by challenging them to a contest. Calling Natalia Toledo's text "a clever little folktale, with well-crafted rhymes," *Resource Links* critic Michelle Gowans added that Toledo's gouache illustrations are "rich and possess a strange beauty," although their darkness might frighten smaller children. In *School Library Journal* Tim Wadhams agreed with the "frightening" quality of the images and recommended *Light Foot = Pies ligeros* as an "appropriate" addition to "collections of Mexican fine art."

Biographical and Critical Sources

BOOKS

Manrique, Jorge Alberto, and Verónica Volkow, *Francisco Toledo,* Smurfit Cartón y Papel de México (Los Morales, Mexico), 2002.

PERIODICALS

Américas, December, 1998, Caleb Bach, "Francisco Toledo: Art of Magical Mutations," p. 22.

Art in America, February, 2001, Christian Viveros-Faune, "Toledo's Metamorphoses," p. 130.

Geographical, January, 2004, James Blackman, interview with Toledo.

Resource Links, December, 2007, Michelle Gowans, review of *Light Foot = Pies ligeros,* p. 13.

School Library Journal, March, 2008, Tim Wadham, review of *Light Foot = Pies ligeros,* p. 192.

Social Justice, summer, 2006, Edward J. McCaughan, "Notes on Mexican Art, Social Movements, and Anzaldua's 'Conocimiento,'" pp. 153-154.

ONLINE

Francisco Toledo Home Page, http://www.franciscotoledo.net (February 2, 2009).*

V-W

VAUPEL, Robin

Personal
Married. *Hobbies and other interests:* Cooking, walking in the woods, reading.

Addresses
Home—CA.

Career
Young-adult author. Has worked as a public-school English teacher for twenty years.

Writings

My Contract with Henry, Holiday House (New York, NY), 2003.
Rules of the Universe by Austin W. Hale, Holiday House (New York, NY), 2007.

Sidelights
After working as an English teacher for over twenty years, young-adult author Robin Vaupel turned her hand to writing books, publishing her first novel in 2003. *My Contract with Henry* relates the story of an eighth-grade-girl named Beth Gardner and follows Beth's experiences with a group project on Henry David Thoreau. After reading about Thoreau's experiences at Walden Pond, Beth and the other members of her group decide to try to live as the famous American philosopher once did, constructing a small cabin deep in the Michigan woods. Even after the school assignment ends, the four continue to meet, foraging in the woods for food, observing the natural beauty around them, and reflecting on their own existence as well as their relationships with others. When a developer looks to build on the land, however, Beth fights to preserve the hideaway, forcing herself to overcome her natural shyness and stand up for the serenity of Wayburn Woods.

For her first effort, Vaupel was commended for her ability to capture the thoughts and feelings of preteen students. According to *Booklist* critic Carolyn Phelan, "Vaupel creates a painfully accurate portrayal of middle-school social dynamics." While finding the book's ending a bit too neat, a *Publishers Weekly* critic nonetheless called Vaupel's voice "crisp and often lyrical." A *Kirkus Reviews* contributor wrote that the author offers "an excellent introduction to Thoreau" in *My Contract with Henry,* and in *School Library Journal* Susan Cooley concluded her review of the novel by dubbing Vaupel's debut "a credible story that most students will enjoy."

Another student interested in learning outside of the classroom appears in Vaupel's second young-adult novel, *Rules of the Universe by Austin W. Hale.* Facing the loss of his beloved grandfather to cancer, thirteen-year-old Austin distracts himself with a gift he received from the ailing relative, an award-winning scientist. Experimenting with his grandfather's gift throughout the summer, Austin discovers that the object can alter living things, making them gain or lose years. Grandfather's mysterious gift can even transform the structure of organisms, giving legs to water creatures. After returning his moody adolescent sister to her more-cheerful preteen years, the budding scientist changes his elderly dog into a puppy and his cabin mates at summer camp into old men. However, Austin's ultimate desire is to restore his grandfather's health, a goal the dying man warns him against pursuing.

Many reviewers noted that *Rules of the Universe by Austin W. Hale* is much more than a book about a boy's comical science experiments. For readers able to look past the obviously unbelievable events, Vaupel's novel

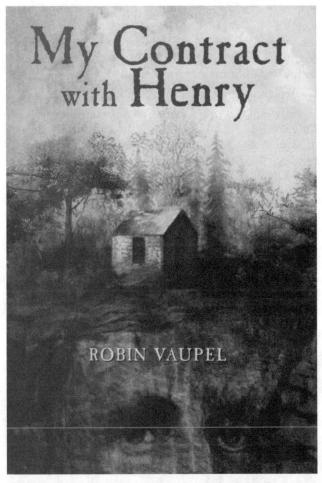

Cover of Robin Vaupel's My Contract with Henry, *featuring artwork by Guy Spalenka.* (Holiday House, Inc., 2003. Jacket art copyright © 2003 by Greg Spalenka. Reproduced by permission of the illustrator.)

"smartly addresses the ethics of altering something's molecular structure," as well as "the meaning of death and friendship," observed *Booklist* reviewer Suzanne Harold. Writing in the *Bulletin of the Center for Children's Books,* April Spisak commended Vaupel's "blend of scientific research and magic," finding them "effectively balanced against the stark realism of a boy facing his first significant losses" in life.

Vaupel told *SATA:* "I've had a fascination for Henry David Thoreau since I was fifteen, when, like Beth Gardner, I studied an excerpt from *Walden* in a textbook. Many years later, as an eighth-grade teacher, I noticed that selections from Thoreau's writings were rarely included in classroom anthologies. I worried that my students would graduate from high school never having heard of Henry Thoreau, let alone knowing what an interesting and original person he was. I wrote *My Contract with Henry* not only to introduce young people to Thoreau, but also to indulge my own desire to live in a tiny cabin in the forest. Naturally, I also hoped that meeting America's first and most passionate environmentalist would inspire readers to try their own experiments in essential living. I was thrilled when I found an

agent and later a publisher who liked Henry as much as I did. My proudest moment was being invited to Walden Pond to sign books, not far from where Henry's famous cabin stood.

"I encourage young writers in my classroom to keep journals and often wish that I had been a more disciplined and steady journal-keeper. Maintaining a work journal helped me grow tremendously as a writer, providing a place to experiment and play with ideas, safely away from the actual text which can be intimidating. Both my protagonists record their thoughts as their stories unfold. Beth Gardner gains insight through her journal in *My Contract with Henry* and even allows it to be published in the school newspaper, while Austin Hale in *Rules of the Universe* uses his lab notes to analyze the mysteries of science and magic."

Biographical and Critical Sources

PERIODICALS

Booklist, July, 2003, Carolyn Phelan, review of *My Contract with Henry,* p. 1892; November 1, 2007, Suzanne Harold, review of *Rules of the Universe by Austin W. Hale,* p. 47.
Bulletin of the Center for Children's Books, January, 2008, April Spisak, review of *Rules of the Universe by Austin W. Hale.*
Kirkus Reviews, June 1, 2003, review of *My Contract with Henry,* p. 812; September 15, 2007, review of *Rules of the Universe by Austin W. Hale.*
Publishers Weekly, June 30, 2003, review of *My Contract with Henry,* p. 80.
School Library Journal, July, 2003, Susan Cooley, review of *My Contract with Henry,* p. 135.

ONLINE

Robin Vaupel Home Page, http://robinvaupel.com (January 31, 2009).

*   *   *

WALDREP, Richard

Personal

Male. *Education:* University of Georgia, B.F.A.

Addresses

Home—Glencoe, MD.

Career

Illustrator and artist. Eucalyptus Tree Studio, Baltimore, MD, partner for fifteen years; designer of dozens of stamps for U.S. Postal Service, beginning 1993.

Awards, Honors

Carter G. Woodson Book Award Honor Book designation, 2008, for *Surfer of the Century* by Ellie Crowe.

Illustrator

Claire Rudolf Murphy, *Gold Rush Winter*, Golden Books (New York, NY), 2002.

Ellie Crowe, *Surfer of the Century: The Life of Duke Kahanamoku*, Lee & Low Books (New York, NY), 2007.

Contributor of illustrations to periodicals, including *Men's Health, U.S. News & World Report*, and *Washington Post.*

Sidelights

With a degree in art, Richard Waldrep cofounded the Eucalyptus Tree Studio in Baltimore, Maryland, where he established a successful career as a commercial artist whose advertising and illustration clients included publishers and other businesses. Beginning in 1993, Wal-

drep has also created paintings for the U.S. postal service, and his work has appeared on dozens of stamps in the years since. With the publication of Claire Rudolf Murphy's *Gold Rush Winter* in 2002, Waldrep also added book illustration to his artistic credits.

In Waldrep's second book-illustration project, the award-winning *Surfer of the Century: The Life of Duke Kahanamoku*, he brings to life Ellie Crowe's biography of one of the most famous surfers of the twentieth century. With his record-breaking performance at the 1917 Olympic games, during which time he rode a wave for almost two miles, the twenty-seven-year-old Kahanamoku introduced the sport of surfing to athletes around the world while also breaking racial and cultural barriers. Calling *Surfer of the Century* a "strikingly illustrated picture-book biography," *Booklist* critic Gillian Engberg cited Waldrep's "dramatic colored-pencil-and-gouache artwork" depicting the acclaimed surfer, while a *Kirkus Reviews* critic noted the book's "stunning Art Deco-style airbrush illustrations." "Waldrep's paintings

Richard Waldrep's energetic art for Ellie Crowe's Surfer of the Century ***shows the dedication required to forge an Olympic athlete.*** (Illustration copyright © 2007 by Richard Waldrep. All rights reserved. Reproduced by permission of Lee & Low Books, Inc.)

convey both dignity and dynamism," wrote J.D. Ho in a *Horn Book* review, the critic adding that *Surfer of the Century* features "ocean scenes hurtling from pages awash in sunlight."

Biographical and Critical Sources

PERIODICALS

Booklist, September 1, 2007, Gillian Engberg, review of *Surfer of the Century: The Life of Duke Kahanamoku,* p. 134.
Horn Book, November-December, 2007, J.D. Ho, review of *Surfer of the Century,* p. 695.
Kirkus Reviews, October 1, 2007, review of *Surfer of the Century.**

*   *   *

WINN-LEDERER, Ilene

Personal

Born in Chicago, IL. *Education:* Attended museum school of Art Institute of Chicago and Chicago Academy of Fine Arts.

Addresses

Home and office—Pittsburgh, PA. *Agent*—Heflinreps, Inc., 10 Linden Terrace, Leonia, NJ 07605. *E-mail*—ilene@winnlederer.com.

Career

Artist, illustrator, and educator. Has taught illustration and design at Ivy School of Professional Art and Carnegie-Mellon University. *Exhibitions:* Work included in public and private collections throughout the United States, Europe, and Israel.

Member

Graphic Artists Guild, Pittsburgh Society of Illustrators.

Writings

SELF-ILLUSTRATED

(With Paul Fleischman) *The Binnacle Boy: Investigating Mysteries,* Scholastic (New York, NY), 1992.
Between Heaven and Earth: An Illustrated Torah Commentary, Pomegranate Communications (Petaluma, CA), 2009.
The Alchymical Zoodiac: A Celestial Bestiary, Imaginarius Editions (Pittsburgh, PA), 2009.

ILLUSTRATOR

Dina Rosenfeld, *A Little Boy Named Avram,* Hachai Publishing (Brooklyn, NY), 1989.
Dina Rosenfeld, *Kind Little Rivka,* Hachai Publishing (Brooklyn, NY), 1991.
Kathleen Thompson, *Sometimes I Am a Kite,* Green Tiger Press (New York, NY), 1992.
Dina Rosenfeld, *Dovid the Little Shepherd,* Hachai Publishing (Brooklyn, NY), 1996.
Rabbi Nina Beth Cardin, *The Tapestry of Jewish Time,* Behrman House (Springfield, NJ), 2000.
Dina Rosenfeld, *A Little Girl Named Miriam,* Hachai Publishing (Brooklyn, NY), 2001.
Ellen Kushner, *The Golden Dreydl,* Charlesbridge (Watertown, MA), 2007.

Contributor to books, including *Starting Your Career as a Freelance Illustrator or Graphic Designer,* by Michael Fleishman, Allworth Press (New York, NY), 2001; *Exploring Illustration: An In-depth Guide to the Art and Techniques of Contemporary Illustration,* by Fleishman, Thomson/DelMar Learning Publications, 2004; and *How to Grow as an Illustrator,* by Fleishman, Allworth Press, 2007. Contributor to periodicals, including *New York Times, Wall Street Journal, Progressive, Cricket,* and *Hadassah.*

Biographical and Critical Sources

PERIODICALS

Booklist, August, 2007, Hazel Rochman, review of *The Golden Dreydl,* p. 73.
Pittsburgh Magazine, May, 1989, Harry Schwalb, "Art Review," p. 25.
Publishers Weekly, October 29, 2007, review of *The Golden Dreydl,* p. 59.

ONLINE

Artworks Web site, http://www.theartworksinc.com/ (March 1, 2009), "Ilene Winn-Lederer."
HeflinReps Web site, http://www.heflinreps.com/ (March 1, 2009), "Ilene Winn-Lederer."
Ilene Winn-Lederer Home Page, http://www.winnlederer. com (March 1, 2009).

*   *   *

WOOD, Audrey

Personal

Born in Little Rock, AR; daughter of Cook Edwin (an artist) and Maegerine (an artist and furniture historian) Brewer; married Don Wood (an author and illustrator), November 21, 1969; children: Bruce Robert. *Education:* Attended Arkansas Art Center.

Audrey Wood (Reproduced by permission of Heacock Literary Agency, Inc.)

Addresses

Home—Santa Barbara, CA.

Career

Author and illustrator of children's books, 1978—. The Blue Moon (book and import shop), Eureka Springs and Fayetteville, AR, co-owner and operator, 1970-75.

Member

Society of Children's Book Writers and Illustrators.

Awards, Honors

Children's Choice citation, International Reading Association/Children's Book Council (CBC), Young Reader Medal, California Reading Association, and PEN Los Angeles Center Younger Children Literary Award, all 1985, and American Library Association (ALA) Notable Book citation, and *Booklist* Best Books of the 1980s citation, both 1990, all for *The Napping House;* Child Study Association of America's Children's Books of the Year citation, *School Library Journal* Best Books of the Year citation, and Parents' Choice Award, Parents' Choice Foundation, all 1985, Colorado Children's Book Award, 1987, Washington State Book Award, 1989, and ALA Notable Book citation, all for *King Bid-*

good's in the Bathtub; American Booksellers Association Pick of the Lists citation, 1988, for *Elbert's Bad Word;* Christopher Award, Irma Simonton Black Award for Excellence in Children's Literature, Bank Street College of Education, and Notable Children's Trade Book in the Field of Social Studies designation, National Council for the Social Studies/CBC, all 1988, Virginia Children's Book Award, and Nevada Children's Book Award, both 1989, and Young Hoosier Book Award, 1992, all for *Heckedy Peg;* Best Children's Books of the Year citations, *School Library Journal* and *Boston Globe,* and *Booklist* Editor's Choice citation, all 1991, and ALA Notable Book citation, all for *Piggies.*

Writings

FOR CHILDREN

Moonflute, illustrated by husband, Don Wood, Green Tiger Press (La Jolla, CA), 1980, revised edition, Harcourt (San Diego, CA), 1986.

Tickleoctopus, illustrated by Bill Morrison, Houghton (Boston, MA), 1980, new edition with illustrations by Don Wood, Harcourt (San Diego, CA), 1994.

Quick as a Cricket, illustrated by Don Wood, Child's Play (Swindon, Wiltshire, England), 1982, Child's Play International (New York, NY), 1990.

(With Don Wood) *The Little Mouse, the Red Ripe Strawberry, and the Big Hungry Bear,* illustrated by Don Wood, Child's Play (Swindon, Wiltshire, England), 1984, Child's Play International (New York, NY), 1990.

The Napping House, illustrated by Don Wood, Harcourt (San Diego, CA), 1984, issued with CD, 2004

King Bidgood's in the Bathtub, illustrated by Don Wood, Harcourt (San Diego, CA), 1985, issued with CD, 2005.

The Three Sisters, illustrated by Rosekrans Hoffman, Dial Books for Young Readers (New York, NY), 1986.

Heckedy Peg, illustrated by Don Wood, Harcourt (San Diego, CA), 1987.

The Horrible Holidays, illustrated by Rosekrans Hoffman, Dial Books for Young Readers (New York, NY), 1988.

(With Don Wood) *Piggies,* illustrated by Don Wood, Harcourt (San Diego, CA), 1991, issued with CD, 2006.

The Napping House Wakes Up, illustrated by Don Wood, Harcourt (San Diego, CA), 1994.

(Reteller) *The Rainbow Bridge: Inspired by a Chumash Tale,* paintings by Robert Florczak, Harcourt (San Diego, CA), 1995.

The Flying Dragon Room, illustrated by Mark Teague, Blue Sky Press (New York, NY), 1996.

Bright and Early Thursday Evening: A Tangled Tale, illustrated by Don Wood, Harcourt (San Diego, CA), 1996.

The Bunyans, illustrated by David Shannon, Scholastic (New York, NY), 1996.

Birdsong, illustrated by Robert Florczak, Harcourt (San Diego, CA), 1997.

The Christmas Adventure of Space Elf Sam, illustrated by Bruce Wood, Blue Sky Press (New York, NY), 1998.

Sweet Dream Pie, illustrated by Mark Teague, Blue Sky Press (New York, NY), 1998.

A Cowboy Christmas: The Miracle at Lone Pine Ridge, illustrated by Robert Florczak, Simon & Schuster (New York, NY), 2000.

Jubal's Wish, illustrated by Don Wood, Blue Sky Press (New York, NY), 2000.

A Book for Honey Bear: Reading Keeps the Sighs Away, Little Simon (New York, NY), 2001.

An Alphabet Adventure, illustrated by Bruce Wood, Scholastic (New York, NY), 2001.

When the Root Children Wake Up, illustrated by Ned Bittinger, Scholastic (New York, NY), 2002.

(With Don Wood) *Merry Christmas, Big Hungry Bear!,* Scholastic (New York, NY), 2002.

Alphabet Mystery, illustrated by Bruce Wood, Scholastic (New York, NY), 2003.

Piggy Pie Po, Harcourt (San Diego, CA), 2003.

Ten Little Fish, illustrated by Bruce Wood, Blue Sky Press (New York, NY), 2004.

The Deep Blue Sea: A Book of Colors, illustrated by Bruce Wood, Blue Sky Press (New York, NY), 2005.

Alphabet Rescue, Scholastic (New York, NY), 2006.

FOR CHILDREN; SELF-ILLUSTRATED

Magic Shoelaces, Child's Play (Swindon, Wiltshire, England), 1980, Child's Play (Auburn, ME), 2005.

Twenty-four Robbers, Child's Play (Swindon, Wiltshire, England), 1980, Child's Play (Auburn, ME), 2005.

Scaredy-Cats, Child's Play (Swindon, Wiltshire, England), 1980, Child's Play (Auburn, ME), 2005.

Orlando's Little-While Friends, Child's Play (Swindon, Wiltshire, England), 1980.

The Princess and the Dragon, Child's Play (Swindon, Wiltshire, England), 1981, Child's Play International (Auburn, ME), 2002.

Balloonia, Child's Play (Swindon, Wiltshire, England), 1981, Child's Play (Auburn, ME), 2005.

Tugford Wanted to Be Bad, Harcourt (San Diego, CA), 1983.

Presto Change-o, Child's Play (Swindon, Wiltshire, England), 1984, Child's Play (Auburn, ME), 2005.

Tooth Fairy, Child's Play (Swindon, Wiltshire, England), 1985.

Detective Valentine, Harper (New York, NY), 1987.

(With Don Wood) *Elbert's Bad Word,* Harcourt (San Diego, CA), 1988.

Little Penguin's Tale, Harcourt (San Diego, CA), 1989, published as *The Little Penguin,* illustrated by Stephanie Boey, Dutton (New York, NY), 2002.

Oh My Baby Bear!, Harcourt (San Diego, CA), 1990.

Weird Parents, Dial Books for Young Readers (New York, NY), 1990.

Silly Sally, Harcourt (San Diego, CA), 1992, reprinted, 2007.

Rude Giants, Harcourt (San Diego, CA), 1993.

The Red Racer, Simon & Schuster (New York, NY), 1996.

A Dog Needs a Bone!, Blue Sky Press (New York, NY), 2007.

Contributor to periodicals, including *Horn Book.*

Author's works have been translated into Spanish.

Adaptations

The Napping House was adapted as a filmstrip with cassette, Weston Woods, 1985, as an audiocassette, Harcourt, 1990, and as a book and cassette packaged as *Into the Napping House,* Harcourt (San Diego, CA), 1990; *King Bidgood's in the Bathtub* was adapted as a filmstrip, Random House/Miller-Brody (New York, NY), 1986, and as an audiocassette, Harcourt, 1991; *Moonflute, The Napping House, King Bidgood's in the Bathtub, Heckedy Peg,* and *Elbert's Bad Word* were adapted for audiocassette, Caedmon (New York, NY), 1987; *Elbert's Bad Word* and *Weird Parents* were adapted as animated short films, Think Entertainment/ Universal Studios, 1992.

Sidelights

A prolific author of children's picture books, Audrey Wood combines her interests in art and storytelling in her work. Inspired by such ordinary events such as bathing or napping, Wood's stories have a whimsical air. In addition to writing and illustrating books such as *The Princess and the Dragon, Silly Sally, The Red Racer,* and *A Dog Needs a Bone,* she has also incorporated artwork by her husband, Don Wood, in books such as *Heckedy Peg, The Napping House,* and *King Bidgood's in the Bathtub,* as well as her son, Bruce Wood, in *Alphabet Adventure* and *Alphabet Mystery.*

Born into a family of artists, Wood spent time as a toddler watching her father, then a young art student, repaint murals at the Ringling Brothers Circus in Florida. Wood also remembered painting with her father, who guided her and allowed her to use his art supplies. Her grandfather was an artist as well; as she recalled in an interview published in *SATA,* "I spent a lot of time in my grandfather's studio as a child. . . . I used to love to watch the paintings emerge. Classical music filled the air along with the wonderful scents of paint, turpentine, linseed and a host of other oils. Like a chemist, or a wizard, he mixed his pigments from powders and oils."

Wood plotted her career path early, and by the first grade she had decided to become an artist. She also took lessons in dance, drama, and art; with her sisters, she created and produced plays, using "a little stage and an old set of footlights. We designed and made our costumes and built the set using a lot of our father's paints and materials. A small admission would gain entrance to anyone in the neighborhood," Wood told *SATA.* Later the author became involved in an art and drama institute in Little Rock, Arkansas, that was partially founded by her father and grandfather.

In the late 1960s, Wood moved to Berkeley, California, with the intention of pursuing a career in art. "I was experimenting with my art and teaching children's art part time," she recalled. "My work consisted mostly of narrative paintings and large sculptures. I was also writing stories." In California she met Don Wood, also an artist, whom she married in 1969. The couple traveled for several months in Guatemala and Mexico, particularly the Yucatan peninsula, and brought home sculptures and pottery made by Indian artists. This trip inspired the Woods to open a shop in Eureka Springs, Arkansas, where they sold arts, crafts, and books. After the couple's son was born, however, Wood decided to make a career change. "My childhood ambition to write and illustrate children's books had come back to me in full force . . . ," she recalled. "I spent many hours reading to our son, Bruce, and becoming a part of his child world."

In 1980, after a move to Santa Barbara, California, Wood wrote and illustrated several books, including *Scaredy Cats,* which was based on an episode from her son's childhood. That same year she produced *Moonflute,* the first collaborative endeavor with her husband. The book tells the tale of a young girl named Firen who is unable to sleep and is convinced that the moon is to blame. Restless, she goes outside, where a moonbeam turns into a magic flute as it touches her hand, leading her on a magical journey.

Another joint project was also inspired by the Woods' young son. *The Napping House* describes how a household—including a child, cat, dog, and mouse—gravitates toward Granny at nap time and falls asleep on top of her. Their restful slumber is interrupted, however, when a flea bites the mouse, causing a chaotic chain reaction. The recipient of several awards, *The Napping House* was praised for lyrical text, gentle wit, and skillful teaming of words and illustrations; *Bulletin of the Center for Children's Books* contributor Zena Sutherland remarked that the story's "silliness" contains "just the right kind of humor for the lap audience."

King Bidgood's in the Bathtub is another highly acclaimed work created by Audrey and Don Wood. In it a mischievous king refuses to leave his bathtub despite protests from his court. As each person attempts to persuade King Bidgood to come out, he persuades them to join him in the warm water instead. Finally a young page discovers the solution: he pulls the bathtub's drain plug. Considered lighthearted and humorous by reviewers, *King Bidgood's in the Bathtub* received several awards. *New York Times Book Review* contributor Arthur Yorinks declared that in the book the Woods "express an exuberance that is quite infectious," while in a *Booklist* review, Ilene Cooper predicted that the story's "panache and wit . . . will please children and their parents."

Inspired by a game that has lasted for centuries, *Heckedy Peg* tells the tale of a mother's efforts to rescue her children from the evil witch of the title. By identifying which of her seven children have been transformed into different objects, the poor mother is able to gain their freedom. Describing it as a "nicely bare-boned tale," Patricia MacLachlan observed in the *New York Times Book Review* that Wood's original story has "a feel of a familiar tale told at the fire to young and old alike." While *Horn Book* critic Ethel L. Heins thought the story contained "artificiality and clichés," a *Publishers Weekly* critic termed it full of "playfulness and eeriness" with a "poetic license that effects a looseness in structure." As Betsy Hearne noted in the *Bulletin of the Center for Children's Books.* "there's nothing more gripping than a kidnapping-rescue drama," and the book's "rhythmic vitality [is] characteristic of the Woods' best work."

The Woods team up again on *Piggies,* in which the "inventive collaborators," as a *Publishers Weekly* reviewer called the husband-and-wife team, convert a pair of child's "hands into a unique combination of concept and fantasy." Each of the fingers on the hands becomes a little piggy, each of a different shape and state of cleanliness, until bedtime when all the fingers run away and hide. Jane Saliers, writing in *School Library Journal,* found this picture book to be "an imaginative play on the fingers-and-toes game."

Bright and Early Thursday Evening: A Tangled Tale is another collaborative effort, this one resulting in "the stuff of dreams and fantastical visions," according to a contributor for *Publishers Weekly.* Told in rhyme, the story takes a surreal twist from the beginning when a woman awakens and finds herself dead, then gets

Audrey Wood captures a classic circle of desperation in her self-illustrated picture book A Dog Needs a Bone!

dressed up for her funeral, except that it turns out to be her wedding. "Then things get really bizarre," quipped a critic for *Kirkus Reviews.* Husband Don Wood took his first foray into digital illustration with this title, filling his images with "zany humor," according to the *Kirkus Reviews* critic. John Sigwald, writing in *School Library Journal,* felt that Wood "created a 'Jabberwocky'-like poem," with an "ostentatious surrealism" that is "intrinsically appealing." However, Sigwald also noted that the work's "undeniable dark side may disturb some children." A reviewer for *Publishers Weekly* concluded that the text and illustrations present a "potent combination of technology and creativity."

Less dark is *Jubal's Wish,* a Wood and Wood collaboration in which a bullfrog learns about the power of friendship. Jubal the Bullfrog finds the day so lovely that he wants to go on a picnic with his friends. But Gerdy Toad is busy with her bunch of baby toads, while Dalbert Lizard, an old sea captain, is just not in the mood. Jubal goes alone, but on his way he encounters a wizard who will grant a wish for Jubal. The toad wishes that his friends could be happy. Coming back from his picnic, it seems nothing has changed for his friends, but outside dark storm clouds are gathering and a flood manages to wash Jubal out to sea. When he is saved by Dalbert and Gerdy, they all agree to sail off to a new adventure, making Jubal's friends very happy indeed. Carol Ann Wilson, reviewing the title in *School Library Journal,* called it "wish fulfillment at its most basic" and further noted that Wood's tale "moves along briskly with a simple story line and predictable dialogue." *Booklist* critic Michael Cart also had praise for the book, calling *Jubal's Wish* a "sweet-spirited story of the magical power of friendship."

Because a book's worth of her husband's elaborate, detailed illustrations can often take one or two years to complete, Wood has also teamed up with other illustrators and additionally has written and illustrated a number of picture books independently. Working with her son, she has produced picture books such as *The Christmas Adventures of Space Elf Sam, The Deep Blue Sea: A Book of Colors,* and *Ten Little Fish,* the last a counting story that will "encourage preschoolers to gleefully chant along" with Wood's rhyming text, according to *Booklist* critic Gillian Engberg. *The Christmas Adventures of Space Elf Sam* finds Sam on a mission to deliver presents to the children on Alpha One, a space colony. But when he crashes on Gom, he ends up giving its green inhabitants a lesson about Christmas. Accompanied by computer-generated images, the book was welcomed by reviewers as fine holiday fare. A critic for *Kirkus Reviews* commented that "the energy of the text is duplicated (and sometimes bested) by the illustrations," while Cart found that "Sam is a stalwart hero." A reviewer for *School Library Journal* also remarked that "children will no doubt be attracted to this glitzy package."

Another collaboration between mother and son, *Alphabet Adventure,* is a concept book that a *Publishers* *Weekly* critic dubbed an "unorthodox ABC." Capital T and her twenty-six charges (the lower case letters of the alphabet) have worked hard all summer long and now, just as school is approaching, fear they might be late for class when the lower-case i misplaces her dot. Things seem bleak until Capital I puts things right in the "cleverly conceived and dramatically executed story," according to Linda M. Kenton, writing in *School Library Journal.* Kenton further commented that kids learning their alphabet "will be fascinated by this book." A sequel, *Alphabet Mystery,* focuses on lower-case x, which goes missing during nightly roll call.

Working with illustrator Mark Teague, Wood has also spun tales of magical rooms and dreams. In *The Flying Dragon Room,* young Patrick gets some magical tools to play with while the very special handyman, Mrs. Jenkins, is painting the house. The results are quite amazing, for Patrick takes his startled parents and Mrs. Jenkins on a tour to show them all his special places, which include a garden full of creatures, a room with a bubble machine, and even a room full of every tasty treat imaginable. Carolyn Noah noted in a *School Library Journal* review that Mrs. Jenkins is a "wonderfully wacky Jill-of-all-trades" in this "inventive and refreshing" as well as "nontraditional adventure." Patrick's imaginative creation is "every child's dream come true," according to *Booklist* critic Susan Dove Lempke.

Sweet Dream Pie, which also features Teague's illustrations, is "a suspenseful sugar-shocker about a rare and dangerous dessert," according to a contributor for *Publishers Weekly.* The dessert in this case is Ma Brindle's magic pie, a delicacy that induces sweet dreams. However, if too much of the pie is eaten bad dreams are induced, and no one who eats the pie can resist eating too much. Fortunately, Ma Brindle does not eat her own creation and thus is awake to sweep all the bad dreams away. "This is a funny and clever story," declared *Booklist* critic Elizabeth Drennan. Pat Matthews, writing in *Bulletin of the Center for Children's Books,* had similar praise, concluding that "steam from the gargantuan dessert seems to waft off the page, and the notion of such a baking phenomena creating such hilarious results should prove a mouthwatering temptation."

Wood has partnered with illustrator Robert Florczak on a number of books. *The Rainbow Bridge: Inspired by a Chumash Tale* is based on a legend of the Chumash Indians, a pourquoi tale that is an "impressive production," according to Carolyn Phelan in *Booklist. Birdsong* represents birds of many states, while *A Cowboy Christmas: The Miracle at Lone Pine Ridge* tells the story of a boy who, searching for a father, gets his wish one Christmas. Collaborating with Ned Bittinger, Wood retells an old German tale in *When the Root Children Wake Up.* Featuring the changing seasons, the book depicts Uncle Fall, Aunt Spring, and Cousin Summer as they parade through the months in their finery and then retire for a long winter's sleep. John Peters, writing in

Booklist, deemed the picture book "an engaging way of looking at the seasons," while a contributor for *Publishers Weekly* noted that "the tale's timeless themes of renewal and rebirth have lost none of their resonance" in Wood's retelling.

Illustrating her own words, Wood has also created a number of winning titles. *Detective Valentine* is a wintry mystery about a mole searching for a hat thief; Amy Spaulding wrote in *School Library Journal* that "Wood's cartoon illustrations fit the silly story." Praising the fun aspect of the puzzle, a *Publishers Weekly* reviewer similarly noted that the "overall effect is buoyant—Wood exercises a freedom born of skill and confidence." In *Weird Parents,* a young boy eventually accepts the eccentric behavior of his mother and father, who tend to speak to strangers on the street and blow kisses to him at the bus stop. Noting the "joyous abandon" of Wood's paintings, a *Publishers Weekly* critic termed *Weird Parents* an "oddball and thoroughly captivating book," while *School Library Journal* contributor Susan Hepler noted the book's "outrageous good humor and child appeal."

Silly Sally is a rhyming picture book about a girl walking to town and the host of silly and odd animals she meets along the way, including a dancing pig and leapfrogging dog. A contributor to *Publishers Weekly* felt that the "repetition and vitality" of Wood's text, as well as the "simplicity of the words, makes this ideal for beginning readers." Deborah Abbott, in a *Booklist* review, had similar praise, commending *Silly Sally* as a "neatly packaged gem of a book." Abbott dubbed Wood's text "clever," adding that the book's artwork "explod[es] . . . with whimsy, humor, and zest." *Rude Giants* is Wood's self-illustrated story about what happens when two vile giants move to town. In *Booklist,* Ilene Cooper noted that "kids will be clamoring" for this story of how Beatrix saves her best friend Gerda from being devoured by the ravenous giants.

The Red Racer tells of young Nona and how she wants a fast, red bicycle so badly that she plans to get rid of her own bike in order to get a new Deluxe Red Racer. Ultimately, however, the girl's scheme fails and her old, banged-up bike survives to limp along another day. Lauren Peterson, writing in *Booklist,* lauded Wood's narrative in *The Red Racer,* calling the book a "humorous and witty tale with a wonderful, heartwarming ending." Susan S. Verner, reviewing the same title in the *Bulletin of the Center for Children's Books,* described the story as a cautionary tale about the "eternal themes of greed and lust."

A frisky pup willing to promise his mistress anything due to his characteristic doggy passion is the hero of Wood's self-illustrated picture book *A Dog Needs a Bone!* Featuring a text with what *Booklist* critic Linda Perkins described as "bouyant rhyme," the book also entertains readers with the nostalgic-styled crayon cartoons, drawn on kraft paper, that "find hilarity in all the goofy antics" of the buggy-eyed pup and its loyal mistress. In *School Library Journal* Blair Christolon cited the "homelike atmosphere" created by the author/illustrator's "jovial, cartoonlike illustrations," dubbing *A Dog Needs a Bone!* "a winner."

Wood once described her artwork to *SATA* as "very expressionistic." She explained that, instead of using models, she draws "from imagination and memory. For my work to convey humor, it must be spontaneous and free." In addition, Wood commented, she has "matured as a writer. Not that I'll ever stop growing, but I've reached a point where I feel at home in that mysterious place where stories come from."

Wood explained in *Horn Book* that a large number of ideas are necessary to craft a picture book, because "even after . . . years of creating picture books, I still can't tell which ideas are the good ones." An example of an idea that eventually became a picture book was, as Wood remembered, "the sultan's bath, a magical place, a fantastic bath experience where anything could happen," which was the seed for *King Bidgood's in the Bathtub.*

A prolific writer, Wood clearly enjoys her work. She declared that as an author, "if you do your work well, you can lead your readers into new worlds, worlds of delight and truth, humor and magic, worlds that are as real to your readers as this one. That is the joy of creating the picture book."

Biographical and Critical Sources

BOOKS

Children's Books and Their Creators, edited by Anita Silvey, Houghton Mifflin (Boston, MA), 1995.

Children's Literature Review, Volume 26, Gale (Detroit, MI), 1992.

Wood, Audrey, in an interview with *Something about the Author,* Volume 50, Gale (Detroit, MI), 1988.

PERIODICALS

Booklist, October 1, 1985, Ilene Cooper, review of *King Bidgood's in the Bathtub,* p. 272; March 15, 1992, Deborah Abbot, review of *Silly Sally,* p. 1384; March 1, 1993, Ilene Cooper, review of *Rude Giants,* p. 1227; December 1, 1995, Carolyn Phelan, review of *The Rainbow Bridge: Inspired by a Chumash Tale,* pp. 639-640; April 1, 1996, Susan Dove Lempke, review of *The Flying Dragon Room,* p. 1363; September 1, 1996, Lauren Peterson, review of *The Red Racer,* p. 145; September 15, 1996, Ilene Cooper, review of *The Bunyans,* p. 252; October 1, 1997, Carolyn Phelan, review of *Birdsong,* p. 339; February 15, 1998, Elizabeth Drennan, review of *Sweet Dream Pie,* p. 1021;

September 1, 1998, Michael Cart, review of *The Christmas Adventure of Space Elf Sam*, p. 135; December 1, 2000, Michael Cart, review of *Jubal's Wish*, p. 724; September 1, 2001, Hazel Rochman, review of *A Cowboy Christmas: The Miracle at Lone Pine Ridge*, p. 122; September 1, 2001, Michael Cart, review of *Alphabet Adventure*, p. 118; February 15, 2002, John Peters, review of *When the Root Children Wake Up*, p. 1017; September 15, 2002, Helen Rosenberg, review of *Merry Christmas, Big Hungry Bear!*, p. 247; December 1, 2003, Julie Cummins, review of *Alphabet Mystery*, p. 687; August, 2004, Gillian Engberg, review of *Ten Little Fish*, p. 1946; July, 2005, Gillian Engberg, review of *The Deep Blue Sea: A Book of Colors*, p. 1931; November 15, 2006, Julie Cummins, review of *Alphabet Rescue*, p. 56; October 15, 2007, Linda Perkins, review of *A Dog Needs a Bone!*, p. 51.

Bulletin of the Center for Children's Books, September, 1984, Zena Sutherland, review of *The Napping House*, p. 18; December, 1987, Betsy Hearne, review of *Heckedy Peg*, p. 80; December, 1995, Roger Sutton, review of *The Rainbow Bridge*, p. 145; July, 1996, Susan S. Verner, review of *The Red Racer*, p. 389; October, 1997, Deborah Stevenson, review of *Birdsong*, p. 71; March, 1998, Pat Matthews, review of *Sweet Dream Pie*, pp. 262-263.

Horn Book, September-October, 1986, Audrey Wood and Don Wood, pp. 556-565; March-April, 1988, Ethel L. Heins, review of *Heckedy Peg*, pp. 197-198.

Kirkus Reviews, October 1, 1995, review of *The Rainbow Bridge*, p. 1438; August 15, 1996, review of *Bright and Early Thursday Evening*, p. 1245; September 1, 1996, review of *The Bunyans*, p. 1330; October 1, 1998, review of *The Christmas Adventure of Space Elf Sam*, p. 1466; October 1, 2001, review of *A Cowboy Christmas*, p. 1436; March 15, 2002, review of *When the Root Children Wake Up*, p. 429; November 1, 2002, review of *Merry Christmas, Big Hungry Bear!*, p. 1627; August 1, 2003, review of *Alphabet Mystery*, p. 1025; August 1, 2005, review of *The Deep Blue Sea*, p. 861; August 1, 2004, review of *Ten Little Fish*, p. 751; August 1, 2006, review of *Alphabet Rescue*, p. 799.

New York Times Book Review, October 13, 1985, Arthur Yorinks, review of *King Bidgood's in the Bathtub*, p. 50; November 8, 1987, Patricia MacLachlan, "Magic Good, Bad, and Rotten," p. 50; November 15, 2003, Paul O. Zelinsky, review of *Alphabet Mystery*, p. 37.

Publishers Weekly, August 14, 1987, review of *Heckedy Peg*, p. 102; September 11, 1987, review of *Detective Valentine*, pp. 93-94; April 27, 1990, review of *Weird Parents*, p. 61; March 22, 1991, review of *Piggies*, p. 79; January 20, 1992, review of *Silly Sally*, p. 65; March 1, 1993, review of *Rude Giants*, pp. 55-56; October 23, 1995, review of *The Rainbow Bridge*, p. 69; January 22, 1996, review of *The Flying Dragon Room*, p. 73; June 24, 1996, review of *The Red Racer*, p. 60; July 22, 1996, review of *Bright and Early Thursday Evening*, p. 242; September 16, 1996, review of *The Bunyans*, p. 82; July 7, 1997, review of *Birdsong*, p. 68; February 2, 1998, review of *Sweet Dream Pie*, p. 89; September 25, 2000, review of *Jubal's Wish*, p.

115; July 2, 2001, review of *Alphabet Adventure*, p. 75; September 24, 2001, review of *A Cowboy Christmas*, p. 49; March 4, 2002, review of *When the Root Children Wake Up*, p. 79; September 1, 2003, review of *Alphabet Mystery*, p. 87; August 20, 2007, review of *A Dog Needs a Bone!*, p. 66.

School Library Journal, October, 1987, Amy Spaulding, review of *Detective Valentine*, pp. 119-120; July, 1990, Susan Hepler, review of *Weird Parents*, p. 66; May, 1991, Jane Saliers, review of *Piggies*, p. 86; April, 1992, Virginia Opocensky, review of *Silly Sally*, p. 101; October, 1995, Patricia Lathrop Green, review of *The Rainbow Bridge*, p. 130; March, 1996, Carolyn Noah, review of *The Flying Dragon Room*, p. 184; September, 1996, Kathy Piehl, review of *The Red Racer*, p. 194; October, 1996, John Sigwald, review of *Bright and Early Thursday Evening*, pp. 109-110; December, 1996, Jane Gardner, review of *The Bunyans*, p. 110; October, 1997, Alice Eames, review of *Birdsong*, p. 114; March, 1998, Susan Garland, review of *Sweet Dream Pie*, p. 190; October, 1998, Susan H. Patron, review of *The Christmas Adventures of Space Elf Sam*, p. 46; October, 2000, Carol Ann Wilson, review of *Jubal's Wish*, p. 143; September, 2001, Linda M. Kenton, review of *Alphabet Adventure*, p. 209; October, 2001, review of *A Cowboy Christmas*, p. 71; October, 2002, Mara Alpert, review of *Merry Christmas, Big Hungry Bear!*, p. 65; October, 2004, Blair Christolon, review of *Ten Little Fish*, p. 137; August, 2005, Joy Fleishhacker, review of *The Deep Blue Sea*, p. 118; October, 2006, Marilyn Ackerman, review of *Alphabet Rescue*, p. 131; September, 2007, Blair Christolon, review of *A Dog Needs a Bone!*, p. 178.

Teacher Librarian, November, 1998, Shirley Lewis, review of *The Christmas Adventure of Space Elf Sam*, p. 48.

ONLINE

Audrey Wood Home Page, http://www.audreywood.com (February 2, 2009).*

*   *   *

WRIGHT, Michael 1954-

Personal

Born 1954, in Frankfurt, Germany; immigrated to United States; married; wife's name Cheryl; children: Mason, Sloan, Paxton. *Education:* University of Utah, B.A. (art).

Addresses

Home and office—Manhattan Beach, CA.

Career

Author and illustrator. Previously worked in advertising and designed greeting cards. Also worked in television.

Writings

Jake Stays Awake, Feiwel & Friends (New York, NY), 2007.

Jake Starts School, Feiwel & Friends (New York, NY), 2008.

Sidelights

Michael Wright has always loved to create cartoons, not only drawing, but also writing them. After studying art at the University of Utah, he got a job in advertising, serving as an art director and eventually writing as well. Wright started his art career after his sister found a box of his cartoons, submitted them to a greeting card publisher, and got her brother a contract. Deciding to turn to children's books, Wright created *Jake Stays Awake,* and he has continued Jake's adventures in *Jake Starts School.*

Jake Stays Awake is a rhyming story about young Jake, a boy who refuses to go to bed on his own because he would rather sleep with his parents. Jake insists that all three of them—Mom, Dad, and toddler—try out different places for sleeping—including the roof and the bathtub—before ultimately deciding that his bed is the best sleeping place after all. Wright's "pleasantly rhyming text is paired with droll, stylized full-and double-page illustrations in bold colors," noted Marie Orlando in *School Library Journal.* In *Booklist,* John Peters wrote that the art is "done in a distinctive cartoon style," while a *Kirkus Reviews* contributor observed of the illustrations that "hidden details and the family dog's antics will keep readers in stitches."

Jake Starts School is a "tongue-in-cheek" sequel, according to *Booklist* contributor Krista Hutley. As in *Jake Stays Awake,* Wright's young protagonist does not want to be separated from his parents; when they drop him off at school, Jake clings to them, refusing to let go. When his parents accompany the clinging youngster to class, all three cannot fit into Jake's chair, and the boy misses out on class art projects and recess until his teacher convinces him to let his parents go. Wright's "funny selection will easily transform first-day jitters into giggles," wrote Hutley, while a *Kirkus Reviews* contributor noted that much of the fun comes from "preposterously shaped characters, pithy rhymes and the many emotions expressed by just a few differently drawn lines."

Biographical and Critical Sources

PERIODICALS

Booklist, September 1, 2007, John Peters, review of *Jake Stays Awake,* p. 127; May 15, 2008, Krista Hutley, review of *Jake Starts School,* p. 48.

Kirkus Reviews, September 15, 2007, review of *Jake Stays Awake*; May 15, 2008, review of *Jake Starts School.*

School Library Journal, September, 2007, Marie Orlando, review of *Jake Stays Awake,* p. 179.

ONLINE

Cynsations Blog, http://cynthialeitichsmith.blogspot.com/ (August 5, 2008), Cynthia Leitich Smith, interview with Wright.

Macmillan Web site, http://us.macmillan.com/ (March 9, 2009), profile of Wright.

Michael Wright Home Page, http://www.michaelwright land.com (March 9, 2009).*